FRANCO-AMERICA IN THE MAKING

France Overseas: Studies in Empire and Decolonization
Series editors: A. J. B. Johnston, James D. Le Sueur, and Tyler Stovall

Franco-America in the Making

The Creole Nation Within

JONATHAN K. GOSNELL

UNIVERSITY OF NEBRASKA PRESS   LINCOLN AND LONDON

© 2018 by the Board of Regents of
the University of Nebraska

Acknowledgments for the use of copyrighted
material appear on pages xiv–xv, which constitute
an extension of the copyright page.

Library of Congress Control Number: 2017054272

Set in Garamond Premier by E. Cuddy.
Designed by N. Putens.

Pour Annie qui est si généreusement venue,
comme ses arrière-grands-parents,
vivre dans un monde inconnu, aux Etats . . .

And for Simone and Gabrielle,
Franco-Americans in their own right who
will, I hope, gracefully navigate the worlds that they inhabit

In loving memory of GGD,
for introductions to cultures, francophone and other,
beyond the City of Brotherly Love

CONTENTS

List of Illustrations ix

Acknowledgments xi

Introduction 1

1. Between Dream and Reality in
   Franco-America 21

2. Cultural Institutions and French
   Renaissance in America 61

3. Women's Social Clubs and the
   Transmission of Culture 107

4. Franco-American Cultures in a
   New World Perspective 151

5. Ethnic Identity and the Franco-
   American Press   189

6. Unmasking the Creole Cowboy   233

   Conclusion   279

   Notes   291

   Bibliography   323

   Index   337

ILLUSTRATIONS

1. Monument National, Canadien
   Français, Holyoke, Massachusetts   3

2. Welcome to French neighborhood,
   Woonsocket, Rhode Island   46

3. *La Maison Française*, Assumption
   College, Worcester, Massachusetts   64

4. AF Marianne.   74

5. *La dame de la renaissance française*,
   Nashua, New Hampshire   108

6. École Sainte Jeanne d'Arc/
   St. Georges School, Aldenville,
   Chicopee, Massachusetts   122

7. Fédération Féminine Franco-Américaine emblem, 1951   143

8. Original Jack Kerouac tombstone, "Ti Jean," Edson Cemetery, Lowell, Massachusetts   185

9. *L'Avenir National*, 3 July 1914   207

10. Festivals Acadiens et Créoles poster, 2013   256

11. *Le Journal de Lowell*, June 1995   282

ACKNOWLEDGMENTS

I have many to thank for the help provided during a lengthy intellectual and very real sojourn into French contours of New England and south Louisiana. I am indebted to the specialists who have paved the way for scholars, many of whom shared extensive knowledge personally. In Worcester, Massachusetts, the past and present directors of the Institut Français of Assumption College, Professors Claire Quintal and Leslie Choquette, provided access to archival materials and numerous contacts, read chapters, and spent hours in conversation with me. In Lowell, I had the pleasure of speaking with Marthe Biron Péloquin, longtime leader of Franco-American cultural life in the city. I am very appreciative of the organizers of the Cercle Jeanne Mance of Lowell who invited me (and then invited me back) to participate in the annual June Franco-American celebration. Albert Côté, former editor of *Le Journal de Lowell*, was an excellent tour guide to the city's Franco-American sites during a summer visit and subsequently provided access to virtually the entire collection of *Le Journal de Lowell*. Manchester, New Hampshire, resident Robert

B. Perreault was an equally enthusiastic guide to the west side of his fair Franco city. During research trips, he facilitated a better understanding of both local and wide-ranging Franco-American history and culture. At the Centre Franco-Américain in Manchester, Adele Boufford Baker, Yvonne Cyr Bresnahan, and Christine Davis facilitated access to the library's riches. In Lewiston, Maine, Rita Dube, former director of the Franco-American Center, was equally generous with materials and insights.

I would like to express my deep gratitude to the women of the Franco-American Women's Association of Chicopee, Massachusetts, for allowing me to sit in on their meetings, a first time in 2005, regularly in 2008 through 2010, and more sporadically in 2011, 2012, and beyond. Special thanks to Pierrette Blanchet for sharing music and keeping me informed of Franco-American activities in the area. I had the chance to experience something warmly Franco-American in the group's presence on Thursday evenings. Murielle Banas of the Cercle des dames françaises shared archival materials from the organization, many a conversation, and occasional press clippings about Franco-Americans and Franco-American life in western Massachusetts. Members of these women's organizations not only welcomed me but met on occasion with advanced French culture classes at Smith College, sometimes providing food and entertainment. Father Gérard Lafleur of Assumption Church in Chicopee, Massachusetts, one of the last French-speaking priests in the area (and now deceased), opened his parish to our group during field trips. Local historian and genealogist Elise Bernier-Feely of Forbes Library in Northampton encouraged groups of students to take a greater interest in the francophone culture at their doorstep. She helped arrange a tour of the former "French" church, Sacred Heart. Outside we observed the site established in honor of the French parish school (since removed).

Franco-American folk singer and playwright Michael Parent sang, told stories, and laughed with Smith students and members of the college community. His performances, which I first witnessed fifteen years ago, were a reminder of long forgotten memories of disparaged but vibrant Franco-American cultures. Special thanks to French-Canadian troubadour Josée Vachon for continuing to perform, to remember, and to inspire people of French descent. I very much appreciate her permission to reprint one of her songs. Postcolonial Franco-American author and activist Rhea Côté Robbins also shared many a yarn with students and me about her work over the years. I have been fortunate to include Côté Robbins and Cajun poet Kirby Jambon in our curriculum at Smith College. Jambon read poetry, broke bread, and shared recordings of his verses, formally recognized by the French Academy in 2014. I offer my sincere thanks to French 380 students at Smith who impressed me with their penetrating questions of authors and to the contemporary producers of Franco culture who facilitated our learning.

Through contacts made possible by friends and colleagues, I was able to speak with several leaders of the Alliance Française, a French cultural organization once quite active in Franco-America. Chapter heads in Boston and Lowell, Massachusetts, Portland, Maine, St. Louis, Missouri, Manchester, New Hampshire, and the Lake Champlain region, Vermont, took the time to reflect on group initiatives. For sustenance, I happily joined more informal gatherings such as the Bavards, a French-speaking group organized for many years by Sylvanne Pontin on Saturday mornings at Jorgensen's Café in Waterville, Maine. On the occasions when I participated, it felt satisfying symbolically to bring French back into public places, as used to happen in former French ethnic enclaves in New England. I thank Sylvanne and the Bavards dearly for welcoming my grandmother, Daisy L. Gordon, into their midst for a couple of French lessons. In Louisiana I had the opportunity to chat with French heritage speakers over breakfast several times. At Dwyer's Restaurant in downtown Lafayette, I joined Cajun, Creole, and standard French speakers for coffee and conversation on early Wednesday mornings. Group organizer Lester Gautier has certainly contributed to *la survivance* in encouraging this French table for twenty years.

I traveled to south Louisiana on several occasions for research as well as for pleasure and had the very good fortune to meet people (who knew other people) who encouraged contact with the unique Cajun and Creole cultures. In Lafayette, Elaine Clément, community relations liaison for the Council for the Development of French in Louisiana (CODOFIL), generously connected me to the lively local scene. I thank her particularly for pointing me in the direction of the Blue Moon Guest Saloon in Lafayette, a mecca of French cultural life, particularly music. Former CODOFIL president David Chéramie spent two hours conversing with me about the work of his organization in south Louisiana. Over lunch at Dwyer's Restaurant, Faustine Hillard, also of CODOFIL and the Alliance Française of Lafayette, and Creole poet and teacher Debbie Clifton talked with me about the intricacies of south Louisiana French-language communities. During a first trip to Lafayette, historian Carl Brasseaux discussed hybrid francophone cultures and identified delicious local eateries. On two occasions, it was my pleasure to interact with teacher, storyteller, linguist, and cultural depository Richard Guidry. I spent a wonderful evening with the Smith College Club of Louisiana at Tulane University in New Orleans, talking about marginalized yet resilient French cultures of New England and Louisiana, after hurricanes Rita and Katrina.

To the anonymous readers at the University of Nebraska Press, I offer my gratitude. One in particular made herself known to me, and her careful reading has most certainly improved this book. I am grateful to Eloise Brière for her keen eye and expansive knowledge of North American *francophonie*. Many thanks to Bridget Barry for answering all of my questions from beginning to end of the publication process, and to her assistant, Emily Wendell. Ann Baker and Elaine Durham Otto guided me through copyediting. I am indebted to Frank Citino of Information Technology Services at Smith College for his assistance in formatting illustrations. Funding from Smith paid for copyright expenses and indexing. I would like to formally acknowledge the *French Review, French Cultural Studies,* and *French Politics, Culture, and Society* for copyright permission to reprint the following previously published articles:

"Unmasking the Creole Cowboy: Cosmopolitan Cultures in the Gulf South." *French Review* 85, no. 5 (April 2012): 916–28.

"Between Dream and Reality in 'Franco-America.'" *French Review* 80, no. 6 (May 2007): 1336–49.

"The Alliance Française, Empire, and America." *French Cultural Studies* 19, no. 2 (June 2008): 227–43.

"Franco-American Cultures in a New World Perspective." *French Politics, Culture, and Society* 30, no. 3 (Winter 2012): 96–118.

The story of French cultural survival in the United States is not really my story, but I have discovered that its telling is quite personal. I am not Franco-American, nor French, but I consider myself to be a French speaker curious about the French-speaking world. I spent a part of my adolescence in central Maine, where the predominant ethnic or immigrant experience is still French-Canadian. French could occasionally be heard on the streets of mill towns in our area. Some of the young people at my high school had exotic-sounding names to me—Laverdiere, Coutouriere, Saucier—all unaccented in writing and pronounced in the local northern New England dialect. Our French classes visited area nursing homes to sing carols to elderly French speakers at Christmas time. I would be remiss to not thank one of my first French teachers, Mr. Errol Snipe, who organized these cultural excursions. After my first several months in Maine, I wondered why all the ethnic jokes were about French Canadians? This book is most certainly a tardy response to some of these cultural questions I asked myself as a young person.

Introduction

This book explores the imprint that has been left by members of the diasporic French family on the North American continent since their arrival four hundred years ago. It aims to better understand the francophone components of American society and culture, the United States' fifth largest and forgotten ethnic group. Through a variety of cultural expressions, Franco-Americans have affirmed that they have actively taken part in the francophone world, despite exile and assimilation. A French cultural residue remains obscured yet present in the industrial centers of New England and on the prairies and in the bayous of south Louisiana, generated by the many thousands of people who first settled these areas. Of course, smaller and more isolated French ethnic enclaves can be found elsewhere in the United States, such as the plains of the upper Mississippi and Missouri and the agricultural fields of the St. John's River valley on the northern Maine–New Brunswick border.

The homegrown French of America, or Franco-Americans, were born in the New World, of French, French-Canadian, Acadian, Native American,

African, and Caribbean descent. I will use Franco-American to refer to them all, although their individual group experiences are distinct. They migrated to the United States in the eighteenth, nineteenth, and twentieth centuries, often on a second leg of their transatlantic and trans-American voyage. It is important to note that many Francos came to the United States as Americans. The America in which their descendants were born and have lived is very much a Creole nation as some scholars have asserted recently, particularly so within the distinct spaces where French attitudes fostered a middle ground between continents and cultures.[1] Here European, African, and Native American traditions mingled to a greater extent than in more mainstream Anglo-America and gave rise to hybrid traditions *à la française*.

Franco-America in the Making analyzes what has remained of French cultures in North America, long after the formal end of the empire in the mid-eighteenth century. It explores the evolution of peoples and ideas that crossed the "French Atlantic" to America, leaving behind the *vieux continent* for the New World, and how French cultural identity has come to be defined here. The six chapters examine French written and oral cultures of the United States that remain infrequently investigated, those produced by individuals and organizations, ethnic men and often women. The analysis draws comparison between French cultural forms in New England and south Louisiana. It examines the circumstances that transformed French colonial activity in North America into francophone postcolonial cultures. What does it mean to be French, not simply *in* America but *of* America? Postcolonial studies are actively investigating the traveling bodies, ideas, and cultures that have moved widely across oceans and continents, yet the francophone component of the United States has received little attention thus far. The study of North American *francophonie* is restricted to Canada and almost exclusively to Quebec and New Brunswick (Acadie) in standard postcolonial anthologies.[2] Many Americans today no longer master their heritage language, but there are some twenty million French speakers and people of French or francophone descent in North America. They are French as well as American linguistically, culturally, and in myriad ways that they redefine continually.[3]

The term *Franco-American*, in adjective or noun form, is a confusing

1. Monument National, Canadien Français–Holyoke, Massachusetts. Courtesy of author.

concept. While sometimes used to qualify exchanges or relations between the French and Americans, I use it as French-descended people began to do in 1900, to identify people from French-speaking areas of Canada who had settled in the United States. Since then, Franco-Americans have continually sought to define and calibrate the two distinct parts of their being, the French and the American, the sum of which was altogether unique. In a classic work of cultural anthropology Raymonde Carroll, found French and American attitudes at opposite ends of the social and cultural spectrum.[4] Carroll did not set out to examine the ambiguous places where they meet, intersections highlighted in the present study. At no other time has French culture and cultural life been so readily accessible to people, francophone and otherwise, on the highways, byways, and bayous of French America. How has French, and how have the French, broadly defined, contributed to American life? In what ways is America French today? This study of francophone cultural expression in the United States provides responses. As the symbolic nature of figure 1 suggests, such transnational identities are often fractured.

Culture and imperialism are intrinsically linked, argued Edward Said several decades ago. Without European expansion into the furthest reaches of Africa, Asia, and the Americas, there is no impetus for the modern novel, he asserted, and without driving cultural thirst, there is no leitmotif for colonial expansion.[5] European writers cast their narratives from a shared imperialist past, and a "colonial idea" informed and shaped their translation of the present. Modern writings helped to provide metropolitan citizens—the French, English, and Spanish, for instance—with a global perspective and, at the very least, some sense of an attachment to an extended imperial community. What does culture, and often far-flung bits of cultural driftwood, look like long after empire? This is one of the central questions asked in the context of North America centuries after French colonial expansion and retraction. French postcolonial thought, an oxymoron until quite recently, is beginning to formulate similar questions. French scholars assert that it, *la pensée postcoloniale*, "s'inscrit . . . dans la lignée de *la rencontre entre l'Europe et le monde* [my emphasis] et elle l'appelle (l'Europe) à une éthique de la responsabilité inspirée de ses propres traditions."[6] Meetings between an increasingly distant Europe and the world have continued unabated in the form of violent global migrations and cultural transactions, despite Europe's enlightened past.

What is one to make of fragments of empire, continental detritus in the wider Atlantic realm? *Nations* of all sorts, *regions*, *hinges*, *hubs*, *islands*, and *communities* (imagined and otherwise) abound throughout the region. How can one define the network of places located within the French and black Atlantic?[7] Expanding commercial and cultural routes coalesce and give life to disparate collectivities. What terminology might be best for the framing of Franco-America, more an imaginary place than real? The encompassing notion of *la francophonie* has come under attack, notably from the *littérature-monde* movement recently, for its Franco-French centrism.[8] Anticipating a future change in semantics, prominent scholars in the field opted for "French-speaking world" instead of Francophone.[9] "Does *littérature-monde* offer an all-embracing transnational vista leading beyond the confines of postcolonialism," some of the same researchers ask?[10] Francophone postcolonial studies, as they continue to be called, have attempted to reconfigure the relationship between French and francophone, via exploration of the cultures of France and its former colonies. Curiously, 2005 was something of a watershed year during which greater recognition of postcolonial issues in France occurred. The French could no longer easily ignore a postcolonial condition in their very midst, as violence escalated between young black and brown people and the police in the suburbs, and as French deputies and intellectuals disputed the "positive nature" of colonial activity in Algeria, the highly controversial law of February 23, 2005.[11]

It is clear that for the last decade writers and researchers have sought a greater diversity of expression, with resulting victories and struggles. Globalizing and power-driven concepts of Empire and Nation long served to mask ethnic, linguistic, regional, and religious distinctions, but their dismantling brings cultural fusions and differences uncomfortably into the light. French scholars of the postcolonial, working in isolation as much of the French academy still rejects postcolonial thought as marginal, ideological, and dangerous to the national or republican cause, introduced the concept of *la République coloniale*, an evocative perspective for bridging the distance between colony and *Métropole*.[12] While the nation remains a perplexing entity within a weakened European Union, historian Gérard Bouchard makes the case for examination of the little used lens of the nation in North America.[13] Even an unborn nation of North America, in the context of Quebec, has symbolic importance. None of the mentioned terms in fact—nation, region, island, hinge, or hub—is entirely sufficient in terms of representing the complexities of a Creole Franco-America. Franco-American cultures are both rooted and nomadic, of Old World and New, traditional and modern.

As much of the analysis in the book will be informed by written documentation, print culture and capitalism, as Benedict Anderson labels them, are vital. The notion of his *Imagined Community* is a persuasive one when it is Franco-America that is under the microscope. The prevalence of Franco-American written cultures is remarkable, particularly given the lack of power and minority status of its creators. Their very persistence suggests that nonprofessional writers of prose, poetry, and journalism have contributed significantly to the development of a Franco-American identity. The forgotten Franco-American story (as told by writers) is one of (re)discovery, of redemption, and growing subjectivity. By acknowledging, writing, and rediscovering their own history, they strove to exist and to exist as participating members of *la francophonie*. Réda Bensmaïa suggests that writing can be the only nation to which the exiled nomadic writer pledges allegiance.[14]

Franco-Americans suppressed or hid from the public eye a common French heritage, but it persisted in the living arts of foodways, music, folktales, and social gatherings (*veillées* and *fais do-dos*). These cultural phenomena evoke the thoughts, fears, and joys of Francos, at least as much as ethnic literature and newspapers. Print culture alone cannot fully represent an imagined Franco-American community, although it is clear that Francos are linked by the power of the written word. Oral cultures, those that are performed, staged, sometimes recorded, and consumed by eager audiences, even those recorded only in collective memory, have transformative qualities. They bring to life, both yesterday and today, the Franco-American experience. Questions remain, of course, namely, how has a cultural identity been sustained, over centuries, when it has little to no value, no cultural or symbolic capital? This is a Franco-American conundrum that even sociologist Pierre Bourdieu would be hard-pressed to explain.[15] Franco elites hoping to elevate and prolong the culture are only partially responsible.

My analysis of Franco-American cultures is part of an ongoing interdisciplinary effort to remap America and American studies. As this book was being written, multiple diasporas from across the globe have continued to transform American life. I probe postcolonial, transatlantic, and border theories in order to better understand the French experience in North America. While the French were officially banished as a colonial power from North America by the British in the mid-eighteenth century, with the notable North Atlantic exception of St. Pierre and Miquelon, I invite them back into contemporary ethnic American studies. French entry into the New World narrative took place during France's pre-republican first colonial experiment, during the seventeenth and eighteenth centuries primarily, distinguishing it from other republican colonies of the nineteenth century. French cultural survival in the Americas, *la survivance*, began during the second phase of empire in the nineteenth, after France had largely withdrawn from the New World. The Haitian Revolution and the sale of Louisiana at the advent of the nineteenth century decisively signaled this withdrawal. Dean Louder and Eric Waddell claim that the French story of America has yet to be fully told.[16] We know more of the French experience in other places, in Africa and Asia, for instance, yet the comparison with North America is instructive.

How does a postcolonial Franco-America differ from other regions of France's former empire? What do Franco-Americans share with other francophone populations? Are they an ethnic as well as a linguistic minority? How precisely are francophone populations, some of whom are people of color, defining French America? New work on white ethnic identity stresses its complexities alongside more monolithic definitions (of white privilege, for instance).[17] As French ethnics, Francos periodically articulated an acute awareness of race and disadvantage. Franco-Americans sought lasting substantive relationships with other Francophones; they expressed pride when recognized as fellow French speakers. As we will see throughout the analysis, *francophone* is a problematic term that must be unpacked. Critics as well as advocates of the *littérature-monde* movement have done just that. It is precisely in questioning that scholars will help to problematize the notion of *Amérique française*, or *Franco-Amérique* as it is sometimes called in French, a term reflecting a historic and cultural evolution from French to francophone. Louder and Waddell claim that the break with distant France is definitive, yet becoming American has proven to be difficult for Francos.[18]

A New World francophone cultural study identifies a space where French and (North) American populations and traditions intersect in intriguing ways. It provides a way of making French cultures more visible within the increasingly transnational study of America and drawing attention to infrequently traveled avenues of exploration in French studies.[19] An analysis of postcolonial francophone cultures in North America is naturally scattered, untidy, an exploration of a variety of physical objects, media, traditions, places, and institutions through time. French and Francophone studies, which are increasingly interdisciplinary, combining literary and historical as well as cultural and political analyses borrowed from the social sciences, have much to learn from the models and methodologies of American studies, and similarly American studies may profit from the linguistic, textual, and cultural insight often explored in critical French and Francophone studies. For a postcolonial examination of francophone cultures in the United States, metropolitan France and French culture certainly loom large historically, culturally, and symbolically. Affairs from France periodically poked their heads into the conversations and discussions held in Franco-America. A decentered French studies, inclusive of France yet outside direct metropolitan control, is one of the areas of inquiry of the new postcolonial francophone studies.[20]

An appropriate point of departure for a study of postcolonial franco-phone cultures in America is the transatlantic French port of La Rochelle, "la ville la plus américaine de France."[21] Protestants, slaves, and future *habitants*, settlers of French Canada, began leaving La Rochelle for New World destinations in the seventeenth century. The irony, of course, is that Protestants were initially unwelcome in the French New World. Many of the women destined for a new life in New France, and who were aptly named the *filles du roi* or daughters of the king, left from La Rochelle. While an America-bound Samuel de Champlain would depart from Honfleur, and one finds a small bust in his honor there, it is in the New World that he truly left his mark . It is in La Rochelle, French center of Calvinism, that Samuel de Champlain's partner and scribe Marc Lescarbot published his suggestive poem, *Adieu à la France*. Champlain himself was born just outside of La Rochelle in Brouage around 1570. The waters that once placed Brouage at the center of exchange with the Atlantic world, however, have long since receded.

From such ports as La Rochelle and Brouage set sail not only people but ideas and symbols. Some of these signifiers have embedded themselves in the material fabric of the New World, marking America perhaps indefinitely in the process. On the town hall of La Rochelle one finds a departing ship transporting material, human, and intellectual cargo to American shores.

Favorable winds suggest the future success of transatlantic voyages, however traumatic for the enslaved.[22] The three *fleur-de-lys* symbolize all that was royal and holy about French colonial efforts at that time, commissioned by absolute monarchs who were the reputed representatives of God on earth. Today, that most symbolic monument of French arrivals in the New World, the statue of Samuel de Champlain, greets visitors on the promenade high above the St. Lawrence River at Quebec City. It is a reminder of what has remained on American shores for four hundred years. The *fleur-de-lys* evokes a transplanted French culture and life in America that people have not forgotten. Hence the *Je me souviens* slogan that is so central to Québécois consciousness and that is transported throughout the roadways of North America on French-Canadian automobile license plates.

Modern Quebec is clearly a story of francophone postcolonial success, a vibrant center of transatlantic French cultural life. Its eight million francophones occupy a leadership position not only within Franco-America but also in the wider francophone world. Linguists in Quebec have been at the vanguard of efforts to modernize the French language, to create useful terminology, and to limit the influence of English words. The controversial yet effective Bill 101 promoting French language usage since 1977 is largely credited with revitalizing the Frenchness of Quebec.[23] Some 80 percent of Quebecers are French speakers, and accordingly, the rights of minority English-speaking communities are now periodically raised. The Quebec government has been supportive of efforts to promote North American *francophonie* and has recently turned some of its attention to the New England states that received almost one million French Canadians looking for work a century ago.

Both French America north of the Canadian border and in the Caribbean have been the subjects of scholarly inquiry, but again much less so the United States.[24] Recent scholarship in transnational or international American studies, including influential works such as José David Saldívar's *Border Matters*, challenges narrow, confining interpretations of American society and culture. Even a specialized study of French-Canadian immigrants in the United States makes a case for northern border matters and the comparison with Mexico.[25] While these works indicate a beginning of the "worlding" of American society, twenty-first-century events have illustrated that the process is not complete. Anthropologist Margaret Mead famously claimed that people in the United States are all third generation, alluding to the centrality of the immigrant experience. Despite the increasingly multicultural nature of American society, foreignness is as suspect in the current climate as it has been in the past. The question of how one negotiates ethnic and American identities in the post-9/11 world is still open to debate. In 2005 Hurricane Katrina brought first and third worlds in America together in dramatic fashion. Where else but the United States of America is it possible to be ethnic and French, a place where hyphenated or hybrid identities are part of the national mythology and norm (although also hotly contested at various times in the nation's history). They are largely absent from the republican discourse in France, although this also has shifted somewhat. Third, fourth, and fifth generation Franco-Americans seek to revive or retrieve lost culture, language, and ethnicity. As will be discussed in the following chapters, this has proven to be difficult due to the conscious burying of Franco-American cultures.

All too often, and understandably so, southern borders haunt the American psyche and receive much of the focus in American ethnic, cultural, and border studies. While northern borders do not evoke the same racialized fears as those separating the United States from Mexico, they are real and somewhat porous, although certainly less so since 2001. In the North moreover, distinct French notions of race provide interesting contrasts with Anglo perceptions. Great migrations of black Americans and French Canadians traveled south and north, in the twentieth and nineteenth centuries, respectively, but sometimes simultaneously. It is in Franco-America where French and black worlds join symbolically. I will argue that Franco-Americans are Creole by virtue of their Old World cultures and hybrid experiences in the New World, although many Franco-Americans would probably not self-identify as Creole. Extensive contact with African and Native Americans cultures makes a persuasive case nonetheless for the *creolisation* of French America and of Franco-Americans.[26] The underlying shadow of blackness in Franco-American life is an intriguing and persistent phenomenon. A French ethnic identity has survived the tides of cultural assimilation and oppression well into the twentieth and twenty-first centuries, in contrast to working-class identification that remained ephemeral.[27] Franco-Americans in Lewiston, Maine, refused to give up their ethnicity despite the Ku Klux Klan marching in the 1920s against French Catholics.[28]

America's French past and its more contemporary present are relevant today and offer a substantive reflection on French and American cultural, racial, ethnic, and national identities. Too often French and American are viewed as rival, competing, and altogether different models, but Franco-America provides an avenue for understanding relevant intersectionalities. While cultural, ethnic, and postcolonial studies in the United States have unearthed many underrepresented cultures in America, they have had little to say about the French within the melting pot (or salad bowl). What have saved the French from complete disintegration in the pot are the lively culinary, artistic, and musical cultures, retained and passed along, albeit in slightly different form, sometimes in translation in English. Francophone postcolonial cultures have not yet entirely disappeared, although they are more vulnerable today than they were a half-century ago.[29] In contemporary Quebec, study of the *Americanness* within the French-Canadian province has ignited an ongoing debate about French cultural preservation and identity. Franco-America, however, is a different project, according to Joseph Yvon Thériault.[30]

What does Franco-America have to do with metropolitan French concerns about ethnicity, race, and a troubled French national identity, all postcolonial questions? Examining Franco-America under different lenses will provide insight, as will positioning Franco-America more visibly within francophone postcolonial studies, one of the aims of this book. Franco-Americans pursue questions of identity as do the French in France. Whether in immigration debates, discussions about history and identity, and of course regional and national politics, the French seem perpetually locked in a national dialogue about memory, as the seminal work by Pierre Nora suggested some thirty years ago.[31] Scholars such as Robert Aldrich have articulated criticism concerning the absence of colonial remnants from studies of national memory and attempted to fill the void.[32] The colonial is not, French researchers say, an insignificant part of France's past and cannot be treated as if it were a mere footnote. Recent and influential critical thought contends that the postcolonial offers a penetrating means of observation beyond the superficial or chronological, the *au-delà* or beyond, bringing together past, present, and even to some extent future.[33]

By bringing the margins out of the shadows, by giving voice to the voiceless with the assistance of critical thought, *Franco-America in the Making* sheds light on a minority French population in the United States, one indeed threatened by further obscurity if not disappearance. Had the French won the colonial struggle for power, might more Americans speak French today rather than English? Perhaps, although of course we have no answer to this rhetorical question. As losers in the struggle for imperial dominance, francophones have clearly been relegated to the sidelines of New World power. As much of Franco-America itself is a memory, more past than present in many respects, I pay close attention to Franco-American sites of memory in the United States. They are little known markers of this country's French past, sometimes imposing yet fragile monuments left by churches, schools, and social organizations. The book assembles a representative collection of sites, dispersed in the various regional pockets of Franco-America, in New England, south Louisiana, and Quebec.

America's French history is clouded by the fact that, following the end of empire and the departure of the royal commissions, many of its actors occupied the geographies of the working class, not the stratospheres of the political or intellectual elite, and as a result North American French cultures rarely circulated beyond the gates of hermetic ethnic enclaves. Franco sites of memory are still hidden from view in these historic spaces. Jack Kerouac offers one of the rare exceptions of Franco-American cultures available to a wider public, although his rise to prominence had little to do with his French heritage.[34] Franco elites long shunned Kerouac because they felt that he had turned his back on his French ancestry (he had not) or chosen to air dirty laundry. Thanks to recent work, we know more now about Kerouac's French or Franco legacy.[35] The spicy cultures of Louisiana represent more widely known French cultural phenomena in the United States.

The year 2008 provided an opportune moment for reflection on French intrusions (border crossings) into the American text and context, on what it means to write, to speak, and to be French and American. Not long before midnight on December 31, 2007, at Quebec City, began the official celebration of four hundred years of French presence on the North American continent. Céline Dion and Zachary Richard sang, representing francophone cultures of Quebec, Louisiana, and other French satellites in a colorful (inter)national performance.[36] Celebrations continued throughout 2008 and 2009 in honor of the exploits of Samuel de Champlain and those that followed. Champlain might be regarded as much a symbol of "Euro-imperialism" as Christopher Columbus, but he has been spared the heavy criticism that accompanied the five hundred year anniversary of the Italian explorer's New World arrival in 1992. David H. Fischer demonstrates why in *Champlain's Dream*. Like Samuel de Champlain, Quebec party officials carefully included Native American people and cultures in the four hundred year celebration and in the envisioning of Franco-America today. What helped keep the French New World party under the radar is the discreet French experience in America since military defeat.

For "native" francophones in the United States, for heritage speakers of French-Canadian, Acadian, Cajun, and Creole extraction, Quebec constitutes a benevolent yet sometimes imperious *Métropole*, not unlike France. France is certainly a more removed center than Quebec for many Franco-American groups. As the most immediate French reference point in North America, it is not surprising that people question the imperialist role of Quebec and its French cultural policy. Outside of Quebec, Franco-Americans have complained of abandonment and general ignorance of other francophone cultures in America by the Quebec government and people. The tenuous pockets of French language and culture in other Canadian provinces, the state of Louisiana, and the New England region, represent a sobering perspective for French cultures in North America, generally, if stringent measures to preserve them are not maintained. The ways that Americans of francophone descent and culture remember, celebrate, and perpetuate themselves constitute the primary subject of inquiry in the story that follows. Much remains to be learned about traveling French cultures, about departures, arrivals, and cultural transformations.

Frenchness on North American soil in the seventeenth century required travel, as well as vigor. That original Frenchness is now as sparsely rooted as other minority transplants to the New World. It is significant that people continue to speak French, to create French language, to invent stories, poems, music, and plays in French in North America today that speak of the Franco-American experience. As Franco-America's early modern squires, Champlain and Lescarbot's production of captivating Franco-American image and word represent early and provocative examples of print cultures. They set a cultural precedent in North America that has been widely imitated, yet after the military victory of the British in 1763 and the worldwide onslaught of American culture in the twentieth and twenty-first centuries, this would seem improbable indeed. French language and culture continue to cling precariously to the continent, much as they did a century ago when Louis Hémon, the author of *Maria Chapdelaine*, wrote of voices evoking three hundred years of French presence: "Nous sommes venus il y a trois cents ans, et nous sommes restés."[37] *Clinging* is probably too pejorative a term to describe what has taken place, yet it is a telling phenomenon that the French experience in North America is described in this way, with little agency or legitimacy.

After the 150-year effort of the past to literally graft France onto the American landscape, and in the wake of the powerful American-led wave of globalization in the twentieth and twenty-first centuries, operating in English for the most part, it is indeed notable that something profoundly French has remained. It is the musicians, cooks, social organizers, novelists, journalists, storytellers, and poets who carry the Franco-American banner, very often without any knowledge of taking part in *la francophonie*, in cultural transfer, exchange, or renaissance. They are simply modeling French life to some degree in translation, in the original, as their fathers, mothers, grandfathers and grandmothers, cousins, aunts, and uncles once did. Overtheorizing sustained French cultural life cannot accurately convey the meaning of these everyday traditions because many French Creole cultures are inherently popular in nature, by and for the working people. Franco-American *survivance* might be interpreted as a sign of Franco-America's resilience or perhaps weakness. The Franco glass is either half full or half empty.

The first chapter takes readers on a cultural expedition from the colonial experiment of la Nouvelle-France to postcolonial Franco-America. Almost two centuries ago, Alexis de Tocqueville noted a distinction between French and English mentalities in his study of American democracy. Today, French-Canadian folk artist Josée Vachon sings about the experience of discrimination and minority status, linking all members of the French family. The French did not emigrate in large numbers to any outlying territory, in comparison with other European imperial nations. Nor did they make great colonizers generally, following more advanced overseas powers out of perceived necessity into the race for international influence. Although the British prevailed in the Atlantic world, the French had won the battle for the hearts and minds of indigenous populations. Pioneering Jesuits and *coureurs de bois*, French bushwhackers, are examples of New World French populations that "went native." Colonial New France had been based on an intercultural alliance, "a Franco-Indian America." This middle grounding was one way of promoting French survival through successive imperial regimes (English, Spanish, American). The French chose intimate contact with native populations, but by doing so, they arguably opted out of whiteness. Romantic writer Francis Parkman banished them from the future-driven American trajectory.

The French broadly speaking did more than just name a few towns; they helped facilitate an era of American independence and expansion. The French accompanied Lewis and Clark on their trek westward. Franco-American explorers, priests, entrepreneurs, and professionals settled the frontier. French presence in fact ran north-south down the Mississippi River valley, along the "Creole Corridor," not to be confused with the "Zydeco Corridor" running east west between New Orleans and Houston. The "Franco freeway," running from the St. Lawrence River valley in Quebec to tributaries south in New England and New York, was also a conduit for activity. There is increased attention now paid to such north-south migrations in America. French Canadians traveled south from impoverished Quebec in search of work in the textile and shoe factories of the industrial northeast. They established French ethnic enclaves where life in French flourished. *Les Petits Canadas*, or Little Canadas, have all but disappeared, dispersed and razed by the double whammy of white flight and urban renewal. These ethnic neighborhoods in Lewiston, Maine, Manchester, New Hampshire, and Woonsocket, Rhode Island, were large yet certainly much less well known than the Little Italies and Chinatowns on the urban American landscape. Some of them lasted longer. Franco authors often evoke the notion of group invisibility: neighborhoods, institutions, and people existing unnoticed, underground. Even ephemeral ethnic enclaves produced lingering francophone cultures that warrant attention.

The second chapter examines the institutions that have fostered and supported Franco-Americans who settled in the working towns of New England and Acadiana, as the French parishes of south Louisiana are affectionately known to Cajuns. Franco mutual aid societies such as the Association Canado-Américaine (1896) and the Union Saint Jean Baptiste (1900) already have their stories and historians. Bilingual parochial schools in ethnic enclaves are largely responsible for maintaining French linguistic practices. We know less about smaller supportive organizations, such as the teaching institutions established historically to create an elite among laboring Franco-American populations. The University of Louisiana at Lafayette and Assumption College of Worcester, Massachusetts, are places founded at the beginning of the twentieth century for this very purpose. An older, influential French institution, with an early and unfamiliar American history, is the Alliance Française (AF). Symbolized by the French republican figure Marianne, the AF opened chapters in many parts of Franco-America, benefiting from the French ethnic centers that had been developed. Archives reveal that the French colonies and indeed postcolonies provided a useful and ready-made network for the French national organization's chapters. Later in the twentieth century, French community and cultural centers emerged. I examine the Council for the Development of French in Louisiana (CODOFIL), which has supported French heritage preservation in south Louisiana since 1968 and the Franco-American cultural centers of Manchester, New Hampshire, and Lewiston, Maine, at the service of French-descended populations for the last two decades.

Chapter 3 studies the role that women's social organizations have played in the perpetuation of Franco-American cultures. My examination begins with the *dame de la renaissance française*, a monument built recently to immortalize Franco-American contributions to urban life in Nashua, New Hampshire. The dame of french rebirth statue symbolizes the role that ethnic women have assumed in French America, in a rapidly changing post-colonial and postwar society. I focus on women's groups that have attempted to support Franco cultures in Massachusetts, where they were numerous and organized, for the last century. Men long denied women entrance to Franco-American social organizations, and so ancillary groups emerged. Today, women's organizations are among the most vital in carrying on the Franco-American tradition: Le Cercle Jeanne Mance (1913) of Worcester and Lowell, Massachusetts, as well as Woonsocket, Rhode Island, Le Cercle des dames françaises (1930) of Springfield, Massachusetts, and L'Association des dames franco-américaines (1953) of Chicopee, Massachusetts. Each was part of the Fédération des femmes Franco-Américaines (1951), an umbrella organization for social groups throughout New England. Historically, each catered to different social milieu within the Franco-American community. They hoped to inspire a new generation of Franco women, and indeed many daughters did follow their mothers into group participation. Today membership in associations has dwindled as individuals aged and some groups have folded.

Chapter 4 explores the broad scope of Franco-American literary cultures, the provincial, regional, or ethnic texts produced by individuals seeking to give voice to the French experience in North America, an obscure corner of the *littérature-monde*. Writers established a literature that sought to promote the best of Franco life. Franco-American literature includes *romans de la terre*, regional novels from Quebec, Acadian texts as well as more specifically Franco-American works dating from the late nineteenth to the twenty-first century. The analysis includes comparative readings of classics such as *Maria Chapdelaine* and *Pélagie-la-Charette* that reveal French interpretations of the North American continent, from Canada to the Gulf Coast, as well as the Franco origins of Beat generation author Jack Kerouac. The chapter examines little-known works by contemporary authors of Franco descent born in the United States. They affirm that the French experience of America, that Franco-American cultures continue to exist, in French, in English and in between. Franco-American authors might be included in more transnational notions of francophone literature.

Many Franco-American novels first appeared in the French language press of New England. Press and prose combined did much to articulate a contemporary Franco-American sense of self. As soon as significant numbers of Franco-Americans settled, they organized parishes, schools, and very often newspapers, the subject of the fifth chapter. The Franco journalistic tradition in New England continued until nearly the end of the twentieth century, unlike in francophone Louisiana where it expired. For a century, Franco ethnic centers maintained a daily, weekly, and monthly press written in French. The chapter is based on focused readings of Franco-American newspapers such as *Le Travailleur* of Worcester, Massachusetts (1931–78), *L'Avenir National* of Manchester, New Hampshire (1895–1949), *La Justice* of Holyoke, Massachusetts (1904–64), *L'Etoile* of Lowell, Massachusetts (1886–1957), and *Le Journal de Lowell* (1975–95). I examine the question of identity and nation articulated in newspapers between the two world wars, the apex of Franco-American ethnic identity, and a French language press. How did Franco communities celebrate cultural identity on Quebec's national holiday, Saint John the Baptist Day (June 24), during American Fourth of July festivities, as well as French Bastille Day (July 14)? The analysis includes commentary on suspect French sympathies in Franco-American communities during the Vichy period. Franco-Americans were forced to confront their cultural heritage in a wartime climate hostile to immigrants who maintained French affinities. Some editors of the Franco press were quicker than others to assert their Gaullist colors and to condemn the collaborationist French government. The analysis concludes with an investigation of *Le Journal de Lowell* and its short-lived but determined attempt to promote *la francophonie* within the United States.

The final chapter explores the unique contemporary Franco-American traditions of Louisiana, where cultural fusion or *métissage* took place to a greater extent between more groups than anywhere else in Franco-America. I refer to the Creole Cowboy and Mardi Gras Indian who symbolize the uniqueness of French hybrid cultures that developed in the Gulf South. Cultural expression provided a bridge across the color line, between European, Native American, and African groups in French Louisiana (an unsturdy bridge at best that one traversed at his or her own peril). The southern half of Louisiana is demonstratively French and different from the rest of the South. A French distinction can be witnessed in law and education, ethnic traditions, and voting patterns, despite a conservative push in the twentieth century. It is in French Acadiana that we find the most compelling examples of creolized cultural forms. In the early 1930s, Alan and John Lomax recorded for posterity what they called "tropical French music," all hybrid creations. The chapter focuses on oral and performed cultures: the blended origins of Cajun and Creole music, rural Mardi Gras celebrations, seasoned foodways, layman's poetry, and swamp folktales passed along from generation to generation. These evolving cultures are consumed like gumbo at cultural festivals.

French postcolonial monuments in the Franco-American south and northeast speak evocatively of the remaining cultural residue that marks the New World well after empire. They address the loss, mourning, and resurrection that transform cultural islands into networks. The conclusion to the text examines the meaning of Franco-American Day in Lowell, Massachusetts, where war veterans and civilians raise the seldom seen Franco-American flag (see cover), a contemporary symbol of French ethnic heritage. Francos honor the transnational nature of their experience annually in Lowell with a multitude of French, Canadian, and American symbols. Franco-American Day is one of a few significant remaining cultural and community expressions. Some evocative sites of French memory are included in the ceremony's itinerary each year. Several decades ago, Francos in other mill towns organized ethnic pride fairs, but most have disappeared.

My examination of Franco-America is selective and does not pretend to be exhaustive. The subject is in constant evolution, as will become evident in the body of the argument. I attempt to document some of Franco-America's distinctive features in their current forms. I also hope to have identified underrepresented currents in Francophone postcolonial studies that will encourage others to press on. The analysis can help to illustrate how French and American studies can inform one another more than they currently do without risking being swallowed up by the other. Interdisciplinary and international fields, as explored in French and Francophone studies, are contributing broadly to the American humanities. French is now studied across disciplines and far out into the field. My work intends to make this phenomenon better known. Much of what has been written about Franco-America has been produced by Franco-Americans themselves. Such scholarship produces a cultural insularity with rich attention to detail but also blind spots. While a few studies of Franco-America and Franco-Americans exist, comparative, cultural histories of the French experience in the United States are rare and all the more necessary.

CHAPTER I

Between Dream and Reality in Franco-America

Venez tous, jeunes filles et garçons
Je vais vous raconter
L'histoire de notre immigration aux USA
De grands aventuriers, des pays étrangers
Le long du grand Mississippi, venus coloniser

Et, en mille-sept-cent-cinquante-cinq
Des villages acadiens
Brûlés un soir inattendu, par les anglais vilains
Des familles séparées, en bateaux, exilées
Et par la mer emportées dans un pays lointain

Du Québec vers la Nouvelle-Angleterre, des habitants
Venus travailler l'usine, il y a plus de cent ans
Dans leurs p'tits Canadas
Par leur langue et leur foi
Vivant la survivance mais, au moins, pour le moment

Speak white, on nous disait
Pour enlever notre héritage
C'est par l'assimilation qu'on trouve les avantages
The borders between lands
Are not all that we have crossed
Now, we must be taught the language
That our mothers lost.

   Josée Vachon, "déracinée"

French demographic, cultural, and linguistic roots in North America
are entrenched and widely dispersed, from the Canadian provinces to
Louisiana's Gulf Coast, intones French-Canadian and adopted Franco-
American singer Josée Vachon. Francophone traditions and heritage have
been forged and maintained on the North American continent for more
than four centuries, following the exploratory voyages of Jacques Cartier,
Samuel de Champlain, Robert Cavalier de la Salle, and others, beginning in
the sixteenth century. Today these traditions appear threatened by global,
American-led forces of assimilation. As the song concludes with a subtle
but definitive shift from French to English, so French cultures in the United
States have been transformed, translated, and sometimes practically erased
from memory. Vestiges remain as well as hopes of preserving once vibrant
French ways of life. Vachon manages to capture many aspects of the French
experience in America, past and present, in a three-minute melody: exile,
oppression, preservation of cultural traditions, assimilation, loss of language,
and culture. She makes reference to some of America's diasporic francophone groups: Acadians and their Cajun brethren in Louisiana, Québécois
and Franco-Americans of New England. They are members of the greater
French family of North America, along with Franco-Ontarians, Franco-
Albertans, Franco-Manitobans, Fransaskois, and les Métis.[1] The offspring
of fur traders and Amerindian women, who came to be known as the mixed
races of the Canadian Midwest, les Métis represent a small but significant
creolized population. Each member of the French family possesses a singular
historical experience and cultural particularities, yet shares a language, a
predominant religion, and minority status in North America.

Canadian and American cultural geographers refer whimsically to Franco-Amérique as an entity that loosely groups all of these cultural communities. They define it as an "archipelago" consisting of linguistically and culturally French islands located in an Anglo-American sea.[2] *Franco-America*, cultural geographers claim in recent work, is a broader, more accurate, less Eurocentric term than its predecessor, French America.[3] Invoking the notion of Franco-Amérique, Dean Louder, Jean Morisset, and Eric Waddell have provocatively suggested that the history of America be reexamined to take into account the participation of French descendants. They erect bridges between the various French islands of North America. Bill Marshall suggests that we consider the important linkages that connect the various points, or hinges, in the French Atlantic.[4] The currents that flow through such hinges accentuate similarities as well as distinctions. Many New World French island cultures, Acadian, Québécois, Creole, and others, have established symbols, flags, "national" anthems, holidays, and traditions through which Franco-American identities have taken shape over the last century. They are powerful repositories of memory as well as of present trajectories.[5] Outside of these markers, what particularly connects the Franco-American family members of the United States: Canucks, Coonasses, and Creoles, to use both disparaging and unifying labels for French heritage populations in New England and Louisiana? Older generations of French descent to this day refer to themselves as French Canadians or Francos. Others simply call themselves French. They claim that they frequent the French church, or occasionally attend a French social organization and take part in French social cultural activities, even if they do not speak the language. The French were identified as such from the outside and within, having their own neighborhoods and infrastructure where French language was widely spoken publicly until the mid-twentieth century. This is not, however, a case of attempting to assume a foreign Frenchness. The formation of a Franco-American identity over the course of a century, from 1850 to 1950 roughly, illustrates the attempt to negotiate something else. It problematizes what it means to be French and francophone today in the United States.

To be French in America is certainly distinct from being French in France or elsewhere. Empire and postcolonial migratory currents have removed French identity debates from a strictly metropolitan or national space. The struggle for French cultural and linguistic survival unites groups, but some advocates of Franco-America regret that individuals have not sought to make use of their collective force. They continue to exist as isolated island cultures for the most part, despite the sporadic support given to North American *francophonie*, particularly in Louisiana, by the French, Belgian, and Canadian governments. One must be careful not to exaggerate the resonance of Franco-America, which primarily exists as a collection of wistful ruminations of scholar-advocates. This chapter and book explore why French presence in America is significant despite minority status, despite limited knowledge of it, and despite disparaging remarks about French interest in the New World, summarily dismissed by the Enlightenment philosopher Voltaire's comments about frigidly desolate *arpents de neige* and *déserts glacés*. Postcolonial Franco-America is about the homegrown products of French and francophone descent, the parts of an American nation and people that continue to function to some degree in French, that are culturally "French." The thousands of French nationals living and working in the United States have another story to tell.

Some Franco-Americans choose to live in French, linguistically and/ or culturally, in the United States today, in New England and Louisiana. For others, Franco-America as a lived and spoken ethnic experience is a phenomenon of the past, and traditions are carried on primarily through the lens of folklore. Franco-Americans have one foot firmly in the past and one in the future as a Nashua, New Hampshire, monument to the Franco-American war dead proudly claims: *Du passé, à l'avenir*. Franco-America is still in the making, I would suggest, despite being on life support practically since its inception. Living in French in North America has required passionate dreamers and fighters, people for whom French or francophone linguistic and cultural practices have been worth preserving. One of Franco-America's most vocal spokespersons before and after the physical and cultural ravages of Hurricanes Katrina and Rita has been Cajun singer and activist Zachary Richard. For the several million people of French and francophone descent in North America, many of whom, like Richard, live south of the Canadian border, French culture is a part of daily life, not simply a commemorative gesture.[6] Franco-Americans are professionals, skilled laborers, and teachers— American like other immigrant groups, but with a French twist.

The Internet today places French and francophone images, voices, sounds, and ideas at the disposal of the increasing numbers of Americans who are connected to the worldwide web of telecommunications. Through one such media form (TV5Monde), it is possible for Franco-Americans in New England to hear French as it was and is spoken by their Québécois and Acadian ancestors. TV5Monde has been an active sponsor of francophone cultural life in places such as Lewiston, Maine, and Lafayette, Louisiana. Virtual and traditional media sometimes help to support North American francophone communities, stimulating a continuing demand for French language and culture, which may bode well for the future of Franco-America on both sides of the U.S.–Canada border. TV5, known as TV5Monde since 2005, emerged in 1984 when French, Belgian, and Swiss channels pooled resources. It has since become a successful international French-language television station. The station with an overtly francophone agenda transmits its programs to 160 million households, placing it in third position behind MTV and CNN.[7] It has organized scheduling according to the consumer demands of its varied markets in Europe, Africa, Asia, Canada, and in the United States. Although not available everywhere, Franco-Americans can periodically tune in to a French-language channel that includes productions of particular cultural interest to them.

Three prominent national and international francophone media including TV5Monde have helped to give voice to Franco-American communities in the past and as they have moved into the twenty-first century. They will be referred to occasionally throughout the text. More specialized ethnic media representing French-speaking populations in New England and south Louisiana existed and will be examined in detail. Benedict

Anderson asserted that economic and technological advancements, or the explosion of telecommunications, have served to create the conditions for the birth of national consciousness, none more so perhaps than what he calls "print-capitalism." French radio, television, and the written press form an influential triumvirate within the cultural and commercial contours of Franco-America. The opportunity to speak, read, listen, and observe French and francophone life *in French* has provided inspiration to many. Radio France Internationale (RFI) brings its audience of more than 45 million listeners news in French about France, the French-speaking community, and the wider world around. For audiences of traditional FM radio in large metropolitan areas like New York City, RFI is accessible twenty-four hours a day, seven days a week. It is currently unavailable in much of New England, although connection through the web and live audio streaming offers continual access. Since 2009 RFI has been available to French speakers in south Louisiana via their smart phones.

Comparatively, the written press has suffered in terms of circulation and relevance in the age of virtual media. The newspaper *France-Amérique* long provided a source of news for French-speaking, educated populations in the United States. It is the largest French-language newspaper in the United States and the only one with a relatively wide audience since it fused with its sister publication, the San Francisco–based *Journal Français*, in April 2007. That same year, it underwent a transformation from a bimonthly edition, with a 20,000 print circulation and an alleged readership (according to its own figures) of 60,000, to a glossy monthly format. In 2015 *France-Amérique*, known as the "French paper of the United States," became a bilingual publication in hopes of increasing readership. Since its founding during the Second World War in 1943 and from its headquarters in New York, the "international edition of *Le Figaro*," the center-right French daily, has served as a source of community information for French nationals and has also highlighted America's rich and varied French heritage. From its inception through today, *France-Amérique* has sought to foster relations between the two universalist nations. All such media, radio, television, and print news serve to promote French language and culture, francophonie, in other words, in the United States.

Franco-American dreams and realities offer a different reading of America, a distinctly French take on the proverbial American melting pot and its *métissage* (miscegenation), race relations, and cultural identities. At the same time, the history of French presence in America offers an interesting perspective on seventeenth-century monarchic France, which sought to reproduce itself transatlantically beyond European shores. Early settlers to the New World were to create a promised land exclusively for Catholics.[8] This was to be a New and Better France, and in some respects it was.[9] Despite the real dangers of resettlement and life in New France, we know that settlers were at times better off than in the Old World. European hierarchies were reproduced, but there was more social mobility in New France.[10] In *The Bourgeois Frontier*, Jay Gitlin reminds readers that traders and commercial tycoons accompanied the peasants and bushwhackers—*habitants* and *coureurs de bois*—to French America. Military men were the social category most likely to remain in what would later become a former French colony. While social elites tended to validate and to reproduce Old World culture and cultural distinction, the working classes identified with their New World American surroundings.[11]

The United States of America is indebted as an independent nation to individual French revolutionary war heroes such as the Marquis de Lafayette and the Comte de Rochambeau. Historians rightly contend that French efforts in the New World made it possible for American upstarts to complete their revolution.[12] The irony of French aristocratic aid to our Revolution may be somewhat lost to the general public today, but both Lafayette and Rochambeau have had prominent commemorative sites built in the United States for special remembrance. The popular Broadway musical *Hamilton* has reinserted these two fighting Frenchmen into discussions of the early history of the United States.[13] In 2005 French and American guests in Newport, Rhode Island, celebrated the 225 years since Rochambeau's arrival in America and his subsequent collaboration with the American insurgency. Two years later, the French and Americans celebrated the 250th anniversary of Lafayette's birth. Practically a son to

George Washington, wounded at the Battle of Brandywine, and buried in American soil (in Paris), Lafayette symbolizes like no other French American interconnectedness.[14] More than a dozen cities named Lafayette in states across America represent a symbolic tribute to French assistance, which originated not with any particularly sympathetic enthusiasm for the American upstarts but in order to weaken the British.

When Canadians celebrated four hundred years of French presence in North America, few Americans had more detailed knowledge of French imperial interests in America, or about French makers of American history, or about the descendants of French and francophone extraction now self-identified as Franco-Americans. At that time, *French* and *American* seemed almost to be contradictory terms, so diametrically opposed were Old World French culture and American frontier traditions. This was despite the lengthy colonial history linking the two countries, the similar revolutionary trajectories and democratic principles, and the twentieth-century experiences of French-American world war cooperation. France is the only European nation against whom the United States has never waged war.

The continental divide widened in recent years as a result of acute discord over the war in Iraq, highlighted by the comical movement to replace *French* with *Freedom* as the modifier to beloved (inter)national fries. Recalcitrant French bashers may be dismayed to discover the extent to which the American nation has been marked by French influence. Long before the recent tensions escalated, French sociologist Pierre Bourdieu recognized two linked yet opposing universalisms in French and American cultural, political, and economic models and thus an inevitable collision in the contest for global influence.[15] For this reason, France and Frenchness matter in America in ways that more powerful nations and cultures do not. As both ally and irritant in the last century, France holds an important place in the American consciousness. American interests in France are certainly nourished by representations of French cultural distinction and savoir faire that are continually renewed in the media. Rapture with French high culture will likely continue to draw American interest, physical travel to France, and participation in French language courses in significant numbers in spite of economic woes or political tribulations. Despite fears of French irrelevance in the contemporary world of globalization and a unified Europe, France remains a culture and a model by which Americans like to measure and define themselves.[16] "France is the country most like the United States that differs most from it," asserts Herrick Chapman.[17] France and the French are thus still present within the scope of American interests and have survived (perhaps not entirely unscathed) the recently volatile and competitive nature of French American relations.

Much has been written about the Americanization of France in the twentieth century. We have considerably less information about the *francization* of America, particularly the United States. If Lafayette is one of the most American of Frenchmen, Benjamin Franklin deserves mention as one of the most French of Americans. He was certainly one of the early cosmopolitan Franco-Americans in some regards.[18] In the early nineteenth century, the astute student of American life Alexis de Tocqueville noticed the particularity of French America north of the border. Tocqueville found scant daring and little disdain for class consciousness among French Canadians: "La race canadienne . . . n'a point cet esprit aventureux et ce mépris des liens de naissance et de famille qui caractérisent les Américains," the French aristocrat wrote.[19] The French America that he observed, in other words, did not seem particularly American. Yet since the eighteenth century when French population growth began to stem not from immigration but from birth in the New World, people of French descent had become American while continuing to be French or francophone. In typically French and not American fashion, they intermingled with other groups in the cauldron of New World society. Creolized settlers born in the New World after the eighteenth century became progressively known as *Canadiens*, a term used prior to this in reference to Native Americans. Canadiens, Creoles, and Francos today all provide evidence of the pervasiveness of New World Frenchness.

As an example of such cultural negotiations, a glance across the Canadian border is revealing. Current debates about *Américanité* or North Americanness among francophone cultural elites in Quebec have ignited heated discussion about French and American identities and demonstrate that it is still difficult to reconcile French and American in the New World. How can French Canadians admit their Americanness without being swallowed up by the behemoth to the south of them? "La route de l'américanité ne conduit pas à l'Amérique française, mais à sa perte dans la descente continentale," warns Thériault.[20] There is no *Américanité* without Americanization, he claims. America may indeed be an English-language invention and concept, but so is Franco-American, a qualitative term used to this day by people of French-Canadian descent in the United States. The dilemma continues for Québécois intellectuals who, over the past several decades, have struggled to live their lives in French in North America. This semantic and ideological battle is less pitched among Francos in the United States, but the Frenchness of the U.S. is nonetheless in need of further interdisciplinary study.

One of the early historians of France in America, Francis Parkman, identified two very different projects in New England and New France: "Liberty and Absolutism, New England and New France. The one was the offspring of a triumphant government; the other, of an oppressed and fugitive people: the one, an unflinching champion of the Roman Catholic reaction; the other, a vanguard of the Reform. Each followed its natural laws of growth, and each came to its natural result."[21] Parkman seems to suggest that the attempt to create a transatlantic France could only ultimately fail. New England, on the other hand, plodded on methodically, progressing but without the flair of a French crown that could scale great heights, yet also knew crushing defeat. Parkman continues: "The growth of New England was a result of the aggregate efforts of a busy multitude, each in his narrow circle toiling for himself, to gather competence or wealth. The expansion of New France was the achievement of a gigantic ambition striving to grasp a continent. It was a vain attempt."[22] New France was destined for expiration according to Parkman (and here he was for the most part correct), although New England would become home to increasing numbers of French Canadians seeking better fortunes at the very time that Parkman published his classic work.

This study is in part a response to Parkman and to Tocqueville for whom Frenchness and Americanness appear mutually exclusive. Writing before dreams of a modern francophone nation took shape in nineteenth-century Canada, Parkman alludes to the end of the French era in the Atlantic world. In his book *In This Remote Country* Edward Watts identifies writers such as Francis Parkman as "romantic historians," chroniclers perhaps most interested by intrigue, myth, and the development of a compelling story.[23] In the signature, dramatic tones of a skilled writer and a flawed historian, Parkman tells a mystical tale of the French experience in the New World, an unseemly fellowship of Native American "savages," fearless Jesuit servants of God in the wilderness, and French lords and vassals. "The French dominion is a memory of the past; and when we evoke its departed shades, they rise upon us from their graves in strange romantic guise. Again their ghostly camp-fires seem to burn, and the fitful light is cast around on lord and vassal and black-robed priest, mingled with vivid forms of savage warriors knit in close fellowship on the same stern errand."[24] This motley crew represents the uniqueness of the French experiment on American shores. Despite "romantic" nineteenth-century claims to the contrary, French fires lit on the North American continent have yet to be fully extinguished in the twenty-first century.

Outside of Franco-American individuals, families, and organizations, as well as a coterie of specialists, knowledge of French colonial activity in America is limited. Franco-Americans have nearly disintegrated within the assimilating American system, offering little help. "Francos" have yet to be entirely retrieved from the melting pot by multiculturalists. Before the white ethnic pride movements of the 1970s and 1980s could intervene and recuperate them, French ethnic shaming pushed a people and a culture underground. For decades, people of French and francophone descent have been objects of derision from New England to Louisiana. They have been the butt of ethnic jokes, labeled poor, backward Coonasses and Canucks, and ridiculed for perceived working-class and peasant inferiorities. As a result of this stigmatization, some members of the francophone family rejected French identity altogether, opting not to teach "inferior" French to their children and not to preserve certain cultural or "ethnic" traditions.

French shame intensified assimilation, which had set in naturally by the early to mid-twentieth century and was facilitated by a growing consumer culture bred by television. Franco-American shame contrasts sharply with privileged metropolitan notions of French grandeur and high culture, a markedly Parisian model of distinction, dulled slightly perhaps by the current French economic and cultural malaise. French pretentions of style and grace date back some four hundred years, to the court of Louis XIV, suggests Joan DeJean.[25] In Franco-America, the shift out of French ethnic identity was symbolized by the great American move to the suburbs in the 1960s, flight that signaled the end of many endogamous Franco-American communities. A xenophobic state had accelerated this process with the English-only laws that officials put into place in the early twentieth century in both New England and Louisiana. The French disappearing act in America is related in part to the dilution and defamation of French identity between Old World and New.

New World French ethnicity is quite different from the universalist claims of the French Republic in which national identity is not tied to any racial, religious, or regional sensibility. Since the Revolution, the French Republic has vigorously eschewed any such notion of *communautarisme*, of a rival nation within the nation. Following publication of *The Empire Writes Back*, scholars asserted that postcolonialism sought to reject the universalism that was part and parcel of the imperial project. Spokespeople from immigrant organizations and other *minorités visibles* in France have been quite critical of the French republican tradition in recent years. In French postcolonial thought, we witness rejection of universalism but support for the universalization of expressions: "La pensée postcoloniale montre comment le colonialisme lui-même a été une expérience planétaire, qui a contribué à l'universalisation des représentations, des techniques et des institutions."[26] *Francophonie*, and more specifically the Organisation internationale de la francophonie as an international movement, has provided an extended space for recognition of French linguistic and cultural identities outside and beyond French national borders. The international organization has begun to recognize the wide francophone horizons of the North American continent, assisted by members of the French media.

Assuming a French cultural or ethnic identity in the United States strangely meant that groups of francophone descent became lost from sight, not more easily recognized. Having internalized the negative attitudes about them, people chose to live French or Franco lives in the shadows. They expressed little pride publicly about their French heritage until very recently, and as a result, a cultural identity began to fade away.[27]

There is nothing currently resembling St. Patrick's Day celebrations for francophone communities in the United States, in which people can demonstrate pride in being French, if only for a day. Yet a half century ago, Franco-Americans gathered in many a New England town in June and paraded to celebrate their French ethnic roots on St. John the Baptist Day. The New Orleans Mardi Gras celebration has taken on such surreal, over-the-top dimensions that it fails to convey much of anything about French traditions in the United States, unlike some smaller festivities in rural Louisiana. It seems important to acknowledge French and francophone cultures of the United States, if only to identify an obscure part of American history. One metaphor is readily apparent: these cultures are in peril, as are the Cajun bayous and wetlands in south Louisiana that are rapidly being swallowed up by the rising tides of the Gulf of Mexico.[28]

As some readers will recognize, the themes mentioned in the song by Josée Vachon at the beginning of the chapter are distinctly postcolonial in nature. The victory of the British in the battle for North American supremacy resulted in the deportation and exile of the Acadians. The queen of England officially recognized the tragedy of *Le Grand Dérangement* of 1755–62, in which Acadian homes were burned to the ground, families were separated, and people were dispersed on ships leaving Grand-Pré, in today's Nova Scotia, bound for points south. *Ethnic cleansing* and *genocide* are terms that might arguably be applied to these acts. Recognition had long been an objective of the Council for the Development of French in Louisiana (CODOFIL).[29] In solemn remembrance of the 250 years following the forced exile, Queen Elizabeth announced that beginning in 2005, July 28 would represent an official day of reflection and atonement for British cruelty inflicted on a French population. On that day, a French Mass was celebrated at the St. John's Cathedral in Lafayette, Louisiana, as part of the commemorative events, marking the anniversary of the deportation. Atop the cathedral, the French *coq* or rooster is a small but symbolic marker of the area's French heritage.

Since Henry Wadsworth Longfellow first wrote his epic poem in 1847, *Evangeline* has reassembled the people of Acadian descent, creating perhaps a more impassioned group and nation in the process. Evangeline's odyssey, shining bright like the star of the Acadian flag, continues to lead Acadians back "home." This classic story of fidelity and both romantic and patriotic love remains powerfully relevant today for Franco-Americans of varying descent. In Longfellow's tale, Evangeline and Gabriel are to be wed when news of the deportation arrives. They are separated and wander biblically along the Atlantic coast, as did many Acadians. Just once, their paths cross, oh so close in the night in a Louisiana bayou. Evangeline never forgets her love of Gabriel and Acadie during her long years of exile, and the lovers are finally reunited in death. Lying side by side in a cemetery in Philadelphia, they remain banished from their ancestral land.

The reading of the work and the perpetuation of its mythical message represent a compelling example of Homi Bhabha's *Nation and Narration*, that is to say, a veritable nation forged by the power of fiction. The narration of Franco-America is both extensive and evocative. Scholars have recently attempted to reassert study of the nation, more a European model and history, into the discussion on American society and culture.[30] In 1755 the British had hoped that exile would eradicate the Acadian nation and identity, but instead it only intensified loyalties. Evangeline and her story continue to inspire and unite. Evangeline has been immortalized at commemorative sites like Grand Pré where Acadians boarded ships of no return, and she also rests in points south such as St. Martinville, Louisiana. The Louisiana Evangeline site, donated in 1927 by inspired Mexican actress Dolores del Río, is probably the most popular of Franco-American or Acadian memorials. Massive Acadian family gatherings have occurred every five years since 1994, the year of the first highly successful Acadian World Congress (Congrès mondial acadien).This suggests that transnational Acadian sensibilities are still held dear, powerfully forged through shared hardships. In 2014, the Acadian World Congress held its annual meetings over the course of two weeks at the intersection of

Acadian francophone frontiers and international borders of northernmost Maine, Quebec, and New Brunswick.[31] These events, which include many family reunions on a macro scale, affirm the French Creole nation within the American homeland.

Franco-American identity, as noted, has been significantly shaped by its association with people of color. It is striking that in rejecting slights and reclaiming French cultural identity, some Francos identified with the black experience in America. The Great Migration of large numbers of African Americans to the growing industrial cities of the Northeast, Midwest, and West is not altogether unlike the southbound migration of French Québécois to the smaller industrial centers of New England and New York. Like the six million African Americans who left the South at the beginning of the twentieth century, Québécois moved en masse southward, bringing with them distinct ways of living, worshipping, and speaking. A million people left the desolate farms and inhospitable land of Canada, flocking by train, horse, and on foot to the industrial cities of New England. This trip was not always as harrowing as the voyage north for African Americans, fleeing the violence of Jim Crow, but it was uprooting and could potentially be perilous. There were factors pushing forward both groups but also pulling them back.

There is chronologic overlap between these two migrations, and both sets of migrants brought with them "backward" peasant customs ridiculed by residing urban populations. They cooked, cleaned, worked, and amused themselves differently. They were country bumpkins who sometimes looked and felt out of place in the industrial North of the United States. They did learn how to survive, however, and over time they became less conspicuous. Both relied on Native American assistance in their adaptation. Isabel Wilkerson, author of *The Warmth of Other Suns: The Epic Story of America's Great Migration*, cites Mahalia Jackson's "Moving on up": "Our mattresses were made of corn shucks and soft gray Spanish moss that hung from the trees. . . . From the swamps we got soup turtles and baby alligators and from the woods got raccoon, rabbit, and possum."[32] Rhea Côté Robbins's Franco memoir, *Wednesday's Child*, notes making hog head cheese and creton from slaughtered pigs, "everything but the squeal," consumed by family members.[33] Nothing was wasted within communities faced with migratory upheaval, but everything was remembered. In the wake of French-Canadian and African American collective shifts, stories of customs, food, song, and dance abound. Both groups attempted to remake a bit of "home" in their surroundings, which were sometimes perceived as temporary but were often permanent. Wilkerson argues that an "unrecognized immigration" within the United States should be given its due respect. Franco-American migrations are similarly obfuscated.

Some of the most assertive attitudes of francophone nationalists in America (Québécois mostly) have taken their inspiration from the civil rights movement and from black nationalists particularly. Pierre Vallières famously spoke of *Nègres blancs d'Amérique* (white niggers of America).[34] In her 1968 poem "Speak White," Michèle Lalonde equated speaking French with speaking black or Cajun, with the language of poor, working-class, and sometimes racialized groups.[35] By speaking French, Franco-Americans defiantly asserted their minority status along with other voices of the oppressed in the 1960s. Speaking English equaled erasure of cultural distinction, becoming "white" and losing ethnicity, although some had little difficulty doing this. Becoming "white" in a Franco-American context signals a loss of symbolic capital. Analyses of white ethnic identities suggest that the construction of whiteness had everything to do with survival and establishing supremacy among rival groups.[36]

One can readily identify a lingering postcolonial condition among former colonizers in a British-dominated settler colony. There are, however, a confusing array of colonized/colonizing forces operating in the New World. Marvin Richards indicates four imperial powers: France, the United States, Rome (i.e., the Vatican), and the United Kingdom.[37] Sandra Hobbs has suggested that Quebec is both a colonizer of Native Americans and simultaneously colonized like indigenous populations by the English, "à la fois colonisateur de l'Authochtone . . . et co-colonisé avec l'Autochtone par le Canada anglais."[38] Amerindians of North America make up a colonized group apart from the historical winners and losers. The postcoloniality of North American francophone literatures has been a topic of discussion since the timely conversation begun by Vincent Desroches in 2003.[39] The

United States of America, according to critics, is the postcolonial country par excellence, despite its now independent, arguably imperial status.[40] Theorists are insistently (intrusively, some might argue) pushing postcolonial paradigms into North America for new insights. While contested, a postcolonial condition is a perceived reality for members of the displaced French family. As ethnic minorities, Franco-Americans have asserted their existence from the shadows.

Since the beginning of French colonial activity in America in the early seventeenth century, there have been substantial levels of contact between French and indigenous populations, much more so than between English colonialists and Amerindians. The original French Acadian groups that settled the Maritime Provinces mingled extensively with Micmacs. Nowhere was cultural métissage as widespread as in south Louisiana; this will be explored in further detail in the final chapter. The baby held by the Native American legend Sacagawea on the one-dollar coin is a Franco-American, fathered by a French explorer or *coureur de bois*, an indication of the pervasive melding of cultures. Historians Gilles Havard and Cécile Vidal argue that French America was in actuality an "Amérique franco-indienne." A French empire in North America was possible only through what they call an "alliance interculturelle" between European populations, Native Americans, and African slaves.[41] They are careful to acknowledge that this intercultural alliance was based on inequalities and violence. Settlers certainly used this alliance to their advantage, adopting Native American practices such as *la petite guerre*, rapid ambush tactics followed by retreat into the forest. *Indianization* gave habitants a better chance for a successful existence.

Allan Greer offers a new history of New France in giving voice to the perspectives of women, blacks, and Indian slaves: "In the 17th and 18th century, Catholic immigrants from France, working often in close relations with Natives, Blacks, and Protestants, reconstituted a version of European society on the banks of the St. Lawrence."[42] There are today significant numbers of Native American Indian tribes, members of the Houma nation, for instance, growing up in Cajun French.[43] The Houma began trading and intermarrying with displaced Acadians in the bayous of eighteenth-century

Louisiana. Such distinct French experiences with race and métissage in America, particularly early French models of cultural integration, offer compelling perspectives. The legal system in place in Louisiana is still French (Napoleonic) and quite distinctive. The French *Code Noir,* which established certain rules of conduct for slavery, offers a case in point. The *Code* legislated more lenient treatment of slaves, for instance, although this often proved to be impossible to enforce.

FRENCH TRANSATLANTIC VOYAGES AND SETTLEMENTS

Four hundred years ago, French explorer Samuel de Champlain helped to establish France's imperial foothold in North America with the powerful blessing of crown and church. Champlain's exploits and his detailed essays and illustrations provide colorful, enduring images of the New World. He is the person most frequently (and justifiably) identified in historiography as the founder of French America, although he was only one of many European emissaries to comb North Atlantic shores in the sixteenth and seventeenth centuries. After an unsuccessful attempt to tame its wilderness a few years earlier, Champlain planted the seeds of a lasting French colonial settlement at the protected site of Quebec City on July 3, 1608. *La Nouvelle-France,* more French colonial fantasy than actuality, had been born.

La Nouvelle-France, a sparsely populated settler colony, stretched from the St. Lawrence River valley, throughout the Great Lakes basin, and down the Mississippi River into the Gulf of Mexico. Acadia, Canada, and Louisiana were integral parts of this French imperial space for more than a century before being broken up by the decisive victory of English forces in 1713 and on the Plains of Abraham, just outside the walls of Quebec City, in 1759. With the exception of the North Atlantic islands of St. Pierre-et-Miquelon, North America has not been officially French for some two hundred years since then, after Napoléon Bonaparte sold the immense Louisiana Territory to America in 1803. Nonetheless, a minority francophone presence has held tightly if precariously to American shores. Champlain's figurative and literal descendants have continued to define an original New World sense of Frenchness beyond this gateway to an imagined, transatlantic France of fabulous riches.

French pioneers in the New World, as Francis Parkman called them, were the first to cross into the plains of the West, advancing up to the Rocky Mountains ahead of American explorers Lewis and Clark.[44] They served as guides to the famous American trail blazers. They left their imprint in the naming of places large and small, in cities such as St. Louis, Detroit, and Baton Rouge, but also in smaller municipalities like Des Moines, Iowa, Prairie du Chien, Wisconsin, and St. Geneviève, Missouri. French influence in America is more, however, than simply names imposed on a map. Commemorative sites have been etched onto the landscape. While the French never really "possessed" America to the extent that the colonists from England did, they acquired a superior knowledge of huge tracts of the continent through exploration and close trade relations with Native Americans. *Coureurs de bois*, exploring and clearing paths through the American wilderness for others to follow, are as iconically American as cowboys, more so in fact as they smartly adopted Native American ways instead of fighting them. Like Creole cowboys in the Gulf South, they represent the very essence of Franco-American.

Jacques Mathieu claims that the French opted, to their own detriment perhaps, for expansive efforts over more intensified colonial efforts in the New World. Gilles Havard and Cécile Vidal, in analyzing the imperial holdings of the French, echoed the large scale of the French project in the Americas: "Ils disposaient d'une infrastructure capable de maîtriser correctement l'espace, en acheminant les personnes et en transmettant les ordres et les informations sur de longues distances, du Canada à la Louisiane. La Nouvelle-France, en ce sens, constituait un empire."[45] W. J. Eccles concurred, calling la Nouvelle-France a "river empire."[46] The land and adjacent waters of French America facilitated community, trade, leisure, and escape for a minority population. The descendants of the French in America still live along the banks of the great industrious rivers, including the St. Lawrence, the St. John, the Merrimack, the Connecticut, the Ohio, the Missouri, and the Mississippi. As their numbers dwindle, monuments marking their presence continue to spring up on the shores of places like Nashua, New Hampshire, establishing a more permanent reminder of French life than ephemeral human existence.

The French colonial experiment in the New World represented an attempt to inscribe France onto the continent. Its designers, as noted, conceived of *la Nouvelle-France* as a new, improved, and royal French transatlantic remake. "La Couronne cherchait à transplanter outremer une société française corrigée et transformée dans une optique absolutiste."[47] Missionaries envisioned a "New Jerusalem," a territory blessed by God, more Catholic than France, by the conversion of indigenous peoples. As for its European contingent, Colbert believed that New France should be built from "good seed," not the riffraff often associated with colonial outposts.[48] It is difficult to measure, of course, the success of French society corrected and remade overseas, but historians have noted that New World settlers had greater freedoms, they ate more and better food, and they tended to live longer than they might in the old country.[49] The Coutume de Paris established a social hierarchy with the king at the top, but did not prevent greater social fluidity.[50] Colonial populations spoke a "better," purer form of French as a result of the "linguistic homogenization" that evolved in the New World.[51] Immigrants left aside their regional dialects for the *langue d'oïl* to facilitate communication. The French of America thus began to speak what would become standard French before people in France did. It seems far-fetched to claim that colonial populations became more French than the French, as is sometimes suggested, because French languages, people, and cultures evolved considerably over time in North America. They developed their own particular amalgamated forms of expression.

Why pursue colonial activity far from France in the eighteenth century? Glory, riches, and prestige for the crown as well as trade routes to Asia provided incentive enough for a few adventurers, although the question is justified by the typically lukewarm approach to colonial activity. Canadian historian Peter Moogk argues that "ironically, New France proved to be the most successful effort at overseas colonization undertaken by the French, and its people endured, despite being abandoned by the founder state."[52] Moogk's claim appears dubious if one looks at the ephemeral nature of the French empire in the New World and if one considers the larger scale of development in North Africa, particularly in Algeria. But he is right to highlight the zealousness of a few transatlantic Frenchmen to duplicate themselves. That they failed to convert many Native Americans is another matter, although it is certainly true, as Moogk suggests, that descendants of the French have remained in North America long after France lost its colonial possession. The titles of a sampling of studies of French colonial efforts in the Atlantic world are revealing: *Chasing Empire across the Sea* (2006), *Ghost Empire* (2006), and *In Search of Empire* (2007) echo the ephemeral or halfhearted nature of French colonial efforts from the very beginning.[53] They signify a lack of sustained French interest, making the lingering effects of their activities all the more surprising. According to James Pritchard, author of *In Search of Empire*, disparate settlers and slaves were responsible for the establishment of French societies in the New World, more so than colonial or metropolitan authorities. Organizational and demographic weaknesses proved to be fatal flaws in colonial efforts, hence the elusiveness of French empire.[54]

New France captivated the interest of some of the most powerful men of *ancien régime* France, for a time at least, such as François I and the Sun King, Louis XIV, whose bust sits in the Place Royale at the lower town in Quebec City, where the French experiment began. Yet France entered the colonial game in the New World quite late, well after Spain and Portugal, and most specifically to thwart their aspirations. The French crown was certainly "chasing empire" in the wake of Spanish and Portuguese ships.[55] Moogk describes colonial settlers as "reluctant exiles" who recognized the very real and dangerous obstacles to life in America.[56] Nathan Brecher blames weakened French colonial presence in the New World on the ineffective policies, warmongering, and philandering of French monarchs such as Louis XV.[57] W. J. Eccles notes that French interests lie primarily in the West Indies.[58]

The failure to fully engage in the colonial project is surely related to a monarchy that was not willing to risk its Old World demographic reserves to populate new colonies such as *La Nouvelle-France*, particularly after the colony failed to yield the resources that inspired the transatlantic voyages in the first place (Jacques Cartier's famous *faux diamants*). New France was finally established permanently after several unsuccessful attempts to colonize, namely, by Cartier. Europeans had actually been sailing to the

Grand Banks off of the North Atlantic coast to reap the benefits of its productive fishery long before Samuel de Champlain founded the capital city. The 150 days of the year that the Catholic faithful could not eat meat certainly stimulated the fishing industry and inspired exploration of the Atlantic world.[59] No established colony was needed initially, and as such there was little interest in creating a populous settler colony. Only a small labor source was needed to exploit the natural resources from the American wilderness, the fish and fur industries.[60] Felt top hats, made with the delicate underbellies of beaver, had become all the rage in high European society, creating the parameters of this market.

François I was responsible for initiating the transatlantic ventures that combined the expansionist interests of both the monarchy and religious leaders. Some of the first writings about *la Nouvelle-France* were more accurately about Nuova Francia, as they were written in Italian and based on the voyages of Verrazano in the early sixteenth century. Henri IV later propelled French interests in the Americas, but was apparently most interested in Brazil.[61] Commercial interests certainly directed French activities in the Americas, although the church sent some of the earliest settlers to New France. Louis XIV's penchant for diamonds, a not so subtle sign of his powerful reign, surely fueled his New World ambitions.[62] Under the leadership of Prime Minister Richelieu, the Compagnie des Cent-Associés was responsible for the distribution of land, *seigneuries*, in *la Nouvelle-France* and for the successful colonization of the territory between 1627 and 1663. It was supposed to help establish four thousand people of Catholic faith there in the first fifteen years and assist them in settling for three years.[63] Historians concur that this initiative did not produce the desired results.

Between 1667 and 1685, the French absolute monarch, Louis XIV, had reached the apex of his powers and orchestrated his ambitions in the New World. His interests withered rapidly, however, once the fabulous riches of the French royal imagination failed to materialize. He did maintain the belief that empire bolstered the prestige and power of his regime. With Foreign Minister Colbert at the imperial helm, the state became involved in French colonial activity in the New World. While unwilling to "depopulate" France, Colbert attempted to encourage settler growth by fining settlers whose daughters and sons were not married by ages sixteen and twenty, respectively.[64] There were few women of any age to marry in New France, a phenomenon that certainly accelerated the contact with indigenous groups. Most of the population was made up of soldiers involved in subduing the Iroquois. They traveled to New France with three- to five-year contracts. Some of these soldiers eventually paired with Louis XIV's *filles du roi*, who were granted royal permission to remain and procreate in the French Americas. Female orphans under twenty-five years of age received a dowry and ship's passage for the purpose of finding a husband in New France and having children.[65] Coming from the Île-de-France region, they contributed to French linguistic homogeneity in the New World. These women retained at least some level of personal choice in the matter of marriage and family life. The Quebec government has commemorated their role in the building of Franco-America.[66]

Over a span of ten years, several thousand young women (and some widows) made the voyage to the New World. In a contemporary visual representation of their arrival, rapid marriage in many cases, and child-bearing, artist Cynthia Girard depicts forlorn French soldiers of the Indian Wars patiently aligned and awaiting their future brides with penises erect.[67] Approximately 10,000 immigrants, *filles du roi* and husbands included, had settled in New France at the end of the seventeenth century. Among these early migrants, some 80 percent sustained itself by agriculture.[68] Leslie Choquette has entitled this process *"Frenchmen into peasants,"* a nod to Eugen Weber's classic *Peasants into Frenchmen*.[69] It rightly places emphasis on the transformation of the French in the New World.

New France was effectively a sparsely populated settler colony. At the midpoint of the eighteenth century, when New France would soon be no more, some 70,000 European settlers resided there while well over a million lived in the British colonies.[70] Unsuccessful policies to promote colonization obliged authorities like Colbert to attempt to convert Native Americans to Catholicism. Organizers designed alliances with Amerindians to replicate a French Catholic entity in the New World, as mentioned, but also to pin the British colonies to the coast. Indigenous legions would allegedly help prevent the British from moving west. The Jesuits were insistent in their attempt to convert Native American populations. While their successes were limited, their role in modeling French métissage in the New World is salient. That they did so without sexual relations with Native American women is all the more remarkable. Black Robes, as they were called, fearlessly ventured into the wild, met with native populations, and learned their languages. They were able to integrate indigenous tribes so intimately perhaps because they sought neither native furs nor women; they had a higher calling. With their courage and ability to predict natural cycles, they gained the respect of Indian people if not their conversion. Some mocked the Black Robes, however, who appeared fragile despite their holy imperviousness to the weather, environment, or even torture. Moogk wondered why Native Americans would possibly want to emulate people they found visibly and culturally repulsive.[71]

In becoming progressively *Canadien* after the turn of the seventeenth century, when growth stemmed more from birth on the North American continent than migration, European populations had well learned that survival rates could be enhanced by the adoption of Native American methods of hunting, food production, war, dress, and transportation. The enduring image of pioneering New World masculinity incarnate in the *habitants* and *coureurs de bois*, still so linked to contemporary Québécois identity, is distinctly Amerindian, expressly Creole. After its beginnings as a small settler colony, spectacular natural growth is what led to the development of a sustainable French population that still exists today.[72] That this happened as France was forced to retreat from the New World is yet another historical footnote. Just about everyone but priests married in New France, as it increased survival rates significantly, and when they did marry, they tended to have very large families. Substantial families were certainly blessed by the church, and the average family was made up of 9.5 children, although not all lived long past birth.[73] This is the demographic history of Quebec's traditional, pre-Quiet Revolution (*Révolution tranquille*) family and social structure before the uproar of the 1960s uprooted society from the principles laid down by the Catholic Church, crippled natality, and set the country on a rocky yet modern path.

Even diminished French presence in the colonial and contested New

World was cause for concern for rival imperial nations like Great Britain. The British tried to thwart French initiatives, and it was this massive push that reportedly led to success. *La Nouvelle-France* disappeared in 1763 after the British military victory and the signing of the Treaty of Paris without much commotion or regret among French ruling classes. "The loss of New France would be nothing compared to Britain's loss of her original American colonies" a decade later, concluded Eccles.[74] While Napoléon Bonaparte later sold the vast expanses of la Louisiane française to Thomas Jefferson for a pittance (to weaken the British), French culture lives on and is visible to the naked eye in many places where Franco-Americans settled. In the United States alone, French America is preserved architecturally in at least sixteen states.[75]

A FRANCO-AMERICAN FUTURE

To travel north into New England from the birthplace of the American nation in Philadelphia is to leave Anglo-America (Boston aside). To find New France in New England is perhaps a historical anomaly, but subtle signs of welcome (*bienvenue*) in New England let travelers know that they have entered a cultural niche, both fictive and experienced, Franco-America. The French welcome sign in Woonsocket, Rhode Island, is an invitation into a historic French ethnic enclave (see fig. 2). The misspelling of the word in French on the Woonsocket billboard (it is missing the final *e*) is perhaps revealing of the dilution of French in the United States. It is the subject of some consternation, but according to locals, high cost has long prevented correction. Two hundred miles to the north, the U.S./ Canadian border along the Vermont, New Hampshire, and Maine state lines represents a linguistic and cultural divide between majority French and English speakers in French America. While English dominates in families of French-Canadian descent in New England, in the St. Georges de Beauce region of Quebec, from whence many Franco-American families originate, the language of communication is French. International borders still do matter in our interconnected world.

The welcome signs greeting residents and visitors to French heritage cities and states in New England illustrate a past and present French connection.

2. Welcome to French neighborhood, Woonsocket, Rhode Island. Courtesy of author.

The sometimes prominent position of the word at city/state entrances is a subtle but resonant invitation. It voices the potency of a single word, which for some can evoke a rich history. The bilingual signs represent typically American hybrid or hyphenated identities and are visible markers of francophone postcolonial presence. The backstory is that the French were often far from welcome. They constituted the dregs of society, labored for meager wages, and lived in rundown areas. A late nineteenth-century report identified them as the "Chinese of the East," presumably because of their foreign ways and indifference to assimilation. In the 1880s, Francos resented this unfavorable association with China.[76]

Franco-Americans have had to struggle to post and to keep their signs acknowledging a hidden heritage. The signs in Waterville, Maine, were the result of individuals thinking it important enough to place an invitation to Franco-America at two entrances to town, via land and water (a bridge leading into town). The politics of French posting indicates a precarious practice at best. In 2005 an effort to remove the bienvenue signs from southern New Hampshire was defeated by local activists who wanted to preserve this recognition of the area's franco(phone) heritage and cultural traditions. The welcome signs on U.S. routes 95 and 93 at the Massachusetts–New Hampshire border might be easily missed, as some critics of the efforts to save the signs mentioned, but for others it clearly represents a cultural marker worth defending.[77] While it would be difficult to miss the giant Woonsocket billboard, signs of Frenchness in Holyoke or Lowell, Massachusetts, once influential ethnic centers, are more discreet.

Physical traces of French colonial presence still mark the American landscape in places from east to west. The French participated in that quintessentially American phenomenon, the gold rush, lending their efforts to the expansion west.[78] Lafayette squares, parks, and cities are probably the most numerous and visible examples of French geographic presence. Louis XIV registered an indelible French impression in America's north country and also in the now predominantly "Red" South: the French territory of Louisiana was named in his honor in 1682 as was Louisville, Kentucky. Had the great Mississippi River been named the St. Louis River as originally planned, says Alexis de Tocqueville, perhaps America's French past might be better known today.[79]

The *fleur-de-lys* can be found in many such places where French culture established itself. The French symbol dots the walls of the former Assumption Church in Chicopee, Massachusetts, where people of French descent gathered to pray first in French and then in English. It is clearly visible in Acadiana, in Louisiana's Cajun country. The French iris is emblematic of the region's Acadian university, the University of Louisiana at Lafayette.[80] The *fleur-de-lys* is no longer an exclusive symbol of the monarchy or even of the Catholic Church in the New World. But it is a meaningful, marketable symbol found in the front windows of businesses and on billboards, municipal signs, brochures, and other printed materials.

The cities of Manchester, New Hampshire, Lowell, Massachusetts, Woonsocket, Rhode Island, and Lewiston, Maine, mill towns built along the rivers that harnessed the energy that fed America's industrial revolution, have been home to working-class and middle-class peoples of French and francophone descent since the early nineteenth century. To the trained eye, their French ethnic identity can be seen in the smokestacks and steeples dotting the horizon.[81] Some historically French neighborhoods have disappeared entirely, fallen victim to the municipal bulldozer. All that remains in Lowell of the French ethnic enclave is a commemorative stone, although social clubs still dot the local landscape. A century and a half ago (1875), a fire consumed Precious Blood Church in a Little Canada neighborhood in the flats of Holyoke, Massachusetts. Today, echoes of the once vibrant parish are preserved in a solemn local burial site of Franco-American memory.[82]

A half century ago, New England mill towns supported daily French-language newspapers, but today only the obituaries speak of French presence in the local press and the extent to which the French came to occupy parts of Anglo-America. Local Francos read them as they once read French ethnic newspapers, for community news. While French surnames of the deceased convey the general state of French America, a glance through the phonebook also indicates the lingering pervasiveness of French influence in these same places. French names abound in print, and many more are hidden by changes made in spelling to mask foreignness.[83] Non-French-speaking officials sometimes permanently altered names on documents, both consciously and out of ignorance. Written grammatical accents were often lost in the translation of names, and oral accents have receded from speech as a result of assimilation, although they can also continue to identify Francos. Some remain French solely in name, while others identify more closely with the French tradition through preserved cultural or linguistic practices. French cemeteries are a poignant reminder of the status of Franco-America. In French Catholic cemeteries from the Northeast to the Gulf of Mexico, one finds row upon row of Richard, Dragon, Lafleur, Papillon, Charlebois, and Ducharme, names that can be traced back to regions of Old France. Some of the traditions that immigrants brought with them have ended with their passing. Cemeteries are among the most densely populated, evocative parts of French America.

In south Louisiana today, Acadians and their descendants, Cadiens or Cajuns, as well as Creoles and Native Americans have formed another component of French America, one that perseveres with the assistance of a state-supported French educational and cultural program. In nineteenth-century Louisiana, a francophone Creole culture produced by black elites and refugees from St. Domingue dominated cultural life in New Orleans. Scholars have access to the work of writers who published the first collection of black poetry in 1845, *Les Cenelles*. The tragic history of New Orleans devastated by Hurricane Katrina is a reminder of the Crescent City's historic yet infirm French existence. Even a battered Big Easy is unlike any other city in North America, at the intersection of European, African, and Native American cultures, an important hub in transatlantic French space.[84] As anthropologist Nick Spitzer says, "The best way to begin thinking about New Orleans as the rarified cross-roads of artistic development in this hemisphere is to adjust our sense of geography and visualize the city not as the bottom of the United States but as the crown of the Caribbean."[85] Spitzer suggests that creolization can be a creative stimulant in a postcatastrophe world, modeled by the return of Mardi Gras Indians to the city.[86] Creolization reveals more of Franco-America than simply New Orleans and its festive celebration. The quest to reconnect with ancestral lineage and language has renewed interest in the hybrid French roots of America.

New France could perhaps only ultimately fail as a colonial project given its deficiencies, but curiously, this did not prevent implanted French influences from remaining in Anglo-America long after the severing of formal ties to France. Franco-American cultures, identities, and experiences persisted and sometimes even flourished. That French cultures still exist in the heart of puritan New England today is noteworthy. In order to better understand the transformation of the French in the United States, we will examine now in more detail the experience of Franco-Americans of New England. People of French descent left southern Canada in the mid-nineteenth century and not long thereafter sought to actively establish their own communities in the United States. Almost a third of Quebec moved south to work in the American textile mills of New England, leading to bitter criticism by religious and political elites in Quebec. They spoke of *la saignée*, the bloodletting of Quebec, and accused emigrants of being traitors to their country, language, and religion.[87] Others stated ruefully that it was the rabble-rousers who were leaving, "c'est la canaille qui s'en va." Toward the end of the century, though, when Quebec officials proved powerless to stop the exodus, the flux was painted in starkly different terms. These same elites described a reconquering of Anglo-America or the extending of French America south into the United States.

In becoming part of the working masses, migrating French Canadians did not fully abandon their peasant traditions of old. The descendants of habitants maintained ancestral, rural ways of life. They may never have developed a working-class consciousness, asserts William F. Hartford, unlike Irish immigrants in the industrial North. Franco-Americans tended not to join unions, and they maintained an "enclave consciousness," further explaining their cultural distinction from other "white" groups.[88] Immigrants, according to their former detractors from the church, were remaking New France in their divinely assisted movements. A Catholic journalist asserted that the blessedly prolific French "race" was expanding in America, transgressing the borders of Quebec and marking America as French: "Elle est en voie de créer quelque chose de plus vaste. Le Canada français; que dis-je? L'Amérique française."[89] In less than a decade, migration to the United States had run the gamut from apocalyptic seizure to utopia in its interpretation.

Life in French flourished in towns all over New England, where francophone migrants settled between 1840 and 1930. The Great Depression, the relocating of the textile industry to the South, and greater restrictions on immigration ended this flux. By this time, the easing of the economic crisis in Quebec meant that fewer emigrants traveled south to American industrial centers. For decades during the late nineteenth and early twentieth centuries, within the homogeneous Petits Canadas that formed Québec d'en bas, or Lower Quebec, French was spoken in the streets, shops, and community organizations of several U.S. states, by members of the French and francophone diaspora. Once communities were established, French-speaking priests arrived to set up parishes that would become the centers of Franco life. After first representing an Old World anchor in the wilderness of New France, the church represented the cornerstone of Franco-American identity. Families saved money to contribute to the building of French parishes, and their names are still inscribed in the individual stones and windows of some of these buildings. In addition to offering regular masses to parishioners in French, the church organized bilingual schools in which French was the mode of communication in the morning and English in the afternoon, or vice versa. The Catholic Church was the primary subscriber to the motto "He who loses his language loses his faith" (Qui perd sa langue, perd sa foi). This made for an unusual and compelling alchemy of religion and language. The church was one of the leaders of cultural resistance to assimilation. Religious elites headed this spirited but ultimately unsuccessful effort to hold Anglo-Saxon forces at bay and maintain French moral and cultural values. Schools, parishes, the ethnic media, and the Franco family represented a bulwark against the current of mainstream Anglo-Protestant society.[90]

French churches, as they were called both within and without the Franco community, existed alongside other ethnic, national churches. Sunday morning was the most segregated hour in America, said Martin Luther King, a reality most certainly echoed by the insularity of the ethnic French, Irish, Polish, and Greek Orthodox churches that once dotted New England. The Irish had arrived first and built the dams and canals that facilitated the American industrial revolution. Sometimes acrimonious rivalries developed in factory towns with large immigrant populations, particularly between Franco-Americans and Irish Americans who disagreed on the language in which prayer would be recited in church. The authority to lead was also at issue within various parishes and communities. Disputes came to a head with the naming of bishops and an alleged Irish monopoly on religious authority. Rivalries were sometimes expressed politically with Francos voting Republican in local elections because the Irish voted Democratic.[91] National elections, however, could display another electoral dynamic.

Voters in Rhode Island elected the state's very first Franco-American governor, Aram Jules Pothier, in 1908. Franco-American mayors served in municipalities throughout New England alongside Irish clergy and police. Controversies arose when English-speaking priests were named to French parishes or when parishioners were asked to contribute to school districts where French was not taught. The church excommunicated individuals when they refused to comply. For them at least, religion appeared to be no more central to Franco identity than language, although this was not necessarily the case for religious leaders. This was the basis of the *Sentinelle* affair in Woonsocket, Rhode Island, which ripped at the Franco-American community and moral code in the 1920s. As younger generations became increasingly assimilated and monolingual English speakers, mass in French disappeared. In the 1960s, Vatican II signaled the eventual end of French and other national parishes.

The term *Franco-American* first appeared in print in 1888, with the publication of the newspaper *Le Franco-Américain*, serving the French community of Fall River, Massachusetts.[92] Several early papers in New England bore the same name, and by the advent of the new century, use of the qualifier *Franco-American* had gained currency. Like the press, a Franco-American literature emerged in the late nineteenth century. Both spoke on behalf of the French population in America, on bettering the French "race," and on ameliorating often dismal social conditions. Within journalistic and literary circles, a Franco cultural elite hoped to inspire the greater community. New World French cultures were often stigmatized, but elites both produced and advertised uplifting Franco-American traditions.

While being Franco-American has traditionally meant a person of French-Canadian descent (from Quebec or sometimes the Maritime Provinces) who speaks French, identifies as Catholic, and preserves cultural traditions, this has changed substantially in recent years. Francos today may no longer practice their faith or speak French. Acadians have historically had a distinct relationship with the Catholic Church, a factor that may be related to geographic exile and cultural isolation. As noted, Francos have long "suffered" from a sense of inferiority generated by cultural hostility, both real and imagined. Franco-American identity has generally always been split, hyphenated, hybrid. In terms of national affinities, people have divided allegiances between France, Quebec, and the United States. While radical Francos of the FAROG Forum identified strongly with nationalist Quebec in the 1960s, the post-Quiet Revolution, nonconformist Quebec alienated conservative members of the Franco-American community for whom traditional values mattered. Historian François Weil suggests that Francos aligned themselves more with a certain conception of France, *la France éternelle*, and with the French than with geographically closer Québécois cousins.[93] He noted that in some Franco homes, the ideas espoused by Marshal Philippe Pétain and the Vichy regime held appeal. For a time, some Franco-Americans and Americans found themselves on opposite sides of the Second World War front, although this did not linger beyond the early 1940s (see chapter 5).[94] War memorials indicate proud participation by Francos in American military efforts.

The cultural hybridity of the Franco-American population is apparent within the social organizations that served them. Various institutions along with the church have assumed responsibility for the spiritual and material well-being of Franco-American populations. L'Association Canado-Américaine (ACA) of Manchester and L'Union Saint-Jean Baptiste d'Amérique of Woonsocket are two of the oldest mutual aid societies.[95] The first and still extant "people's bank" in the United States, La Caisse Populaire Ste Marie (1908), was a Franco institution also established in Manchester. It, along with the others, provided a number of financial, social, and cultural services to community members. One of their most important objectives was the preservation of French language and cultural traditions for immigrant populations. The imposing architectural structure of each suggested that the mutual aid society would always stand as a protector of Franco-America. "*Religion, Patriotisme, Fraternité,*" the ACA motto, long echoed the cultural ideal of Franco-American survivance today. The forced 2009 sale of the ACA to the Royal Arcanum represented a figurative and literal deflation to Franco-American perpetuity.[96]

FRENCH ETHNIC REVIVAL?

Much of the contemporary Franco experience in America is relegated to memory and folklore, articulated in history books, noted within the walls of institutions, and carved into commemorative stones. Still a French cultural renaissance in New England and Louisiana has taken shape over the last two decades.[97] People of francophone descent in Maine and the

Gulf Coast have begun efforts to reconnect with their scorned heritage. A relatively newfound pride in being French or Franco-American has driven this renaissance. Some have found inspiration for cultural renewal among francophone African immigrant populations in transforming mill towns. African Catholics sometimes fill pews at French mass, as well as the pulpit. People organize discussion groups where they can speak French, especially their very own ethnic vernacular, in a comfortable setting. Others take classes in order to revive their birth language. It would be difficult to accurately identify the numbers of French speakers who gather regularly around tables, but weekly and monthly meetings in New England and south Louisiana advertise in local media. Community leaders have invented or reintroduced Franco-American festivals in New England towns in recent years, drawing attention to the cultural roots of immigrants of French-Canadian descent. Such festivals including Cajun/Creole music, food, dance, and language have been a part of the cultural landscape in south Louisiana for several decades. People are clearly thinking about what can be lost culturally when an ethnic group assimilates and what is worth salvaging. They organize because it is no longer easy to express cultural identity; it requires making a conscious effort.

In the 2006 Maine state legislature, in commemoration of International Francophone Day on March 20, representatives conducted sessions symbolically in French to honor the state's ethnic heritage.[98] For many years, Franco-American Day has been similarly celebrated in Maine. In 2015 state officials announced Franco-American Day in Connecticut, and the Quebec Government Office in Boston sponsored a 2017 FrancoConnexions Conference at the University of Vermont to celebrate International Francophone Day. While some people of French-Canadian descent might not consider themselves Franco-American or francophone, they are members of the French family with lingering ties to the language and culture. There is certainly no fluency standard to distinguish between beginning, intermediate, and advanced speakers of French. The definition of *francophone* is purposefully vague, enabling the Organisation internationale de la francophonie to tout the greatest number of members possible. In 2006 the Maine francophone event was highlighted by the singing of "The

Star-Spangled Banner" in French by a young Franco-American girl from Fort Kent in northern Maine, just across the river from officially bilingual New Brunswick.[99] The event took place a few weeks before demonstrations to liberalize immigration law and facilitate naturalization for Mexicans began, when word of singing the national hymn in Spanish raised hackles. It is worth noting that after the singing of the national anthem in French, Maine state officials also sang the anthems of France ("La Marseillaise") and Canada ("O Canada"). The French of New England still express their hybrid existence today, both publicly and privately. Louisiana's French heritage is more recognizable than its counterpart in New England, for it has been increasingly cool to be Cajun since the 1980s, and savvy marketers and business owners have attempted to exploit this commercially.

After centuries of migratory flows, immigration is still, most certainly, a weighty, controversial, and politically perilous topic in two similar lands built by immigrants, France and the United States. Despite a long-standing tradition of liberal naturalization law, these two countries never welcomed immigrants, but people came anyway and in significant numbers. Immigrants to France and to the United States have had to withstand violence, overcome considerable disadvantages, and prove their worthiness. French immigration to the United States is an interesting, if atypical, phenomenon. Given popular notions of French prestige and culture, French and immigration might appear to be contradictory terms. The French of France emigrated in far fewer numbers than did other European groups to the United States or elsewhere; relative wealth kept these flows to a minimum.[100] While others left their home countries to seek fortunes or refuge from political oppression, the French remained largely within their borders. French Canadians did travel to the United States, as Americans, and today we witness the remains of a distinctive immigrant history.

Since the eighteenth century, the French of America had established themselves on the continent, living increasingly as New World *Canadiens* rather than Old World French. Like Mexicans today, their American odyssey was not legitimized by passage through Ellis Island where immigrants symbolically became recognized as being a part of the American fabric and on the road to inclusion in the citizenry. Still the Statue of Liberty would remain a beacon to them, as it would to others; journalists in the French ethnic media often honored it. Unlike immigrants (and slaves) who departed on a long, often arduous transatlantic voyage, people of French-Canadian descent could theoretically return "home." Some participated in frequent border crossings, a fact dictated by seasonal agricultural work that continues to control the ebb and flow of migration, clandestine and otherwise. Being white and close to their ancestral land, Francos could relatively easily settle, disperse, or disappear, a factor that certainly contributed to their "Quiet Evolution" and invisibility. Like other immigrants to America, French Canadians maintained the desire to save money, provide for their families, and eventually resettle, in death if not before.

Despite the inroads of cultural assimilation in the United States, the French remain an important linguistic and cultural presence. According to the 2000 census, there are more than 1.6 million speakers of French in American households nationally, which put French in the position of fourth most spoken foreign language in the home other than English.[101] If one includes speakers of French Creole, there are more than 2.1 million francophones in the United States, placing it in third position, ahead of Chinese and behind Spanish. Spanish represents by far the most spoken language other than English, 60 percent; French languages combined constitute only 4 percent. The 2010 census data suggest that the number of U.S.-based French speakers is relatively stable, although somewhat in decline compared with the 2000 census. What is interesting is that there were still slightly more than 2 million French and French Creole speakers within American borders, in 2000 and 2010, while in 1980 there were more than 1.5 million francophones, and in 1990, 1.9 million. Despite a slight drop in the last ten years, this represents an increase overall in numbers between 1980 and 2010. The data make clear that it is growing French Creole populations that offset a decline in the numbers of other French-language speakers. Between 2000 and 2010, French Creole speakers over the age of five increased in number by 60 percent while French speakers (including Patois and Cajun) fell by 20 percent. This would certainly seem to indicate the importance of la francophonie, in North America and elsewhere, in the future of French.[102]

Almost 80 percent of French speakers claim to speak English very well, while only 57 percent of French Creoles can make this claim. Accents, traditions, and cultural differences certainly remain, but the evidence suggests that Franco-Americans are well integrated in comparison with other immigrant populations. The questions posed to individuals remain the same from the 2000 census, although they are now asked annually in the American Community Survey, not the decennial census. Is a language other than English spoken at home; if yes, what is this language, and how well is English spoken?[103] According to American Community Survey reports, the questions identify those that may require resources to foster understanding English and integration. The data suggest that people tend to become increasingly Anglophone in their communication over time in the United States, yet the foreignness of French populations has often worried officials.

The 2000 census affirmed that the state of Louisiana had the largest number of French speakers (not including creolophones) in the United States, with almost 200,000 individuals who identified as Cajuns, Cadiens, or Cadjins (all deformations of the word *Acadian*). It also distinguished four thousand individuals as creolophones in the state. Maine and Massachusetts had significant numbers of French heritage speakers, 63,000 and 84,000, respectively. The state of Maine had a higher percentage of French speakers than any other state in the country in fact in 2000, 5.3 percent, whereas Louisiana had 4 percent. Approximately 70 percent of Maine's non-English speakers are francophone to varying degrees, indicating lingering cultural homogeneity. The French are still the predominant "minority" element in Maine and many parts of New England. New Hampshire and Rhode Island have a lower percentage of French speakers, 3 and 1 percent, respectively, despite the presence of cities like Manchester and Woonsocket with a deep French tradition. In some of the ethnically Franco locales of America, Maine, New Hampshire, and Louisiana, there are currently more French than Spanish speakers, although this will likely change.

Francophone linguistic and cultural trends within particular states are again confirmed in the 2010 decennial census data. The first five states where U.S. French rank first in ancestry population percentage are Maine,

New Hampshire, Vermont, Louisiana, and Rhode Island, respectively. In the three northern New England states, French is the first in ancestry population with over 25 percent of the state population, 27.7, 26.7, and 26.4 percent, respectively.[104] Louisiana and Rhode Island have an 18 percent French ancestry population, and Massachusetts, in sixth position, has 13 percent. These percentages are greater even than those noted on the 2000 census, most likely a result of the aging of the population. It is noteworthy that within areas of historic French and francophone settlement, French linguistic patterns are still clearly marked.

There are increasingly large numbers of francophones in areas outside the historic areas of influx for French-speaking populations. "Snowbirds," or wintering Québécois in south Florida, and Haitians in Florida and other areas have changed the composition and geography of Franco-America. They emerge on the maps of postcolonial francophone cultures accessible via the MLA Language Maps. While the number of native French creolophones in Louisiana is small, speakers of Haitian French Creole in Florida make up more than 200,000 in and around Miami. Snowbirds themselves contribute to a growing French-speaking, non-Creole population of 129,000 based on 2000 data. Franco-Americans in south Florida have created a demand for services in French and represent another extension and remodeling of Franco-America.

Franco-America continues to be imagined and constructed by the preservers, makers, and transmitters of the culture. Michael Parent sings traditional French-Canadian songs, in French and English, for Franco children, reminding them of their heritage.[105] The aptly named Parent offers young people a few words of their often lost, ancestral French language, even mixing in a traditional Cajun lullaby. He and other folklorists demonstrate that culture, albeit in different forms, can be transmitted without mastery of the "mother tongue." Can heritage languages be relearned? Can French linguistic practices established at birth and sometimes forgotten over decades be awakened? This is the underlying assumption in the film *Waking Up French!... Réveil.*[106] Self-identified postcolonial writer Rhea

Côté Robbins asks, "Am I a cultural dead-end?"[107] Or will she be able to pass on traditional culture, linguistic or otherwise, to future generations? One of the questions to which her work and *Waking Up French* allude is whether Franco-Americans are still Franco or "francophone" if they no longer speak the language of their ancestors. Can they still accurately express the Franco-American nation in English? Abby Paige addresses this question in her recorded one-woman show exploring the existential state of contemporary Franco-Americans young and old, male and female, and predominantly anglophone.[108] One of her ten characters states that the only remaining tangible cultural expression for some is eating French-Canadian meat pie during the holidays. Each is based on interviews Paige conducted with Francos themselves, and only one speaks French.

Franco-Americans yesterday and today are no less francophone than other francophones around the world, with differing levels of access to and facility with the language. Switzerland, Belgium, and Canada are certainly franco-phone in practice if not entirely in popular conception. Francos of America have been affected by the French national and international project, with all of its inspirations, inadequacies, and impositions. Francophonie today is sometimes and erroneously synonymous with French-speaking people of color, people neither expressly French nor from France. Franco-Americans of New England and Louisiana, however, offer another interpretation.[109] La Francophonie nord-américaine exhibits an interesting point of convergence, a meeting of French language and cultures on the American continent, a collision of Old Worlds and new, white and black. The cited 2000 and 2010 census information on domestic French language practices indicate that creolized American francophonie, while relatively small, is far from insignificant. Continued study of North America's French experience offers an underexplored, pertinent case, not simply another example of global American assimilation. Today the French and francophones of America are still in between languages, places, and cultures. All Francos of North America are hybrid mixes, living amid continents, languages, traditions, and ethnicities. Some will indeed have to be taught the language that their moth-ers lost, at the Alliance française and elsewhere, but only if they so desire.

CHAPTER 2

Cultural Institutions and French Renaissance in America

Since the defeat on the Plains of Abraham outside Quebec City in 1759, signaling British winners and French losers in the quest for power in the Atlantic world, French teaching institutions have assumed increasingly greater importance. Not only military defeat but also ensuing minority status and assimilation into mainstream Anglo currents thrust franco-phone teachers, schools, and organizations into the position of cultural preservation. A French identity no longer officially sanctioned as native or national would have to be taught when possible or permitted; it had to be nourished to remain vital, by those to whom it remained important, largely within postcolonial francophone communities. The teaching of French was at times forbidden in the United States, for instance, during the puni-tive English-only period during and following the First World War.[1] This chapter will demonstrate how Franco-Americans, systematically excluded from the opportunity to learn in French, assumed responsibility for their own education, through participation not only in more formal teaching institutions but in the collective efforts of community and cultural centers.

Franco-Americans hoped to avoid enduring an experience of cultural erasure in the overriding narrative of American assimilation. French ethnic parishes and bilingual parochial schools in particular long promoted cultural preservation.[2] Some notable Franco success stories can be identified outside these traditional spaces, dynamic places where francophone and francophile synergies meshed. Franco-Americans partnered with individuals and associations in order to create an ethos of permanence. Francos have continually striven to create community access to French culture through print, audio, and visual technology.[3] Through their websites and more traditional media forms, Radio France International (RFI), *TV5Monde*, and *France-Amérique* have been marketed and sold to prospective buyers as teaching tools. Each has also played a historic and contemporary role in the perpetuation of French America. The tools at the disposal of creators of French culture today can be persuasive indeed, but as we will see, early twentieth-century instructors and institutions relied on none of them.

The French *fleur-de-lys* is the centerpiece of the official logo for the "Université des Acadiens," the University of Louisiana at Lafayette. Situated at the heart of the campus in Louisiana's French southwest, la Maison Française today serves as a formal entry into the university and its history. The university was founded a century ago to educate people of French descent, Acadians turned Cajuns, and thus to uplift a people who had suffered socially, culturally, and economically. Like other social groups, Cajuns experienced upward social mobility since 1900 and especially since 1950, yet older generations still bear the stigma of the downtrodden. The founders may very well have wondered if teaching institutions could help to change a Franco-American culture of shame. The names of graduates and donors to the University of Louisiana in Acadiana (ULL) indicate that the institution has indeed enlightened Franco-Americans of the Gulf South, helping them to transcend socioeconomic hardships. They have left a lasting physical trace of appreciation on the brick walkways of the ULL campus for an education received. The Broussard, Richard, Guidry, and Thibodeaux families listed could very well be of Cajun, Creole, or mixed origin.

Assumption College of Worcester, Massachusetts, was founded by French priests in 1904 to educate the French "race" in New England, some three hundred years after the foremost New World French *habitant* Samuel de Champlain's first exploratory voyages. Assumptionist priests groomed the cream of the Franco-American crop here.[4] An American flag flies outside the rolling greens of its prominent entrance, where another Maison Française greets visitors and takes them back into the college's past. The American national symbol is not uncommon but is noteworthy because Assumption once served expressly to promote French *survivance*, to instill in young Franco-American men knowledge of the moral duties of perpetuating Franco traditions in America. French-language proficiency was a requirement for entrance until the 1960s. The school paper of this traditional Catholic institution is called *Le Provocateur*, but it is neither particularly provoking nor is it written in French. While the college has since shifted its focus, no longer teaching to a majority student body of Franco-American descent, the Institut Français (1979) has carried on the French tradition, indeed inviting scholars to devote scientific attention to its study.

ULL and Assumption are the best-known institutions of higher learning educating America's indigenous French and francophone populations, but others continue to open their doors to younger generations. Rivier College (1933) of Nashua, New Hampshire, has long educated Franco-American women, and neighboring St. Anselm of Manchester, New Hampshire, recently began sponsoring the Centre Franco-Americain of the same city. Just after the Second World War, the Sisters of Saint Anne established Anna Maria College (1946) for women, now a coeducational institution. American International College (AIC) in Springfield, Massachusetts, has an intriguing yet obscure Franco-American history of educating and promoting the assimilation of its youth. The Reverend Calvin E. Amaron founded it as the Collège Franco-Americain, a Protestant institution, in 1885.[5] Amaron believed that women should be given the same access to education as men, and Franco women entered beginning in 1892, making it the first coeducational institution in the region.[6] Today that French immigrant past has receded to the background, leaving the forefront to the educational needs of new immigrants to Springfield. AIC currently assists more recent Third World transplants to Springfield to receive an education and expand opportunities if not ascend the American social ladder.

3. *La Maison Française*, Assumption College, Worcester, Massachusetts. Courtesy of author.

The list of Franco colleges and universities, linking a historic ethnic past and a more hybrid future, is a surprisingly long one. On a distinct and more recent teaching plane, Franco-Americans have transformed former places of industry into educational sites exhibiting expressions of French ethnic life in the late twentieth and early twenty-first centuries in several mill towns. These facilities are not museums in the traditional sense or hermetic containers of minority francophone cultures. Builders have reconstructed crumbling mills pedagogically with a hands-on approach to teaching and learning about the Franco-American experience. They are places of both elite and popular culture. Public representations of a culture in museums, expositions, and fairs convey some sense of the value it has gained in Franco-American circles. While many such cultural institutions are not well known outside of their Franco locales, they welcome individuals, organizations, and schoolchildren and facilitate learning about the French history of America. The factories-turned-museums expressly preserve a part of this history, as many residential and laboring quarters have been razed. It is perhaps only as the work in mills became increasingly rare that it could be reintegrated into the annals of culture. It is particularly striking that places such as the Millyard Museum of Manchester, New Hampshire, the Museum L-A of Lewiston-Auburn, Maine, and the Museum of Work and Culture in Woonsocket, Rhode Island, draw attention to both an ethnic and a working-class identity for a French-Canadian immigrant population of mostly peasant stock.[7]

More prominently, the national historical site at Lowell, Massachusetts, helps to tell the story of Franco-Americans within the context of a twentieth-century industrializing nation. Since 1989 the Mogan Cultural Center at Lowell facilitates exploration of the Franco-American experience, as one cog in the city's rich immigrant history.[8] The center resides in the former boardinghouse of the Lowell mill girls, at least some of whom were Franco-American. Franco mill girls such as the protagonist Vic in Camille Lessard-Bissonnette's *Canuck* come to life in the ethnic literature that will be examined in chapter 4. The permanent Museum in the Street exhibit located throughout New England is distinct in offering pedestrians a walking tour of the remnants of the ethnic enclaves, the

Little Canadas where Francos lived, laughed, prayed, and died.[9] In several New England cities, maps take walkers past a series of illustrated panels providing glimpses into municipal and state history, in both English and French. In working with historical societies and individuals, the Museum in the Street project intends to unearth previously hidden groups and their collective experiences from oblivion. While there are few supporting state institutions in the New England region, Franco-Americans and Franco cultures benefit from a network of associations that rejects the forgetting of past traditions and folk cultures.

From French sociologist Pierre Bourdieu, we know that institutions are typically in the business of reproducing the cultures of dominant or elite social groups.[10] Yet even organizations such as the Alliance Française have stimulated ascension within the working classes. While there have been successes as well as failures along the way, many grassroots Franco organizations have set out explicitly to encourage minority cultures. They emerge suggesting a longevity and sustainability. The preservation of French language has long been at the heart of their mission; they hope to embody still living cultures and not to become home to static museums of dead ones.

THE ALLIANCE FRANÇAISE IN AMERICA

Well before organizers set most teaching structures in place, the Alliance Française (AF) offered comparable but sometimes quite distinct opportunities for learning French. The Alliance has existed for more than 130 years, since 1883, and is, more than any other single institution, responsible for disseminating global knowledge of France, French language, and culture. There is no larger such nonprofit, independent cultural institution in the world, which illustrates the persistent international place of the French language. The most comparable organization might be the Goethe Institute, which has served Germany and German culture on a smaller scale since the Second World War. The Alliance currently has more than 1,000 chapters, many of them teaching institutions, in over 130 countries.[11] To its approximately 400,000 students and several million members worldwide, the organization offers an abundance of cultural offerings: not only the trademark language classes, but conferences, lectures, discussion groups, concerts, films, theater productions, art exhibits, and even scholarships. The larger AF branches have their own, sometimes quite elaborate facilities, providing meeting space, libraries, and multimedia centers to their dues-paying members. In the last half of the twentieth century, the institution established a dense network of programs throughout the world. The AF became particularly well implanted in Mexico and South America, where some of the largest branches are located.[12] In recent years, the organization began pushing to make French language more known and relevant elsewhere, through initiatives in Eastern Europe and China.

Since inception, the institution has completed public relations work for France, not as a partisan political association but one nonetheless in tune with French national concerns. In many parts of the world, it is to the Alliance that people turn to learn about France, its language, and its culture. The organization may have materialized from the late nineteenth-century belief that French required promotion.[13] It is through this thoroughly Parisian institution that members have been able to learn about the wider French world. As we will see, the Alliance Française relied on Franco-Americans to establish its North American base. The Alliance functions as a quasi-official representative for France abroad, often working alongside embassies, schools, and universities. What I will suggest at the outset is that the French national institution, both inadvertently and purposely, helped to promote Franco-American cultures, despite tensions between socioeconomic groups. Francos did not always feel welcome at the institution. The Alliance has helped, however, to perpetuate awareness of the international role that French language and culture have played in the last three centuries. While the French court at Versailles may have set the standard for French culture, language, and etiquette, both the *littérature-monde* movement, as well as the field of postcolonial francophone studies today, have attempted to demonstrate the international scale of "French" culture. Many francophiles and francophones today know something of the elite institution, but its transnational past is much less known. The history of the Alliance Française in the United States is particularly unfamiliar. Six years after the original AF de Paris was founded in 1883, the first American branch opened its doors in San Francisco.[14]

Reference sources on the organization are not numerous, and monographs are rare. Maurice Bruézière's centennial tribute to the institution provides detailed information on the origins of the Alliance Française while Alain Dubosclard offers a more recent and critical examination of the Federation of Alliances in the United States.[15] What one discovers in closely examining the AF is that each branch has its own distinct trajectory apart from that of Paris or any of the various regional federations. This is not very French at all. The Alliance has a long respected tradition of autonomy for its individual chapters, in contrast to the administrative tradition in France. Dubosclard writes, "The French Alliance was conceived of a simple idea: letting foreigners disseminate French culture themselves, partially relinquishing the responsibility of France's cultural efforts."[16] Given France's historically centralized political apparatus, in place since at least the French Revolution, this clearly *de*centralized perspective is extraordinary. The *rayonnement* of French culture has certainly benefited from this. Every Alliance branch is guided by a similar mission to promote knowledge of French, as established in the bylaws of the *AF* de Paris, albeit subject to local jurisdiction.

We begin with the American story, which was marked by the particular ethos of the organization at the latter part of the nineteenth century, during the French Third Republic. The Alliance Française was established within U.S. francophone communities that existed at the beginning of the twentieth century. The institution might be thought of therefore as helping America and Americans to recognize a long existing French heritage dating back to the seventeenth-century imperial construct, *la Nouvelle-France*. By giving voice to several constituencies within the French diasporic family in North America, and by creating a space for cultural exchange, the Alliance has helped to shape and define the contours of New World francophone identities.

America was, of course, "French" long before the Alliance was created on its shores. Remaking France in the New World was one of the earliest and most fanciful of French colonial initiatives, financed by kings seeking fantastic and largely illusionary riches to be reaped. The Alliance Française itself has a colonial past, but the AF did not have imperialist objectives.

The decision to establish an American network of chapters did not come from the Paris headquarters. This determination, per the philosophy of the organization, came from the francophile and francophone grassroots, from Americans interested in exploring and indeed fostering French heritage cultures themselves. The autonomous tradition continues, in central Maine in 2016, as Franco-Americans and francophones from West Africa consider collectively whether to open a chapter of the AF.[17]

The Federation of Alliances Françaises, USA celebrated the centennial of its birth in 2002, and is still the representative body for more than one hundred branches.[18] The Federation presides over AF teaching institutions and cultural centers, large and small, urban and suburban mostly, in forty-five states, including Puerto Rico.[19] The American Federation was a North American one for almost the entire twentieth century and included several Canadian chapters until 1992, when a separate Canadian organization emerged. Through its close collaboration with students, teachers, and departments of French, the Alliance is very much at the center of French cultural and linguistic exchange in the United States. The AF and the American Association of Teachers of French (AATF), with its 10,000 members, form a particularly powerful voice for engagement with French in the United States. Federation president Jane Robert specified in 2004 that the collective body grouped the vast majority, 112 of the 130 American chapters of the Alliance.[20] The advantages of belonging are clear. Membership provides financial assistance, development grants, and a network of affiliate branches able to share experiences and resources. According to Robert, the umbrella organization offers a useful support system for the diverse and autonomous chapters. The annual meeting each fall allows representatives from across the country to pool energies and more effectively promote study.

Historically, the institution has catered to an eclectic and sometimes volatile mix of francophile Americans and francophones of various nationalities seeking to study French, reconnect with their lost language, or find a community of French learners and speakers. Partly deriving from the close associations of the French language with high culture and intellectualism, the institution has had the reputation of being elitist and of gearing its activities toward privileged social groups. French prestige has indeed been the source of periodic conflict between members of differing class status. A disconnect appeared between largely working-class Franco-Americans and the wealthier social groups affiliated with the Alliance Française, but areas of intersection are revealing. Elevated notions of France, French language, and culture have served for decades, one should mention, to attract students to the institution, as well as to French departments in high schools and colleges in the United States and around the world. Some Francos hoped that the Alliance would elevate their own social status and indeed that of their ethnic group as a whole.

One of the elements that set the American Alliance apart from other branches is that most students and members express interest in French language and culture for personal enrichment, as opposed to direct professional gain. The academic certificates issued by the Alliance in other parts of the world have not been as relevant in the United States. The typical AF student in the United States is an older, retired woman or a young professional (also female), both of fairly comfortable socioeconomic means. For such individuals in the twenty-first century, France still has cachet and its language opens up avenues to global cultural appreciation. People want their children to have access to French culture and to the international perspective that it offers. French classes and even summer camps for children have grown in popularity. With American public schools offering fewer French classes, people have sometimes turned to the Alliance where available for excellent albeit expensive language instruction. Alain Dubosclard is only partially correct in asserting that the AF in the United States is a distinctly American institution with American governance and concerns. This portrayal does not capture the transnational complexities of the organization, for while chapter presidents are often, but not always, American, the teaching corps is almost entirely composed of native French speakers from the postcolonial world. Jane Robert expressed the desire that more French (and francophone) people living in the United States would participate in the organization.[21] It would set a symbolic example of French-American collaboration.

The Alliance Française has promoted harmonious, mutually enriching French-American relations from its inception, to counter backlash from French opposition to the Iraq War in recent years. The Alliance supported the work of the Congressional French Caucus in this initiative. Beginning in October 2003, the AF pursued a policy of educating the American public about the history of French-American collaboration and friendship.[22] In the more than two hundred years of history between the eighteenth-century Republics, from the French and American Revolutions until the Iraq War, relations have run the gamut from highly cordial to hostile. Several sources suggest that while the AF in some areas of the United States, notably in the Midwest, experienced a drop in attendance in the early 2000s, many other chapters, even in the so-called "red states," did not seem to be affected. Former French ambassador to the United States Jean-David Lévitte, in a presentation made at Yale University, described improving French-American relations due to political consensus on reform in the Middle East.[23] Experts identified a thawing between France and America since 2012 as political systems have been more in line than in the recent past.

FRENCH REPUBLICANISM AT WORK

It is important to emphasize the ideology of the French Third Republic that was a determinant in the formation of the Alliance Française in 1883. Still the most enduring French political regime more than half a century after its demise, the Third Republic was established in 1870 as a patriotic call to arms during the Franco-Prussian War. It came to an abrupt end with French capitulation to Hitler in June 1940. Germany, accordingly, is as powerful an influence as any for the Alliance. It is significant symbolically that there is no Alliance Française in Germany today, although similar French cultural institutions have operated there (Die Französichen Kulturinstitute). Soon after the victory of German forces in June 1940, the Alliance was almost immediately identified as a French nationalist propaganda machine, its 101 Boulevard Raspail offices were shut down, and its archives were transferred to Berlin. The institution reemerged in London, seat of the Free France movement, and consequently followed the Resistance back across the English Channel, as well as the Mediterranean

Sea, to Algiers.[24] Charles de Gaulle, honorary president of the Alliance Française and Free France leader, spoke eloquently in its name in 1943 in Algiers, at the sixtieth anniversary of the organization's founding, claiming that the institution kept alive the French flame.

The resistance activities of the *AF* de Paris leave little doubt of its politics during the Second World War. Those of the American Alliance, according to Alain Dubosclard, were much more clouded. He says that the Federation of Alliances Françaises could be accused of implicitly supporting the collaborationist Vichy regime by not taking a principled position between 1940 and 1945. American Federation officials remained adamantly neutral. "If the fight against Nazism was a fight in defense of French culture," Dubosclard asks, "did the American federation not fail in its efforts?"[25] He identifies a self-serving American insistence on autonomy.

Returning to the Franco-German conflict of the late nineteenth century and the nascent French Third Republic, a defiant nationalism was clearly its defining trait. Political leaders set out to shape the French citizenry on the perceived Prussian model of devotion and zeal, in the obligatory, free, and secular schools established by the Ferry Laws of the 1880s.[26] National needs provided a ready-made platform for the Alliance Française. The organization could encourage the crystallization of nationhood and identity through French language learning worldwide. This points to an inherent contradiction within AF philosophy, the promotion of French language outside the physical borders of the nation, made possible of course by colonial activity. With empire, French language and culture could be extended to the furthest reaches of the planet, the realm known as Greater France, *la plus grande France*. From its very early days in fact, one could identify the specifically francophone aims of the organization. Promoting global French usage was the objective of its Comité général de propagande.[27] One might ask today why in fact people continue to want to study French despite the country's partially tarnished national and international image.[28] Alliance leaders devised strategies to encourage even the French to study the language and to become teachers, linguistic and cultural ambassadors of sorts. Such visions of internal colonization were organized not only through the Paris operation but also at the dozen provincial AF chapters located throughout provincial France.

Language teaching was not always the driving force of the increasingly global organization. The early AF did not have to offer formal language instruction in places, for instance, where colonial institutions were already carrying this out. It was through cultural initiatives that the Alliance could also promote the spread of French. By 1900, the French Republic had constructed a colonial network through which it could transmit French linguistic and cultural practices in North Africa, West Africa, the Antilles, and Indochina. Such exchange was certainly celebrated in the offices of the *République coloniale* and the AF.[29] At the advent of the twentieth century, a critical mass for the future Federation of Alliances in the United States also existed within the postcolonial residue of the former French Empire.

Many of the Alliance Française's early leaders were either civil servants within the national education system or high-ranking colonial officials under the Ministry of Foreign Affairs. The list includes Paul Cambon, resident general of France in Tunisia, and Paul Bert, former minister of public instruction. The institution's *mission civilisatrice* is succinctly expressed in the statement that adorned its very first bulletin in April 1884, "National association for the spread of French language *in the colonies* [my emphasis] and abroad" (see fig. 4). It is certainly not without import that Marianne the generous republican provider, Marianne the emblem of France's civilizing mission, was chosen to represent the Alliance. The two are quite literally synonymous, as Maurice Agulhon affirms.[30] A helmeted Marianne is a reminder of the military nature of her colonial endeavors, of cultural transmission made possible by force. The comparison with the militant female representation of liberty made famous by the French painter Eugène Delacroix in *La Liberté guidant le peuple* (1830) is self-evident. After empire, Marianne officially retreated from the scene of her activity, but not without leaving profound traces in her wake. French language and culture continue, in varying degrees, in West African postcolonies, but the contemporary Alliance Française has been inactive there, perhaps as a result of the reaction to violent colonial history with France. AF officials have seen a need for increased activity in Africa to counter the inroads made by English.[31]

ALLIANCE FRANÇAISE

ASSOCIATION NATIONALE

POUR LA PROPAGATION DE LA LANGUE FRANÇAISE

DANS LES COLONIES ET A L'ÉTRANGER

(Approuvée par arrêté du Ministre de l'Intérieur en date
du 24 janvier 1884)

BULLETIN N° I

AVRIL 1884

SIÈGE SOCIAL

2, RUE SAINT-SIMON (215, BOULEVARD SAINT-GERMAIN)

PARIS

4. AF Marianne. Reprinted with permission of the Alliance Française, Paris.

TV5Monde has made clear that future strategic initiatives focus on Africa from whence the majority of the world's French speakers will come.

More examples of republican imagery used by the Alliance Française illustrate the usefulness of the colonial territories. A bare-breasted Marianne carries the banner of the Alliance, bringing the French language to people of varying creeds and colors at various historical moments. Representations of Amerindian populations make reference to French influences having penetrated New World frontiers. Another figure shows a recently arrived Marianne (her ship is still in port) already at work. Here she is an attentive teacher reading to her receptive students, both Christian and Muslim, boys and girls.[32] Such imagery is omnipresent in Alliance Française documentation, in France and abroad. Marianne may very well be more French than Franco, but she symbolizes the transatlantic diffusion of culture. The image of Marianne as bearer of books and knowledge to an unlettered world is relevant to the twentieth-century Alliance Française in the United States. The Alliance has a long history of distributing books and establishing libraries in the areas it serves. The institutions cited at the beginning of the chapter similarly transmit knowledge to contemporary Franco-American generations. Alliance leaders clearly viewed collaboration between Marianne and the organization as synergetic and mutually beneficial. The organization was a vehicle in the Republic's push for greater influence worldwide.[33]

The Alliance Française attempted to publicize its global efforts and the colonial successes of Marianne at the elaborate expositions of the twentieth century. The organization sent representation to the Universal Exposition of 1900 where it established a working classroom complete with teacher and natives. At the 1931 Colonial Exposition of Paris, often described as the zenith of French imperial might, the Alliance organized a congress to transmit its ideas. It was also present at the 1937 Universal Exposition.[34] Influential Parisian publishing houses, Nathan, Delagrave, Colin, Calmann-Lévy, Alcan, Flammarion, Hachette and Belin, were among the many financial supporters of the organization at these venues. They too hoped to benefit from the spread of French language and literacy. A traditional representation of Marianne symbolized Alliance efforts in the United States.[35] Individual chapters such as that of Worcester, chose Marianne as their emblem, as did the American Federation of Alliances Françaises, of which they were a part. Transatlantic Marianne is in motion in both instances, depicted by her flowing hair. She is actively sowing the seeds of liberty, that is, of Frenchness, in the New World. She is fostering collaboration between Americans, Canadians, and the French. The smaller American Stars and Stripes and Canadian Union Jack are on top, while the French tricolor flag bears the largest influence, of *la Métropole*, on the bottom. Later versions of the same Alliance emblem display only the American and French flags. The female allegory is quite accurate in the context of the American Alliance. Women have played, and continue to play, a leading role in social and cultural organizations available to francophones in the United States.

THE ALLIANCE FRANÇAISE AND FRANCO-AMERICA

Since its foundation, the Alliance Française established an institutional presence in the communities of Franco-Americans, although Francos did not necessarily make up a large part of individual club membership. In the French-speaking neighborhoods of New England, the AF was one institution among many providing cultural, social, religious, and economic services to the one million French Canadians who left the province of Quebec to work in the paper, shoe, and textile factories of industrial New England and New York in the mid-nineteenth and early twentieth centuries.[36] Two-thirds of the founding chapters of the Federation of Alliances Françaises that met in New York City on March 4, 1902, were located in French-speaking, largely working-class Franco communities. They met in New York City with Jules Cambon and other *AF de Paris* leaders to officially recognize the birth of the Federation. James H. Hyde, a wealthy American francophile and member of the AF in New York, was responsible for its formation.[37] Nineteen of the existing AF chapters that met in New York came from places such as Hartford, Connecticut, Worcester, Lowell, Lawrence, Boston, Lynn, Salem, and Fall River in Massachusetts, Biddeford and Lewiston in Maine, Pawtucket and Providence in Rhode Island, all places where Franco-Americans represented a sizeable minority. In some industrial areas, there were also significant Acadian populations.

Other founding chapters were connected to colleges (Dartmouth, Smith, and Wellesley) and had neighboring francophone and francophile communities in Hanover, New Hampshire, Northampton and Wellesley, Massachusetts, respectively. Still other original chapters had ties to French or Franco-America: New Orleans, Lafayette, Indiana, and Detroit. The state of Massachusetts had many chapters, as this was the state with the greatest concentration of Franco-Americans.[38] The Alliance's objectives for the dissemination of French language and culture coincided with the *survivance* movement in Franco-American communities, that is, the effort to preserve a distinctly French cultural, linguistic, and religious identity from American influence. We know that this charge was taken up primarily by the clergy of the Catholic Church, keen to preserve its authority. It is ironic that the Alliance Française would emerge in predominantly working-class, francophone enclaves, given its generally elite status, and it is singular that an institution founded in a secular, republican culture would develop in devoutly Catholic communities in the United States.

There remain many questions about the early history of the AF and the role that it played in Franco-America. Much of the physical evidence of the organization's activities has disappeared from record. Existing Alliance archives indicate that many of the early Franco chapters were not teaching units but rather social and cultural clubs. As French was already widely and fluently spoken in French-Canadian neighborhoods, the small club format was the organizational structure that best suited members. Prominent Franco-Americans headed branches in places like Fall River, Lowell, and Worcester.[39] Antoine Clément, secretary of the Alliance Française de Lowell, provides an uncommon account of the history and activities of an Alliance chapter. He published a compilation of the lectures sponsored by the Alliance in Lowell in the 1930s that were the focal point of activities.[40] Eminent scholars from France, Quebec, and local institutions of higher learning such as Assumption College and Harvard University prepared the lectures. They spoke about literature, art, music, French history, French-American relations, Quebec, and the Franco-American experience generally. Reviews of these lectures appeared in Lowell's *L'Etoile*, one of the many French ethnic newspapers that operated in New England. The Alliance profited from this publicity and from the fact that Clément also edited *L'Etoile*.

By perpetuating the vitality of French language and culture in America, the AF played an advisory role within Franco-American communities in New England. The Alliance added luster to the image of Franco-Americans in the United States, who were most often ignored or associated with the uncultured classes. In a 1934 *Etoile* article, Clément described the Alliance as "an instrument of culture for all of our elite and a means of fulfilling the needs of the most cultivated spirits within the element of French-Canadian descent. Conserving amongst us the love of the French language and elevating the prestige of Franco-Americans in the eyes of other American groups who surround them, that is the objective increasingly achieved by the revived Lowell group for five years."[41]

Through contact with the esteemed Parisian institution, local French cultural standing might be given a boost, perhaps even among those at the lower end of the socioeconomic ladder. In Lowell at this time resided 35,000 people of French-Canadian descent and a wide representation of Franco-Americans in the educated and professional classes. Franco-American priests, doctors, lawyers, and merchants had followed migrating laborers in smaller numbers to offer their specialized services in the Little Canadas.

The Lowell chapter is representative of Alliance cultural centers in early industrial New England, as is the AF de Worcester, another founding Federation chapter with a similar orientation. Organization archives illustrate that official Alliance lecturers provided the core of activities in Worcester, along with films, excursions, plays, and performances.[42] This was an organization catering to a Franco-American membership, but that also included "war brides" (French women who had wed American servicemen after the Second World War) and assorted francophiles. The group maintained an active core of several dozen members who organized and profited from the cultural activities. The annual Mrs. Homer Gage lecture, an endowed fund, brought in prominent scholars from France to profess on Franco-American topics.[43] The Worcester group's presence was acknowledged in the columns of *France-Amérique*, an affiliate of the French newspaper *Le Figaro* in the United States, in the 1960s and 1970s.[44] The New York–based paper solicited the patronage of such French cultural organizations each year around New Year's Day, and simultaneously illustrated the breadth of French presence in the United States. The Franco-American newspaper of Worcester, Massachusetts, *Le Travailleur*, also relayed information about Alliance activities, among other events of interest to the community. As in the case of *L'Etoile*, the editors of *Le Travailleur* were group members. The AF had integrated one of the most influential Franco-American institutions, the French-language press.

While some Alliance Française chapters saw an amplification of their activities in the 1960s and 1970s, they often became more francophile than francophone as the century progressed.[45] As Franco-American populations aged, assimilated, and moved out of urban areas, and as younger generations spoke more and more English, branches in many mill towns in New England began to disappear. The decline of the founding American Alliances is certainly linked to an evolving Franco-American community. Francos were increasingly Americanized, despite *survivance* efforts, with a significant number of them moving out of French ethnic identity almost entirely. There were still four Massachusetts AF branches in the late 1970s and early 1980s.[46] But by the 1990s these chapters had all but ceased to exist, even the founding Worcester group. The opposite might have been anticipated. As some Francos moved into the middle classes, might the Alliance and its "high culture" not interest them more? The organization had to contend with the general decline in interest in foreign language that has plagued American society and institutions for the last few decades.

One Alliance Française chapter continues in Massachusetts (in Boston), the state once home to many ethnic Franco chapters. Maine, New Hampshire, and Vermont each maintained an existing chapter, although they vary greatly in activity. Three offices currently exist in Rhode Island, although none in Woonsocket, which once vied for the distinction with Manchester, New Hampshire, and Lewiston, Maine, as the Frenchest town in America. The Portland, Maine, chapter became virtually defunct in the early twenty-first century, but the Lake Champlain region, Vermont, branch sought to promote cultural and linguistic exchange between heritage and current speakers of French on either side of the Canadian border.[47] Farther south, the Alliance Française maintains a chapter, one of the American originals, in Hartford, Connecticut, where there was a significant Franco-American population until the mid-twentieth century. After a thirty-year hiatus, the Manchester Alliance chapter reopened in 2005, having received authorization from the *AF* de Paris (see following section). In current American Federation of Alliances literature, those interested in opening a chapter in New England are encouraged to look into the history of their area. There very well may be an AF affiliate on record that can be "revived," as in Manchester.

With far fewer chapters today, can the AF help to promote a cultural and linguistic renaissance in New England? Can the Alliance facilitate a return to lost cultural roots? This and other institutions convey the need as well as the desire for reconnection with a threatened French linguistic and cultural heritage in America. The AF is in many respects an intermediary between French America's past and present. Not only does it foster contemporary understanding through language and culture; it refers back to *la Nouvelle-France* and its postcolonial remnants. By working alongside cultural heritage associations in New England and the Upper Midwest, or celebrating Cajun and Creole cultural traditions in Louisiana, the AF promotes knowledge of America's fifth largest and forgotten ethnic group, the French (defined broadly).

As we will see, the recently reopened Alliance Française of Lafayette, Louisiana, has been involved in this initiative, as has the Council for the Development of French in Louisiana (CODOFIL), out of whose offices the Lafayette AF was initially run. There are several million people of French descent in North America and thus many potential clients for the organization.[48] Schools and universities continue to provide a feeder for Alliance students seeking local or more specialized knowledge, although the decrease in demand for language instruction in recent years has led some institutions to dismantle French programs. Despite widespread and historic ties to Franco-America, it is unclear whether the *AF* de Paris is interested in encouraging the kinds of smaller chapters that existed in the twentieth century. There have been episodes of discord concerning the autonomous branches that did not always sufficiently or accurately reflect the tenets of the Parisian institution. The current emphasis seems to be placed on developing teaching branches in urban areas that can bring in revenue. As the AF has faded from the Franco universe, other institutions have stepped in to fill the void, to reactivate a French language that has long lain dormant and to which some Franco-Americans are returning.[49] Some have even managed to survive the most recent economic recession of the early twenty-first century.

THE *ALLIANCE FRANÇAISE* AND FRANCOPHONIE

From its late nineteenth-century birth through its contemporary operations, one can trace an evolution within the Alliance Française network from a context of empire to one of francophonie. While France continues to be attractive to American AF members, francophonie is perhaps equally seductive, offering the allure of French culture mingled with the exoticism of Africa, the islands, the Orient, and the Canadian North. For the last few decades, the AF has been actively promoting francophonie through its initiatives, instructors, and courses. This seems to be a general trend, not simply a politically correct American phenomenon. Study of *la francophonie* associated with the Alliance Française in the United States is particularly important because French cultures outside of Quebec remain a minor and largely unexamined subject area within postcolonial francophone studies.

It is certainly in the interests of those promoting the spread of French to tap into an existing postcolonial network of countries and cultures. While French colonialists during the twentieth century sometimes boasted of an imperial France made up of 100 million bodies on five continents, known also as *La France des cinq continents*, contemporary advocates of francophonie claimed that French-speaking populations numbered more than 200 million (2011 OIF figures). In 2014, officials bandied about the inflated figure of 275 million francophones, many of whom reside in Africa. Ten years ago, during the March 20, 2005, "Journée internationale de la Francophonie," organizers listed the number at 175 million.[50] It is interesting to note that the postcolonial francophone world has thus far exceeded empire demographically, more than doubling it, although the actual number of French speakers is very difficult to identify and varies considerably depending on how closely one associates francophone with fluency. In a heavy-handed critique, Richard Serrano identified the dangers of terminology such as *francophone* or even *African*, which through their homogenizing effect reduce all to a monolithic state.[51] Patrick Manning claims that it was only in the 1980s that people in French-speaking African countries began to describe themselves and their countries as "francophone."[52] Francophonie advocates clearly view the Organisation internationale de la Francophonie (OIF) and its global initiatives as amounting to an intra-national and alternative superstructure, to a veritable reordering of the world by language, the French language, of course. The American Alliance has every reason to embrace a francophone world found within the borders of the United States. A 2004 edition of the AF newsletter featured the Senegalese president of the OIF, Abdou Diouf, acknowledging the relevance of francophonie for American members.[53]

Current members of the Alliance in the United States are increasingly connected to diasporic francophone populations. Branch instructors are of Belgian, Haitian, Québécois, Ivoirian, and French descent. They teach standard French but certainly illustrate its varied linguistic influences. The American Alliance has made extensive efforts to reach francophone heritage speakers. The AF named 2005 the "Year of Languages," with the Federation sponsoring numerous activities promoting French cultural heritage.[54] Community outreach efforts in Boston, Chicago, and San Francisco achieved some success. A program named "Crossroads" organized by the Boston AF facilitated contact between students from urban francophone immigrant communities (from Haiti, the West Indies, and Africa) and students of French in suburban settings.[55] The idea was to promote empathy and appreciation of different cultures as well as improved usage of both French and English. The Boston AF offered courses in English to nonnative francophone speakers, in addition to its French language curriculum. Critics may see the French cultural and imperial model at work here, but the AF in Boston, and in the United States generally, has indeed been at a cultural, ethnic, and socioeconomic crossroads for a long time.

The Alliance Française has been a leader, an imperfect one no doubt, in the preservation of historic Franco-American ties and continued goodwill between the two nations. The Alliance's American initiatives bring together several different institutional and media outlets capable of widely projecting its interests. *France-Amérique, Radio France internationale*, and *TV5Monde* have served as the quasi-official newspaper, radio, and television outlets for the organization. They have long formed a complementary cultural network informing and perhaps even advancing francophone cultures in the New World and elsewhere. This media relationship is symbiotic. Alliance Française documentation has carried advertisements for *France-Amérique*, and the newspaper similarly printed advertisements for the organization. *France-Amérique* has also promoted *TV5Monde*. All, of course, stand to profit from the spread of interest in France, the francophone world, and French language. Together they serve not to impede globalization or Americanization but to remind people of the French and francophone presence in North American society and culture.

FRENCH OUTREACH IN THE GULF SOUTH

The Council for the Development of French in Louisiana (CODOFIL) is a much more recent organization than the *Alliance Française*, but one that for fifty years has aspired to teach and preserve French cultures of south Louisiana. The institution, founded in 1968 by James "Jimmie" Domengeaux, still offers its linguistic and cultural services, after myriad political and policy changes, budget crises, and the devastation of Hurricanes Rita and Katrina. Former Louisiana governor Bobby Jindal cut cultural budgeting some 40 percent in 2012, but the organization persisted. CODOFIL is a state-run institution, hampered by the fluctuations of state budgets unlike the Alliance, but also an organization with a very similar message of linguistic and cultural pluralism. Its primary objective is to support, and perhaps even grow, the approximately 200,000 people that claim French heritage status in South Louisiana.

According to Act 409 of the state legislature, CODOFIL's mission is to "do all that is necessary to encourage the development, the utilization, and the preservation of French as expressed in Louisiana for the greatest cultural, economic, and touristic good of the state."[56] It is very difficult to assess precisely how effective the organization has been in its promotion of French, however loosely defined *francophone* or *French-speaking* truly is. French as expressed in Louisiana (*français tel qu'il existe*) is a complicated component of the group's objectives. Embedded in CODOFIL's legislature is not only the cultural importance of French instruction but also its economic vitality. Lawmakers, teachers, and business owners understand that maintaining Louisiana's French cultural distinctiveness can add to the state's tourism dollars.

The legal status of CODOFIL has been updated and slightly modified by new legislatures and governors, but amendments do not substantially alter the legal act explicitly recognizing linguistic expression in response to past decrees forbidding the use of French in schools in the United States, the English-only laws of 1916 and 1921. Both the South and Northeast drew up and maintained legislation meant to discourage speakers of French at a time when fear of the foreign immigrant had reached a crescendo. Fears are perhaps no less pervasive today, but French is a sanctioned language in Louisiana. Louisiana is the only officially bilingual state in America. Today CODOFIL contends that the state's francophone populations of Acadian, Creole, and Native American descent should maintain access to an education in French and that they as well as non-native French speakers benefit from exposure to an (inter)national language.

The economics of French cultural instruction is foremost in CODOFIL laws and regulations: "To oversee the . . . expansion of the state's economic development and tourism activities designed to promote our French culture, heritage, and language" is the first of the organization's priorities.[57] This was clearly a strategic initiative for CODOFIL organizers to assert. By tying Frenchness to the state's economic health, they have emphasized its essential qualities. Second, CODOFIL stressed the importance of the region's francophone connections to "countries, provinces and states that share historic French heritage, culture, and language." Its francophone objectives are noted explicitly in the legislature and the organization actively promotes forming relationships with culturally similar countries that might provide teachers. Third, French language instruction and immersion are emphasized, in cooperation with the state education board. These three objectives have varied in definition and priority since 1968 (between first, second, or third positions on the list), but they remain steadfastly within the mission of the organization.

The prioritizing of objectives is certainly political in nature, and in the current climate an economic imperative is persuasive. An earlier manifesto cited pertinent educational ambitions: "To provide elementary, secondary, and college-level students, teachers, and administrators with opportunities to engage in and profit from French language learning experiences." Practically since inception, CODOFIL set out to increase the number of French-immersion schools throughout Acadiana's twenty-two parishes and even east to Baton Rouge and New Orleans. According to the Council, its "Foreign Associate Teachers touch the lives of nearly 80,000 students in 31 parishes throughout the state every day."[58] These schools would ideally create legions of French speakers and even potentially French teachers. The executive director of CODOFIL had to be a French speaker as was expected of the twenty-three Council members. Today, membership includes appointees by the governor and representatives from state colleges and universities, the city of New Orleans, the French-American Chamber of Commerce, the Louisiana State Bar Association Francophone Section, the American Association of Teachers of French (AATF), and the United Houma Nation.[59] These varied constituents echo the wide diversity of Frenchness in the state. CODOFIL has served as official liaison to the Organisation internationale de la francophonie (OIF).

Louisiana state senator and veteran of the political trenches James Domengeaux had hoped initially to correct the legions of "bad speakers of French" in Louisiana by promoting standard or metropolitan French, not French as spoken locally. For this, critics attacked him. Domengeaux claimed to want to do this in his own Cajun or "pidgin French," a local variant of French with a host of other, more unsavory names.[60] Like many other Americans of French descent, Domengeaux had grown up thinking that his French dialect or patois was inferior. Many in Louisiana still remember receiving physical reprimands for speaking French publicly. After attending a local cultural festival in the 1970s and hearing the authenticity of the

Cajun experience expressed in Cajun French, Domengeaux is reported to have experienced a change of heart. Since then the Council has not only encouraged young people of French descent to speak Louisiana French but to be proud of their heritage. Cajun, Creole, and "standard" French are now embraced and taught by program instructors as well as University of Louisiana professors. The *Alliance Française* of Lafayette has been a strong supporter of the state's diverse francophonie.

In the early 1980s, CODOFIL's operating budget hovered around $1 million. Subsequent state legislatures reduced this by three-quarters in the 2000s to $250,000, well before the Jindal administration applied cuts in 2012. The reduced budget of $150,000, not nearly enough to cover all costs, forced the organization to seek a short-term gap of donations to pay for activities, an unsustainable measure. In 2012, a reduced CODOFIL supported four thousand schoolchildren in French immersion classes and another fifty thousand who took part in French as second-language classes, according to the executive director.[61] The CODOFIL office is located in the center of Lafayette, next to the Lafayette Parish Courthouse. The nearby bilingual municipal building signs, as well as street names throughout the region, are a testament to the Council's efforts to make French a part of daily life for area Cajuns and Creoles. The French-English signs in front of the building, like the local McDonald's hoisting both state and Cajun flags, convey the complementary and sometimes competing cultural sensibilities in Franco-America. Such demonstrative efforts are part of a calculated project to reclaim parts of the United States as French, such as the southern half of the Pelican State, that have French minority status but majority appeal.

French is a desired part of both public and private space in Acadiana (a fusion of Louisiana and Acadia), as inhabitants have known this French heritage area of south Louisiana for the last half century. Area families have demanded access to French culture and language for their children, directly resulting in the development of immersion programs in primary schools. Annual cultural festivals, highlighting French musical and culinary traditions, have also helped to create Acadiana's local, national, and even international appeal. Marketing this French legacy (and delicacy) is most certainly a means of attracting people and dollars to places outside of New Orleans where many Acadians settled and where Cajuns and Creoles currently live. A CODOFIL signature sign, "Ici, on parle le Français!" (Here French is spoken) became a popular public statement in Acadiana storefronts and homes after the Council was founded in 1968. New ones created for the anniversary celebration in 2008 boasted that life begins at forty.[62] One of the latest CODOFIL campaign strategies in 2014 was the marketing of "Proud to be Cajun/Creole" license plates. The French connection is not cited on every license plate as in Quebec (*Je me souviens*), but those willing to pay can affirm a Louisiana French heritage. The proceeds are reinvested in the development of French in the state.

The Council sponsors traditional teaching of French language and culture in the classroom and also makes them tangible through interaction, encouraging people to think about French culture through the experience of song, dance, and food. It has combined traditional as well as more innovative methods of learning French. The Council helped launch the Alliance Française de Lafayette from its former rue Principale Ouest street address. The Lafayette operation offers an example of cooperation between the French national organization and local francophone groups that culminated in the opening of the Alliance chapter in 2005. The Alliance Française of Lafayette set the ambitious objective to foster learning of standard French, Cajun French, and Creole French. Its stated mission is to "enrich, develop, and support the francophone community of greater Lafayette by the teaching of French in its local variants, by the acknowledgment of French heritage in its multiple expressions, thanks to a varied and adapted cultural program."[63] The operations of the AF and Council have clearly been linked.

In 2005, the emerging AF de Lafayette had a number of supporting institutions, both francophone and francophile, at its disposal, which gave its candidacy particular strength. Partnering with CODOFIL was vital given its physical space in the center of Lafayette, the availability of classrooms, and a library stocked with traditional printed, visual, and digital materials, and a network of resources. The other affiliated institutions illustrated the extent to which a new *Alliance* was entering into an established francophone community and network. In its letter of support, the Acadiana Arts Council and Center stressed the fact the chapter would not have to teach French to beginners, but could in fact depend on local francophone leaders.[64] CODOFIL itself, notably through its teaching initiatives, was built upon francophone solidarity and collaboration. "CODOFIL offers scholarships to foreign students and works to consolidate community relations among francophones."[65]

Lafayette's Université des Acadiens (University of Louisiana at Lafayette) listed its numerous francophone programs, resources, and interested faculty in support of the local AF candidacy, as did other local francophone and Franco-friendly offices. The Cité des Arts, Louisiane à la carte, and Louisiana Folk Roots all lent their resources and commitment to promoting interaction, cultural diversity, and francophonie. Le Centre International de Lafayette, though most closely invested in promoting economic interests for the city, could not fail to support the AF, as collaboration would create the possibility for exchange with the network of cities in the United States, Canada, and Mexico. Le Centre International gave the AF a line to the mayor's office. The AF stood to benefit substantially from supporting the Festival international de Lafayette, the major U.S. francophone cultural event for music and performance.[66] Associates have indeed stressed the teaching of Franco-American language and culture through music, since the founding of CODOFIL. By way of such assistance, including that of the Consulat général de France in New Orleans, the AF became operational almost immediately, offering a plethora of classes and cultural opportunities within an already established infrastructure.

Its supporters and the CODOFIL director believed that the Lafayette AF could be a flagship chapter, reflecting the interests of the national organization, perhaps even its best practices. It could highlight its richly unique and creolized musical, linguistic, and culinary cultures. At its chapter location in the heart of *l'Acadie tropicale*, the proposal boasted of not just the typical AF fare of classes for children, beginners, conversationalists, and heritage speakers, but authentic Cajun and Creole experiences with living culture. The Alliance chapter offered its patrons local Louisiana fare with hands-on cooking classes. Courses offered local French speakers and learners the opportunity to discover francophone connections with other parts of the world. French summer immersion camps for the children of French ancestry rounded out the special offerings of the Lafayette office. As its mission stated, the linguistic and cultural programming reflected the diversity of area francophone cultures of south Louisiana. After the opening of the Louisiana chapter of the Alliance Française in 1902, it would be a full century before Acadiana, the state's largest francophone area, would have a branch.

People other than James Domengeaux might have been surprised to see the Alliance Française and CODOFIL collaborating to maintain Cajun and Creole patois, in addition to supporting standard French. Both organizations are participants in the development and recognition of distinct forms of French, reflecting the francophone perspectives maintained by historic migrants to south Louisiana. Supporting all of them simultaneously, however, was and remains a formidable task indeed. Fortunately Louisiana francophones have had not only the support of the noted institutions, but that of different media sources. Beginning in October 2009, French Louisianans gained access to Radio France Internationale (RFI), like the denizens of mostly larger metropolitan areas of the United States.[67] Distributers designed RFI access especially for mobile phone devices and represented another means of promoting North American francophonie. TV5Monde has also actively promoted the cultural life of Acadiana.

The core component of CODOFIL's cultural work supports the French immersion classes that have existed in area primary schools for the last several decades. The majority of CODOFIL's long-standing $250,000 budget helped to run the French teaching and mentoring program through the Lafayette office. With the intensive language program of CODOFIL taking the lead in schools, progressing French speakers and future members of the AF might be encouraged. A potential rivalry among cultural organizations could develop thus into a more synergetic relationship. CODOFIL is responsible for orchestrating French teaching in Acadiana's many parishes west of the Mississippi River, as well as the French *lycée* in New Orleans. The teaching program has not been too adversely affected to date by swings from right to left in the governor's mansion. Each year, 250 young, energetic teachers from around the francophone world converge in south Louisiana to form the CODOFIL teaching corps. They typically obtain three-year contracts to teach a variety of subjects in French in area primary schools, from pre-kindergarten through eighth grade.

The first teachers arrived from France and Quebec just after the Council's founding. A few years later, Belgian teachers began working with area children. In the early twenty-first century, the majority of these young cultural ambassadors were from France, Belgium, and Canada, former colonial powers in the first two cases and a postcolonial in the latter. Recruiting teachers from the formerly colonized world became more difficult, politically and economically, especially after the attacks of September 11, 2001, and the No Child Left Behind education policy was set in place. Obtaining visas for teachers from Africa posed problems for the CODOFIL administration.[68] Still the organization's recent teacher ranks include individuals from Tunisia, Niger, Mali, Ivory Coast, Benin, Burkino Faso, Algeria, Haiti, and Switzerland. The Council claimed to be the only group recruiting experienced teachers to take part in the French-immersion experiment in south Louisiana.[69] CODOFIL expected teachers to bring experience, enthusiasm, and ideas to primary schools of Acadiana, not just native French fluency.

In 1990, the organization hired its first teacher from francophone Africa, and in 2000 the first Haitian teacher joined the francophone pedagogic corps. In 1991, the Council began hiring teachers of Acadian descent. One of the objectives of CODOFIL from the very beginning, and still proclaimed in its current legislation, has been rendering the arrival of a francophone corps of teachers obsolete. The organization would ideally promote from within the local population of francophone descent, harvesting teachers from the ranks of pupils who would in turn serve as role models for young schoolchildren of French heritage. This represents a lofty dream indeed that would require many to have had a real impact in Acadiana. CODOFIL has had a handful of local francophone teachers working with language students, after having been students themselves. While their numbers have increased, Cajun and Creole primary schoolteachers, including Haitian instructors, represent a small number of the total number of teachers in local schools. CODOFIL has not yet attained the objective of cultural self-sufficiency.

If we look at a representative school year, 2004–2005, the vast majority of CODOFIL teachers came from France, then Belgium and Canada.[70] Long-range planning for the institution included the organization of missions to France, Belgium, Tunisia, and Canada every other year to encourage the collaboration of teachers, researchers, and mutually beneficial relations.[71] Teachers from francophone African countries typically numbered one per country, although Niger and Tunisia each sent several French instructors.[72] Contact with this diverse francophone teaching group could be culturally enriching, but also be disruptive for the children. Immersion school children might be exposed to several different accents, personalities, and ways of teaching French over the course of their primary school education. They could encounter sympathy to their minority cultural status from their teacher or resistance. The Council claims that "Louisiana students receive a better education due to exposure to a greater variety of French accents, expressions, and diverse teaching methods."[73] Critics question whether francophone teachers can help to both promote the French language among heritage speakers and help to heal historic wounds.[74]

French teacher associates themselves state that the variety of French speakers can be confusing for young learners. The organization expects its corps of teachers to be sensitive to the local francophone situation, because children can indeed have different French teachers in successive years, forcing them to face each year anew their fears about Louisiana French. One young instructor acknowledged the tricky adjustment to new accents.[75] She said moreover that the children in St. Martin's Parish only spoke in French during the topic sessions that she taught. English was spoken in the assorted subject classes for the remainder of the day. She personally found it difficult for children to gain fluency in the language with such limited contact. Not all of CODOFIL's programs are equally intensive or immersion-style, as mentioned earlier. In some schools, all subjects are taught in French, and in others, French instruction is one part of the day's curriculum.

Young women make up a large part of the ranks of the CODOFIL teachers working with area children. The number of years of teaching experience among them tends to vary considerably. The three-year contract in Louisiana provides the mentors with a paid job, an important cultural objective and an opportunity to explore a new culture themselves. In many respects, they are each mini-ambassadors for francophonie in the United States.[76] It is no small challenge to accept the French cultural work that they have undertaken, even for an energetic and ambitious group of young people. Incoming CODOFIL teachers spend a summer weekend in Baton Rouge becoming acclimated to the Louisiana heat as well as learning about the unique Cajun/Creole heritage of schoolchildren. This is a short albeit important orientation for French teachers who must be sensitized to the particularities of the French experience in South Louisiana. Some school-age children and their families grew up having ingrained the pejorative notions associated with French cultures in south Louisiana as well as in the United States more generally. CODOFIL instructors must combat these historic experiences and wounds.

The results achieved by CODOFIL programs have subsequently come under criticism, often by Cajuns themselves.[77] To ask of it to produce a cohort of native French speakers in its relatively short history is certainly a tall order. The curriculum runs through eighth grade only, although high schools and the University of Louisiana at Lafayette do provide access to higher and more specialized learning in French, as does the Alliance Française. The pressures on teachers and students to achieve success in national testing can also take time and focus away from study of French. CODOFIL is, in sum, a small operation, offering a wide assortment of cultural opportunities by agents with limited resources. The organization has raised awareness and generated a documented interest in French language and culture that can be measured in the demand for French immersion schools and in the organic development of French cultural and social exchanges in the area. The Council has sponsored two events that have become significant in Acadiana: the Festival international de Louisiane in the spring and Festivals Acadiens et créoles in the fall (discussed in more detail in the final chapter). These events bring culture to life in ways that are not always possible in the classroom.

A former director stated that CODOFIL is a facilitator, promoting French language and culture and putting people in direct contact with

French heritage.[78] Whether through the establishment of French street signs or the fostering of French language tables, CODOFIL has helped to make French culture a more visible, lived, and felt experience. It is difficult to imagine what the state of French in Louisiana would be without the work of the organization, despite its deficiencies. Cajuns and Creoles make up a small percentage of the population, and a good many have lost touch with their French roots as in New England. The French of Louisiana are no longer a majority even within many towns in Acadiana such as Lafayette. A whole generation of Louisianans of francophone descent had grown up almost exclusively in English before French immersion programs began in the early 1970s. CODOFIL continues to remind them that their French culture is worth preserving.

The Council long maintained a website instructive for people searching out francophone activities in the area, including French language tables, which have grown in number and in popularity in Acadiana, as they have in New England. The Council listed dates and locations for meetings. In Lafayette and surrounding towns, residents, tourists, students, and professors gather in restaurants and cafés, as in the days when French was more often heard in public. One of the groups has met in downtown Lafayette every Wednesday morning for more than twenty years.[79] The local public radio station KRVS ("Radio Acadie" since 1963) regularly advertises this on its daily program *Bonjour Louisiane* as well as other events where French is spoken. People do not need formal structures or organizations in order to assemble and find French culture. The former CODOFIL director suggested that while some Franco-American associations have been successful in New England, they fail to generate much enthusiasm in Acadiana.[80] People tend to find the culture that they crave in other, more spontaneous settings, although in 2006 the Richelieu Club and the Association Canado-Américaine collectively attempted to set up offices in Lafayette.[81] Thanks in part to CODOFIL and the revitalization of Franco cultural life through music and food notably, local French expressions are still present in people's lives.

For many years, the community relations office of CODOFIL orchestrated a regional as well as national and international cultural network, putting area residents in touch with French and francophone cultures near and far. Like CODOFIL as an entity, this small bureau fully embraced the multicultural nature of French traditions in south Louisiana. "We will respect our past to enrich our future by affirming the distinct components of our multicultural Francophone identity through education, community outreach, and international exchanges."[82] The office issued weekly bilingual Cajun French and English bulletins, *Le Bulletin du Calendrier CODOFIL*, which informed francophones and francophiles about an active French cultural life in south Louisiana that had outlived the devastation of xenophobia, assimilation, and hurricanes. It offered tributes to resilient French music, vocabulary, foods, and organizations.

This was a cultural lifeline in some respects that connected isolated and vulnerable Francos to the wider francophone cultural world. CODOFIL made more visible to readers the contours of Franco-America, linking local French initiatives with those in New England and New Brunswick. The Council's weekly bulletin became *Patates nouvelles* in the summer 2009 with even more accessible news of local francophone lectures, music, Alliance Française events, tastings, and assorted happenings. *Patates nouvelles* added a translation into Louisiana Creole to the regular French and English bulletin, creating a trilingual forum for area francophone affairs.[83] The politics of black versus white, of Cajun versus Creole, periodically crept into local French conversations in south Louisiana, but CODOFIL and its regular bulletins served as interpreter, filter, and arbiter, acknowledging differences but also reminding communities of their shared pasts and cultures. This was important when conversations intensified over the possibility of changing the name of Lafayette's Evangeline Thruway to Martin Luther King Expressway.[84]

Through its community relations office, CODOFIL has made notable strides toward Cajun and Creole collective engagement in their heritage culture. The African American Museum and the Acadian Memorial of St. Martinville, Louisiana, stand side by side today, symbolically linked in many regards yet representing often painfully separate francophone communities and experiences. The organization has reportedly not been able to make inroads into the Native American community through its francophone teacher corps, although many Native Americans still speak Louisiana or Cajun French. Cultural and scholastic programming has had an impact on African Americans. Many have successfully attended immersion schools, and one can surmise that participating parents sought out this specialized teaching. The children who have gone through immersion programs tend to achieve better scholastic results, CODOFIL reports. There has been no targeted partnering of francophone children of Creole descent with francophone teachers, although sometimes a third of a particular class is African American.[85]

Jimmie Domengeaux's wish to help preserve Louisiana's unique cultural heritage has certainly taken root. The Louisiana congressman and CODO-FIL founder passed away decades ago, but his institution has remained vital to the area. A symbolic tree and monument were planted at Girard Park near the University of Louisiana campus to honor Domengeaux's efforts to develop French roots and call attention to the stewardship of French culture in Acadiana. The Festivals Acadiens et créoles, sponsored originally by CODOFIL, are held on this same site each year bringing to life Domengeaux's dream. French life takes center stage in Lafayette and is part of public discourse. France's participation in the preservation of French Louisiana is a delicate but necessary one, particularly since the hurricanes of the 2000s. French ambassadors have had the difficult task of supporting local French initiatives without ostensibly imposing cultural norms, for local francophones are sensitive to Parisian snubs and initiatives smacking of colonialism.

AT THE FRANCO GRASSROOTS IN NEW ENGLAND

The short-lived CODOFINE (Council for the Development of French in New England) attempted to duplicate what was happening in Louisiana in the northeastern quadrant of the United States. A problem lay, however, in the fact that Franco-Americans in New England are spread out over several states.[86] The modern oil industry took many Creoles and Cajuns into neighboring Texas, extending a French Gulf already reaching eastward into coastal Mississippi, but a large contingent of Franco-Americans of the South are still located in Louisiana. Dispersed as its population was throughout Maine, New Hampshire, Vermont, Massachusetts, Rhode Island, Connecticut, and New York, CODOFINE never became firmly established. CODOFIL did have a representative that they briefly sent to New England as a delegate. Two decades after the founding of CODO-FIL, two autonomous cultural and community centers built from below in Manchester, New Hampshire, and Lewiston, Maine, began to offer cultural and pedagogical activities to New England Francos. The Alliance Française has also been engaged in this development.

The Franco-American Center or Centre Franco-Américain (CFA) in Manchester has been in existence since 1990, gathering Francos, informing them of their history, recording their past, and facilitating their future. The Center received its charter as a nonprofit cultural institution in New Hampshire. Founders claim, "The mission of the Franco-American Centre is to preserve the rich heritage of our French communities. We promote History, Culture and Education with an understanding of their historic contributions, cultural and artistic expressions, both past and present."[87] The cultural center facility long maintained an extensive library of Franco-American novels, histories, French language, and children's books, as well as a collection of Franco-American newspapers, including many of the daily French-language newspapers that served New England mill towns. The center was open to researchers as well as genealogy buffs, a national sport among Franco-Americans.

For most of its history, the organization operated out of the Association Canado-Américaine (ACA) building in downtown Manchester. Inside, ACA members could make use of a bowling alley and theater. Visitors found walls filled with commemorative tributes to the numerous Franco-Americans who served in the military. Plaques written in French honored those fallen for their American homeland (*la patrie*) during the First and Second World Wars. "A la mémoire de notre société-morts au service de la patrie américaine—et de la cause des Alliés." These commemorations are not unlike the *monuments aux morts* that emerged on the metropolitan French landscapes after 1918 and 1945. While the foreignness of Franco-Americans was at times suspect, like other immigrant groups, these plaques articulate that Francos viewed themselves as patriotic Americans. American and French flags periodically flew outside the imposing pillars of the ACA, signaling the international (yet loyal) activity within the establishment.[88]

Today, Franco-American veterans associations continue to draw attention to military service. At another site in Manchester, city leaders have immortalized the patriotism of Franco lieutenant René Gagnon. He was one of the five soldiers who planted the American flag at Iwo Jima in 1945 in an epic battle. Gagnon's story was recounted in Clint Eastwood's 2006 feature film *Flags of Our Fathers*, as was a Native American from the Pima tribe in Arizona whose tragic life was immortalized in a 1968 Johnny Cash song "The Ballad of Ira Hayes." How distinctly American, that a Franco-American and a Native American were at Iwo Jima in 1945, raising the flag in one of the defining moments of twentieth-century American history.[89] The participation of Franco-Americans in the transformative wars of the twentieth century is remembered in other places like the noted Nashua, New Hampshire, city monument. At its center is a plaque dedicated to Amédée Duchêne, who died on the battlefields in World War I. Surrounding this site are stones indicating the city's fallen heroes in the numerous wars in which America has participated, from the revolutionary battle through the current and ongoing "war on terror." On the bricks that pave the path leading visitors throughout the space are still more French engravings of family names. Physical bricks, or building blocks, inscribe French participation in American history, giving a sense of the permanence of their contribution.

The CFA opened some twenty years after Manchester's Alliance Française affiliate went dormant. It also welcomed its rebirth and helped to cultivate excitement about the possibilities for French language and culture in an area where francophone communities had long been established. The coordinated efforts of local enthusiasts resulted in the inauguration of the revived Alliance Française de Manchester on July 22, 2005, and the American Federation of Alliances Françaises recognized the reopening of this historic chapter.[90] In the 1920s and 1930s, the Manchester chapter of the French national organization had been active. CFA artifacts include a sixty-year-old Alliance Française certificate noting the organization's historic presence in the city, dated 1948. The Manchester Alliance was like the small New England groups discussed at the beginning of this chapter, founded by Franco-Americans. After a thirty-year existence, the chapter became inactive in 1970, to the displeasure of the Federation. In 1967–68, the group still had seventy-five listed members, virtually all of whom were of French-Canadian or Franco-American descent, but interest had waned.[91] Ten years following its twenty-first-century inauguration and renaissance, the Manchester AF is again inactive, but the Centre Franco-Américain organizes classes for various levels of French learners. A still integrated CFA and AF might have fostered increased French fluency while also respecting the local vernacular and cultural traditions, as has happened in Lafayette, Louisiana.

The $40 annual membership fee gave CFA supporters access to a range of cultural activities including regular French movies. The Centre sponsored exhibits by Franco or French-Canadian artists in its own gallery until 2011, not to speak of the annual celebrations of local Frenchness, St. John the Baptist Day. Wine tasting and Bastille Day celebrations still attract large groups of people today. The organization continues to promote Franco cultural life and increasingly encourages its patrons to draw connections to the wider francophone world. The organization has annually sponsored Francophone Day in March with the support of the Organisation internationale de la francophonie (OIF). A former executive wondered if the organization might more fully engage in francophone as well as Franco-American culture as the ethnic center in Lewiston, Maine, had begun doing, which had garnered some financial success.[92]

Like CODOFIL, the Centre Franco-Américain has faced an incessant search for funding made necessary by a recovering economy and subsequent belt-tightening. It provided a cultural space where French could be spoken and heard by community members in the city center. Such places are rarer in Manchester than in the past. One local Franco-American meeting space is a restaurant where patrons can still be understood in French, especially between masses on Sunday, but during the week, one can no longer count on being able to find a French-speaking waitress. A local bookshop has long been another local cultural hub. Franco-Americans and francophones in

Manchester can still listen to French radio broadcasts on Sunday mornings and evenings.

The CFA vacated its historic space and moved in April 2011 to the nearby St. Anselm College campus, a move necessitated by the 2009 sale of the ACA building to the Royal Arcanum of Boston. The sale represented a symbolic and literal shock to the Franco community of Manchester as noted, with the disappearance after more than one hundred years of the very organization whose mission it was to provide assurance to community members in time of need.[93] The move meant no more downtown presence for the organization or public access to its collections. Francos could no longer congregate in a designated ethnic space in the heart of Manchester. The organization's rich and varied assembly of documents, objects, and materials are now held at the ACA/Lambert collection at the St. Anselm College library, used more by scholars. The current CFA is more virtual than real, still offering a variety of pedagogic and cultural services but without the physical space to host them.

A decade after the founding of Manchester's CFA, Franco-Americans in Lewiston, Maine, established the Franco-American Heritage Center (FAHC). It emerged at the former St. Mary's Church on July 1, 2000, soon after the last French-language mass was celebrated. A century prior to this development, Lewiston residents had organized one of the founding chapters of the American Federation of Alliances Françaises. In 2000, local Franco businessmen and prominent citizens contacted the Diocese and suggested that the building be given to the community in order to establish not only a cultural center but a museum and performance hall as well.[94]

Housed in one of the expansive religious buildings constructed by and for Franco-Americans at the height of their presence, the space carries considerable cultural weight and thus requires significant support. Franco-American community leaders knew, however, that they wanted to save this space, which local families had helped to build in 1927 with their savings. The Franco community of Lewiston, once living in a tightly knit, endogamous enclave, had become more dispersed socioeconomically and geographically and could no longer fill the pews of the large church. Organizers purchased it for a symbolic dollar with the understanding that they would raise the necessary resources to preserve it.[95] The FAHC received a $1 million grant from the state of Maine to pursue its cultural activities, and it has sought additional funding since then.

The organization emerged as a Franco-American heritage center, but today is known as the Franco Center for Heritage and the Performing Arts.[96] The restored place of worship houses a gallery display of Franco-American cultural expression and a vast performance hall with a Steinway piano given to the Center by an anonymous donor. "The mission of the Franco-American Heritage Center is to celebrate and preserve the Franco-American heritage while welcoming the cultures of our neighbors."[97] According to the founding FAHC executive director, twenty-five percent of the performances are in French.[98] Musical events, plays, and weddings round out the varied calendar of activities. Its cultural mission is still only possible if it can pay for the necessary building upkeep. French cultural heritage has at times been profitable in Louisiana, and Francos in New England have similarly explored the connection between profitability and French culture. At Center performances, there is often a subtle insertion of culinary culture. For instance, crêpes have been a signature sales item at FAHC events.[99] As in other parts of Franco-America, the industrial center once inhabited by Francos now houses immigrant populations from the Third World, some of them from francophone countries. A Somali community has developed in the former French ethnic enclaves of Lewiston since 2000, and Somali weddings are held at the FAHC.

The Franco Center is under new direction since the retirement of its first director in 2011, but it maintains the same cultural agenda. All board members speak French. They meet regularly with representatives from the French and Quebec consuls to support francophonie, and so communication in French is an imperative. Perhaps equally important to the direction of the organization are the fund-raisers and grant writers employed. Like its Manchester equivalent, the Franco center offers an assortment of events that highlight Franco-American life in the city but also serve to embrace multiculturalism. The institution expresses a commitment to diversity described in Alliance Française and OIF initiatives discussed earlier. The Franco Center/FAHC received the support and sponsorship of television station TV5Monde beginning in 2007, meaning that area Franco-Americans attained access to the largest French-language cable network. TV5Monde installed a satellite dish and large-screen monitors in the performance hall lobby so that patrons could see and hear French while on the premises.[100] The Center has continued to sponsor the annual Festival Franco Fun event, featuring traditional music, crêpes, meat pie, and pea soup for Franco families.[101]

Outside of festival time, local French speakers can take French classes at different levels on-site at the Franco Center. The community center organizes a summer French immersion experience for area youth. Middleschoolers travel to Quebec, where they stay with host families. The Center also supported an after-school French program. For adults in search of French-speaking opportunities, the monthly Rencontre draws two to three hundred people for a meal, music, and French conversation.[102] Attendees pay twenty-five cents every time they speak English at table, a historic reversal from the days when Francos were made to pay physically for speaking French.

Food and music bring Lewiston's Francos together for other events. Four times a year, they attend *la soirée canadienne*, with the C'est si bon ("It's so good) band and share supper. The former director herself shared recipes for *tourtière*, the traditional meat pies offered at events. The organization long maintained an active website illustrating its many activities as well as a widely circulated newsletter. *Le Messager d'aujourd'hui*, a monthly bilingual newsletter, projected the mission and agenda of the organization to some 2,800 readers in 2010.[103] The publication exists as a sequel to the former Lewiston daily paper, *Le Messager* (1880–1968), which some residents still remember from its regular circulation in the 1950s and 1960s. The newsletter informed readers of center activities and performances, sponsoring initiatives, donors, and improvements to the facility. It also aimed to promote teaching and learning through cooking, a French-Canadian vocabulary lesson *le parler de chez nous*, and an Instant French column providing phonetic sampling of useful French phrases.[104]

The permanent collection of Franco-American memorabilia housed at the Franco Center offers more opportunities for engagement with the culture and with Francos' past. The exhibit displays popular snowshoe club souvenirs including attire worn by members. They are particularly evocative of an earlier period when people lived by French tradition. The walls of the building are adorned with murals that illustrate Franco contributions to the life of the industrial city. FAHC organizers have raised millions of dollars to support the center and its Franco initiatives by bringing people into the facility at St. Mary's. At the same time, they have helped to revitalize a city by stimulating business.[105] Organizers dreamed of bringing prosperity into an area long known locally as the armpit of Maine. As Francos now share urban space in Lewiston with members of many immigrant groups, the Center has shifted its extended message of community through French. The Franco Center sponsored peace walks in the neighborhood. It has joined the movement for diversity and call to action for greater understanding among groups. Francophone African groups attend La Rencontre and help to promote French linguistic and cultural life in the city.[106] Franco-Americans of Lewiston share in the sporting success of immigrant high school neighbors and friends. This symbol of francophone unity contrasts jarringly with the politics of Maine governor and Franco-American Paul LePage.

Franco-American cultural centers such as Franco Center/FAHC play an important role in acknowledging the historical import of sometimes crumbling ethnic neighborhoods in early industrial mill towns. Franco-American social clubs as well as vestiges of tenements are located just across the street from the former church. As in other industrial centers of New England, there is not much left that is clearly visible of French communal life except for those who choose to pay careful attention. Not far from the Franco hub of Lewiston is the terminal station of the Grand Trunk Railway line, once linking Montreal, Quebec, Portland, Maine, and other points for French-Canadian emigrants. The station even in its current state of abandonment still recalls the importance of north-south migration to the city.

The existence of the Alliance Française, CODOFIL, and Franco-American cultural centers conveys the transformation of the French (Canadian,

Creole, Acadian) diaspora of the United States. The continuity of French ethnic life has required such spaces where an education in French can be obtained. Former French parochial schools, with instruction conducted in French and English, are no more. In the case of the center in Lewiston, occupying the historic and hallowed space of Franco-Americans has meant renewed life in an era of razed or vacant churches, emptied ethnic enclaves, and bought out insurance companies. Francos have developed strategies for maintaining these ethnic establishments and created pulpits from whence to teach and learn about guarded, little known, or denigrated cultures. While some notions of Alliance Française may be frozen in a nostalgic representation of the past, these institutions demonstrate that Franco-America can be a forward-looking concept. A subtle but strong French past is powerful indeed, and this is witnessed in the Franco-American memory and museums. These sites stimulate ongoing conversation about the past and present; they foment cultural resurrections. Francos had their past erased in a sense, and returning to it represents a considerable step moving forward. Long denied access to a native language and culture, Franco-Americans have assumed positions of leadership and have been at the vanguard of heritage preservation, from the building of some of the great basilicas and churches of New England to the establishment of mutual aid societies, formed to help the needy, to the creation of dynamic cultural centers. Local historians, activists, genealogists, and simple citizens interested in Franco cultural preservation have joined this effort. Francos have increasingly seen their continued French-influenced future in conjunction with the wider francophone world.

Francos celebrate the factory of old today in renovated museums while remaining attached in some ways to rural traditions. Renovation of the mills has certainly helped to collectively rebuild aging industrial cities by saving historic textile, paper, and shoe factories, now transformed not only into cultural institutions but also restaurants, art studios, and condominiums. We have witnessed that cultural institutions can at times promote economic growth and help to identify undervalued local cultures, but they require resources at times when these are scant. Such centers focus on local life primarily, and so their ability to touch the public consciousness outside their immediate areas is limited. Those listed provide representative examples. Francos continue to forge ahead and found centers in other areas where cultures have remained hidden such as the French Heritage Center in Chicopee, Massachusetts. It has had no physical home, but began organizing for the necessary funds and space to exist. Social networks such as Facebook breathe life into not yet even incorporated groups like this one.[107] The Center sponsored a series of lectures and events in 2014, including commemoration of the participation of Franco-Americans in the attempt to aid a beleaguered France in 1914 and 1944.[108] This effort, during the centennial of the First World War (1914–2014) and the seventieth anniversary of the Normandy invasion (1944–2014), indicate unforgotten Franco ties to France. The Alliance Française operates on a much larger scale, of course, than most of the other cited establishments, but its fundamental and sometimes contested belief in the perpetuation of French and francophone cultures by means of decentralized efforts is exemplified by them in New England and Louisiana.

One can trace the history of Franco-America from seventeenth-century *filles du roi*, to twentieth-century Franco mill girls, to the aging grandmothers or *mémères* who pass on ethnic cultures today. They are repositories of francophone postcolonial thought. In closing, let us consider a small, emblematic, and also virtual initiative designed to further promote the Franco fact in America. The Franco-American Women's Institute (FAWI), L'Institut des femmes franco-américaines in French, founded in 1996, represents a digital acknowledgment of Franco-American achievement, notably that of women. For the last twenty years, the Franco-American Women's Institute has sought to shed light on unknown Franco-American women's experiences. It is a warehouse (and "wherehouse") of Franco women's voices, somehow both archive and parlor, ambiguously placed between past and present in its institutional mission and responses. "Ours is a lived culture," says its founder, Rhea Côté Robbins.

> The Franco-American Women's Institute is an organization of women who gather together for the specific purpose of promoting Franco-American, ethnic women's voices. The women come together in many

forms of presentation, body, soul and creative spirit, as Franco-American women—-Québécois, Acadian, Métis, Mixed Blood, French Canadian, Cajun, Creole and Huguenot . . . Daughters, mamans, and mémères.[109]

FAWI draws connections between generations of Franco women, as well as pointing to ties with women from varied francophone countries.

Robbins insists on the metaphor of a net hauling in quantities of Franco women's experiences, thus seeking increased visibility for these fecund expressions of Franco life after decades of silence. "A NET is designed to capture, and also free the diversity of expression of the women, their mamans, and their maman's mamans."[110] The net is certainly biblical in its efforts to provide nourishment and salvation, and it is still pertinent for women today. The private sphere of Franco women rendered their expression largely invisible.[111] The Women's Collection Process featured on the organization's site boldly advertises Community Women, Academic Women, Women of the Seam, Women of the Pots and Pans, Women of the Hammer, Women Who Farm, and many others. "The reason the net is wide is to make us fishers of women who are all different."[112]

CHAPTER 3

Women's Social Clubs and the Transmission of Culture

Traces of French presence in North America can be observed from particular vantage points, yet they remain hidden to the general population. Pedestrians can unintentionally and quite literally stumble upon French sites of memory established in the centers of American postindustrial cities where small but sometimes formidable monuments constructed in stone speak to a more luminous French past.[1] These objects of yesterday voice articulations of a future Franco life as well. Since its dedication in 2001, *La dame de la renaissance française* oversees the continuity of the French tradition through family and learning, in a small park overlooking the Nashua River in southern New Hampshire. The monument is accented with several *fleur-de-lys* and set against the backdrop of one of the local mills where Franco-Americans worked (fig. 5). A sign at the entrance of the park indicates the French community's rebirth. It is fitting that this testament to French preservation is reconstructed as a woman, like Marianne, a female symbol of the French Republic, and that she is located on Water Street, near the life and industry-producing waters.

5. *La dame de la renaissance française*, Nashua, New Hampshire. Courtesy of author.

Not many women were among the first explorers, fur traders, or soldiers to emigrate and colonize the French New World four hundred years ago, but once the colony had been established, they came in small numbers to help galvanize it. And sustain it they did. Due to the dearth of French women during the early colonial period, Louis XIV sent orphaned and destitute young demoiselles, the fabled *filles du roi*, to wed the early inhabitants in order to create a sustainable French colonial population. Louis Hebert, his wife, and children were among first courageous French colonists in the early seventeenth century, and they have been duly immortalized in Quebec City. The Quebec government recognized the role that women have played in several celebratory constructions. The pioneering French women acknowledged run the gamut from the influential women of religious orders to the more commonplace *filles du roi*.

Women of power and influence certainly did play a crucial if sometimes neglected role in the efforts of the colony alongside Cartier, Champlain, Iberville, and company, the heavyweights of the French New World. Many of these early female advocates for French lives were Church affiliated. The Augustinian and Ursuline orders of high-minded religious Sisters in particular established institutions for the perpetuation of the early French colony, namely, through education and medical care (the Ursuline religious order was established in Italy in 1535). Marie de l'Incarnation, founder of the Quebec Ursulines, represents one of the exemplars of French initiatives in the New World. She set sail like the other New World explorers, abandoning all that she had possessed in the Old World, including a son, in order to offer an education to French and Native American girls in North America.

Another enterprising woman, Jeanne Mance, helped to establish the first hospital in Montreal in 1642. Her example inspired many to serve, not the least of which an early twentieth-century association of Franco-American women taking its name and mission from Mance's example (the Cercle Jeanne Mance). These are just a few of the best-known women to support French life in North America. Others who have contributed demographically, socially, and culturally to French America will never be known individually, despite recent commemoration, yet they have helped to sustain the French flame in the United States.

The immortalization of female figures such as Jeanne Mance and Marie de l'Incarnation represent French generosity globally in the tradition of the French Republican "civilizing mission." Through religious conversion and education, these women sought to realize the colonial objectives of church and crown. Living women today continue to actively promote French culture and life in contemporary America, quietly, behind the scenes. They organize collectively, for personal enjoyment and the better good of their descendants, as they have for more than a century. Franco-American women have organized at least partially due to being barred entry, until very recently, into male social groups such as the Richelieu or Beaver Club. They were particularly active in Massachusetts, founding their own institutions and promoting their own agendas. Franco-American daughters followed their mothers into associations such as the Cercle Jeanne-Mance or the Cercle des Dames Françaises, in Lowell and Springfield, Massachusetts, respectively. Some traditional Franco-American organizations in New England have in recent years opened their doors to women, and this occurrence may very well describe gender sensitivity as well as the tenacious desire for organizational survival. So while women have often been relegated to the sidelines of power, Franco and otherwise, I will attempt to elucidate the significant role that they have played in the preservation and dissemination of New World French cultures.

These cultures are predominantly popular in nature, modest and traditional manifestations of Franco-American life. They represent the joyful articulations of fellowship that derive from communal life, manifestations that alleviate fears or isolation experienced by some in Anglo America. *La vie associative*, the sometimes formalized gathering of individuals in order to share common concerns, is a frequent response to life's recurrent challenges. The minimal fees required for membership are indeed quite small when compared with the benefits bestowed upon subscribers. Association life has been studied from many perspectives and in a variety of places in the French-speaking world. "Voluntary associations, then, constitute an organized and institutionalized form of sociability," writes Alan R. H. Baker about patterns found within the French peasantry.[2] When looking at the French postcolonial world, immigrant workers in industrial cities managed to maintain rural traditions in this way, even when exile removed farmers from their lands. Some of these voluntary assemblies took the shape of *veillées* in which individuals congregated to sing, dance, eat, and commiserate. A modern expression of the traditional veillée, social gatherings provided another way of conceptualizing the collectivities that French ethnic communities create to this day. Lawrence Wylie's classic study of a village in the Vaucluse describes the custom of meeting, particularly in winter, for warmth, amusement (including the French and francophone tradition of card games) and community in Provence.[3] Distinct spaces of women's sociability have existed as well, and we see a manifestation of this in the female Mardi Gras riders of south Louisiana.

Almost every Franco-American parish in New England had an organization for women (Les Dames de Sainte Anne, for instance) including one specifically for young, unmarried women (frequently Les Enfants de Marie). Other clubs that formed under parish leadership promoted sports, musicals, and drill teams. Le Cercle des Dames Françaises, founded in 1930, held its last meeting in 2007, although some of its objectives and activities are still carried on by former members. Several years earlier, the leadership of the New England Fédération Féminine Franco-Américaine brought its association to a close in 2001 after a half-century of coordinating and promoting more than one hundred organizations. A chapter of Le Cercle Jeanne Mance, founded in Worcester, Massachusetts, in 1913, has continued to assemble several dozen Franco women every month. The Cercle Jeanne Mance de Lowell celebrated its eightieth anniversary in 2011 and is the oldest of the Franco social institutions for women. It persists in its efforts to conduct association business exclusively in French. The group maintained three independent branches, in Worcester and Lowell and in Woonsocket, Rhode Island, at one time. It is the only Franco-American women's organization in New England able to replicate itself, and it subsequently became a model for later groups. L'Association des Dames Franco-Américaines (1953) of Chicopee, Massachusetts, the most recent of Franco women's groups, has endeavored to meet monthly in a local church to the present day. Through their efforts, the women who organize French meetings and who promote Franco-American cultural life have not yet been completely relegated to the annals of history.

LES DAMES FRANCO-AMÉRICAINES

As its association banner illustrates, the Franco-American Women's Association's binational loyalties to the United States and Canada (not the more modern and radical Quebec) are prominently displayed. These "French" women of America express their dual sensibilities each month in the repeated rituals of their collective processions, while usually leaving their formal symbols closeted for special occasions. For more than sixty years, women of French-Canadian descent have gathered in Chicopee, Massachusetts, one evening per month for the nourishment of their ethnic identities. Members of the association have had many other occasions to meet over the years, being in an area with a relatively large Franco population, but it is these regular Thursday meetings that help to ensure the transmission of Franco-American traditions and the remembrance of an earlier and much more pervasive French experience in industrial America. In some ways, the ethnic social group is all that is left of the extensive organizational structure within Franco-American communities. The French parish, press, and school have all disappeared, and even larger societies such as the Association Canado-Américaine and the Union Saint-Jean Baptiste are no longer fixtures in Franco-American life.

The Franco-American Women's Association began by meeting in members' homes. For many years, the group met in the parish hall of the Church of the Nativity of the Blessed Virgin Mary in the Willimansett neighborhood of Chicopee, a historic Franco enclave. It was a modern sanctuary constructed with the monies and blessings of the local parish and parishioners. Following the consolidation of ethnic Catholic churches that took place in Massachusetts in 2009, Nativity Church closed, and since 2010 the group has assembled in the Saint Rose de Lima Church in the Aldenville section of Chicopee, another historic Franco area.

This has not been an altogether easy transition, particularly for older members, but they continue to meet on Thursday evenings except during the summer. The group exhibits a remarkably steadfast desire to continue carrying on the French or Franco-American tradition, a resilience that defies the vulnerability of age, sex, and socioeconomic status. The name of the group has been changed for insurance purposes, and they are now officially called the Franco-American Women's Association of St. Rose de Lima Church.[4] Early in its history, they referred to themselves as the "Franco-American ladies," and to most, they are still simply known as *les dames franco-américaines*. Group officials hoped that affiliation with the new church in 2010 might inspire new membership. Club officers issued written invitations to St. Rose de Lima parishioners, but those efforts have not produced many new members. Between 2008 and 2012, membership dropped from forty to thirty active participants.

Participants are almost all residents of the Chicopee-Holyoke-Springfield area with a few members from outlying districts.[5] Many of them remember when intact French ethnic neighborhoods, *les Petits Canadas*, still thrived. These women range in age from forty-five to more than eighty, with the median being over sixty. A few honorary members are no longer able to attend meetings regularly but appear at seasonal events and gather group news as they can. The Association maintained no formal written leaflet, other than their annual member program, and so word of mouth helped to spread information.

All members are "French," whether they continue to speak the language or not. Culturally and linguistically, Francos express their Frenchness in ways that are sometimes more visibly perceptible in social settings. While some still speak French fluently every day, others maintain their French identity through cultural traditions such as preparing ethnic dishes, playing cards, singing French songs during the holidays, practicing their faith in French, or perhaps making a family pilgrimage to Quebec. Some insist that they no longer speak French, but it can resurface spontaneously and rather fluently during festive gatherings. Social theorist Herbert Gans contended that such acts of "symbolic ethnicity" can be performed at will, at little figurative or literal cost to the individual.[6] For older women such as *les dames francos*, not all of whom are in the best of health, simply getting together on a cold evening requires more effort than Gans may have had in mind.

Franco-American Women's Association meetings begin promptly at 7 p.m., late perhaps for elderly members, particularly in winter. Yet some have living spouses for whom they prepare meals before meetings, and so the start time accommodates them. The spiritual director of the organization asks that they rise from their seats to recite a prayer for the group, "une prière pour l'association" to bring reunions formally to order.[7] In taking the lead with the French preliminaries, the spiritual director possesses acquired respect among her peers and also confidence in her speaking abilities. Carefully preserved cue cards help professed non-French speakers among the members to ask God to bless their organization and to help bring peace to the world. For listeners, this is a somewhat rehearsed exercise, but it is clearly repeated in heartfelt fashion. *Le Serment d'allégéance* or Pledge of Allegiance that follows is recited in French like the prayer. This is the American Pledge of Allegiance translated and read in French. All formal parts of the Association protocol are in French. In closing the ceremonial opening, members fervently sing the Canadian national anthem, "O Canada," composed by French-Canadian Calixa Lavallée, in French as well. Sung aloud collectively and in unison, the hymn exemplifies both the ancestral country and language of group members.

No small amount of meaning can be interpreted from these ancient and repeated rituals. The cultural historian must attempt to "see things from the native's point of view, to understand what he [or she] means and to seek out the social dimensions of meaning," Robert Darnton contends, and this is certainly true for an active group such as the Franco-American Women's Association.[8] The French past is honored while the present is performed solemnly for maximum effect. This performance is all the more significant because Franco-Americans, as practitioners or nonpractitioners of the faith, have had to contend with religious rites exercised increasingly outside of French. Members affirm their allegiance to God first and foremost in French prayer, a telling act for a group that is expressly Catholic and that meets in a Catholic place of worship. It is afterward that their American identity is articulated *in French*, followed by an ode to their

French-Canadian roots, the singing of "O Canada." This expresses the hierarchies and dualities that have long governed Franco-American identity. The relationship today between French and American sensibilities among Francos is not fixed but rather fluid.

During one Thursday gathering, Franco-American Women's Association members expressed a yearning for hearing the Canadian national anthem *en français* during the 2010 Vancouver Olympics. For these women, Canadian or Québécois French is both admired for its ties to a cherished past but also disparaged for its earthiness. Members systematically give short shrift to their local variant of French and praise the standard and seemingly superior language spoken in Paris. These public and regularly performed rituals, partially expressed in French, all point to the emergence of a very specific cultural group, one that saw birth in the late nineteenth century. Franco-American women persevere in their willingness to express a part of their cultural identity through coded language, religious faith, and cultural practices. The traditions represent an affirmation of who these women are and want to continue to be today.

Forty years ago, Franco-American Women's Association meetings were conducted entirely in French, but English became the language of discussions and reports as younger less-francophone members took on leadership roles. The second generation gradually lost touch with the heritage language before the third attempted to bring it back. Nonetheless, today many discussions and reports are interspersed with French words that convey perhaps more cultural meaning than clear instruction. Some of the official ceremonies are still conducted in French, such as the induction of new members at May meetings. In the *Programme de l'année*, which is distributed every fall to dues-paying members and that highlight the group's upcoming activities, bilingual French and English descriptions such as "Duties-Privileges-Good Deeds" or "Devoirs-Privileges-Bonnes Oeuvres" announce club activities in unaccented French.[9] The written accents typically begin to fade as foreign language usage diminishes over time, although spoken accents remain more permanently imprinted. The French in the annual members' brochure contains some grammatical errors, but it is an important reference source to members of their ethnic heritage, as are the cue cards. The Association literature, like the culture, is very much bilingual.

A switch is made to the English language and American side of Franco-American life during the discussion and subsequent close of official association business. After the French traditions to begin meetings, almost all group communication is conducted in English. This shift is noticeable to an outside observer, but is perhaps felt less so to members; recitation in French and English is simply part of the regular routine that is both bilingual and intercultural. The beginnings to association meetings convey the *mélange* of language, faith, and transnational traditions that are so expressive of the Franco-American experience. To do this once a month is significant for persons for whom this is one of the few ways of expressing Frenchness, in French sometimes, publicly today. There are fewer opportunities to hear and speak French today in community parishes and elsewhere.

Every other Wednesday, Chicopee area parishioners were able attend a French-language mass at St. Rose de Lima Church, although religious leaders added that it took place in *Franglais* more than French. This nonetheless provided some satisfaction to congregation members for whom connection to God is facilitated by the French language. Periodically in the state of Massachusetts, parishioners have organized special French-language masses, during Franco-American festival activities in Lowell, for instance, but they are now the exception. The cue cards used by the Franco-American Women's Association remind one of the fleetingness of such cultural connections. They are very important for members who have grown distant from French language practices, serving as a comforting mechanism in some regards for women who have been uttering phrases in French for years and certainly know the lines by heart, even if they think that they do not. As French is increasingly a foreign language, the cue cards represent a desire for cultural longevity. They are now well worn around the edges, and members carefully distribute and then collect them after each recitation. They are a collective ethnic treasure and respectfully preserved.

At one of the regular meetings when the cue cards had mistakenly been left at home, everyone in attendance recited the Lord's Prayer in French, fluent French and English speakers alike, at the beginning of the meeting instead of the usual prayer. They also sang "O Canada" in French without difficulty. Members recited a French Hail Mary at the end of official business to bring the meeting to a symbolic conclusion, instead of the common prayer, along with "God Bless America" in English. These cherished words from people's pasts had been etched more or less permanently in many Franco-American minds and could be recited easily by all. Despite the loss of French fluency, French words, prayers, rites, and traditions continue to be perpetuated. Members may find solace in the relative permanence of this cultural transmission.

After the symbolic prayers and song in French, meetings continue with a roll call of officers. The administrative hierarchy includes a president, vice president, treasurer, and secretary. The president gives her report followed by updates from other leaders. Minutes from the previous meeting are read (in English). Both old and new business is discussed. At some meetings, the secretary reads thank-you notes from the recipients of Association scholarships. It serves as a reminder to members of their good deeds. The treasurer's report is often a central component of the meetings. Members discuss the funds that they have collected and the activities that will bring in money for their assorted initiatives, such as the annual card party and Christmas party. Fund-raisers primarily generate income for the annual merit awards that the organization gives out to the children and grandchildren of members attending college. Each year the Association clears enough money, raised by earned interest in a certificate deposit, to award several scholarships. Since formal record keeping began in 2001, they have distributed fifty thousand dollars in aid to seventy students. There are fewer committees than before, according to some, but members assemble to organize their special events and to prepare the sandwiches that accompany each of the monthly meetings.

During the business part of meetings, the president asks if anyone knows of sick members or of those who have passed away. The group thus keeps in touch with ailing participants, visiting them in the hospital and sending cards. Every November it honors Franco-American women who have died. As women who lived in French, they similarly want to pass in French as well, and it is indeed important that the funeral celebration be performed at least partially in French. There are fewer moments as ritualized as death, and Franco women have made sure their own ceremonies are culturally relevant. Because there are fewer and fewer French-speaking priests, the women of French organizations have also had to be flexible in the organization of their funerals.[10] While an English-speaking priest presided at one memorial service, Franco-American club members surrounded the deceased member and sang in French. Living participants know that a French or hybrid French ceremony will be part of their own last rites. This is both culturally and linguistically important as family members sometimes travel from Quebec to attend funeral services. For these reasons alone, it is perhaps comforting and a compelling reason to enter into a relationship with les dames franco-américaines.

While English conversation tends to predominate during Association meetings, there is a free-flowing bilingualism that lives during the smaller group discussions. Conversation at individual tables often takes place in French as well as in English, as members eat sandwiches and play cards. While some tables are monolingual, others switch from English to French and back again continuously depending on the conversation topic. As members code switch, they repeat informally at meetings that the French that they grew up hearing and still partially speak in their French-Canadian families, "Canuck French," is different from Parisian French. French from France is usually taught in schools and validated, and so people often defer to the Parisian "norm," although the Alliance Française has become more cognizant of the imperative to recognize a diversity of French forms of expression. Many Chicopee children have heard at least a few French words uttered by older relatives. At the group meetings, ethnic or regional spoken French reappears in starts and stops, when intimate, family, or community issues come up. Some people listen intently to the French being spoken, clearly understanding everything, but contribute to the discussion in English only. This back and forth poses little problem for Franco-Americans, who again are located between the two cultures in many respects. While some members may be uncomfortable speaking French around strangers, they have heard it all their lives and can easily participate in English or in French conversations.

Some members are Canadian citizens for whom French expression is still a part of everyday existence; they travel regularly to Quebec to see family and continue to speak in French after decades of life in western Massachusetts. They are more fluently francophone in some respects than other Franco-Americans. Some of these women followed husbands to Massachusetts who had come in search of work, well after the larger southward migration of French Canadians ended in 1930. These more recent emigrants came in the 1960s and 1970s. Some adherents are thus still traditional *Canadiens français* in many regards, not Franco-Americans, nor a part of the more modern Québécois movement that developed at about the time that people came to the United States. As Mark Paul Richard underlines in his case study, some emigrants to New England mill towns maintained their Canadian nationality while others adopted American citizenship.[11] Lewiston's French-language newspaper, *Le Messager*, advocated for naturalization a century ago as French Canadians became settled in Maine's Spindle City.

The accents that many such people have maintained when they speak in English are audible markers of a North American French ethnic identity. Despite their assimilation, some have maintained a French-Canadian voice that is clearly heard in the articulation of certain words. *T*'s are pronounced like *D*'s for holders of Canadian and American passports. Accents are indeed prevalent among the Canadian citizens in the group, but also among older Franco-Americans born in the United States who were brought up culturally and linguistically French in *les petits Canadas*. Cultural and literary studies suggest that accents can raise questions about foreignness or difference; unlike the *Garcia Girls*, some Franco-Americans never lose them.[12] The value placed on certain accents is certainly connected to willingness to dispose or preserve them. Individuals might prefer to speak in accented English rather than speak in French with people deemed to speak a "superior" variant of the language.[13] Association women periodically express concern about preserved ethnic colloquialisms.

Being Québécois is part of a sometimes politicized and polarizing French identity of America with which not all persons of French-Canadian descent have been comfortable. As modern Quebeckers distanced themselves from the Catholic Church during the Quiet Revolution of the 1960s, Franco-Americans maintained religious as well as cultural traditions. Many Franco-American Women's Association members are Franco-Americans of the second and third generation, still closely tied to Catholicism, culturally French in some ways but thoroughly U.S. citizens. More are Americanized English speakers, although they still know a good bit of French, much more than their children. French prayers and swear words (all religious in nature) continue to be a part of an individual and family vocabulary, which illustrates playful coexistence between the religious and the secular.

The Franco ladies' association program remains the same from year to year, with meetings running from September to May. In summer, members take time away from work and away from Chicopee for vacation. In September and October, the group begins preparing for the Christmas party in December. The November meeting includes the formal worship service for the departed in the attached sanctuary of the church. Following the closing of Nativity Church in 2009, members selected the St. Rose de Lima sanctuary for the memorial service. From January through March, members begin the organizational work for the card party in April, which is the biggest fund-raiser of the year. In 2010, members raised two thousand dollars to support the scholarships that the organization grants to college students.[14] The year ends with the May meeting that signals the group's continuation with the induction of new members. Members meet as a group nine times overall during the year, although the December meeting is more festive than formal. Some mobile women meet more regularly and converse in French in other settings, for instance, at the card-playing events held at area churches. There are a few younger members who represent a possibility for leadership within the organization. Children rarely attend meetings except for the final May gathering, when the children and grandchildren of members awarded scholarships attend.

In May 2008, thirteen $250 scholarships were awarded to family members. The association distributed nine scholarships in 2007, five in 2009, and six in 2010. This signals some variability, but in 2011 and 2012 the total number of prizes awarded increased again. These scholarships are intended to help pay for books on college campuses, and due to the rising costs of education, members raised the amount of the scholarships to $300 in May 2010. In 2015, the award amount increased again to $350. The group requires official notice of school enrollment for the funds to be issued. At one time, these scholarships were designated for students who were studying French at the college level, but this tradition has faded. The group still does contribute to the education of Franco-American youth, however; young winners glean some connection to a Franco-American organization and identity through their scholarship. Fund recipients are invited to the last meeting to accept their awards and thank the association. Their pictures are proudly displayed on the buffet table by grandmothers and great-aunts. Some of the recipients appear in person to accept the award and tell the association what it means to them personally. For an evening, these young people witness a continued French cultural heritage, a more public expression of the old ways of family members and the extended community. The May meeting brings together old and new Franco-American traditions more than other meetings.

At this final spring meeting, new members are inducted in a bilingual and evocative celebration echoing the group's French heritage. After a full year of attending meetings, at least four, and taking part in activities, new members are formally eligible for induction. The ceremony is conducted in French and English, the French statements serving as a symbolic testament to the period when all association business was conducted in French. New members solemnly declare their loyalty to the association in French and English, pledging to be faithful, dues-paying members. It is significant that French again plays a prominent role in the formalized rituals of new life and continuity. As cultural traditions recede, French practices may very well gain in appreciation. New members receive flowers, applause, and welcome from the assembled group and an official group badge, which is worn during more formal gatherings. In 2008 and 2009, one to three new members were received into the organization.

L'Association des Dames Franco-Américaines gives a small prize to an eighth-grade student from the St. Georges School, the only local school

6. École Sainte Jeanne d'Arc/St. Georges School, Aldenville, Chicopee, Massachusetts. Courtesy of author.

that continues to teach French as a heritage language to children of Franco descent. Once there were many French parish schools across Massachusetts and throughout New England, but virtually all have closed their doors and in some cases have been physically removed.[15] The St. Georges School is housed in an impressive site of French memory in the Aldenville section of Chicopee (fig. 6), the former École Sainte Jeanne d'Arc. Its façade celebrates the seemingly disparate Franco-American ideals of truth, science, and virtue; the association represents a Christian quest for knowledge. Just above the school name is a symbolic trinity of sword, crown, and two *fleur-de-lys*. The richness of the façade and building suggest the past status and importance of the French element in this working-class community.

The St. Georges School recognizes and promotes the study of French even as it has become less used by Franco-Americans collectively. Since 2003, young people at St. Georges have been able to study with a native speaker of French for an hour a day, a far cry from the half-day once devoted to instruction in French.[16] Association members invited the St. Georges French teacher to regular meetings to report on teaching strategies. The impetus for this initiative came from the lack of language classes in the parochial school system. The Franco-American Women's Association pledged its financial support to the French program at the St. Georges School in 2009 and 2010. In January 2009, Franco folksinger Josée Vachon performed in Chicopee at a benefit concert for the St. Georges School, and 10 percent of the proceeds went to the institution. By performing regularly in area parishes and senior centers, Vachon continues to provide Franco-Americans access to their culture. Her itinerary throughout New England and New York provides cultural nourishment to the remaining French ethnic islands. In November 2014, Vachon headlined the one hundredth anniversary of the St. Georges School, an event that combined music, prayer, and traditional foods.

In the past, les Dames franco-américaines organized activities that were meant to celebrate and preserve French linguistic, cultural, and ethnic identity. Association organizers also intended to encourage French participation in local politics, so as not to relinquish power to other ethnic groups such as the Irish and the Polish. More recently, the politics of the group are revealed in activities such as the invitation of a pro-life supporter to a meeting in January 2009. The Association agreed to make a financial contribution of fifty dollars. The Franco-American Women's Association serves, on the whole, to maintain the informal ethnic ties of a more dispersed community. In gathering, people of French heritage can continue to feel part of a culture that has lost some of its meaning in the twenty-first century.

FRENCH NITE

Since the 1970s, and increasingly in the past two decades, Franco-Americans have been inspired to search out their roots, like Alex Haley and African Americans, and to reclaim a culture that has long been stigmatized.[17] Unlike Cajuns, Franco-Americans of New England do not have a spicy, exotic cuisine or music that draws national attention and popularizes cultural traditions. They do have hearty and satisfying regional fare that they value. Francos also have folklorists such as Josée Vachon who have maintained cultural traditions and continue to transmit them throughout Franco-America. In songs, skits, and one-man/woman shows, performers bring Franco culture directly to audiences in schools, festivals, associations, and community centers throughout New England. They talk about well-known Franco subjects of interest: work at the mill, unemployment, food, sport, and family life, and the populations of New England states offer a ready-made public.[18] Television producers unveiled Franco-American ethnic identity to a wider audience in the popular series *West Wing*. In a January 2005 episode, the presidential candidate Matt Santos, played by Hispanic actor Jimmy Smits, commented that New Hampshire is not significantly representative (i.e., ethnic or not white) of the country generally. This offends a potential financial supporter who demands a public apology. He claims that New Hampshire was 30 percent Franco-American and thus as ethnically legitimate as any other immigrant American community.[19]

Several Franco-American Women's Association members regularly attended and helped to organize a large regional gathering of Franco-Americans, where an ethnic identity could be expressed publicly by many. For almost a decade, from 2001 until 2009, French Nite was held every winter in the large parish hall of the Church of the Nativity in Chicopee, Massachusetts. The event drew hundreds of people from Massachusetts and neighboring states who made time for an evening of French-Canadian music, food, and fellowship. It offered an opportunity for the community to be together, to hear and speak French, and to surround themselves in Franco culture. The crowd sang French songs and enjoyed the *soupe aux pois* (habitant pea soup, available in cans at New England and Canadian markets) and *tourtière* (French-Canadian meat pie). A band played traditional French and French-Canadian music (cue cards provided for singing), and dancing could be spontaneous. Afterward, people divided into groups for the intense and familiar Franco card games. French Nite was a clear success if the longevity and popularity of the event are taken into consideration; it provides a telling example of *la vie associative*.

Franco-Americans sometimes traveled a considerable distance annually to enjoy the food, music, and comradery of French Nite. The food itself had pertinent cultural meaning, as its preparation constituted a significant act of being Franco-American. In sharing the Franco dishes, participants continued to eat as family members had once done regularly in Quebec. People thus not only consumed food but participated in a common, collective practice of "culinary citizenship."[20] The particular meat pie recipe used in a given year at French Nite was a subject of animated conversation. Participants energetically compared it with past recipes, both positively and negatively. The subject of whether or not it was served with traditional Anglo gravy could elicit ardent responses. In 2009, a member of the preparation crew mentioned that the peas used for the pea soup had been purchased in Canada, clearly a culturally significant transaction. This acknowledged the importance of substance and sustenance from the mother source, like Franco families sparing no expense by ordering marble from Italy for the building of local churches.

One can assume that there must have been no small matter of pride associated with the oversight of such a large community event for Association and community members.[21] The demise of French Nite must also have been a source of some distress. The last area French Nite was held in 2009, as a result of the restructuration of the local Catholic parishes by the bishop of Springfield. While Nativity Church could accommodate several hundred people, other area churches could not. Now people organize smaller *soupers canadiens* or *soirées canadiennes* instead, with food and music still central components of the festivities.

In November 2008, Franco-American members discussed putting together a book of Franco-American recipes to sell as a fund-raising event, and the vice president asked people to dust off their mother's and *mémère's* cookbooks. Members attending that night discussed with some interest the languages of the proposed cookbook and thought that optimally recipes should be written in French on one side of the page and English on the other. This would be culturally appropriate reflecting the bicultural and binational affinities of the group. The interest underscores that family recipes are cherished, and food is also clearly a part of maintained French cultural identity.[22] Food is certainly at the heart of what it has meant to be French in America since Samuel de Champlain's famous banquets and festivities in the early seventeenth century. The celebration of nature's bounty and of the annual harvest is another example of borrowing from old French tradition. Although passionately discussed, the Franco-American Women's collection of recipes has yet to be assembled.[23] Other books of traditional grandmère cooking do exist. Traditional music and food both clearly keep Francos who are less fluent linguistically in touch with their culture. The revelers at French Nite might have had a hard time deciding which was more important to them, the pea soup, the meat pie, or the music.

GOOD NIGHT, MY FRIENDS

Meetings of the Franco-American Women's Association end rather symbolically with the change to English language for a prayer and the singing of "God Bless America." This shift in communication refers back to the influential American side in Franco dual sensibilities, an assumed and underexplored part of their identity. While some may very well feel attached to their adoptive or birth home, some still struggle to converse and pray in English. Mass in English has become the weekly standard. Priests now deliver the ceremonial November homily for the deceased in English.

Among the English-speaking members who play cards and eat sandwiches after meetings, French memories flow back. Words in the language believed lost return. One evening, a group broke spontaneously into French song while playing the card game "31," which they had played since youth. They began to sing "Bonsoir, mes amis, bonsoir" from memory, mentioning that they had no idea what the lyrics meant (this is questionable).[24] But they did remember instinctively singing this song in French, probably at the end of social gatherings.

The objective of "31" is to get your hand of cards as close to thirty-one in value as possible, in rounds, picking up and discarding cards as the game progresses. Card playing is clearly a cherished part of Franco-American cultural life, through which certain aspects can be expressed. Not all Francos like playing cards, however, and are certainly no less Franco as a result. Whether singing songs or playing games, these activities help to tell the story of Franco-America, past and present. Sociologist Kristen Langellier's work discusses personal narratives and performative identities of such Franco-American women.[25]

"Screw your neighbor" is another popular game, in which players gain advantage by besting others. The symbolic nature of the game is not missed on anyone. Playing brings people closer together, relieves stress, and renders cultural identification possible. At every meeting, members pass around a small wicker basket or *petit panier* to which they can add dollars in exchange for lottery tickets. Several members go home as "winners" after playing, although others love to gripe that the game is rigged. The Franco sense of joyfulness, joie de vivre, over hardship is cultivated. One of the card players mentioned to me that this is why they leave their homes every Thursday night, even in the dead of winter, to experience the Franco culture to which they are still connected on a personal and emotional level, with the people who share the same French family heritage.

Some people may not have known precisely what all of the words to the "Bonsoir" song meant, or how to pronounce them, but it was evidently a part of contemporary Franco-American expression. Michael Parent sings the traditional Franco-American song that came back instinctively to members on his bilingual CD "Chantons—Let's Sing." The refrain goes "Bonsoir, mes amis, bonsoir, bonsoir, mes amis, bonsoir, bonsoir, mes amis, bonsoir, mes amis, bonsoir, mes amis, bonsoir. Au revoir." "Good night, my dear friends, good night. And good-bye."[26] "Until we meet again" would be a more literal translation of the end. Clearly something of Franco-American culture is being preserved outside of fluent expression in French during these meetings.

Some women still think it is important to come together, to express their common French-Canadian or Franco-American identity. They pay the yearly ten dollar dues every September and come to monthly meetings. This is a small amount indeed in exchange for the cultural rewards provided. Within the group, nationality as well as language divides members into distinct groups: *Canadiennes françaises*, French Canadians by nationality, and Franco-Americans who are primarily American but of French-Canadian descent. While these two identities can be quite different, the group has found ways to bring members together. French speakers turn to English when addressing the group and English-speakers add a French word or two to demonstrate affinities and enliven conversations. The active French listeners can move between groups. Some English speakers are quite capable of conversing in French when inspired to do so. French language skills are maintained among friends and family, some of whom reside in Canada.

Individuals express some bitterness about not having taught their children to speak French, or in some cases, their efforts at transferring French culture proving to be unsuccessful. A few members married outside the French ethnic enclave, making more difficult the continuation of French language practices. Franco-American communities generally remained more closed than other immigrant groups, resulting in preserved ethnic identity, but individual experiences certainly varied.[27] Some former members of Le Cercle des Dames françaises, an older and more socially prestigious French organization, joined the Franco-American Women after the Cercle disbanded in 2007, providing important cultural and group leadership. They have not found the same linguistic fluency that their group maintained, but as one woman said, they appreciate the more informal atmosphere of les Dames francos.

One member stated succinctly that the group's raison d'être comes from the scholarships that they distribute to family members. While this may partially be the case, the demand for Franco identity exceeds these material concerns. The scholarship program forms a bond between old and young and at its origin identified the importance of maintaining language to one's ethnic or cultural identity. The group's meaning and relevance to the wider Franco-American community is still signaled at the annual card party, which generates a portion of the income for scholarships. Les dames franco-américaines express a variety of shared experiences in informal conversation: the memories of a youth spent singing and praying in French, the echo of disappointment in the loss of language and culture from one generation to the next, the isolation that can result from marriage outside the ethnic group. These subjects all emerged during exchanges while eating or playing cards. They are all expressions of being Franco-American today.

Le Cercle des Dames françaises, until the early twenty-first century, was an active organization with a busy social calendar promoting French language and culture among women of francophone heritage. By designation, it was a selective organization requiring that its two hundred registered members be nominated by their peers from the same professional classes. In other words, membership recognized social and cultural status already attained. Locally women of Franco-American descent regarded the Cercle as reserved for a social elite in comparison with the members of the Franco-American Women's Association. It is a subtle, symbolic distinction that the Cercle was *French* and culturally dominant while the Association was *Franco* and less cultured. Linguistically, as we have seen, Francos attributed superior value to what they considered authentic Frenchness. The Cercle did have some members from France before its demise.

The Cercle des Dames françaises was originally created as an offshoot of the Club Passe-Temps, a book club for unmarried women of French-Canadian descent.[28] These women regarded themselves as guardians of the language and supporters of French traditions by their very actions. The Cercle took inspiration from an earlier association of Franco women, the Cercle Jeanne Mance. Many early members wanted to continue meeting after they had married, and so they formed the Cercle, assembling for the first time at the Kimball Hotel in Springfield.

A dynamic woman by the name of Clémentine Poirier is credited with the group's formal founding in 1930.[29] An educator by profession and philosophy, she participated actively for a half-century in the group's many activities, until her passing in 1984. Poirier was especially interested in encouraging area children of Franco-American descent to take an interest in their heritage language and culture by offering scholarships. That all Franco social groups in the area emphasized this is a tribute to Poirier's foresight.

The Cercle's mission did not waver from the early focus defined by Poirier. Article II of its constitution stated: "The objective of the Circle is to encourage French cultural life and correct spoken language, to promote the interests of its members and the Franco-American community by way of gatherings and philanthropic work."[30] Throughout its more than seventy-five-year history, promoting not only French language but correct French ("le bon parler français") was primordial. This concern was at the forefront of the organization's official meetings and cultural activities. Officers were determined to set an example by modeling proper French language usage at all association functions. The undercurrent that propelled this concern forward was the inferior status of French identity and Franco-Americans in the United States, a social stain of which Cercle members were keenly aware. But as one recent member described it in a local newspaper article, participating in the Cercle allowed her to maintain her own French, which was perpetually threatened by the dominant Anglophone environment.[31]

By the early 1960s, the Cercle des Dames françaises had attracted two hundred members, primarily from the Springfield area, but also from other towns in western Massachusetts and Connecticut. Placing social exclusions aside for the moment, when putting this group in perspective, it is important to emphasize that far-thinking French ethnic women wanted to look outside of their homes in order to sensitize the youth of Franco-American families, instructing them on the importance of preserving the French language, faith, and culture that their ancestors had brought with them from Quebec. In essence they wanted to develop more than what the original book club had encompassed. A new generation of the more recent Cercle members followed their mothers into the organization and reinvented it. These homemakers, some of whom were employed in leadership positions, were curiously positioned between tradition and modernity. Association documents cite the Cercle prayer to the Holy Spirit, "Prière au St-Esprit," repeated in print and chorally at meetings:

> Holy Spirit, King of Light and Love, kindly grant us your support. Help us to fully understand our duties and give us the strength to act with wisdom in order that we may always strive to work in a Christian and patriotic spirit. Bless our sisters, bless our work so that we may be worthy to receive the reward of success. Amen.[32]

Faith is never far removed from Franco-American conceptions of ethnic identity, yet while awaiting God's blessing, these women were not opposed to working to attain their goals. A keen sense of mission is clear in this opening prayer. Christian charity was motivational for French women of America striving to better others in their ethnic community as well as themselves.

From its inception, the Cercle sought to maintain a certain decorum. Members systematically referred to themselves as "Madame" and addressed others by using the formal "you" (*vous*).[33] This is likely a cultural reiteration that crossed international borders, echoing acceptable forms of polite conversation that made their way from French Canada to *les petits Canadas*. The Cercle reproduced a certain formality often voiced in social settings. The association was similar to the social organizations in other ethnic communities, for instance, African-American social clubs such as Jack and Jill, which announced that an elevated social position had been attained.[34] They encouraged individuals and families from more privileged backgrounds in the community to intermingle. In order to become a member, one had to be Franco-American by at least one parent, be sponsored by two Association members, and be properly vetted by the board of directors. Applicants were required to fill out a membership survey in French in which they discussed their reasons for wanting to join the group. The form required the signatures of two members of the Cercle. By 1999, the strict membership rules had loosened considerably, and one could become an auxiliary member if one had studied French and had demonstrated an interest in the language and culture.[35] Members later abandoned the practice of vetting in hopes of facilitating new membership. The organization opened itself up to a wider francophile as well as francophone body, a strategy for survival as the group attempted to reconfigure itself. All Franco-American social groups were forced to rethink what it meant to be French, as they sought to reinvent at the end of the twentieth century. The new organizing measure does not seem to have had much effect as numbers continued to dwindle during the 1990s. At least one francophone African woman was recruited by a former member, but there is no record of francophone women of color having joined.[36] The formal and elitist nature of the Cercle des Dames françaises may ultimately have led to its demise. Advancing age was certainly a factor.

Like many cultural and intellectual elite social groups, putting the best collective foot forward and uplifting the ethnic group was essential. The Cercle served to promote the very best of Franco-American culture and to provide a space where it could fully develop and be appreciated. The modeling that the group orchestrated for others was primarily linguistic in nature, but also more broadly cultural. The Cercle endeavored to inspire others who had not yet reached the same socioeconomic heights to recognize and perhaps even emulate its distinction. Being a dame française meant that one partook of the finer elements of cultural life and spoke clearly and with elegance. Frenchness as interpreted by the group in industrial New England meant that proper etiquette should be demonstrated for ongoing participation in Franco-American society. Cultural theorist Homi Bhabha asserts that it is "the desire to emerge as 'authentic' through mimicry" that repeats more than re-presents.[37] Group members attempted to reproduce the esteemed French status that they identified with the natives of France. There had been Cercle members from France, as noted, during the group's distant as well as more recent past, along with French Canadians and Franco-Americans. Society groups welcomed some "war brides" who had wed American soldiers during the Second World War and who wanted to maintain contact with French culture. In the early twenty-first century, other French women joined the organization, and Franco members sometimes demurred to them.

Debutante balls were an important social event for the young women of the Cercle from the 1960s through the end of the 1980s. In 1984, nine young women were formally presented to the community in the Franco adaptation of Anglo-American tradition. The Franco-American media publicized the coming out of these young women, their families, and the institutions where they would be pursuing their education with scholarship assistance. This period constituted the Cercle's peak in many respects, when the group had attained its symbolic maximum of two hundred women, including many matrons representing the Franco elite. Members hoped that Franco-American young women had been sensitized to the extent that they would consider returning to the organization after they had completed their studies and married. Their children could thus carry on the tradition.

Some indeed did, but cultural transmission between generations, or lack thereof, has remained a sore spot for Francos.

Through the promotion of *le bon parler* and French cultural distinction, the group actively combatted the often disparaging connotations of Frenchness in America. That they perpetuated a certain French elitism was not necessarily an unattractive component. The group's emblem extolls the virtues of friendship and mutual aid (the shaking of hands), generosity as demonstrated through scholarships to encourage French study (the bourse), and the all-important origin of French influence, the royal flower (*fleur-de-lys*).

Four flags represent the four principal cultural and national influences for the Cercle: French, Québécois, Canadian, and American (Acadian connections are affirmed by other organizations). It is telling that both the original Québécois flag and national Canadian flag are shown. In later Cercle documents, only the Canadian maple leaf appears, likely an indication of a more politically neutral or conservative philosophy. These four competing influences were expressed at official functions of the Cercle when "La Marseillaise" (in French), "O Canada" (in French), "The Star-Spangled Banner" (in English), and sometimes "God Bless America" (in English) were all listed and sometimes sung. Performances of anthems typically followed this particular and symbolic order, from French to Canadian to American. Similar to the Franco-American Women's Association, the singing, language, and order of song echo the evolving, transnational nature of the Franco-American experience. In commonplace Franco-American fashion, Cercle members celebrated Bastille Day transnationally among themselves with a *pique-nique patriotique* in later years, with hot dogs and hamburgers.

The calendar year of Le Cercle des Dames françaises was typically made up of six monthly meetings or cultural events beginning with a fall gathering and concluding with the spring annual meeting. Members organized the monthly meetings of the Cercle in area restaurants, museums, and establishments during the year, with a several-course meal as a centerpiece, echoing the French tradition of gastronomy, which the Cercle went to considerable lengths to perpetuate. Gatherings were intended to be extravagant affairs with detailed menus written out in wavy French script for the pleasure of members. The monthly menu stood out prominently on the first page of the monthly French-language *Bulletin*. Following meals, the Cercle invited speakers from prestigious institutions to enlighten members on French cultural life. Singers performed, and area French-speaking clergy gave their perspective on the continued French presence in postcolonial New England. Cercle members also traveled to various sites of memory, and officers periodically organized lengthy trips to France. Members attended the yearly gatherings of the Fédération Féminine Franco-Américaine to which they were regularly invited and which they periodically hosted. They celebrated Christmas each year with a holiday extravaganza, *une soirée du Temps des fêtes*, as well as other annual religious and secular affairs. Members planned Mardi Gras celebrations in order to raise money for the scholarship fund. The association had hopes not of remaking *la Nouvelle-France* in New England but of fostering French cultural *rayonnement* that went beyond *survivance*.

The monthly *Bulletin* informed the group of French activities in the area and later commented on how members experienced them. All group activities were recorded in French and signed usually by the editor and the president of the organization. A secretary carefully recorded the minutes of previous meetings. The *Bulletin* was typically a one or two-page program summary of past, present, and future activities, as well as a descriptive commentary, which until the very end was written entirely in French. An exceptional summary was printed in English. For members no longer physically able to attend meetings, the *Bulletin* was their only connection to an organization they had attended for years. These newsletters became more quarterly than monthly toward the end of the group's existence. In the early 2000s, it was difficult for members to find a secretary fluent enough in French to convey Cercle activities in the *Bulletin* without publishing many mistakes. French members from France and French Canada provided assistance by assuming editorial responsibilities.

One of the major preoccupations of the group, according to Cercle participants, was the organization and annual distribution of scholarships to young people. The Clementine Poirier Scholarship Fund specified that applicants be enrolled in a college or university and actively speaking French. The funds for successful applicants would be distributed upon completion of the course and the submission of the grade to the organization. According to the application instructions, applicants had to be of Franco-American heritage, and students applied using either the French- or English-language forms. Members distributed the $300 scholarships to recipients in February of each year. Fund-raising events for the Clémentine Poirier Scholarships attempted to make use of popular North American French traditions. The Cercle remained true to *survivance* ideals through its educational enrichment activities. Philanthropic activities of the group aimed at uplifting by way of example, exhibiting models from the cultural elite to which others could aspire. Debutantes already had areas of study in sight and ultimately institutions where they would find employment. They would not necessarily become traditional homebound mothers like their own. It is again revealing to note how education remained at the forefront for matronly yet forward-thinking women. Following the ideal set by Poirier, they opened other potential paths for their daughters.

On October 2, 2005, the Cercle celebrated its seventy-fifth anniversary with a French mass, a meal, and a song in West Springfield, Massachusetts. Franco-American historian Claire Quintal addressed the Cercle members and their guests in a bilingual lecture. She stated that "the Cercle's cultural and charitable achievements demonstrate how women of earlier generations, most of them dedicated to their role as homemakers, recognized how they could overcome the limitations of such a function, glorious though it was and is on a certain level, by putting their organizational and creative skills to use for the betterment of the Franco-American community."[38] Quintal recognized the many achievements of the group and offered advice about continuing their good works by making the remaining group funds available to local students of French.

At this same time, members had begun discussing the possibility of closing the organization. Membership was down to several dozen devoted women, some of whom were tiring of organizing all of the activities for small numbers of attendees. The Cercle newsletters in the early 2000s periodically noted the presence of more guests than members at events.[39] After becoming a social organization primarily for young unmarried women after 1930, one that carried on a tradition of debutante balls for daughters into the 1980s, the members of the Cercle now constituted an aging group of established women, not all of whom could attend meetings independently due to infirmities. According to the 2004–2006 Association program, there were fifty-one active members, and presumably fewer by the end of this period. The association president sent out a survey in the fall of 2005 asking members whether they wanted to continue meeting and whether they were willing to take on a leadership role.[40] Members preferred to gracefully fold rather than attempt merely to survive and jeopardize the legacy of the institution.

On June 24, 2007, the national holiday of the Quebec province, the Cercle assembled for a ceremonial and culinary farewell, an *adieu* and *banquet de fermeture*. Two years after their seventy-fifth anniversary, leaders organized a final French mass and a meal to remember the good works of these women of the Franco-American elite. The celebration was purposely held on the day marking St. John the Baptist as the patron saint of French Canadians, as decreed by Pope Leo XIII in the late nineteenth century. The local press acknowledged the celebration and passing of Cercle.[41] The Springfield Valley Historical Museum obtained the Cercle archives, which were to be displayed every year in June.

After the dismantling of the Cercle, and following discussion of other alternatives, leaders directed Cercle monies to the maintaining of French instruction at the St. Georges School in Aldenville, Chicopee. The organization had distributed the last of its Poirier Scholarships in 2006. After the adieu, the Cercle president circulated one last edition of the *Bulletin*. She thanked the ladies for their devotion, informed them that all bills had been paid, and reminded members that remaining funds would be sent to the École Sainte Jeanne d'Arc/St. Georges School, to assist with the French language curriculum.

LES CERCLES JEANNE MANCE

One chapter of the Cercle Jeanne Mance, another historic and active Franco-American women's social organization of Massachusetts, continues to meet in Lowell on Wednesday evenings at a local church. The group celebrated its eightieth anniversary in a hotel in Chelmsford on October 23, 2011, with 140 people in attendance. The event included a French mass and entertainment by the omnipresent Franco folklorist Josée Vachon. The Cercle Jeanne Mance de Lowell maintains approximately seventy-five Franco "Lowelloises" as members, and forty-five to fifty gather regularly for the Wednesday meetings.[42] This is significant as potential group members today have many social and cultural organizations from which to choose, including the Rotary and Kiwanis. Members join the Cercle Jeanne Mance by choice, like any other social group, and inclusion comes with costs and benefits. Members must pay a fifteen dollar annual fee to join, more than the Franco-American Women's Association dues, but still a relatively small fee. Women can also join the Lowell branch of the formerly all-male Richelieu Club, although it consists of a smaller group of members and a more expensive sticker price (sixty-five dollar annual membership dues in 2010). According to a Cercle member, it is not truly welcoming to Franco-American women.[43]

Unlike the wives of lawyers, doctors, and other professionals who once ran the Lowell Cercle, many members now work. As in similar organizations, the same group officers have presided for years and wish others might assume organizational responsibility. Many members are elderly and cannot always attend meetings, and so they carefully follow the minutes of the monthly newsletter and perhaps join the final June meeting. The Lowell Cercle meets September through December and then March through June, a total of seven times during the year. A French mass inaugurates the association year in September and another typically concludes meetings in June. According to bylaws, meetings are run in French, but informal conversation often turns to English once the officer reports end. People meet regularly to speak in French, to organize various group activities, and to take part in humanitarian endeavors. They help maintain the cultural ideals sacred to their French-Canadian forefathers, but also express a distinct Franco-American experience. Members of the Lowell group have gone online with the promotion of Franco-American Day and Week Committee (Comité de la semaine franco-américaine) activities.

Word of the Cercle program and other group events circulate via blog. This is the only women's association that I examined making use of digital technology, perhaps boding well for the group's future. Area Francos can listen to traditional French-Canadian music on the radio, although such broadcasting no longer has the support of the monthly newspaper, the expired *Journal de Lowell*.

The Cercle takes inspiration from Jeanne Mance, who herself was moved by the idea of re-creating France in the New World. She was one of the daring women who set sail for uncharted territories and took part in the founding of Montreal in 1642. As organizational materials cite, Mance was instrumental in developing the first hospital in *la Nouvelle-France*, l'Hôtel-Dieu in French, a precocious and necessary institution. Mance is thus an important figure of material and spiritual service in the name of French colonial expansion. She cross-crossed the Atlantic Ocean three times in her lifetime, and far surpassing her own humble beginnings.

A group of ten women, *les dix fondatrices* (founders) representing the city's four French parishes, were present at the inauguration of the original Cercle Jeanne Mance in Worcester, Massachusetts, on October 12, 1913.[44] The independent Lowell branch was later founded in 1931, and another Cercle soon existed in Woonsocket. The Cercle Jeanne Mance, all three of its branches, predates the other Franco-American organizations examined here and assumed a leadership position as a result. Other groups set out to reproduce its organizational structure and mission. The familiar French *fleur-de-lys* emblem of the group is set within a Canadian maple leaf, as designed by a former Cercle president. According to article II of its constitution, "the objective of this association will be to promote the advancement of its members in the study of the French language, religion, sciences, and literature."[45]

Beginning with the first year of formal activities, the Cercle carried out its agenda with biweekly instead of monthly meetings.[46] It organized cultural events, galas, conferences, and excursions as did the other Franco-American associations, in order to promote the French element of New England. Group activities included more formal lectures for the intelligentsia and cultural offerings designed as popular fare. These comprised the social card games that many Franco-Americans enjoyed.[47] The group experienced success early in its history. It claimed to have attained more than one hundred new members in its first year.[48] The Worcester branch maintained some one hundred and fifty members into the mid-1950s. In 1938, when the Cercle de Worcester celebrated its twenty-fifth anniversary, newspaper articles portrayed members as traditional Franco matrons from more elite socioeconomic circles of central Massachusetts who took on the role of disseminators of culture. French- and English-language area newspapers reported on the glories of the organization, attended by the French consul in Boston.[49]

One of the characteristics that set the Cercle apart from other Franco organizations was the emphasis that it placed on formal language instruction and specific disciplines. Early in its history, Article II of the association's constitution specified the teaching of diverse subjects *en français*, representing a compelling Franco conception of a liberal education. The Cercle insisted that French classes occupy the core of its mission, apart from its social activities. Learning as such was central to the group's existence. The opening of weekly French classes in the fall made clear the essence of its curricular programming.[50] It is important to mention, however, that Cercle members were no less "French" than other organizational women, despite the emphasis on teaching, quite the contrary, in fact. As members of the Franco elite in the early to mid-twentieth century, their mastery of French had reached its highest point. Article III of a later version of the group constitution stipulated that members be of French-Canadian, Franco-American, or French origin. Members also had to be at least seventeen years old and Catholic.[51] Membership hinged officially on the acceptance of one's candidacy by the governing board, another vetting process used to ensure Frenchness.

Like the Cercle des Dames Françaises later, the Jeanne Mance group adhered strictly to French language use in its proceedings. This served as an important exercise, reinforcing the pedagogic influence of regular language usage. The group adopted a distinct method of bringing to life, for members and their friends, not only French language but French culture, notably through the performance of French recitals, musicals, and plays.[52] While the early years saw a great many musicals by Cercle members, the staging of elaborate plays requiring Franco-American women to perform publicly in French became a part of their cultural offerings.[53] This benefited the group as well as the wider community. Members were at times accomplished artists who embodied education through cultural performance. They sometimes assumed historical roles in performances that explored French experiences in the Americas. French culture was not merely a theoretical notion for the group but one they actively practiced through *les belles lettres*. The original Cercle Jeanne Mance was the Franco organization most closely resembling a literary society. In comparison, the current organization has clearly shifted. While French acting and speaking, the Cercle expressed an American patriotism that perhaps soothed nativist fears when it emerged at the advent of the First World War. Members filled more than four hundred Christmas bags in 1917 for soldiers from Batteries B and E from Worcester.[54]

The second article of the Cercle's 1952 constitution perhaps best articulates the ethos of the organization. "The goal of the Cercle Jeanne Mance is to encourage the study of the French language, to highlight the role of French culture and of religion in American life, to support the work of charity and of education, and to favor the social life of its members."[55] By staging a variety of performances, the group could promote French language and culture, while raising money for its charitable causes. The Cercle began really as a social welfare group aiming to ensure the well-being of French-Canadian immigrants. But more so than other organizations, leaders were interested in the material as well as intellectual and moral welfare of its members. During the group's twenty-fifth anniversary celebration, Worcester's French weekly, *Le Travailleur*, noted the pervasive objectives of the ambitious seventeenth-century woman, Jeanne Mance. Elise Rocheleau, Cercle organizer, and her sister, Corinne Rocheleau-Rouleau, a teacher of high school French in Worcester, wrote a lengthy piece for the group inspired by Mance's zeal.[56] Elise Rocheleau was the first Franco-American woman to receive France's prestigious Palmes académiques.[57]

In the 1950s, the Cercle Jeanne Mance continued its active cultural and philanthropic activity, but not always directly associated with the

Franco-American population. In an English-language text, leaders stated that it should be named an "honor club." "While organized primarily to foster French educational, cultural, and social interests, it had broadened its scope to include many undertakings of community and civic benefit." The United Nations, with its projects of mutual gain beyond linguistic and national borders, was their standard. For an ethnic, national organization most committed to preserving cultural identity, this international bent is interesting. The Cercle believed that it could engage in broader initiatives without sacrificing the ideals upon which it had been founded, specifically *la survivance française*. The group had raised money through bridge parties, fashion shows, and film screenings to benefit Assumption College, a senior citizen home, and recreation centers for area Franco churches. It sent a child lacking financial resources to camp for a month. It distributed scholarships to students and awards at local French parochial schools. These charitable acts affected not only Franco-Americans but the wider community as well.[58]

Beginning in 1953, the Cercle Jeanne Mance offered its members a published bulletin listing its many activities, classes, and services.[59] The group had likely reached the height of its influence at this time. In 1963, fifty years of collective action resulted in a *historique* written to acknowledge individual and group accomplishments. In looking at the Cercle Jeanne Mance in Lowell today, the organization has succeeded in promoting French and francophone activities. Eighty years after inception, and through the use of new technologies, the Lowell chapter still encourages French cultural learning within the Franco-American population. The group has attempted to recruit younger people into its organizational ranks. It is less representative of elite social classes than in the past. It persists in fostering public expression of Franco-American identity.

LA FÉDÉRATION FÉMININE FRANCO-AMÉRICAINE

For decades, Franco-American women's organizations such as the Cercle Jeanne Mance sent delegates to the Fédération Féminine Franco-Américaine. At its apex, over one hundred organizations were affiliated with the association, totaling some 47,000 members.[60] The Fédération may thus have had more collective influence than any single Franco-American group or publication, although it primarily existed as an umbrella organization. Each Franco association had allotted space in the Fédération's lengthy written biannual bulletins, which served as a forum and platform for all Franco-American women's groups. The Fédé expressly stated its respect for the autonomy of individual Franco women's groups.[61] The Fédération's insignia included the usual *fleur-de-lys* associated with other organizations of French heritage, but also a beehive conveying a harnessing of the intense activity of many individual groups for the collective best interests of the Franco-American community. While the *fleur-de-lys* represented French ancestry, the star made reference to the double allegiance, the French and American patriotism of Franco-Americans. The Catholic faith of members is also prominently displayed by way of the cross, formed by the horizontal and vertical bars at the top of the emblem. As noted by their chosen symbolism, these were highly organized, motivated ethnic women of faith. While their motto, "Protect our homes" (*Protégera nos foyers*), taken from the Canadian national anthem, "O Canada," made reference to women's traditional role in the household, these post–World War II women thought it necessary to later add "and our rights" (*et nos droits*) to their organizational representation in the 1970s when they became more acutely aware of their evolving position and power as women.[62]

In 1951, a group of Franco-American leaders thought it important to collectively draw strength from the various organizations that existed throughout New England and even to promote women's rights. A large contingent of both men and women met in Lewiston, Maine, at the second congress of the Comité d'orientation franco-américaine, to form the Fédération Féminine Franco-Américaine.[63] They included one Pauline Tougas, who had been the U.S. organizational head. "American from birth, perfectly bilingual, spouse, mother, social host, lecturer, artist, pianist, initiated even to public service, she brought to the founding movement a complete knowledge of the terrain and knows how to propose practical methods for the net consolidation of the female network."[64] Madame Tougas was the esteemed leader and first president of the organizing committee. The first elected president was Alice Lemieux-Lévesque, a French

Fédération Féminine

Franco-Américaine

Fondée en 1951

7. Fédération Féminine Franco-Américaine emblem, 1951.

Canadian woman and published poet who settled in New England and artistically elevated her ethnic group. A half century later, at the group's demise, the Fédération was led by noted historian Claire Quintal. She and other prominent Franco women such as journalist Marthe Biron Péloquin provided leadership for consecutive terms on more than one occasion. The Fédération benefited from effective leadership throughout its fifty-year history.

The group was expressly Catholic, as articulated in the first article of its legislation, but had greater civic ambitions: "The Franco-American Feminine Fédération has as its objective the banding together of Catholic, Franco-American women, as well as francophone women of New England, in order to strengthen their activity within the family and society by uniting on behalf of the French language and culture."[65] Spiritual advisors would serve to ensure the Catholic authenticity of all activities.[66] It is unusual for an expressly Catholic institution to be situated politically and culturally at the avant-garde in some ways, but such is the case with the Fédé. Its sister organizations were marked by an evident conservatism. While recognizing their religious affiliation, the Fédération promoted women as keepers and transmitters of French language and culture, not just in the home, but in more public roles and spaces as well. This was more explicitly stated than in other organizations. A former leader affirmed that the Fédé was ahead of its time in 1951 at its founding.[67]

Members took inspiration from the role that women had played during the Second World War. Later the institution must have been influenced to a considerable degree by the civil rights and women's rights movements. The second part of its motto (*et nos droits*) suggests this. In its legislation, the Fédération insisted that women who formed its ranks assume positions of authority. Leadership felt that even those exterior groups with whom the organization was to work should send women delegates to Fédération assemblies. This was especially important for the women coming from organizations with male and female members. "Any mixed group of individuals can also be affiliated to the Fédération, but it must be represented by a woman," stated article 12.[68] These women would perhaps not have considered themselves feminists per se, but they clearly wanted to assert the imperative of female leadership in the bylaws. Women might assume more responsibility publicly, as they already were active in the home. The distinction between a traditional experience in French Canada and a "modern" Franco-American existence for Fédération women is striking. Freed from the constraints of rural life, "liberated" women in industrial New England benefited from deliberate access to opportunity, opportunity for women that would later reach Canada.

Like other organizations, the Fédération Féminine Franco-Américaine had a structural hierarchy of leadership including a president, vice presidents, a secretary, and a treasurer. It also had a board or *Bureau de Directrices* made up of members of the executive committee (*le Conseil d'administration*) as well as sixty-two directors from the six New England states, especially Massachusetts and Connecticut.[69] The Fédération produced a lengthy, in-depth bulletin that came out quarterly for many years before scaling back to twice a year. *LE BULLETIN de la Fédération féminine franco-américaine* began to circulate in 1953 and continued until the end of the group's existence in 2001. It often contained more than fifteen pages reporting on the varied activities of affiliated Franco-American organizations, as well as sharing recipes. *Le Message de la Présidente*, featured on the front page, reflected on the current state of Franco-America and announced collective actions taken by the Fédération board.

Le Bulletin existed as "a link among affiliated groups. It will keep them informed of goings-on in the Franco-American community. It will speak to you of their activities. The more our activities grow, the more the Bulletin will be interesting."[70] Given its comprehensive approach to Franco-American social and cultural life, it was held in high regard.[71] As the president stated in the first *Bulletin*, simply speaking French was at the heart of the Fédération's mission: "The recipe is quite simple: we want French? Well, let us speak French then, especially in our homes! This is the first way, the principal way, the only way to begin our work, as noble as it is necessary."[72] Speaking is in essence being. When contemporary working women, as well as war veterans, spoke or translated French publicly in the wider world, recognizable French, they expressed both surprise and pride. Association legislation stated that French was the official language of the Fédération.[73]

The New England chapters of the Alliance Française, those either led by a Franco-American woman or having substantial Franco membership, lent their support and their devotion to the French language and to the Fédération during its existence.[74] French linguistic and cultural activities of the Fédération benefited from the support of the French consul général and the Quebec delegation in Boston. These officials also attended many of the Fédé's functions. Franco-American women's organizations were clearly participating in a wider francophone movement.

In the second issue of the fledging *Bulletin*, the editing team expressed their gratitude to the various groups and individuals who had made its publication a success. It signaled the fact that several French-language newspapers had taken notice of the edition. Its launching had been acknowledged not only by the Franco-American press, but even a long-standing and influential Montreal daily newspaper, *Le Devoir*.[75] In turn, *Le Bulletin* of the Fédération encouraged its readers to support the Franco-American press, which actively strove to maintain *la survivance* in New England through its linguistic, cultural, social, and moral influence. "We solemnly ask each member of the Franco-American Feminine Fédération to subscribe to a Franco-American newspaper and to identify at least one other subscriber to the journal of your choice. . . . All of our papers are Catholic, patriotic and devoted to our interests."[76] The second issue of the publication provided a list of Franco-American newspapers available to readers, including *L'Etoile* of Lowell, *La Justice* of Holyoke, and *Le Travailleur* of Worcester, Massachusetts. All were reportedly in need of support.

Every two years, the *Bulletin* served to draw attention to the main body of work of the organization, which took place at the biennial congresses of the Fédé. As stated in the bylaws, "The Congress constitutes the supreme authority of the Fédération."[77] It was here that the group hashed out its policies, politics, and agenda and executed all of its functions and duties. In fact, these congresses allowed members of the dozens of Franco-American groups to physically assemble under one roof for discussion of common issues. The themes of these congresses give a detailed picture of the twentieth-century concerns of women of French-Canadian descent: "La femme dans le mouvement de la vie française" (1954), "Education franco-américaine" (1956), "Le français dans la famille, à l'école, chez les jeunes" (1965), "L'enseignement du français dans les écoles paroissales et publiques" (1967), "La femme, son épanouissement et son action sociale" (1975), "La femme franco-américaine, son rôle, ses droits et ses responsabilités vis-à-vis du bilinguisme et du biculturalisme dans notre société" (1979), and "La femme francophone aux États-Unis (1984).[78] We find a broadening of the scope of interests of Franco-American women's organizations over the years. They increasingly saw themselves as advocates for women within a greater social, economic, and cultural context. Again, the Fédération was at the forefront for change, for amplified Franco-American subjectivity, for accessible francophone female voices specifically. Anniversary years were devoted especially to women's role in the preservation of French language and culture in America: 10e anniversaire—"Convaincre et agir pour notre refrancisation" (1961), 20e anniversaire—"Renaissance du français au 20e siècle" (1971).[79] The Fédération affirmed the reawakening of the French of America, a phenomenon led by women.

The Fédération held its congresses at various sites of French life in America. These included Springfield and Worcester, Massachusetts, Manchester and Nashua, New Hampshire, Lewiston, Maine, Waterbury, Connecticut, Quebec City, and Montreal. The group turned noticeably more toward specific women's rights and their engagement in society. The 1984 congress held over a late April weekend on the Rivier College campus in Nashua was exemplary. Conference panels drew parallels between Franco-American women and other francophones of America, namely, Canadiennes françaises. Official guests from the French consul's office reminded Fédération members of their distant but unforgotten connection to France. The presence of the honorary consul from Monaco represented a symbolic gesture to the *congressistes* at the sixteenth biennial meeting in New Hampshire, reinforcing the francophone theme of the conference.

After nineteen successive congresses, the organization opted for yearly reunions beginning in 1991. The congresses were busy, elaborate affairs requiring a considerable amount of organization for active but senior women. The Fédération began publishing a condensed version of its *Bulletin*, now called *Le Petit Bulletin*.[80] A report from the 1993 edition mentioned that while showing signs of difficulty, the Fédération still attracted young women of French descent.[81] The publication mentioned seventy members who had attended a recent event, which did not represent all dues-paying members. Like the other organizations, dues were minimal. Ten dollars per year guaranteed a subscription to the *Bulletin* and voting rights at congresses. Not every member, however, received the *Bulletin*, reducing its visibility. Fédération literature noted that not all Franco-American women were involved in cultural and social organizations despite a real need for their assistance.

Fédération leaders decided to disband in 2001 after a half century of supporting the efforts of affiliated Franco-American women's groups in New England. Dissolution of the group had already been conceived in the original constitution. In the event of the formal closing of the Fédération, board members would direct all remaining resources to students in need of financial assistance for the study of French, highlighting a transcendent cultural gift pervasive in Franco social organizations. The Cercle des Dames Françaises noted this act of generosity in its own monthly *Bulletin*.[82] Education remained at the core of the Fédération mission, as at its affiliate organizations. One might conclude optimistically that the group had fulfilled its mission, as more women were being educated and attaining seats of power and influence. For more than a decade, the numbers of new and old members had dwindled. The 2001 Fédération president wrote that aging members could no longer assume all of the needed administrative and executive responsibilities.[83] Capped by a celebration of fifty years of activity, the final formal meeting at Salve Regina University (1934) in Newport, Rhode Island, provided a jubilant ending to a proud institution.

It is not constructive to speculate how long Franco-American women will want or be able to continue their leadership role in the transmission of culture. Each time that they have been counted out, they have managed to persist because of a prevailing willingness to assemble and to simply continue living Franco-American lives. The organized women of Massachusetts provide a key to the past of Franco-American social and cultural life, as well as a window into the preservation of these traditions. They have helped to perpetuate francophone life in New England in the twenty-first century. The Fédération, in pooling together the resources of all Franco social groups, may have promoted the expression of ethnic identity that transcended social, geographic, and class differences. A unifying Franco identity indeed seemed to trump socioeconomic distinctions that might otherwise loosen ties. As seen among the various groups, Franco women demonstrate a patient and enduring approach to the recognition of ethnic culture and to engagement with cultural life. Franco-American women are certainly at the intersection of tradition and modernity, between past and present of the French experience in North America. As protectors of the language, faith, and traditions, they are simultaneously conservative and avant-garde in many respects, perhaps best exemplified by the Fédération. The Franco-American Women's Institute is in some respect a continuation of the Fédération, allowing women to participate in cultural creation and transmission, virtually and from afar. Although much smaller in scale, FAWI fosters the production, distribution, and consumption of Franco cultures without requiring the physical movements of bodies and formal organization.

CHAPTER 4

Franco-American Cultures in a New World Perspective

More than forty prominent *auteur(e)s* from around the world signed a media petition in 2007 expressing their support for a cosmopolitan new definition of literature written in French. Rejecting the categorization "francophone" as devaluing, they demanded recognition of a *littérature-monde en français*, a world literature in French attentive to new voices from the postcolony, or what I will call transnational literature in French.[1] A book quickly emerged following the manifesto, reassembling petitioners and rearticulating their positions, which call into question the French republican narrative.[2] Is French cultural production too narrowly defined? In response, scholars began organizing conferences and special journal issues to further explore this broad conception of French literature.[3]

If writers, journalists, and even politicians have made much ado over the *littérature-monde* debate, it is because what is at issue is how French culture and identity are to be defined in the twenty-first century. "Official" French culture has typically emanated from narrow channels in Paris, from the metropolitan seat of power and prestige. For this reason, it is significant that Parisian literary circles have recognized French cultural production from outside the establishment in recent decades. Can French literatures from without transform the way in which French and francophone cultures are conceived? This question is part of an ongoing and lively debate, one that includes the *littérature-monde* discussion. In my study of Franco-American literatures and cultures, a New World phenomenon within the postcolonial French realm, I suggest that written texts challenge underlying assumptions about la francophonie and Francophone Studies, two ambiguous and distinct entities. They equally call into question the meaning of French culture more broadly. A more inclusive or transnational conception of culture can perhaps provide a framework for understanding obscure and often ambiguously francophone literatures, works outside the accepted corpus of texts that make up the French canon. Cultural production from an often forgotten corner of the French-speaking world, especially francophone North America south of the Canadian border, is now beginning to receive more scholarly attention. This fourth chapter focuses most specifically on the diasporic and discursive francophone cultures of New England, with a short foray into Quebec and less attention paid to Louisiana (see chapter 6). A fully developed concept of *littérature-monde en français* might recognize the cultural work that writers from these areas have contributed in the four centuries since French settlers first came to the New World continent.

In the journal *Contemporary French and Francophone Studies*, Marvin Richards suggested that examinations of French presence in North America be put on the map,[4] while special issues of the *French Review* explored the past and present of French influence in the United States.[5] Diasporic populations and cultures of North America are positioned between French and francophone; they are souvenirs of a French past in the New World dating back to the sixteenth century and a twenty-first-century francophone and American present and future. Two current intermediate French language textbooks, *Pause-Café* and *Réseau*, literally situate "Franco-America" on the map of the greater francophone world, which may help to inform American students about French influence in the New World, outside of Quebec and Louisiana.[6] *Heritages Francophones* is another contemporary

French text that specifically explores the diversity at the heart of lives lived in French in the United States.[7]

Readers will find descriptive nouns and adjectives such as French and francophone, French Canadian, and Franco-American used throughout such texts and this analysis. We have seen that writers inscribe an assortment of more derogatory French ethnic markers, Canuck and Coonass, in their fictive and non-fictive texts. Both real and imagined characters inhabit Franco-America, a place found on no map but that exists nonetheless in the minds of people of French descent in Canada and the United States.[8] It is a space in which French heritage is acknowledged, sometimes begrudgingly, and where residents can still express elements of an ethnic or cultural life. The French came to the New World in small numbers in the seventeenth century; a few remained, built homes and towns, and produced large families. Allan Greer argues that spectacular reproduction is largely responsible for continued New World French presence today.[9] In sum, hundreds of thousands who became known as Canadiens français and later Québécois left the impoverished province in the nineteenth and early twentieth centuries in search of work and better lives. The British also forced Acadians into exile and ultimately resettlement in Louisiana (as well as other places) much earlier, in the mid-eighteenth century.[10] Migrants and exiles created French ethnic neighborhoods where a growing sense of self could be cultivated. A constructed notion of Franco-American identity, shaped most notably by French language, Catholic faith, and cultural traditions, emerged in their recorded stories of material and cultural survival. The Franco-American experience is a familiar immigrant experience in many ways, similar to that of other hyphenated American groups juggling cultural preservation and assimilation throughout the twentieth century, but it is also distinct. The cultures of *les petits Canadas* of New England remain obscure within the American urban landscape, yet recognizing Franco-American cultures within a transnational literature in French can perhaps help free them from their ethnic confinement.

On March 16, 2007, during the Salon du livre in Paris, forty-four writers made a plea for a change in the cultural status quo in France's center-left daily newspaper *Le Monde*, denouncing French (e.g., Parisian) culture as a dominant force either blind or patronizing toward cultural production beyond France's economic, political, and intellectual center. That previous fall, several of the most prestigious literary prizes went to authors who choose to write in French or for whom French is not a birth language: Léonora Miano and Alain Mabanckou (Africa), Jonathan Littell (United States) and Nancy Huston (Canada). That trend continued later in 2007 when Vietnamese novelist Linda Lê received the Femina and Médicis Prizes. In the lengthy manifesto published in *Le Monde*, novelists refused the marginalization that too often came with being labeled and marketed as Francophone authors. Non-colonial white authors like Samuel Beckett and Eugène Ionesco have had little difficulty landing on bookstore shelves as "French" authors. "Fin de la francophonie," *littérature-monde* advocates asserted. "Et naissance d'une littérature-monde en français."[11] Signees proclaiming the end of official francophonie and birth of a more global literature in French included many prominent francophone writers such as Tahar Ben Jelloun, Maryse Condé, Edouard Glissant, Jacques Godbout, Nancy Huston, Dany Laferrière, J.M.G. Le Clézio, Amin Maalouf, Alain Mabanckou, Erik Orsenna, and Gisèle Pineau.

The *littérature-monde* manifesto prompted a quick rejoinder from Organisation internationale de la francophonie (OIF) general secretary Abdou Diouf in an opinion piece published four days later, also in *Le Monde*. Clearly feeling his organization under attack, he replied:

> Nous partageons tous le même éclatant et stimulant constat, à savoir que diverses sont aujourd'hui les littératures de langue française. Mais vous me permettrez de vous faire irrespectueusement remarquer que vous contribuez dans ce manifeste, avec toute l'autorité que votre talent confère à votre parole, à entretenir le plus grave des contresens sur la francophonie, en confondant francocentrisme et francophonie, en confondant exception culturelle et diversité culturelle.[12]

The OIF had placed its energies in the promotion of cultural and linguistic diversity, wrote Diouf, French diversity expressly, in opposition to American-led globalization. Critics, however, labeled this promotion of French as an old form of imperialism in a new bottle. The authors of the *littérature-monde* movement contended that their novels and essays, which convey francophone cultures from several continents, represent equally valid expressions of *French* literature. But as Dominic Thomas has suggested, this group of authors may themselves contribute to a new kind of cultural hegemony.[13] While their national origins vary, they are all established authors whose works are published almost exclusively in France. Thomas remarked notable omissions from the movement, such as *Beur* literature, the contemporary texts written by novelists of North African descent born in France. One could argue that the same thing has happened to Franco-American literature, although certainly a lesser-known entity. The Franco-American cultures examined here are located well outside the French literary establishment. They represent authentic and rather uncommon examples of transnational experiences from the French postcolony. The American continent and cultures have been marked profoundly by French influence, even mid-America and points west, asserts historian Jay Gitlin.[14] Cultural geographers, we have seen, have been influential in helping to publicize the "French fact" in America.[15] This fact, recorded explicitly and repeatedly in Franco-American literatures and cultures of North America, will now be explored in further detail.

TRANSCRIBING LA FRANCO-AMÉRICANIE

Has the last French-language novel of the French experience in the United States been written, the last piece of fiction or nonfiction *en français* expressing the life and culture of diasporic French groups? There have been several such "lasts" identified over the final decades of the twentieth century as people of French descent and cultural traditions have dissolved into the American melting pot. The answer, however, is no, if one considers an active contemporary author like Normand Beaupré. Critics wondered if the end of a French era had been reached when Beaupré published *Le Petit Mangeur de fleurs* in 1999.[16] It is an intensely personal coming-of-age memoir in French, as well as a sometimes stinging portrayal of Franco-American life. Since 1999, Beaupré has written and self-published more novels in French, some in Canada and others more recently in the United States.[17] Fifteen years earlier, Robert Perreault's *L'Héritage* (1983) received similar critical attention, as it was the first Franco-American novel written in French in half a century.[18] Both Perreault and Beaupré describe the lives and labors of French-Canadian immigrants who settled in mill towns in New England in the nineteenth and twentieth centuries. Quebec was a first stop after their initial transatlantic voyage from France, as thousands of immigrants continued on foot, horse, and train to industrial America. Many remained permanently, establishing lives, businesses, and organizations.[19]

The novelists cited above indicate that while French Canadians assimilated like other immigrant populations, they retained French cultural traditions. The National Materials Development Center for French in New Hampshire published Perreault's novel in a broad effort to recognize and preserve ethnic identity in a rapidly changing United States. In comparison to Parisian publishing houses, this was a tiny and now defunct effort to print literature from the French diaspora by the U.S. government. The last Franco-American newspaper written entirely in French in New England, the monthly *Journal de Lowell* of Massachusetts, ceased printing a decade after publication of Perreault's *L'Héritage* in 1995. This is likely a more definitive last edition of the traditional Franco-American newspaper, given the difficulties experienced by the written press in the Internet age. A French ethnic press had existed for a century, with daily editions in several mill towns.[20] They are not as easily found now, although municipal public libraries contain valuable collections of foreign-language ethnic presses.

In the south of Franco-America, in Louisiana, one also finds indigenous French cultures in decline. Nothing will likely come close to matching the production of Creole elites in nineteenth-century New Orleans who created a rich cultural life in the Crescent City. After a century-long run, *L'Abeille de la Nouvelle-Orléans*, the city's French-language newspaper, disappeared in 1925. To this day, however, Cajun and Creole storytellers transcribe postcolonial French cultures of the American South.[21] Some forty years ago, Revon Reed's *Lâche pas la patate* (1976) and Jean Arceneaux's *Cris sur le bayou* (1980) represented a watershed in Cajun and Creole expression and identity affirmation. Some publication in French continues (Les Cahiers du Tintamarre) as do the linguistic and cultural programs of the Conseil pour le Développement du français en Louisiane (CODOFIL), supported by the state university system of Louisiana.

As French cultures in the United States have become increasingly endangered, the *littérature-monde* debate offers a rationale for the understanding of their written record. They provide evidence of perhaps no longer always living, but no less richly varied French and francophone cultures outside of France. Many literatures of the world written in French from the far-reaching periphery are not "world literatures," with appeal outside the sphere of French influence, but rather local phenomena reflecting degrees of Frenchness in the postcolonial period. As novelist Alain Mabanckou asserts, it is through the writing from the periphery of the francophone realm, one that is not uniformly or fluently French-speaking, that some sense of a universal, human thread can be woven: "Et c'est là précisément qu'intervient la littérature-monde, celle qui fonde les complicités au-delà des continents, des nationalités, des catéchismes et de l'arbre généalogique pour ne retenir que le clin d'oeil que se font deux créateurs que tout semblait éloigner dès le départ."[22] These complicities extend to those who talk about the world through a French-colored lens. It is notable that *littérature-monde* advocates evoke a kind of universalism achieved through French language usage, a discourse quite similar to one adopted by the Organisation internationale de la francophonie, yet at odds with postcolonialism, which often rejects the concept of universalism.

While the word may be fairly recently minted (1992), *littérature-monde en français* is not a new phenomenon.[23] Nor is it the first to separate the French language from the nation-state. While the March 16, 2007, manifesto brought media attention to the concept, the "world" has been writing in French for some time, since French power—represented by absolute monarchs, Napoléon Bonaparte, and colonial empire, for instance—made French culture international through conquest and influence. The New World has certainly been involved in this production. Well after the great explorers and associates established *la Nouvelle-France* in the seventeenth century, native or Creole French born in the New World have written about their American experiences in Canada, the Caribbean, and in the United States.[24] These writings add new complexities to the term *American* by introducing

Franco perspectives. They serve to expand notions of Frenchness, which until most recently, during French opposition to the American-led war in Iraq, seemed hostilely opposed to American culture. As noted, Alexis de Tocqueville and more contemporary thinkers such as Pierre Bourdieu examine inherent competition and tension between French and American universalist cultural models.

Writing about French cultural life in America and beyond offered settler populations an opportunity to describe a world in which largely marginal groups attain greater recognition. In fiction and nonfiction, there was a constant flow, a continual exchange of ideas between *le vieux continent* and the New (French) World. Franco-American authors and editors were born in France, Quebec, and the United States. They wrote in French as well as in English, more so in English as the twentieth century advanced. Today their writings and their reading publics are located on both sides of the Atlantic Ocean and throughout the world. France is not a frequent stopover on this Franco-American odyssey (it is more a distant memory and symbolically relevant), yet Franco-Americans today continue to talk specifically about themselves and the spaces that they occupy as "French."

A Franco-American identity was first articulated in the French-language ethnic press of New England.[25] Most were filled with information about life in Quebec, about the society and people that French-Canadian immigrants had left behind in their move to the United States. The daily newspapers that circulated in many of the early industrial cities where Franco-Americans congregated describe in considerable detail how the population from Quebec evolved culturally over time following migration and resettlement in the United States. *Le Travailleur* of Worcester, Massachusetts, a weekly publication, expressed the most important assertively Franco-American viewpoint among the ethnic newspapers. A first edition was founded in 1874 by Ferdinand Gagnon, a staunch objector to American assimilation. Gagnon has remained an imposing if virtually unknown figure outside the Franco-American cultural elite. A statue dedicated to him stands today in Manchester, New Hampshire's Lafayette Park. Its plaque gives an indication of his stature within the Franco-American community, as founder of the French ethnic press, including Manchester's first French paper: "Ferdinand

Gagnon—1849–1886—Journaliste, orateur, fondateur de la presse franco-américaine publia en 1869 La Voix du Peuple, premier journal français à Manchester, NH et Le Travailleur à Worcester, Mass. de 1874 à 1886." The paper Gagnon founded, *Le Travailleur*, began a second phase in 1931 under the helm of Wilfred Beaulieu, who directed it until 1978 and continued to espouse the ideals of *la survivance française*.

Franco-American newspapers were the first to bring works of fiction to the attention of readers. The first formal Franco-American novel, *Jeanne la fileuse*, written in 1878 by Honoré Beaugrand, appeared in segments in the Fall River, Massachusetts, newspaper, *L'Echo du Canada*, before being published as a whole. The writer and journalist Beaugrand was born in Quebec but stationed in Fall River, among other places in the French Atlantic world.[26] His novel depicts life in the textile mills, and as Beaugrand claimed in his preface, it was a response to the critics of emigration. He rejected the notion that it was social outcasts who left Quebec, "la canaille qui s'en va," an 1867 declaration attributed to Canadian statesman and critic of emigration, Georges-Etienne Cartier.[27] The story *Jeanne la fileuse* begins in Canada before moving south to describe the protagonist Jeanne and the Franco community in Fall River, Massachusetts. The title is deceptive in that Jeanne is a *fileuse* (or female textile worker in America) only temporarily before returning to Canada to lead a more traditional life. This return to a bucolic French identity is quite evocative, for Franco-American identity is not entirely defined by industrial labor begun following immigration.

Beaugrand was taken to task by his detractors for not sufficiently defending the national and moral duty of repatriation and for recognizing the permanence of Franco-American communities and cultures before most in industrial New England. Yet several of his characters follow the mythical (and for some illusionary) path back to the French-Canadian homeland. Only Jeanne's brother remains in Fall River where factory life offers him better prospects. While many Franco-Americans did remain in their new homes, Franco-American literature also describes a northbound journey at the end of life. Burial in Canada, the fatherland, was imperative for many Franco-American families. Beaugrand challenged Ferdinand Gagnon to a duel for having abandoned the ideal of repatriation. The rival editors traded barbs in the press but did not come to blows, for Gagnon believed his pen too important to the Franco cause to risk his life.[28] For lay and religious elites, migration was a highly sensitive issue as more than 30 percent of the Quebec population had left the impoverished province in search of jobs.[29] Again, when closely observed, the ideas Beaugrand expressed in the novel are fairly nuanced. Jeanne and her husband ultimately return to a traditional way of life in Quebec. People like her brother Jules, who remains in Fall River, became increasingly American, some without any culturally distinctive prefix.

Canuck, a story of factory life in Lowell, Massachusetts, provides a fuller account of Franco-American life in the twentieth century. Camille Lessard-Bissonnette published the text in 1936, which first saw print in serial form in Lewiston, Maine's daily newspaper *Le Messager*. Canuck is a derisive label for French Canadians and often used by fellow French Canadians, part of the dismissive and derogatory Franco-American vocabulary noted earlier. The author, Lessard-Bissonnette, was born in Quebec in 1883, but her family moved to Lewiston in 1904 to work in the mills and improve their lot in life. It is a more substantively Franco-American work of fiction because it revolves around life in an ethnic Franco enclave, much more so than *Jeanne la fileuse*, which has little to say about conditions in Fall River. Much of the novel *Canuck* is taken from the author's existence in Lewiston in the early twentieth century, although the narrative setting is Lowell. *Canuck* is Lessard-Bissonnette's only published work, but she also delved in education and journalism. She took a particular interest in women's issues and edited a *pages féminines* column for *Le Messager*, providing another example of Franco-American women leading from a position of authority.[30]

Canuck recounts the transformation of Victoria or Vic (for Victory, undoubtedly) from exiled country girl to accomplished young independent woman.[31] This woman of peasant stock is somewhat surprised by her first visual impressions of America, purported land of milk and honey. Spreading out before her on the horizon are the sooty tenements and factories of industrial America. "So this is the United States," says Vic on several occasions, disappointed, as she takes in her new surroundings.

This was certainly not the America of her imagination. In addition to confronting the reality of life in a New England mill town, Vic must face the jealous rage of French-Canadian immigrants who had come before her and for whom she is a freshly arrived, wet-behind-the-ears, Canuck. She is physically and verbally attacked by them, a mob of angry women, and saved from an even more severe beating by the man who would become the great love of her life.[32]

Canuck tells the story of an enlightened Franco-American womanhood. Lessard-Bissonnette speaks of Vic's emancipation or liberation from the more traditional, subservient position occupied by her mother, who remains unnamed and virtually nonexistent in the text.[33] Vic's triumph must be achieved in opposition to the sullen violence of her father, Vital Labranche, who resents her independence of thought and action. Vic escapes to enjoy the intoxicating freedoms of other young working women of Lowell, *les demoiselles de Lowell*.[34] For the first time, Vic experiences independence, the joys of making and spending her own money, as well as solitude away from her family. Far from frivolous, Vic puts aside money for the education of brother Maurice, who is destined for the priesthood. One of the first things that Vic does in this new phase of her life is to enroll in an evening English course.[35] Better use of English would grant her increased mobility; it would enable her to attain an even greater level of freedom. It would also cement her newfound status as a Franco-American. Vic does ultimately return to a more traditional mode of life, but on her own terms. She returns to help support the family after a debilitating accident cripples her father in Canada (the family had remained there after having buried frail son Besson in the cherished soil of the homeland).

Vic takes to farming with all the reputed pride and determination of her position. In this sense, she continues to identify as New World French despite her own personal transformation. Happiness, which had long eluded her, eventually and somewhat surreally, becomes attainable. After having spent years pursuing the sly rascal Jean, who happens to be French, not Franco-American, a heartbroken and distraught Vic is reunited with Raymond, the kind man who had saved her from her tormentors in Lowell many years before. Brother Maurice, now a priest, presides over their wedding. The couple sets off for adventures in Central America. This is a fantastical ending to a popular novel that traces the realm of the Franco-American imaginary.

Canuck is no literary masterpiece and thus uncomfortably included in the *littérature-monde* category, at least as defined by the cited forty-four French and francophone luminaries. As one of the first and instructive Franco-American texts, it does reveal pertinent elements of Franco life, although this has sometimes constituted the bane of Francophone literature generally, more often cited for sociological than for literary value. There are other, more elegantly crafted Franco-American texts that appear later.

The Franco-American novel extends geographically well beyond *Canuck*'s industrial New England. The genre encompasses classic works of Québécois literature also written during the early part of the twentieth century, the so-called *romans de la terre*, which frequently cross the border into the lower United States. Franco-American literature invites readers into the southernmost reaches of America's French expanses, into the bayou country of Louisiana. The story of the Acadians and Cajuns is perhaps the most evocative of the Franco-American journey, and 1979 Prix Goncourt winner Antonine Maillet's *Pélagie-la-charette* is exemplary. After forced expulsion from l'Acadie (later named Nova Scotia by the British), separated from lands, dwellings, and families, and dispersed along the eastern coastline of North America, Acadians are left to wander like biblical folk in search of "home." Pélagie, heroine of the narrative, leads the expelled back to their ancestral land, to their paradise lost, Grand Pré. "Quelle femme, cette Pélagie! Capable à elle seule de ramener un peuple au pays." Toward the end of her sojourn, and near death, Pélagie looks behind her to witness that stragglers had become her people. The author compares Pélagie's people to salmon or geese whose bodies are programmed for the homeward journey.[36]

Despite the return "home," Pélagie points to a sensibility linking displaced Acadians along the Atlantic seaboard. Acadians carry a little piece of Acadie with them wherever they are. Pélagie discusses a shared consciousness linking uprooted and displaced Acadians found all along the eastern coast of North America. "C'est les hommes qui faisont la terre, et point la terre qui fait les hommes. Là où c'est que je marcherons, nous autres, il faudra bien qu'ils bailliont un nom à l'endroit. Je l'appellerons l'Acadie."[37] Acadians could lay their hat wherever they created home, for it was men who transformed the land and not the reverse.

Antonine Maillet presents an interesting turn from traditional French-Canadian rootedness that readers observe elsewhere, in *Maria Chapdelaine*, for instance: "We have been here for three hundred years and have remained. Our prayers and our songs brought overseas are the same." So expresses the voice of French Quebec, the voice that ultimately convinces Maria Chapdelaine (1913), heroine of the quintessential French-Canadian *roman de la terre* by Louis Hémon, to remain true to her roots:

> Nous sommes venus il y a trois cents ans, et nous sommes restés. . . . Nous avions apporté d'outre-mer nos prières et nos chansons: elles sont toujours les mêmes. Nous avions apporté dans nos poitrines le coeur des hommes de notre pays, vaillant et vif, aussi prompt à la pitié qu'au rire, le coeur le plus humain de tous les coeurs humains: il n'a pas changé. Nous avons marqué un plan du continent nouveau, de Gaspé à Montréal, de Saint-Jean d'Iberville à l'Ungava, en disant: ici toutes les choses que nous avons apportées avec nous, notre culte, notre langage, nos vertus et jusqu'à nos faiblesses deviennent des choses sacrées, intangibles et qui devront demeurer jusqu'à la fin.[38]

Maria is tempted to leave the land so laboriously toiled by her ancestors, the land that proved so costly to her own family and friends, for the "bright lights" of industrial America.[39] She realizes in time, however, that this would constitute treason to cultural elites such as Beaugrand, a betrayal of French colonial efforts begun some three hundred (four hundred now) years ago. She opts to marry the staid but steady tiller of the soil, Eutrope Gagnon. The French colonial stakes in North America are clearly evident in this novel from the early twentieth century, which transports readers considerably beyond the geographic confines of Quebec.

Frequently cited and debated one hundred years after its original publication, *Maria Chapdelaine* is indeed a rich site for exploration of identity in the French fiction of North America. Ironically, the work very often taken to represent the foundation of Québécois literature was written by a young man born in France and who had spent a short period of time in Quebec. How does one, in fact, read a novel written by a Frenchman for a French public, as critics have asked?[40] Louis Hémon's novel appeared posthumously after he was killed in a train accident in Ontario in 1913 at the age of thirty-three. Scholars since then have argued about the author's intent and whether Hémon attempted to ridicule or negatively stereotype Quebec and its settlers. A dispassionate reading of the tale indicates that it is more overt homage to French colonial efforts in the New World and to the hardy, simple (in the most positive of senses) pioneers and purveyors of French culture in the wilderness. The depiction is also a caricature to some extent, likely shaped by the flights of the author's colonial fancy. Maria, Father Chapdelaine, and others nobly and patiently carry on French traditions as their forbears did before them, while also creating new cultural forms.

The narrative revolves around the ubiquitous ideals of sentimental and patriotic love. Maria, the comely, dutiful daughter of the père Chapdelaine, is courted by three representative suitors whose names are astonishingly evocative. François Paradis, the rugged *coureur de bois* and perhaps the most symbolically French-Canadian, seeks her favor and is clearly the frontrunner in her young heart. He disappears into a snowy blizzard, never to be seen again, an almost inevitable fate for such an adventurer, especially one named Paradis, "heaven" in English translation. Maria is slightly dazzled by the elegant Lorenzo Surprenant, a newly minted gentleman who had emigrated to *les Etats*, otherwise known as early industrial New England, and returned to Quebec a materially and figuratively transformed man. He promises her an easier, more satisfying life than the desolation of the North woods can provide. Maria is also desired by the timid, simple (again in a good sense of the word) *habitant* Eutrope Gagnon. Gagnon appears a distant third in her esteem, but as his name indicates, he does ultimately triumph (after the disappearance of Paradis), like the proverbial tortoise that starts the race slowly but through steady perseverance prevails.[41] *Maria Chapdelaine* could end, really, no other way.

While tempted at first by the promises of a less burdensome and a more consumerist life in New England, Maria cannot but remain in the

Canadian North, as does symbolically French culture. The author teases readers into thinking that Maria might leave Quebec, especially since it seemed responsible for the deaths of her mother and her beloved François. Maria's hatred of winter, her "haine des hivers du Nord, du froid, du sol blanc, de la solitude des grandes forêts inhumaines" seemed to turn her against choosing Eutrobe Gagnon as her betrothed.[42] The hesitations of the heroine disintegrate, however, upon hearing the voice of Quebec mentioned earlier, that arrives suddenly, unexpectedly. The compliment paid by Louis Hémon to the *Pioneers of France in the New World*, as Francis Parkman calls them, is that she remains in Quebec.

Patriotic trumps romantic love. This account of fidelity to country is thus reminiscent of Henry W. Longfellow's prose poem *Evangeline*. Maria is a French-Canadian heroine of almost Evangeline-esque proportions who steadfastly embodies the most valued in French tradition despite her trials and tribulations. She is patient in love, strong, faithful in the religious and romantic sense, the quintessential, perhaps stereotypical French-Canadian woman firmly entrenched in the soil of these romans de la terre.

In referring to her sober willingness to wait for François Paradis, who is doomed never to return, the author refers to the "infinite patience" of the Canadian people.[43] Like other *habitants* and most particularly women, who bring French life to a "barren" New World, Maria represents the continuity of the stubborn French race in America. Their French faith is exaggerated and untypically American in some regards. Alone in an infertile wilderness and far from France, faith, God, and prayer represent a compelling and enduring component of French identity in the New World, along with French language. French settlers like the Chapdelaine bring with them the cultural and social aspects of regular Sunday worship. Commenting on the women's notable French attire during the exit from Sunday mass, Hémon writes: "Un étranger se fut étonné de les trouver presque élégantes au coeur de ce pays sauvage, si typiquement françaises parmi les grands bois désolés et la neige, et aussi bien mises à coup sûr, ces paysannes, que la plupart des jeunes bourgeoises des provinces de France."[44] A transplanted French cultural distinction stands out alongside the rugged natural setting of the American North. In marrying Eutrope Gagnon and claiming as her own this land, in quietly assuming the ways of her forebears, in having a traditionally large French-Canadian family, and thereby carrying on *la revanche des berceaux* (revenge of the cradles), Maria represents the continuity of an incongruous Frenchness on American shores.

We see in many such traditional Québécois novels from the twentieth century an affirmation of the vitality of French traditions in North America. People of French origin, their lives lived in French, had survived against all odds. Frenchness often appears to be clutching the rocky shores of the continent. These stories bristle with a trenchant, sometimes jarring nationalism for contemporary readers. Maria remains French-Canadian with a serenity that practically opposes the defiant tone in *Menaud, maître draveur* (1937), another classic from Quebec's literary canon by Félix-Antoine Savard. Menaud is determined to fight to preserve French presence in North America. "Un peuple qui ne sait mourir," claims Menaud who takes inspiration while reading lines from *Maria Chapdelaine* ("Nous sommes venus il y a 300 ans et nous sommes restés"). This statement, repeated throughout the novel, is a call to arms. The French race has refused to die.

The protagonist Menaud is profoundly offended by the arrival of foreigners *chez lui* who threaten to become its masters.[45] He objects to being pushed off land settled by his French ancestors and attempts to organize a peasant revolt. He refuses to allow his daughter Marie to marry the sell-out le Délié, to whom she has been promised. Marie, moved by the patriotism of her father, can only choose the brave and loyal Lucon as her mate, provoking the jealous outrage of the rejected le Délié. Both Marie and Lucon follow Menaud in his battle against the powerful outside Anglophone forces that corrupt le Délié. Marie, like Maria Chapdelaine before her, embodies French-Canadian or early Franco-American resistance. Gerard Bouchard, in his comparative historical works, asks why such fierce resistance did not lead to the founding of an independent French nation in North America, as happened in Spanish or English-speaking colonies.[46] This question has formed the basis of the nationalist scholar's work and has fueled the ongoing polemic of Quebec's autonomy.

Savard's *Menaud, maître draveur* is full of nationalist fervor and patriotic clichés that echo ominously in the world in which we live. It is indeed difficult to read this novel without our twenty-first-century lens, sharpened most certainly by sensitivity to cultural offense. There is blunt, repeated reference to the heritage and "race" of the French ancestors who labored to carve out an existence. "Tout cela vient de nos pères, les Français!" claims the author. "Menaud devait à ses pères de ne pas abâtardir sa race." The contamination of blood is strictly forbidden, at least with Anglos, for the race of the defeated must be perpetuated. Menaud, Lucon, and Marie uphold the race while le Délié threatens to dilute if not contaminate it. The men of the story, the protagonist, his son Joson, and his son-in-law le Lucon, represent the most authentic and seductively appealing of French-Canadian manhood, the *coureur de bois*. Marie, again like Maria, is representative of strong, defiant French-Canadian womanhood. Menaud cannot allow his daughter to marry a traitor who has sold his soul to the highest bidder. This would risk degenerating the future of the French race. Their blood boils at the thought of outsiders controlling their country. "Etre jaloux du sol tout entier, vibrer tous et chacun à pleins bords de pays, défendre le patrimoine de la première à la dernière motte, telle est la loi reçue, telle, la loi à transmettre! C'est ainsi que j'ai toujours compris le devoir du sang," exclaims Menaud. As Menaud has understood it, the responsibility that each has to every inch of his homeland, as well as to one's blood or race, is heavy indeed. He and those that follow his lead are obliged to protect a cherished French liberty established on American soil. "Etre libre, sentir sous ses pieds, le son de la terre répondre aux battements de son coeur."[47]

This is the driving force of the narrative. Body and homeland (not mind) are in perfect unison. Individuals so moved by a French rootedness that they can feel pulsating beneath their feet and in their hearts must labor to protect it. Félix-Antoine Savard provides a most singular literary example of French-Canadian nationalism. Since the nineteenth century, claim editors of *Histoire de la Littérature Québécoise*, the distinctly national trajectory of Quebec literature has been well established.[48] Franco-American literature more broadly allows readers to visualize the international parameters of the genre. One can identify Acadian, Québécois, and indeed other currents within the Franco-American literary stream.

In *Menaud, maître draveur*, it is men and women, French blood, that symbolize a French America that knows not how to die. We see a slightly different take on French identity in America in *Trente Arpents* by Ringuet. Philippe Panneton, alias Ringuet, was a noted Canadian diplomat, academic, and physician as well as an author. In his 1938 novel, "la patrie, c'est la terre, et non le sang." Frenchness is inscribed onto North American soil in the rectangular swaths of farmland cut out perpendicularly along the banks of the St. Lawrence River in the North and the Mississippi River in the South, the very arpents described by Ringuet and that embody the first French colonial initiatives in the New World. Ringuet notes in his narrative that the earth could only be generous: "la terre, elle ne fait rien que de grand et large."[49] But it could also be cruel. The lives of men and women are insignificant in the ongoing cycle of life. This ode *à la terre* is reminiscent of French marshal Philippe Pétain, his infamous phrase "la terre, elle, ne ment pas" ("the soil, it does not lie") and a staunch conservatism affirmed by Vichy's National Revolution. Many such *romans de la terre* sing the praises of a traditional peasant life and are organized thematically by season, as presumably would be the travails of the habitants.

In this third classic example, sacred land can generously nourish the soul and physical needs of its people; but man removed from this soil is no longer as unwaveringly French. Race, bloodline, French language, and culture tend to fade on foreign land. This sums up the life experiences of habitant Euchariste Moisan, whose story is recounted in *Trente Arpents*. Moisan embodies the challenges that face French efforts to trace their designs on American soil. "Qui pourtant mieux que lui la connaissait et l'aimait, la vieille terre des Moisan? Qui donc comme lui en savait chaque motte et chaque arbrisseau?" Despite a lifetime of diligence and devoted tilling of the soil, he can expect no return of sympathies: "la terre était immuable et insensible, sans tendresse comme sans compassion."[50] Moisan watches with dismay as his favorite son, Ephrem, leaves the land to seek work in the mills of New England, as did so many French-Canadian settlers. Ironically and tragically, Moisan himself is obliged to leave Quebec and his cherished thirty *arpents* of land because of difficulties on the farm. Far from the affirming presence of the land, he is akin to the proverbial fish out of water in industrial America. The closest Moisan comes to feeling himself occurs when cultivating a small garden while living at his son's home. By contrast, Franco-American texts *Jeanne la fileuse* and *Canuck* assert with greater confidence that in some New England towns, not the countryside, immigrants were able to reconstitute distinctly French cultural communities within tightly knit urban and ethnic enclaves.

Becoming a factory worker and leaving the land is equal to committing the most serious of transgressions, the rejection and indeed the sabotaging of one's French *habitant* status, as not just cultivator but steward of the land. In *Trente arpents* as well as other *romans de la terre*, there is a juxtaposition between the pristine French-Canadian soil and its loyal habitants with the degenerate American city and rootless factory worker. Perilous American working cities, *"villes laborieuses et villes dangereuses,"* threatened to corrupt the faith, values, and language of French-Canadian immigrants.[51] These principles were indelibly tied to traditional notions of identity. "Qui perd sa langue, perd sa foi" (He who loses his language loses his faith), quipped the religious establishment.[52] The sprawling factories of Manchester, Lowell, and Lewiston had greedily devoured many French-Canadian men, women, and children, spitting them out as culturally disinfected Americans. Ringuet comments in the narrative that "les usines étaient insatiables de bras." He compares life in the factory towns of New England to easily tainted yet alluring snow, an American mirage that had entranced many French-Canadian sons (and daughters): "Une neige qui sitôt touché terre n'est bientôt que flaques d'eau boueuse où se délaye une pâte grise. C'est donc cela, les Etats, les Etats dont le mirage a fasciné tant et tant de fils de paysans!"[53] There is at times a quite overt critique of the allure of immigration which some church officials lambasted in apocalyptic terms, as the "hemorrhaging" of mother Quebec. In Louis Hémon's narrative, Mother Chapdelaine is happy that more well-off, established habitants no longer have to leave the French-Canadian heartland to earn their way in the world. This promises to reconnect the descendants of immigrants to their land and identity.

Given the threats on the homeland and the visceral desire to preserve it at all costs, there is no room for migration southward in *Menaud, maître draveur*. A New England priest in *Trente arpents* states earthily that tillers of the soil were the real Canadians, real men in the eyes of God: "que c'était nous, les habitants, qu'étaient les vrais Canayens, les vrais hommes. I'a dit qu'un homme qu'aime la terre, c'est quasiment comme aimer le Bon Dieu qui l'a faite et qu'en prend soin quand les hommes le méritent.[54] Moisan faces a forced and seemingly interminable exile far from familiar French linguistic, cultural, and socioeconomic life. No longer able to speak French, work the land, or identify as a typical habitant, Moisan experiences post-colonial malaise or uncertainty about his identity in the 1930s. He is lost, between worlds.

Moisan had hoped to be able to locate a New French world among exiles like himself in the United States. He had expected to find a more visible and audible French presence, a life that could be lived in French in the mill towns of Anglo America. His son Ephrem explains to him in the local vernacular that such ethnic communities could be found elsewhere: "icitte à White Falls, tous les Canayens i's sont éparpillés. I'a des *places*, comme Lowell, Worcester, ous' qu'i's sont ensemble en *gang* dans leu' p'tit Canada. Mais icitte, c'est pas pareil." The syntax is certainly French-Canadian, but the author's italics point to the fact that far from Quebec, the grip on both French language and cultural identity is loosening. We witness here an early written example of *joual*, of the distinctly Franco-American idiom later popularized by Québécois novelist Michel Tremblay. Ephrem's children are not able to understand their odd, foreign-speaking grandfather. Moisan does connect with the few in White Falls who seem to have preserved their language and culture after crossing the border. He is relieved to find that Franco-Americans, named as such in the text, had not entirely forgotten their French-Canadian heritage.[55]

These are French stories of survival, but also of visceral love of one's country, of a *patrie* created in the New World. Franco-American literature is simultaneously an expressly *trans*national literature, transcending borders, reminding readers of the wide-ranging French "nation" in North America, of French descendants who settled in many parts of Canada and the United States and who preserved French cultures. They carried on in French far beyond the purview of cultural and institutional elites in France. French

Canadians and their descendants participated in frequent physical border crossings until the 1950s (restrictive laws in 1923 did not apply to them), dismantling national frontiers within Franco-America, and perpetuating cultural traditions in ways less commonly observed among other ethnic groups. In several different texts, we find the same French cultural traditions practiced in Quebec, New England, and Louisiana. We know that what remains of the former French empire in North America are obscure and scattered atolls adrift in an Anglo sea, one that is landbound.[56] The French nation of America is indeed in some respects an imagined community inspired in part by the written word, by works such as *Maria Chapdelaine* and Longfellow's emblematic *Evangeline*. As such, Franco-America is both powerfully felt yet tenuous. Not even greater recognition attained by way of a widely encompassing literature of the world in French will change the minority status of the Franco-American experience.

French cultures transplanted in the New World became, as we have seen, associated with a racialized way of constructing French identity outside of France. The French race as it is described in literature and the press has less to do with biology and more with class and culture. The French race of America is also synonymous with Gallic conceptions of the nation. As Ernest Renan wrote at the end of the nineteenth century, one is French because one wants to be, one remembers it, one cultivates memory of it.[57] In North America, one is French by virtue of preciously guarded linguistic, cultural, and religious traditions. This is a key component of transatlantic French identity, but it is important to also remember its non-fixed and evolving makeup. In written works, Franco-Americans articulated a desire to uplift and perhaps even improve the French race in North America, perennially defeated and downtrodden.

In France, race could be invoked by elites to identify those at the top of the social hierarchy. The French outside of France, at the bottom rung of society, were nonetheless all the more French in some regards as a result of their heroic efforts. The authors of Franco-American postcolonial novels depicted a threatened French race persevering outside the Hexagon. It is the intensity of this desire that perhaps led historian Peter Moogk to make the questionable claim that empire in the New World represents the most successful of French colonial initiatives.[58] The desire to proclaim the preservation of French culture on the part of Louis Hémon, author of *Maria Chapdelaine*, echoes a colonial attitude and speaks to the pride of having successfully replanted a cultural seed, despite the outcome on the battlefield. While French cultures in the New World endured, they also experienced a metamorphosis and became something altogether original, strikingly different from their ancestral country and culture. It is the *créolité* of the French peoples and cultures in America, of the French and francophone experience, that renders them distinct. After that very first colonial incursion into the forests primeval of the New World, a prolonged stay, and pervasive contact between European and indigenous peoples, Creole futures emerged.

Since the earliest days of French settlement, New France founder Samuel de Champlain and Marc Lescarbot, her equally adroit historian and scribe, as well as an assortment of others, began documenting French America on the printed page, America written and illustrated in French. Writing represented a distinct French effort to claim its quadrant of the colonial New World. "Ecrire en Nouvelle-France, c'est participer directement à cet effort de colonisation."[59] Some critics would identify an independent and "national" literature written in French later, culminating in the publication of *Maria Chapdelaine*.[60] It was several decades before this that François-Xavier Garneau, responding vehemently to British Lord Durham, stated that a French-Canadian people and history did indeed exist. Literary works offer evidence of purposefully preserved French sentiment and signal the persistence of a Franco nation in contemporary North America. Franco literature can be read as an interpretation of what it means to be French in North America or to be American living in French.

The authors of Franco-American literature have defined it through the lens of identity politics since its earliest manifestation. It is the singleness of this focus that has led some to question whether one can indeed speak of a Franco-American literary tradition per se, with variations, distinctive voices, and styles. Franco-American literature is more a minor, an ethnic, or a regional literature in that sense; few texts have gone on to arouse any particular national attention, not even the French works of Jack Kerouac.

I identify here some of the common themes in Franco cultural communities, the shared French qualities in written expressions of the French diaspora in North America, the narrative threads linking these various parts of Franco-America.

Based on his travels in French Canada, we know that Alexis de Tocqueville found French and American to be mutually exclusive.[61] Francis Parkman, the early American historian of French efforts in the New World, found some of these same distinctions as described in the introductory chapter. Contemporary scholar Joseph Yvon Thériault, in his critique of *américanité*, suggests that Americanness is incompatible with French identity. It is a profoundly English and English-language invention, he concludes, and the *survivance* of the French nation of America is a refusal of américanite. Américanité without Americanization is an illusion and can only lead to the demise of French or francophone cultures.[62] The cited authors convey that there is no cultural compromise possible, yet I believe that literature of the French nation of America, Franco-American literature, asserts that matters are not so clear-cut. Historian Gérard Bouchard writes the following about French culture and its producers in the New World:

> "sauf exception, les élites socio-culturelles y ont été littéralement hantées par le sentiment d'appartenir à une société improvisée, d'une grande pauvreté culturelle par rapport à l'Europe, sans racines et sans traditions, privée de la consistance et du prestige que confère l'ancienneté. *On pourrait même dire qu'elles se sont fait une vocation de combler ce déficit de civilisation par la littérature et par les arts*, dans la construction de la mémoire et le développement de la pensée, pour qu'un jour le Nouveau Monde puisse enfin se prétendre l'égal de l'ancien [my emphasis]."[63]

Bouchard argues that literature and the arts more generally constitute a purposeful reflection of the French national impulse in America. An imperial and culturally superior French shadow continues to haunt Franco-Americans and inspire them to create. Bouchard writes elsewhere that "la société québécoise, elle, s'est longtemps perçue et constituée comme une vieille société, s'installant et se représentant dans des visions et des projets de conservation et de survivance."[64] Franco-Americans in the United States may have had no such French existential struggles or concerns propelling forward their French cultural agendas. If New World French cultures in fact emerge out of a sense of inferiority and yet a desire to equal if not surpass *la mère-patrie*, then they are not mere reflections. They are profoundly Franco-American designs, products of cultural transformation.

CULTURAL FISSURES AND FAULT LINES

The discovery of unpublished works by Jack Kerouac, the most acclaimed American author of French-Canadian descent, raises interesting questions about contemporary Franco-American cultures and Kerouac's own publishing language and literary domain. After a half century spent in the archives of the New York City Public Library, a brief novel written in French by the Beat Generation author was discovered several years ago.[65] *Sur le Chemin* is the most significant piece of prose by Kerouac written first in French. Kerouac wrote it rapidly in Mexico City in 1952, before going on to write the similarly titled but distinct *On the Road* in 1957, which not only attained cult status but transformed the life of the struggling Franco-American author. Kerouac grew up speaking French in his working-class French-Canadian neighborhood of Lowell.[66] During Kerouac's childhood, Massachusetts still had a richer Franco-American cultural life than any other New England state.[67] Yet his counterculture associations and publications have, perhaps definitively, obfuscated his francophone origins. In *Sur le Chemin*, he tells the story of French-Canadian roadsters traveling to New York, writing in the local Lowellois vernacular from his neighborhood, in both dialogue and narration. It is a transcription to the written page of a predominantly oral French form. The subsequently published *On the Road* is not an English translation of *Sur le Chemin*, despite the recurring themes.[68] Kerouac later translated his short novel as *Old Bull in the Bowery*, which remained unpublished as well. The French-Canadian publisher Boréal reached an agreement with the Kerouac estate in 2015 to publish more of Kerouac's early French works.

A broad conception of francophone or world literature in French might well embrace an author such as Kerouac, especially now that he has been discovered in French. His French and English works can help to identify

Franco-America as part of the greater francophone world. Franco author David Plante has suggested that the quintessentially American *On the Road* might be read in actuality as a *Franco*-American narrative.[69] An American classic might thus best be understood when its French and jazz-inspired inflections are read aloud. Kerouac acknowledged his creolized Franco-American status, identifying as "the Iroquois *Canuck* of Breton ancestry."[70] He had always hoped to write (and publish) a great American novel in French (presumably a considerably longer text). He did not realize this aspiration during his lifetime, but several of his works can be considered Franco-American in terms of their subject matter, setting, characters, and language. Portions of dialogue sequences in novels such as *Doctor Sax* (1959) are written in the French idiom of Lowell along with the English narration. *Visions of Gerard* (1963) highlights the haunting French memories of the death of Kerouac's beloved older brother in Lowell. Other mill towns with a large Franco-American presence such as Manchester, New Hampshire, arguably had their own distinct French dialect (see Perreault's *L'Héritage*) and cultures. For one reviewer in the Franco-American press, Kerouac's first book, *The Town and City* (1950), did not refer enough to a postcolonial French presence in New England, although the novel is often identified as a part of Kerouac's Franco-American or Lowell series.[71] The particular reviewer in question clearly wanted more recognition of Franco-American culture and cultural life.

Such works highlight the precariousness of French letters in the francophone world. The French disappearing act has been at work in the United States for at least the last century, as the contours of French as a living language and culture have shrunk. Yet Jack Kerouac provides an example of the important connection between French-language and English-language literatures of the French experience in North America. The Franco-American literature typified by Kerouac is one of evolving French diasporic populations and cultures. The transitional period during the Second World War, when French expression shifted increasingly to English in Franco-American communities, is particularly revealing. The Second World War era represents the most important moment of cultural transition in Franco-American life. Since then, English has become the primary vehicle for Franco-American written cultures, with the occasional forays into French mentioned earlier in the analysis.

This English-language transition, nonetheless, must be qualified. French-Canadian expressions and ideas are still found within many works written primarily in English. The editors of Quebec literature today have similarly had to contend with the English writers in their midst.[72] Much English-language Franco-American writing is highly personal, and the personal leads authors invariably back in one form or another to an "original Frenchness" that is both stated and understood, as seen in Kerouac's writing. In French or English, autobiographical fiction is the genre of choice in Franco-American letters, addressing concerns about cultural, social, economic, and political realities. One of the criticisms *littérature-monde* supporters level is that metropolitan French literature is too infatuated with itself and with literary theory, too disengaged from the world. Without leaving its navel, Franco-American literature depicts an intercultural voyage from Old to New World, from the North of the American continent to the South, from French to English. Franco-American authors demonstrate a capacity to create complex fictive realms in French and English, capturing a sense of cultural moments as they once were and are today, even with stylistic flair.

Contemporary Franco-American writing is peppered with French sayings, thoughts, prayers, songs, and recipes from either an idealized or maligned individual past. It is filled with original characters, voices, and culture. Whether one loved or hated one's French past, it rises back to the surface in prose. In two Franco-American novels, *Forgive Me Father for I Have Sinned* (2005) and *Thy Will Be Done* (2006), Dr. Louise S. Appell recounts the life of a French-Canadian family in Northampton, Massachusetts, during the Depression and Second World War. While family members have largely assimilated, some continue to maintain the traditional French-Canadian ways and those too eager to reject these customs are the subject of ridicule. The third and final novel in the series, *Forever and Ever* (2009), as the others, is self-published, and in the author's note Appell mentioned the Franco-American demand in western Massachusetts for the telling of a familiar story. Appell herself is a local woman of French-Canadian descent, born Louise Fortier, who attended Northampton's Smith

College. She asks her readers to believe that while mostly English words are inscribed on the pages, it is actually French that is being spoken by the characters. This is an interactive and figurative sort of francophone literature. The French that does make its way into the dialogue is sometimes incorrect. Its presence in the text, nonetheless, is a demonstration of French identity preserved within Franco-American cultures.

The publications of newspaper editor and author Jacques Ducharme indicate the cultural transformations that took place nearly eighty years ago as a second world conflict began. In 1939, he published *The Delusson Family*, a fictional account in English of a Franco-American family in Holyoke, Massachusetts. *The Delusson Family* tells the French version of the American Dream, a rags-to-riches tale in industrial America that mirrors the trajectory of his own family. Socioeconomically, culturally, and geographically, the Delusson family had moved up the hill, to the higher, more rarified Anglo air at the heights of Holyoke. Ducharme acknowledged the sharp criticism that his writing in English, a result of this multilayered migration, aroused within the traditional Franco elite. The latter regarded it as a betrayal of *la survivance*, of Ducharme's fathers and forefathers, for whom French cultural identity in Anglo America was paramount.

English is also the means of communication in *The Shadows of the Trees*, a sequential travelogue of the Franco-American experience that Ducharme published four years later. Here the author makes immediate mention of Franco-Americans as an ethnic group, which was never formally articulated in *The Delusson Family*. Backtracking a bit, he claims that it will take time for the descendants of the French and Americans to fuse culturally, despite the fact that French-Canadian immigrants had been self-identifying as Franco-Americans in the United States for almost a half century, since the last nineteenth century. At the very moment that the term emerges in Ducharme's writing, its meaning is shifting. He writes *in English*, "The Franco-Americans, exiles or émigrés as the case may be, have adopted the American way. . . . The final half of the word Franco-American is all that matters, and allegiance is given where it is asked."[73] The pressure to demonstrate one's American patriotism had certainly intensified during the First World War and continued during the second global crisis.

While writing books in English, Ducharme also wrote editorials in French, further demonstrating the fluctuating, hybrid nature of Franco-Americans like himself at the time. In 1940, Ducharme edited the weekly French-language newspaper of Holyoke, Massachusetts, *La Justice*, founded in 1904. He had attained some notoriety within the Franco-American community as the author of *The Delusson Family*, which newspaper directors hoped would mean increased readership of *La Justice*. In his first column as editor, Ducharme wrote, "Notre devise de Canadiens-Français reste toujours le même: 'Langue, Foi, Traditions,' car dans cette trinité se trouve l'essence de notre personnalité, de notre survivance."[74] French language, Catholic faith, and religious and secular traditions, as we have heard, are the instrumental components of Franco-American identity. It is noteworthy that Ducharme addresses the question of cultural traditions and *survivance* in French here while writing elsewhere in English. His explanation is nuanced: "Survivance, ce n'est pas simplement dire notre persistence comme entité ethnique. Survivance, c'est plutôt dire l'existence éternelle de notre caractère. Nous sommes un mélange de France, de Canada et des Etats-Unis." He notes the French strategies of cultural accommodation on the ground, of French tolerance for and integration of other cultures. In this instance, writings from the francophone periphery, in Franco-America, echo a relevant perspective on cultural hybridity.

Ducharme's regular, concise editorials continued to be written in French, but his statement above previews the subtle changes made during his tenure as newspaper editor, which included the launching of a column on Franco-American life in English. His actions underscored the fact that second-generation Franco-Americans were no longer monolingually French like their parents and were rather increasingly Americanized. Holyoke's half-century-old paper, *La Justice*, would continue to circulate weekly in French into the 1950s and monthly until the 1960s, but Ducharme himself had become an Anglophone writer of Franco-America. His real and metaphoric children, of the pivotal third generation, are even more fully Americanized, English speakers (and often cognizant of cultural loss). This does not imply, however, that Franco-Americans today are no longer at least partially "francophone," a cultural and linguistic category that the *littérature-monde* movement rightly problematizes. Clearly no one speaks "francophone," and Francos are not the only marginal or marginally French-speaking "francophone" group of authors. A Franco-American corpus of texts that *is* organically French, but not necessarily always written in the language of Molière, reveals pertinent aspects of francophone cultural identity in North America. Franco-American novelists evoke what remains in the wake of historic French influence in North America.

Franco-American literature in any idiom is far from monolingual and very much intercultural in scope. As I have argued, these works translate an obscure francophone life and culture in America and trace the continental drift of French groups from France to New France and Franco-America. Lost in migration and assimilation, Franco-Americans are periodically omitted from official francophonie documentation, which again has positioned itself ideologically, in opposition to dominant American culture. From this perspective, leaving Franco-Americans out of the picture of transnational French literature is counterproductive. What better strategy than to identify what is francophone at the heart of imperial America?[75]

Making Franco-American matters all the more uncertain is that authors frequently did their best to forget their French heritage. Novelist Rhea Côté Robbins wrote in virtual space (her Facebook wall), "Born French. Went away. Back home."[76] "Someone lost the map of France," she quips in her work of creative nonfiction, *Wednesday's Child* (1997). Like many Franco-Americans of her generation, preserving culture was not on her priority list when she was a young woman in search of herself. Later in life, she began to fear what gets lost in translation culturally when groups adapting to life in a new country abandon a heritage language. Unattractive, working-class feet do not allow Côté Robbins to leave behind her French past entirely for the "pure" English identity and sensibility that she admires. She deems it worthy of admiration, for Englishness seems neither hybrid nor contaminated. She blames her father, who identified inexpensive shoes as the cause of his French foot deformation, but notes that her mother's feet were no beauties either. "A whole history of a people written on these ugly, ugly feet."[77] The author reveals a wry Franco-American sense of humor, making light of sometimes difficult socioeconomic conditions. She writes, tongue-in-cheek, that she was so preoccupied with her feet that she took no notice of Woodstock and the social and cultural upheaval of the 1960s.

The fact that Rhea Côté Robbins's English prose is largely shaped by French is another part of this unconscious cultural remembering. "Perfect, present, future tense. In French. Everything in French. Even if it is in English, it is still in French. A layer of French living laid over by layers of popular culture or popular culture covered by living done in English. Intertwined."[78] French culture erases time and distance, creating a link between past, present, and future. Everything that matters in Côté Robbins's account *is* French, as it came to be defined in New England, the family stories, the heirlooms, the recipes, the shame. Only the language is English, although the author claims it is French influenced. Coming back to French is part of becoming whole again, re-membering, or reconnecting with one's feet in Côté Robbins's case, as well as culture. A cultural awakening explains why some Franco-Americans, in Louisiana and New England, are informally trying to resume their ancestral French language practices.[79] They have reclaimed an identity long denied them.

David Plante, author of the memoir *American Ghosts* (2005) and one of the more esoteric Franco-American intellectuals, spent a good part of his life trying to lose his Frenchness, a cultural identity closely associated with the Catholic Church. French Catholic prayers and hymns are enduring rituals that still punctuate Franco-American life to some degree. Yet in reaction to the perceived intractability of church doctrine, a postcolonial French ethnic identity in North America went into a lengthy hibernation before resurfacing more recently. David Plante and others like him became ghosts, invisible. Losing their Frenchness is an attempt to shed this invisibility, a part of the reason that Plante became a writer, to try to render the invisible visible. For Plante, like Côté Robbins, it is, however, not so easy to forget. The French words from his *Premier livre de lecture* are etched eternally in his memory. In Plante's seventh-grade classroom, the Mère Sainte Flore led recitations of the Canadian national anthem, "Ô Canada, terre de nos aïeux." She told him and others "the truth of the geography of North America," of the French discovery of America.[80]

To us, French meant French Canadian, for we were, in our parish, from France by way of French Canada, but at a time when Canada was called La Nouvelle France. Not one of us would have been able to make an ancestral connection beyond Canada to La Vieille France. Yet we called ourselves French in the way Italians in our school called themselves Italians.[81]

In an attempt to become visible later in life, Plante tries to transform his parochial Canadian Frenchness into a more worldly French Frenchness (i.e., Parisian), through travel and the consumption of great literature.[82]

The bicultural Franco-American base from which David Plante writes is evident in *American Ghosts*. "Though I wrote in English," he notes, "there remained within this language the baptized letters of my French religion, letters that always promised the invisible."[83] As in Côté Robbins's novel, French culture is omnipresent, albeit sometimes sub rosa. The reference to invisibility in Plante's passage reads as an indication of worldly suffering and eternal salvation. It is almost surprising that in his exploration of French invisibility in America, there is no implicit or explicit recognition of African American novelist Ralph Ellison, author of *Invisible Man* (1952). Plante does, however, evoke the *Nègres blancs d'Amérique* (1968) famously asserted by Pierre Vallières. Being French in America to Plante equals being a White Nigger, a failure, a Canuck, incapable of success:

> Why should I feel success in anything, when, as a Canuck, it was forgone that I would not succeed? . . . We were the White Niggers, the Canucks, the people for whom this very term was thought up. We came down from Canada, from the forests of Canada, to the states to do the jobs the blacks wouldn't do. And we did the jobs well; we performed our duties; we never complained, and there was no bitterness in us against injustices. We were invisible.[84]

He acknowledges the great difficulty that he had shaking the sense of being a loser, like the French in the transatlantic battle with England for power in the eighteenth century.

Similarly, Jack Landry, alter ego of author Ernest Hebert in the contemporary novel *Never Back Down* (2012), seems doomed to fail in life, in love, and in baseball because of his hybrid French heritage. He had always associated his dark skin with the French experience in America, namely, the coupling of French explorers with Native American women. At the end of her life, Jack Landry's mother reveals the secret behind their darker complexion: a mixed Irish ancestry.[85] This echoes what studies of white ethnic identity have suggested about groups such as the Irish and Italians who were "colored" differently before becoming "white" in America.[86] Landry and other Francos might very well expire in search of impossible victory, given the inflexibility of the motto "Never back down," a contemporary and more aggressively sporting twist on the traditional Cajun yet also Franco-American *lâche pas la patate*, meaning "Don't give up." Ultimately Landry and Hebert learn to appreciate the dignity of the traditional working-class Franco-American experience.

Today, people of French descent in the United States may know or care little about this heritage or being on the losing side of history. The century-old term "Franco-American" carries some meaning for older generations, but little for many young people. Still the possibility for discovery of what remains of French influence is important, and Franco-American written cultures are thus a valuable resource. The question of language is thorny and likely to remain so. Without an authentic French voice speaking with representative authority, cultures may risk erosion or diminution, although as Côté Robbins illustrates, writing Franco culture through the medium of English constitutes an original contribution. Even the Catholic Church, still one of the community pillars, had to break with language, with French, in order to remain relevant in mid-twentieth-century America. Francos similarly have had to decide whether to follow paths of tradition or modernity in their ethnic lives. To what degree can Frenchness be perpetuated? Choosing to be French may not in fact be an option for all. The degree to which assimilation can be avoided is ambiguous. French cultural dilution has, still, proven to be a protracted process in Franco-America, ongoing for several generations and indeed centuries. There is something still palpably "French" about English and French-speaking Franco-Americans. The forgetting is still not yet complete.

It is in the writing about self primarily, in the autofiction of Franco-American novels, that the French essence is maintained, even in English examples. In a contemporary memoir like Fran Pelletier's *Little Pine to King Spruce* (2003), the author tells family stories through the conduit of English, as they were once told by parents and grandparents in French. His stories include memorable characters like Baptiste Michaud, who speak English in French syntax and whose pronunciation is expressly French as well, with emphasis on the second syllable. "Pull you basTARDS," he yells (lovingly) at his workhorses. "PULL! YOU STOP NOW, I, BAPTISTE MICHAUD, KILL YOU ALL DEAD! Go-go-go-go!"[87] A republished English-language novel like Gérard Robichaud's *Papa Martel* (2003), which examines Franco-American life between the two world wars, retells an old French story of the past to new listeners or readers for whom this history is unknown and inaccessible in the heritage language. Bill Schubart's *Lamoille Stories* (2008) provide a poignant portrayal of a lingering francophone culture expressed through daily American life. More popular or commercially successful novels such as those by Carolyn Chute expand knowledge of Franco-America, although the public airing of Franco dirty laundry represents yet another reiteration of group shame.[88]

French and francophone cultures forge links throughout the Atlantic world that bridge linguistic, geographic, demographic, socioeconomic, and ethnic gaps. The politics of French preservation are responsible in some measure for maintaining ties between contemporary Franco-American literature written in English and the classic French-language *romans de la terre* of early twentieth-century Quebec. Novels such as *Maria Chapdelaine* tell the story of the development of a French-descended race in North America, an ethnic or national identification still present a century later. Subsequent Franco-American novels take up the narrative of migrant French-Canadian factory workers in the United States and evoke the powerful desire of return to Quebec. Physical borders may separate Quebec from New England and French from English speakers for the most part, but culture knows no bounds. Honoré Beaugrand's *Jeanne la fileuse* indicates the important role that train travel played in migratory fluxes and the development of a transnational Franco-American culture:

"C'est au moyen des chemins de fer que l'on est parvenu à abolir en grande partie les préjugés ridicules et les haines séculaires qui existaient entre les races française et anglaise en Amérique."[89] Snow-shoers, members of *Clubs des raquetteurs* who trekked from New England to Quebec in winter, in the tradition of the French-Canadian bush whackers, represent a slower moving but nonetheless border crossing Franco-American culture.[90] They helped meld these two seemingly distinct traditions.

Despite the cultural assimilation that inevitably transformed francophone communities in America, transnational French culture continued to be demonstrated through dance, music, and food. In *Maria Chapdelaine* as well as twenty-first-century Franco-American text *Forgive Me Father for I Have Sinned*, people of French descent congregate to share a meal, a game, a tune, in order to create community. We have seen that these gatherings, *veillées* in French, are a staple of first French-Canadian then Franco-American collective life, an identity-shaping divertissement that perpetuated itself throughout Franco-America after arrival from France (we see specific mention of them, for instance, in *Maria Chapdelaine* and *Canuck*). *Trente Arpents* and *The Shadows of the Trees* indicate the presence of typical French-Canadian dishes and recipes, the commonplace *tourtière* and *soupe aux pois*, prepared by families on both sides of the U.S.-Canadian border. Eating meat pie and pea soup can still label you today as Franco-American in cities like Chicopee, Massachusetts, where French ethnic pockets remain. For the younger generations who are more removed from cultural traditions, calling your grandparents *Mémère* and *Pépère* at family meals may reveal that you are part of the postcolonial francophone world.

In Franco-American literature, one observes how writers defined being French in the contemporary American context, how markedly Franco-American culture developed despite assimilation and the onslaught of the English language. In order to survive in America, the French had to be clever, like the fictive figure of lore "Ti-Jean." Both he and other Franco-Americans maintained the *coureur de bois* audacity, an adventurous French spirit that borrowed extensively from indigenous Native American cultures, and is mentioned in *Maria Chapdelaine* and *The Delusson Family*. In Antonine

8. Original Jack Kerouac tombstone, "Ti Jean." Edson Cemetery, Lowell, Massachu-setts. Courtesy of author.

Maillet's *Pélagie-la-charette*, we find reference to an Acadian "Tit-Jean" and in *Trente Arpents*, a Québécois "Ti-Jean." Ti-Jean, meaning Petit or Little John, is an everyman of French ancestry, capable of impressive exploits despite his diminutive name and stature. In his ever-evolving adventures, "Ti-Jean" typically overcomes socioeconomic disadvantage, defeats superior adversaries, and manages to attain the heights of power through deception and intrigue. Similarly, "Leuk le lièvre" of the Wolof folk tradition, who later metamorphasized into a Creole Br'er Rabbit and American Bugs Bunny, outfoxed adversaries. Franco "Ti-Jean" is no slave to power and often fails to maintain it in fact. Reference to the Franco-American underdog is widespread, a French-Canadian as well as a heroic Caribbean and transatlantic myth that emerges in literature. Storytellers Julien Olivier and Michael Parent have assembled several "Ti-Jean" stories, as told from one Franco-American generation to another, once in French, now in English.[91] They are quite evocative of the French postcolonial paradigm in North America; they transcend the historic complex of the French Canuck or White Nigger. It is convenient that "Ti Jean" is Jack Kerouac's nickname as well as his character name in *Sur le Chemin*. It had been inscribed on his original tombstone in Lowell, Massachusetts, a reminder of his forgotten French origins (fig. 8).

SURVIVANCE

The story of Franco-American life in New England can be told in at least three languages, French, English, and the hybrid form, Franglais. Each is a vehicle for communicating transnational francophone cultures. Even Franco-American writing in English remains true to the *survivance* ideal, of acknowledging and preserving French cultural identity in Anglo-America. It is a postcolonial francophone literature, ever attentive to an evolving French experience in the New World. It evokes a distinct universe that included mostly defunct institutions like French ethnic schools and churches, newspapers, associations, and neighborhoods. While sometimes marginal in terms of art or influence, Franco-American writing is vital to understanding the French history of North America. Franco authors write not only to exist, in myriad forms, but to render the invisible visible, as David Plante asserted. North of the border, in intellectual circles of Quebec, the *américanité* debate will certainly continue to divulge the uniqueness of Frenchness as defined in North America.[92] For some, being an American *à la française* is not a contradiction in terms, despite the "failed" colonial experiment of a French settlement in Quebec. Prolific and original novelist Dany Laferrière, a contributor to the *littérature-monde* movement, is arguably one of the most respected and *American* of contemporary francophone writers. "Je choisis l'Américain" (I choose the American), claimed the author taking an ideological position in French in postcolonial North America.[93] The French Academy immortalized the Haitian writer of *Américanité* in 2015.

Franco-American literature refers often to a more culturally homogeneous French past, yet a transnational Franco present in the United States is still evident. The "francophone" literatures examined in the chapter demonstrate this phenomenon. The 2008 Nobel Prize winner for literature, transcultural author J. M. G. Le Clézio, points to a convergence of

French and francophone, a *littérature-monde en français* in many senses of the word. Le Clézio's worlds transport readers throughout France and its postcolonial appendages, with a predilection for the diverse cultures of the author's native Indian Ocean.[94] Still, French and francophone continue to coexist independently. The 2007 French literary prize selection overall demonstrates a metropolitan cultural life that is still very much vital. William Cloonan rejects the constraints of a zero-sum cultural model, the idea of a poor, unimaginative hexagonal French literature in contrast to a rich francophone literature.[95] Nothing prevents each from thriving, in fact, or failing. French and francophone will likely continue to coexist uncomfortably despite the elucidating efforts of scholars in postcolonial studies.

While Francophone authors have long sought inclusion and recognition, the advocates of a *littérature-monde* dwell on Franco-French distinctions, the reordering of the French world, and the problematic definitions of French, francophone, and la francophonie. They insist that it is French literature, a national literature, which must integrate international, francophone currents of artistic production. Perhaps even the notion of *littérature-monde* must be decolonized. Franco-American literatures and cultures constitute an intriguing narrative within a larger and often volatile French-speaking sphere. They offer not only glimpses of a fading yet influential French past, but also forms of cultural expression and representations of social realities that are important on their own terms irrespective of their linkages to France or Quebec. Franco-American literature, in short, occupies an important place in a truly decentered *littérature-monde*, by granting access to the unusual realities of the North American francophone experience.

CHAPTER 5

Ethnic Identity and the Franco-American Press

Many of the transnational Franco-American novels examined in the last chapter appeared first in regular installments in local newspapers. From the late nineteenth throughout most of the twentieth century, French ethnic hubs in New England maintained a daily, weekly, and monthly press with titles such as *L'Etoile* of Lowell, Massachusetts, *L'Avenir National* of Manchester, New Hampshire, *Le Messager* of Lewiston, Maine, *Le Travailleur* of Worcester, Massachusetts, and *La Justice* of Holyoke, Massachusetts. The newspaper titles evoke the solemn nature of their intent: acknowledgment of Franco-American presence, heritage, and dignity. New England's French-language newspapers did not circulate widely and are little known outside of their geographic zones. They not only remain a pleasant memory for an ever diminishing number of people who read them but are significant for their historical and cultural content. They remind that immigrants of French-Canadian descent in the United States have very much been a part of the French-speaking or francophone world. In this way, they provide an informative road map to Franco-America and its inhabitants in the twentieth century. These texts are similar to the serial novellas that they featured, in their purposeful representation of the needs and desires of the Franco-American community. In some of their editions, they might not seem very different from typical American newspapers printed in industrial centers in 1900, 1920 or 1950, with the exception of their being written in French. This is perhaps the most persuasive indication of their being distinctly Franco-American.

The Franco-American press refers specifically to well over 200 French-language newspapers printed in New England for French-Canadian emigrants from 1850 through almost 2000, although only a few papers managed to survive into the 1970s, 1980s, and 1990s. Ernest B. Guillet suggests as many as 250 French ethnic newspapers existed in New England and 350 throughout the United States.[1] In several notable cases, they were serious affairs produced by trained journalists, respected editors such as founding Franco-American newsman Ferdinand Gagnon and later Wilfrid Beaulieu at *Le Travailleur*, Louis-A. Biron at *L'Etoile*, and Joseph Lussier at *La Justice*.[2] These individuals devoted their professional lives to publishing quality Franco-American newspapers, and they leave a remarkable French written record in New England. Newspaper presses in the United States provided employment to journalists coming out of Quebec's Collèges Classiques. One of them, Honoré Beaugrand, Fall River journalist and founder of the Montreal daily *La Patrie*, has a city Metro stop named after him.

Between 1860 and 1880 alone, more than forty Franco-American papers appeared with more than half circulating in Massachusetts mill towns.[3] While they were primarily intended for the inhabitants of particular urban spaces, some papers did take an active interest in the greater Franco-American experience, as we will see. The French-Canadian diaspora created ethnic hubs throughout North America, and the Franco press sent correspondents to several outposts. The French journalistic tradition persevered in New England and fostered along with it an enduring cultural and ethnic identity. Louisiana had its historic press centered in New Orleans primarily, but shut down production for the most part by the early twentieth century. French traditions in the Gulf South carry on today in other forms, as noted.

Many Franco-American newspapers, such as the weekly *L'Impartial* (1898–1964) of Nashua, New Hampshire, and the monthly *Le Courrier* (1907–81) of Lawrence, Massachusetts, were ostensibly shaped by their affiliation with the Catholic Church. *L'Impartial* was quite partial in fact to French-Canadian national and religious sentiment, devoted as it was "aux intérêts de l'Eglise et de la patrie" (to the interests of the Church and homeland). It claimed, however, at the top of every paper to be "Indépendant en politique." Virtually all of the Franco press regularly reported on church affairs such as the assignment of priests and the organization of parishes, as this was a subject of particular interest to the community. It is quite difficult to disentangle Franco-American identity from its pervasive ties to the Catholic faith and the institution's cultural traditions, as is made clear in the ethnic press. Ferdinand Gagnon believed French-Canadian and Catholic to be synonymous. One noteworthy historical event served as a litmus test for the fidelity of Francos to religious hierarchy. The *Sentinelle* affair in Woonsocket, Rhode Island, pitting ethnic lay demands against church authority became a politically and emotionally charged affair within the Franco-American community, in part due to the role of an increasingly influential press.[4] From inception, the Franco-American press was very much a local or community-based set of newspapers rather than one of general information. While world news certainly made its way into Franco-America from time to time, particularly during events that broadly affected all ethnic communities in the United States, at other times one could read papers and learn very little about life in mainstream America outside of French enclaves. *Le Travailleur* of Worcester was particularly focused on cultural affairs within the Franco-American community.

The Franco-American press began in earnest as concentrated populations of French Canadians settled in mill towns. Ludger Duvernay founded the first Franco newspaper, *Le Patriote canadien*, for the French-speaking population in Burlington, Vermont, in 1839, for those who had in fact taken up arms to establish independence in Canada.[5] Many more French ethnic newspapers began to circulate in developing Franco communities in New England in the following decades. *Le Jean-Baptiste*, printed in Northampton, Massachusetts, in 1875, represents one such early

Franco-American newspaper. This western Massachusetts town was home to several French-language newspapers with titles such as *Le Citoyen*, *Le Ralliement*, and *Le Rateau*.[6] The first congress of French-Canadian journalists of New England took place in 1875 in Northampton.[7] Although the city did not have the heavy industry of other French ethnic centers, it maintained a smaller yet cultured Franco population, with proximity to larger French ethnic enclaves in the Holyoke, Chicopee, and Springfield areas. Towns such as Northampton or Waterville, Maine, to the north put out dozens of fledging newspapers, most of which were short-lived, many entitled *Le Franco-Américain*.[8] What French newspapers did was attempt to call attention to the so-called Franco-American fact, and the persistence of French traditions in North America at the turn of the twentieth century. Maximilienne Tétrault contended that establishing an independent ethnic press was a collective priority and developed before churches, parishes and schools.[9]

In its first issue on September 16, 1886, *L'Etoile* informed its readers, "Qu'est-ce qu'un Canadien Français" (What is a French Canadian). The Lowell, Massachusetts, newspaper listed the French qualities held dear among emigrants: life in Canada, French ancestry, traditions, faith, language, respect of authority, humility, gratitude, and patriotism. A patriotic French Canadian stopped working and adopted festive attire to celebrate St. John the Baptist Day, the publication affirmed. The Franco press offered the best example of French-Canadian cultural *survivance* in the United States. In his comparative study of nationalism, Benedict Anderson noted the role that newspapers played in the Americas in fostering "an imagined community among a specific assemblage of fellow-readers." Such "Creole" publications transmitted, in addition to news of the metropole (Canada in this instance), the hybrid particularities of the New World in which settlers lived.[10] While the French press as a whole began to experience a decline by the early to mid-twentieth century, the francophone press of New England carried on with very often limited resources. From revolutionary Paris to Franco-American ethnic enclaves in early industrial America, the press has long been connected to the fabric of urban life, a vital part of artistic, ethnic, and democratic expression. The United Nations World

Intellectual Properties Organization prediction of the disappearance of physical newspapers by 2040 may prove to be correct, if the relationship between the city, its cultural, social, and political vibrancy, and the printed page is not reaffirmed. Since 2008, a Newseum located in Washington harbors collections of defunct publications.[11] Smaller houses of cultural artifacts in New England maintain copies of the region's historic French-language publications.

Lowell's *L'Etoile* was the oldest Franco daily newspaper, and it also had the longest run of daily printing, from 1893 to 1943.[12] Lowell's large population of professional Franco-Americans gave the city both a pool of potential editors from which to choose as well as an educated reading public. It is reasonable to assume that the influence and circulation of *L'Etoile* was one of the most elevated as a result, although we do not know a great deal about circulation levels for most Franco-American newspapers, particularly during the early period. In the 1930s, approximately nine to ten thousand copies of *Le Messager* circulated daily in Lewiston's French ethnic community.[13] A half-century later in the 1980s, the bilingual, bimonthly newsletter called the *FAROG Forum* (now known as *Le FORUM*) reached a large number of people throughout the New England area. Published out of the University of Maine's Centre Franco-Américain from 1972 until 1985, it notably supported a sovereign French nation in Quebec.[14] The publication had always been something of a different entity, offering its readers a selection of bilingual articles, historical accounts, and poetry from the Franco-American experience, rather than strictly journalistic interpretations. My focus here will be on some of the traditional and lesser-known Franco media.

The first Franco-American newspaper of both substance and influence was the original edition of *Le Travailleur* of Worcester, Massachusetts, directed by journalist, cultural activist, and lawyer Ferdinand Gagnon from 1874 to 1888. A charismatic young man, Gagnon set the standard for the emerging French ethnic press. The founding of Worcester's weekly and its continuation, in a new and independent edition by editor-in-chief Wilfrid Beaulieu in 1931, garnered it a considerable amount of prestige in the Franco-American community. It was the Franco-American source of information for the social and cultural elite. Lewiston, Lowell, Fall River, Woonsocket, and Manchester were the largest, most important Franco-American centers, along with Worcester, and the papers printed in these cities competed for influence. For a half-century, several of these Franco-American centers maintained a lively daily press in French.

Manchester's traditional *L'Avenir National* began circulation in 1895 and had almost as long a daily run as *L'Etoile*, published every day but Sunday from 1900 to 1949. The Manchester paper was first published as *Le National* for a short time in the late 1890s, and as with other newspapers, it was not always clear to which "nation" it was devoted. What would the future (*l'Avenir*) hold for *Canadiens Français* or immigrant populations becoming progressively Franco-American? Timing would be everything for evolving groups. As the demand for French-language newspapers fell after the Second World War, with more and more Franco-Americans growing up in English, the Franco press was pushed to more irregular weekly and monthly printing. Lewiston's daily *Le Messager* may have been the most influential paper during the first half of the twentieth century. It could not match the extended daily circulation of other newspapers, but it is the only regularly printed paper appearing into the 1960s. Editors published it at least three times a week for some sixty years (1906–66). It had the most current daily edition of the Franco press, for thirty years from the 1930s through the mid-1960s. It was often an outspoken mouthpiece for the Spindle City's burgeoning francophone Catholic population in the twentieth century.

La Justice of Holyoke, Massachusetts, was another respected weekly Franco-American newspaper with an influential constituency and a similar lifespan, stretching from the early to mid-twentieth century (1904–64). It was the predominant printed edition for the industrial centers of western Massachusetts, read by Franco-Americans of the Northampton, Easthampton, Holyoke, Chicopee, and Springfield area. Holyoke reportedly produced the largest number of French-language papers of any city in New England in the early twentieth century.[15] Editorials in *La Justice* offer a telling reflection of the cultural transition between generations in the Franco-American community around the Second World War, as noted in the previous chapter. Lawrence, Massachusetts's *Le Courrier* continued publication monthly into the early 1980s, along with the final effort to continue the Franco-American journalistic tradition, in Lowell, Massachusetts, the twenty-year experiment of *Le Journal de Lowell* (1975–95). Virtually all Franco-American newspapers were beset with problems, the high cost of printing and the generally small numbers of papers distributed being the most troubling. These challenges ultimately contributed to their disappearance.

The present chapter will focus attention first on the inward or ethnic reflections of this press during the period between the First and Second World Wars when Franco-American newspapers as a whole had reached an apex of circulation and influence. At this time, all of the Franco ethnic centers maintained endogamous enclaves and French-speaking populations that supported daily editions. While looking inward and actively constructing a contemporary sense of Franco-American identity in the twentieth century, Franco-American newspapers were also increasingly gazing beyond the geographic confines of their specific *petits Canadas*. They looked to other examples from the French diaspora of lives lived in French throughout the United States and Canada. They sought recognition and support from the greater francophone population. Beaulieu at *Le Travailleur* collaborated with French and Belgian journalists. Nowhere else, again, is the case for North-American francophonie outside of Canada made more strongly than in the pervasive French ethnic journalistic tradition in New England between 1900 and 1950. It remained an explicitly, almost exclusively French-language press, highlighting the development of cultural distinction and strength.

The written press in Montreal and Quebec City reported widely on the four hundredth anniversary of French presence in America in 2008. One hundred years earlier, several Franco-American newspapers in the United States reminded francophone readers that it had been three centuries since the French explorer Samuel de Champlain had arrived and established a permanent settlement. *L'Avenir National* paid homage to the founder of *la Nouvelle-France* with a series of articles on the establishment of a French colonial outpost in Quebec.[16] *L'Etoile* and *Le Messager* also noted the historical significance of Champlain's founding of a community in Quebec City in 1608.[17] *L'Etoile* paid particular attention to the history of Quebec and encouraged physical contact between Lowell's Franco population and "la belle province." Ads for train travel to Quebec appeared regularly in the Franco press. Frenchness on the North American continent would be perpetuated long into the twentieth century by Franco border crossers, transcribed by the Franco-American press. It would be tested by events such as the world wars, which served to render borders more formidable and accelerate the process of assimilation of many ethnic groups in the United States.

Many individual newspapers were members of the Alliance des Journaux Franco-Américains de la Nouvelle-Angleterre and of the New England Foreign Language Newspaper Association. Journalists from the Franco-American press convened in places like Northampton, Massachusetts, to discuss the issues that were central to their papers. The mission of the Foreign Language Newspaper Association was "to help preserve the ideals and traditions of our country, the United States of America, to revere its laws and inspire others to respect and obey them, and in all ways to aid in making this country greater and better."[18] Freedom of expression was particularly relevant to editors of the Franco-American press. During wartime, such a policy statement made clear the belief that the Franco press was not a threatening, foreign source of information, but rather patriotically American. The cited public statement stands out all the more because of its English-language composition in the midst of a French edition. This was a rare phenomenon indeed.

All Franco-American newspapers had recurring columns entitled "les Centres" or "Nouvelles locales," calling attention to French-Canadian ethnic hubs in New England towns. They recount news of births, deaths, vacations, marriages, both the banal and the extraordinary, in the old neighborhoods. They most certainly helped to project the commonality of Franco-American experiences as well as to provide an outlet for news of specific events. The Franco-American newspaper almost always invariably sent readers back to Canada, the country of the ethnic group's ancestors. The regular "Nouvelles du Canada" column occupied an important place in the hierarchy of information regularly articulated. Subscriptions could be obtained on either side of the border to enable those with family members in American mill towns or "back home" in Quebec to gather cherished community news. Through shared reading practices and traveling cultures, individuals participated in the building of Franco-America.[19]

This focus was of importance to the significant female readership of the French-language newspaper. Franco-American women homemakers often first received it, and indeed anticipated its arrival, living somewhat isolated lives geographically and culturally. In many ways, women depended on the French press for news that stretched the confines of their existence. So says former newspaper editor Jacques Ducharme in his work of nonfiction, *The Shadows of the Trees*. At the beginning of the Second World War, Ducharme edited the weekly *Justice* of Holyoke and so spoke from a privileged position. He stressed the female reading practices evidenced by the family matriarch, often a monolingual French speaker.[20] Franco women found a veritable almanac on ethnic daily life in the press with information on where community members could purchase (in French) cough medicine, ointments, and fuel for heating or join mutual aid societies. Columns dispensed advice of all sorts to their Franco-American readers including their duty as members of the French race of America to purchase items from members of their own ethnic community.

As women in the home tended to assimilate less quickly and remained French-dominant linguistically longer than men who worked, and who sometimes needed English for employment, they represented an important clientele for the Franco press.[21] The Franco-American woman typically began her day with glances at the news from Canada in the columns "Nouvelles locales," "Nouvelles du Canada," or "Nouvelles des Centres" in *L'Avenir National*, for instance. They are the representative columns first consumed by readers in search of information. The Franco-American woman might also linger on the daily segment of the novella of the moment or "Pages féminines" of Lewiston's *Le Messager*. She read the regular literary *feuilleton* (women's section) before moving on to the obituaries.[22] The newspaper was a familiar object, Jacques Ducharme asserted, typically found in the kitchen or living room in Franco-American homes. In this sense, the Franco paper was an omnipresent cultural object conveying the accessibility to ethnic life beyond its physical columns.

The presentation of fictional stories in the press, divided into manageable parts for readers such as the Feuilleton de *L'Avenir National*, does indeed seem to indicate that women were a targeted audience. Gendered discussions on subjects such as love were frequent topics in the columns of the Franco press. In July 1918, patrons could read "Le Baiser au clair de la lune" (The moonlit kiss) in *L'Avenir National*. At the beginning of the newspaper's life, when it was still called *Le National*, editors selected the feuilleton presumably to satisfy loyal female readers.[23] In other columns ostensibly devoted to women, such as "Pour vous Madame" in *L'Avenir National*, subjects such as health and hygiene, children, religion, and language were broached, all topics that women could raise in the home. Holyoke's weekly feuilleton was intended for women, if the titles are any indication, and every Thursday, Franco-American readers (including many women) could expect to find a similar array of subjects in *Le Travailleur*. At *L'Etoile*, long-running fictional series for women appeared frequently. Most articles assumed that women were homemakers, although articles and novellas sometimes discussed the freedoms that women as new wage earners experienced.[24]

So Jacques Ducharme's claim about a strongly female readership of the Franco-American press appears to be well founded. Children had their designated part of the Franco paper as well, with regular interventions and stories such as "Conte du soir" and "Pour Lire aux Petits."[25] Editors clearly targeted the Franco-American family as a whole. They intended the paper to be of service to all within the traditional family unit.

LE TRAVAILLEUR AND FRANCO-AMERICAN ADVOCACY

Le Travailleur is as influential and as emblematic a newspaper as any among the Franco-American publications. Its beginnings underline the cultural objectives of an ethnic press and an active community-oriented cultural project. Both versions of the paper strongly and persistently affirmed Franco-American cultural identity, led by enterprising editors Ferdinand Gagnon and Wilfrid Beaulieu. I will focus on the twentieth-century publication that

Beaulieu produced. *Le Travailleur* explored with its readers not only the internal dimensions of the French-Canadian "race" but also the diaspora of French peoples throughout North America. The French language bound many far-flung populations of French descent, as articles in the newspaper attested ("La langue française dans le monde" was a regular column). The sympathies of Franco-American editors and perhaps even readers were clarified in "Grandeurs et misères coloniales," a group of articles supportive of even less than exemplary colonial efforts on the part of France. *Le Travailleur* attempted to explain the loss of empire in the 1932 series.[26]

Beginning with the very first issue of the new paper in fall 1931, Beaulieu asserted that *Le Travailleur* would be in the trenches for Franco-American people and their issues of concern. When the resurrected paper came to print, homage was first paid to Franco-American press founder Ferdinand Gagnon. "On vénère sa mémoire," stated a commemorative piece.[27] In Beaulieu's opening editorial column, "Notre premier numéro," he laid out a strategy for Franco-American cultural efforts. "*Le Travailleur* est un journal militant," Beaulieu insisted. "Militant veut dire pour nous: tout équipé, prêt au combat et à la défense de nos droits, sans pour cela hurler sans cesse le cri de guerre."[28] Its militancy and fervor would not spill over into messy squabbles. The paper was "un journal à idée," the editor continued. *Le Travailleur* would interrogate ideas relevant to the community and forcefully advocate for Franco-Americans. Beaulieu openly discussed some of the difficulties experienced by a small ethnic press. The newspaper first appeared in print as promised on September 10, 1931, but in a shorter version than anticipated. Beaulieu announced more pages of French text to Worcester's French readers, but they did not arrive until the following year. Launching a newspaper during the Depression era was clearly no easy affair.

Self-sufficiency was a component of the overall mission of the newspaper to promote Franco-American cultural life. *Le Travailleur* encouraged the building of an ethnic economy by circulating promotional ads for Franco-American businesses and encouraging people to keep their dollars (or *piastres* in the colloquial French-Canadian patios) in Worcester's Little Canada. Beaulieu found there to be sufficient advertisements for local businesses in the first edition of the newspaper, and ads of course helped to offset the cost of printing. First issue headlines claimed, "Nos hommes d'affaires sollicitent votre clientèle."[29] These businessmen were perhaps particularly interested in retaining the Franco-American women who managed households and tended to be the most steady consumers. The idea to keep money in Franco-America and to develop Franco-American commerce would be repeated throughout the first few editions of *Le Travailleur*. Patrons could find furniture, clothes, jewels, eye care, and funeral services within the Franco-American community, as advertised in the paper. There was no need to spend elsewhere when shoppers could purchase their desired items in French.

The word and self-identifying label *Franco-American* echoes throughout this first edition of the newspaper. An article entitled "Franco-Américanisme et Catholicisme" explained the close relationship between religious faith and identity. Catholicism is cited as the end-all in the article while being Franco-American is the means.[30] French language was a sometimes disputed but important link in Franco identity formation. Franco-American children in factory towns throughout New England received religious instruction in French in the parochial schools organized by local churches. One-third of all the parochial schools that existed in New England mill towns in the early twentieth century were French-Canadian.[31] Articles in the second issue of *Le Travailleur* took on the role of education in the formation of Franco-Americans, a subject that reflected the ethos of the ethnic press more generally. "A qui nos Ecoles? A nous!" asserted the newspaper.[32] In his article, Dollard, a pseudonym used by Beaulieu, reiterated the fine line that existed between faith and Franco-American identity, but noted that French instruction was essential. It was not enough that young people receive religious instruction. The author claimed that Francos had the right to request that bilingualism be adopted, that "nos enfants soient formés en bons Francos-Américains sachant le français aussi bien que l'anglais." This demand for French-language instruction and fluency, sometimes at odds with the dictates coming from the Catholic Church, described the battleline of the previously mentioned *Sentinelle* affair in Woonsocket in the 1920s. *Le Travailleur* straddled the fence, but ultimately made its position known that language was as important an element as faith to Franco-American identity. This was a bold and independent cultural affirmation. The newspaper articulated the importance of French education for a largely unlettered group. Many if not all Franco-American newspapers reported on the extent to which French culture was maintained and how immigrants from the north transformed it. In the late 1930s, Manchester, New Hampshire's Franco-American daily newspaper, *L'Avenir National*, published a series entitled "Action de la Race Française aux Etats-Unis," the same French race that had hugged the American continent for four hundred years, as depicted in literary works. Both journalists and novelists served as effective narrators of a francophone and Franco-American nation that had outlived the demise of French empire on the North American continent.

French language was vital to maintaining the distinctiveness and the cultural traditions of the race, but its usage was also controversial. Editors placed themselves in the slightly uncomfortable position of guardians of the language. Columns such as *L'Avenir National*'s "Nos fautes contre la langue française" in the late 1930s provided regular information on correct French usage. The Franco cultural elite were in constant pursuit of the amelioration of the "race," notably by way of language. The column set out to present examples of French language from *A* to *Z*.[33] Journalists both prided Franco-Americans on their French language usage, but their articles also sometimes derided the community for lapses. An article appearing in *L'Avenir National* asked readers why conserve the French language, "Pourquoi conserver la langue française."[34] Editors and columnists reminded them that their linguistic heritage was a gift, an advantage, although one not always seen as such if measured by the numbers of children who received it from parents. The low social value of French culture as defined in North America had much to do with this. The defensive nature of some regular columns like the "Parlons bien" section of Holyoke's *La Justice* echoes this New World French inferiority complex, far from the metropolitan center. What is interesting is the precocious nature of efforts to monitor correct French-language usage in the *petits Canadas* of Franco-America, well before language consciousness emerged in Quebec during the 1960s.

This sensitivity to language, particularly to the usage of dialect among Québécois, later entered debates that fed the Quiet Revolution.[35]

Some journalists came to the defense of Franco-American French speakers whose language received criticism from those who themselves showed no particular mastery of the language.[36] In a series entitled "Le patois canadien-français," *Le Travailleur* defended Franco-American linguistic traditions.[37] It was in fact not a patois, the article stated. Columns sometimes exhorted people to remain French, to not forget their cultural heritage. They should not depend upon their children for English to French translation, claimed an article from *La Justice*.[38] These interventions echo the predicament of Frenchness and French cultural identity in the contemporary twentieth-first-century United States of America. Franco-Americans struggled to identify as a French heritage group at a time when they were assimilating culturally at a greater pace and when the American nation was responding collectively to international crises. The editorial board at *La Justice* brought publication to a close because its second-generation leader did not feel sufficiently francophone to continue to publish a French-language edition in the 1960s.[39] Writing in French, an exercise central to the expression of the Franco-American imagination, was taken seriously by journalists in ethnic enclaves.

What did it mean to be both French and American? An article in *La Justice* located Franco-American identity in the hearts and minds of French-Canadian descendants:

> Nous nous adressons à des Franco-Américains, c'est-à-dire à tous nos compatriotes de descendance canadienne française, à tous ceux qui ont encore dans leurs veines du sang de leurs aïeux, dans leurs cerveaux une tournure d'esprit particulière à leur race d'origine, dans leur Coeur le sentiment de fierté de faire partie de cette phalange de bon Américains que l'on appelle des Francos.[40]

This kind of traditional rallying cry around French blood and family did not prevent Francos from asserting simultaneously an American identity. This is detailed quite assiduously in the Franco-American press. Papers such as *Le Travailleur* suggest that for many, a hybrid French and American cultural identity was possible. As the economy improved in Quebec, fewer French Canadians migrated to the United States in the early twentieth century. As the influx decreased, the American side of Francos gained strength and French language practices slowed. A declaration in *Le Travailleur*, "La langue et la race," further described the linguistic contours of Franco-American identity: "La langue tient étroitement à la race. Elle en est l'expression la plus nette, la manifestation la plus haute."[41] As language was key to Franco-American notions of self, ethnic identity would become more problematic as populations became more dominant English speakers.

Throughout its history, editors and readers of the Franco-American press returned time and again to the question of a French "race" in America, a strongly felt sense of ethnic or cultural identity. Education could certainly uplift the Franco community, journalists claimed. An article on post-secondary instruction at Assumption College, by an author known as Sainte Thérèse, called on the Franco community to send their young adult children to the Worcester institution created at the turn of the twentieth century. Or would they become an inferior race incapable of producing an intellectual elite? "La race Franco-américaine serait-elle une race inférieure, incapable de posséder une élite intellectuelle?" Sainte Thérèse asked.[42] If Franco-American leaders were to be fully educated intellectually, morally, and linguistically, Assumption College was to play an important role, asserted the Franco press. *Le Travailleur* advertised classes at Assumption College as bilingual, offering both French and English languages to Franco-Americans who would enter the professional classes. While the Worcester paper was at the forefront of the cultural battle to assert a Franco-American reality, many of the other French newspapers engaged as well, if less explicitly. As militant Franco-American elites, the team led by Wilfrid Beaulieu at *Le Travailleur* served as a model in the shaping of a contemporary ethnic identity. The weekly newspaper was distinct in its openly subjective and proactive Franco viewpoint. "VIVE NOTRE RACE!" exclaimed a front-page headline in *Le Travailleur* in 1932.[43] This viewpoint was reportedly observed by the paper's 50,000 weekly readers, the largest circulation for a Franco-American paper, even if somewhat exaggerated.[44]

It is the faith and moral fiber of the Franco-American community that kept its members American (and not so French in this instance), holding at bay worrisome political philosophies such as communism. In a 1932 article entitled, "Les Etats-Unis Désunis," a *Le Travailleur* correspondent described the racial, religious, linguistic, and political diversity of the American nation as a potential point of weakness.[45] The author returned to an American motto, E pluribus unum (Out of many, one), which was not entirely true in his estimation. The balancing act between French and American sensibilities was not always an easy or natural process due to social, political, and national pressures. War would pit French against American in some regards, forcing people to choose one over the other. Franco-American for others still meant neither French nor American, but a distinct amalgamation of the two. Despite the combative French stance of the paper, the American sensibility located increasingly within individuals appeared in the columns of *Le Travailleur* as it did in other newspapers. It is this American identity that has tended to be underemphasized in scholarship focused on *la survivance française*. While French cultural traditions were expressly maintained in the press, Franco newspapers could not help but record the transformation of a people who had begun to honor annual American rites of passage. As early as the turn of the century, when the Franco-American press was first asserting itself and proclaiming the existence of Franco-Americans, the Americanness articulated regularly during holidays was rapidly transforming French Canadians who had traveled to industrial America in search of work in the nineteenth century.

The celebration of Christmas should not be underestimated as an affirming rite of Franco-American (French and American in other words) traditions expressed in the home, in church, and in retail shopping. For the Franco-American press, Christmas was a time to acknowledge the importance of family ties and friends.[46] *Le Travailleur* articulated the centrality of the holiday in the construction of Franco-American religious and cultural identity. "Les traditions, mais c'est toute la manifestation de l'état d'âme de la race dans sa vie intime."[47] Franco-American Christmas holidays and their depiction in local newspapers helped to define the hybrid French ethnic and religious community on an annual basis. For several weeks during the Christmas season, individual, association, and business readers of the Franco-American newspaper took the opportunity to extend their holiday wishes, in French, to the community. Religious holidays and rites were highly connected to ethnic identity. In December 1931, for example, Franco businesses offered their "Souhaits de Noël." Many pages of the paper were devoted to these holiday wishes, which both announced the existence of Franco-America and advertised services available to its inhabitants. Non-Franco merchants offered their holiday greetings to potential clients in French in an effort to gain a corner of the Franco market. Well wishes continued into the New Year, reminding readers of personal, commercial, and ethnic ties. At the top of each newspaper, a quote from the Vatican and various popes offered sacred and seasonal food for thought to readers. Many Franco newspapers struggled to tow the religious line while also promoting more modern cultural conceptions.

From the days of his youth, author and editor Jacques Ducharme remembered when the St. John the Baptist Day festival, a cultural and religious celebration resembling the contemporary St. Patrick's Day parade, with floats, community banners, music, and crowded streets, lasted two hours in downtown Holyoke.[48] The ethnic parade has emerged as an expression of American pluralism, very often articulated by minority groups within the mainstream.[49] French historian Mona Ozouf has thoroughly examined the symbolic representation of parades in the French context, which serve as platforms for the expression of cultural identity. Ducharme's local newspaper, *La Justice,* echoed the festivity of the event just before the First World War. The newspaper headlines on June 25, 1914, announced the public expression of Franco-American ethnic identity in Springfield on St. John the Baptist Day when guests could choose from an assortment of cultural activities: "Fêtes de Springfield—Un Triomphe Franco-Américain—Affirmation d'une race forte et vivante—Parades. Messes. Concert. Banquet. Discours." This was a community-nurturing event, a modern ethnic pride parade *avant la lettre*. It provided Francos the occasion to publicly affirm their presence and culture alongside early immigrant arrivals like the Irish. Holyoke's English-language newspaper also acknowledged the importance of the French parade.

What became the national or provincial holiday in Quebec was celebrated by Franco-Americans with considerable fanfare throughout the
mill towns of New England. Franco editors made an annual and extended
subject of commentary how St. John the Baptist Day proceeded throughout
the region. The morning to evening schedule of events always appeared
in newspapers like Lewiston's *Le Messager*. In June 1919, Saint John the
Baptist Day celebrations in Holyoke included the honoring of Franco-
Americans who had served in the First World War. A long list of names
appeared in *La Justice*. A few years later in the spring of 1922, despite the
lingering gloom of an extended labor strike in Manchester, *L'Avenir National*
reported that the religious holiday provided a time to reflect on French
civilization in North America. The article insisted on preserving ethnic
and linguistic distinctions, all the while remaining American. During the
1926 St. John the Baptist Day celebrations in Lewiston, four thousand
children marched in the annual parade.[50] Lewiston's Francos were careful to
emphasize their French and American identity. French cultural preservation
subsisted carefully and intentionally along with English. *L'Avenir National*
lamented the fact that traditions were disappearing too rapidly, while also
proudly insisting that Francos were patriotic Americans. Historian Mark
P. Richard has argued that Franco-Americans of Lewiston, Maine, were
loyal but French.[51] Editors printed a special issue of *L'Avenir National* for
the ethnic celebration in Manchester, in addition to the daily edition in
1939. In 1940, *La Justice* noted that St. John the Baptist, patron saint of
all French Canadians, was celebrated in more than seventy New England
industrial centers.[52] Following the war, the Franco press indicates that
people of French descent could indeed "assimilate" or adopt American
culture while retaining at least some French traditions as well. This is still
the essence of Franco-American identity today.

NATIONS, NATIONALISM, AND THE PROBLEM OF VICHY FRANCE

While local newspapers strategically encouraged Franco-Americans to
think of themselves as both French and American in the early twentieth
century, the papers were forced to assure worried governmental agencies
about their Americanness during the period's global conflicts. On the

9. *L'Avenir National*, 3 July 1914, Manchester, New Hampshire.

Fourth of July in 1914, French and American converged as the nation's holiday was celebrated not long before France and the United States would become allies. Papers serving French-Canadian immigrants like *L'Avenir National* refuted their foreignness. A July 1914 headline explained why they celebrated the Stars and Stripes well before the outbreak of war: "Pourquoi nous célébrons—Liberté et le drapeau étoilé à jamais!"[53] Was this an affirmation of the immigrant roots of Francos, who had not come to America as others by way of Ellis Island and the Statue of Liberty? They came as Americans well established on the continent for hundreds of years. In the accompanying photo, with the Statue of Liberty and a large American flag as backdrop, Franco-Americans illustrated an ongoing French-American relationship.

During the First World War, the Franco-American presses responded with affirmations of simultaneous French cultural and American national identity. Even earlier, *Le Messager* encouraged Francos to naturalize and shield their ethnic communities from scrutiny. By this time says Mark

Richard, "Lewiston's Franco-Americans opted . . . to fight the war under the U.S. flag."[54] As mentioned, the interwar period was likely the zenith for Franco-American communities and their newspapers. *Le Travailleur* noted in 1931 that mutual aid societies had flourished in French ethnic enclaves and played an important role in the preservation of ethnic and cultural values.[55] The Little Canadas of New England towns had reached their greatest cultural influence by this time. The Depression marked the end of the southward migration of French Canadians, and so ethnic enclaves ceased to renew themselves with new people and cultural life.

Later *L'Avenir National* would manifest its support of France in the war effort.[56] At the end of the war, around the American national holiday again, the paper emphasized the American half of Franco-American culture to its readers. Patriotic American song lyrics from the "Battle Hymn of the Republic," "The Star-Spangled Banner," and "America" took center stage.[57] The paper even translated "La Marseillaise" into English to render French revolutionary heritage more accessible to Yankees. This is evocative given the distance in time and space from France. "Victoire!" exclaimed Manchester's daily to French-speaking residents, along with metropolitan French papers, signaling the desired outcome on both sides of the ocean.[58]

On the eve of war, in early July 1939, *L'Avenir National* translated the U.S. Declaration of Independence into French for its readers, making American colonial history more pertinent to French diasporic groups.[59] "Célébrons notre fête nationale," claimed the paper on July 4, but in actuality making reference to not one but two nations. Truly a binational people, the possessive *notre* (our) changed meaning periodically depending on the date and national holiday. The Statue of Liberty, a French gift to a young American nation and symbolic light to the world, would soon be thrown into darkness by Adolf Hitler. In an October 1931 piece, certainly tempered by the First World War experience but well before the second, *Le Travailleur* took on the question of hyphenated Americanness and the myth of being 100 percent American. "Qui est le plus 'américain?'" the author somewhat ironically asked. "Le descendant de l'Anglais, qui a combattu pour l'Angleterre contre les Colonies Américaines, ou le descendant du Français qui s'est battu pour ces dernières?"[60] Is the English descendent more "American" in fact than the French? Nativists questioned the foreignness of all immigrants.

From its inception, *Le Travailleur* committed itself to examining the contours of *la patrie* or homeland for Franco-Americans. When editors identified la patrie, they were generally referring to Canada and more specifically to Quebec. They continually stated to Franco-American readers that they should be proud of their ancestors, heritage, and language, despite any understood or stated shortcomings.[61] They should remain French, or *rester Français*, as the Franco press claimed, in their particularly American way of doing so. As French diasporic populations in the New World, this required some effort, but the French spirit lived on even in American citizens: "La Patrie vit encore même si on est Américain."[62] *Le Travailleur*'s "Patriotisme à l'école" suggests how schools helped to cultivate or preserve a sense of national or cultural identity particularly through the teaching of French.[63]

To what nation were Franco-Americans most devoted, when, and why? Such questions are again difficult to answer and certainly varied by individual, place, and time. Between June 24 (St. John the Baptist Day), July 4 (American Independence Day), and July 14 (Bastille Day in France), Franco-Americans celebrated their connection to their ancestral homeland France, to the Canadian birthplace of their families, but also to their adopted American nation. Québécois nationalism had not yet come on to the radar in the early part of the twentieth century, but Franco-Americans were nonetheless already a transnational people and population attuned to events both north and south of the border. Franco-American ties to France were more distant than the connection to Quebec, stated Worcester's weekly *Travailleur*. France took on the role of grandmother, "elle est la grand-mère," while the province of Quebec was maternal, "elle est la mère."[64] France was perhaps more powerfully compelling for some editors and reading communities than others in Franco-America, but not any "France." Historian François Weil asserts that Franco-Americans maintained strong ties to a traditional notion of France.[65]

For editor Joseph Lussier of Holyoke's *La Justice*, "La France éternelle" was primordial. "La France éternelle, ce n'est pas la France d'un Caillaux, d'un Clémenceau ou d'un Viviani, mais c'est la France d'un Saint-Louis, d'un Godfroi de Bouillon ou d'une Jeanne d'Arc."[66] It is an ancient France of patriots, of tradition and of faith, still devotedly loyal. French intellectuals, it should be mentioned, had long disputed the contours of "True France."[67] Where does this leave the country of adoption, the United States? As we have seen, the American identity of Francos was also translated in the French-language press, even one as culturally combative as *Le Travailleur*. These relationships certainly evolved and were in perpetual flux over the course of the twentieth century. By the 1950s even an overtly French newspaper such as *Le Travailleur* was obliged to publish comics in English, with French translation, to its increasingly Americanized readers.

Bastille Day is the most modern commemoration in the Franco-American public sphere. The Franco-American press did not make much of this holiday throughout much of the twentieth century. It was in the 1970s and 1980s that the French national holiday began to be observed by more people in the United States, not necessarily as a French heritage celebration but one meant to encourage tourism to France. Companies such as Air France sponsored advertisements that appeared in the Franco-American press, such as *Le Journal de Lowell*. Today's "Festival de la Bastille" held in Augusta, Maine, is an invented tradition, a pleasant occasion for area Franco-Americans to remember French heritage while celebrating France.[68] June 24, the day of "national" celebration in Quebec, was the most commented upon in the Franco press, with the Fourth of July drawing increasing and strategic interest. The relationship to France described in the Franco-American press is an intriguing and volatile one indeed. While the language of the ancestral country was praised by elites, politically Francos and the French sometimes found themselves on opposing ends of the spectrum.

On Bastille Day just before the Second World War, *L'Avenir National* published an editorial that specified its support of a generous, patriotic, and eternal French bastion of culture:

> Oui, vive la France éternelle, la France toujours prête à favoriser les bonnes causes, la France généreuse qui ne veut jamais de mal à qui que

ce soit, la France aimable patronne de tous les beaux-arts, la France à qui nous devons le meilleur de nous-mêmes: notre foi, notre langue, notre âme nationale, même l'indépendance des Etats-Unis, que nous aimons.[69]

This celebration was marked by the one hundred and fiftieth anniversary of the French Revolution. France is gendered in the above statement, as is often the case, harking back to the personification of a republican France born in the throes of the Revolution, distinctly feminine because of the male king of old.[70] Marianne would literally be run out of French schools and city halls a year later when the Republic was democratically ended and Philippe Pétain came to power. In some traditional Franco-American families, Marianne had also been become tainted, weak, and undesirable when compared to German might. Francos and the Franco-American press demonstrated an interest in this Franco-French debate, in the question of fidelity to True France. French intellectuals had engaged in a prolonged debate about the country's essential character. An example of French patriotism appeared during the July 14 printing of "La Marseillaise" in Franco-American papers, in French and English. Some newspapers voiced a move away from French fidelity during the Second World War as questions arose about the democratic principles of the Vichy government.

Franco-American newspapers found themselves in a predicament during the dark years, *les années noires*, between 1939 and 1945, which extended across the Atlantic Ocean. With French tendencies becoming increasingly dubious in the early 1940s, the Franco press was at the most exposed point of its existence, forced to defend itself because of its French connection. What did not help matters was that Franco papers, often serving socially conservative constituencies (although some politically more liberal), devoted congratulatory articles to Pétain, war hero, emblem of an age-old France in the early 1930s, and also Nazi sympathizer.[71] He symbolized all that was traditionally and authentically French to French groups throughout the world. Pétain lauded French Canadians for their preservation of French culture in the New World even after the defeat of 1763.[72] Such laudatory comments appeared in papers such as *Le Travailleur* and *L'Avenir National* until 1940. In the fall of 1940, after Pétain had made clear his intentions and had shaken Hitler's hand, *Le Travailleur* had still not yet clearly decided for whom it lent its support and for which France, Pétain's antiquated, collaborationist version or Charles de Gaulle's modern, independent variant.

The French cultural barometer of Worcester, Massachusetts, republished a very ambiguous piece at this time, opting for "La France entière" ("Whole France") neither rejecting nor really endorsing Pétain's National Revolution or de Gaulle's Resistance.[73] It seemed as if the editorial staff sought to support the Allied effort generally, but without taking a principled stand. As a result of this ambiguity and of generalized Franco-American sympathy toward France, the French-language press came under increasing scrutiny. If Franco papers such as *Le Travailleur* translated any of the Pétainisme originating in conservative circles in Quebec, it would become increasingly perilous to do so. *La Justice* editor Jacques Ducharme alluded to a Franco-American critique of the elite in Quebec that failed to fall in line with wartime America.[74]

On May 29, 1941, newspaper editor Wilfrid Beaulieu was forced to make a perfectly clear declaration, one that would leave no doubt about the politics of *Le Travailleur* for readers from the U.S. government. The title of the paper was now printed in English to help clarify. In an editorial entitled "La Politique de Vichy," Beaulieu claimed that while remaining attached to the language, literature, and culture of France ("nous restons attachés à la langue, à la littérature, à la culture de France") we cannot sympathize with a France governed by Vichy. Beaulieu spoke not only for the newspaper but in the name of all Franco-Americans. He claimed that the ethnic group would continue to express its French cultural identity, but that Pétain and his National Revolution had to be defeated. During the June 12 celebration of St. John the Baptist Day, editors accompanied coverage of the holiday with an American flag, perhaps to make clear to worried state authorities of Franco-America's true colors, an American "Red, White and Blue," and not the inverted and now contaminated French *Bleu, Blanc, Rouge*. Francos directly addressed the embattled French marshal to disclose group anguish. In an open letter to Philippe Pétain printed on July 17, *Le Travailleur* announced that Franco-Americans suffered from a forced and difficult separation from ancestral France and that they were pained to see France soiled and stripped of its moral authority.

In September 1941, an English-language supplement appeared reprinting the editor's declaration in order to emphasize the paper's stance. Prominently positioned and entitled "To Our Readers and Advertisers: *Le Travailleur*'s Policy toward the Vichy Government," the document introduced the Franco-American paper to suspicious new bureaucratic readers and repeated that its editor had made clear the paper's position on May 29. "It may interest you to know that as early as May 29, 1941, *Le Travailleur* published an editorial by Wilfrid Beaulieu, publisher and managing editor, stating clearly the attitude of Franco-Americans of New England toward the spirit of Nazi collaboration on which the official French government is based." In the city where the paper had its headquarters, Beaulieu's article was translated and published in its entirety in English in the *Worcester Evening Gazette* on June 9, 1941. A Franco-American perspective was also transmitted via shortwave radio to France and her colonial possessions on May 31. The statement about Franco-American sentiment contained in the article drew on a survey taken within several areas of Franco-American concentration in New England.

Thus despite a love for French culture, Franco-Americans could only distance themselves from the Nazi affiliations of Vichy France:

> Just as the downfall of France last June struck us to the heart, made it bleed abundantly and caused many tears to be shed, just as the loss of France's prestige in the world doubles the difficulties that we must now surmount to perpetuate her spirit and culture on American soil, so on the other hand is it impossible for us to conceive of a France collaborating with Nazi Germany.

Beaulieu went on to say (in translation), "The Nazi ideal radically opposes itself to our democratic ideal." While asserting the right to continue to live as free French-descended people, the editorial recognized that this option had become more difficult. The editor made repeated declarations of the American patriotism of Franco-Americans. Small colorful American flags appeared on either side of the French-titled newspaper in 1941 and 1942.

Beaulieu began collaborating with a group of Harvard University professors on a statement sent to the president of the United States affirming the American sympathies of the French-descended population.

Le Travailleur's choice had been made, hesitantly it would seem, by this time: Gaullist republican France. Charles de Gaulle makes his appearance in the Franco-American newspaper in the 1941 commemoration of Bastille Day. He now represented what was morally beyond reproach, what was good about France. This was a fairly late choice, when compared with other Franco press decisions. *Le Travailleur* reprinted de Gaulle's wartime speech for the Franco-American reading public on July 24. It is striking, given the historic traditionalism of readers and editors, to see Gaullist symbols and revolutionary concepts such as "Valmy" and "Liberté" make a very distinct and visible entry in the newspaper. On September 11, in an editorial marking the ten-year anniversary of the relaunching of Worcester's French weekly, Wilfrid Beaulieu described a French "sacred duty," still dear to the hearts of Franco-Americans despite the turmoil: "la défense, le maintien et la conservation de la culture française, qui reste et restera toujours la culture des cultures, quoique parfois obscurcie par les nuées de la politique." The devotion to French culture, *the* culture among cultures, even that marked by partisan politics, stubbornly remained.

Beaulieu's statement of denied support to Vichy in Franco-America is echoed emphatically in other newspapers. This is noteworthy because scholars have sometimes stressed the overtly conservative tendencies of Franco-Americans generally.[75] Analysis of the Franco-American press suggests something more nuanced about the Franco-American reaction to Pétain's National Revolution. Vichy is in fact vehemently denounced, in more unforgiving terms than those printed in *Le Travailleur*. *La Justice* of Holyoke, under the direction of Jacques Ducharme in June 1940, stood clearly on the side of the Allies, as did *L'Avenir National* of Manchester, well before Wilfrid Beaulieu's public statement a year later. On July 11, 1940, immediately following the official vote on the future of the French republic, Ducharme and his writers responded with a front-page headline claiming, "Dissolution de la Troisième République française. Une France fasciste." There is no lukewarm or delayed response here. Historians consider French fascism ambiguously benign by European standards, but this bold Franco-American public statement is revealing. The July 10, 1940, vote in France is forever etched in the historical record as the day that French lawmakers voted down the Republic by an overwhelming majority, giving full political powers to Philippe Pétain.[76] The French daily newspaper of Manchester, *L'Avenir National*, made explicitly critical declarations about the abdication of the French republic, identifying the ominous beginnings of a dictatorship in its July 9 headline: "UNE DICTATURE EN FRANCE." This early and quite belligerent rejection of Vichy France, in papers other than *Le Travailleur* suggests that moral authority may have resided elsewhere than Worcester, Massachusetts, at least during the summer of 1940. In their close reading of metropolitan French history as it unfolded, Franco-American editors made clear their French connection and identity by disassociating themselves from Vichy France, and upholding their ideal of *True France*.[77]

La Justice editor Jacques Ducharme continued the attack on (grand) motherly but proto-fascist France and consequently his support of the democratic United States. "La France devient fasciste. Il ne reste au monde qu'une grande démocratie: les Etats-Unis."[78] In comparison with this blow at Vichy France and rally to the American democracy, *Le Travailleur*'s 1941 statement indeed seems tepid. The denunciation made by *La Justice* was very likely facilitated by the changing of the guard, the arrival of a new generation at the newspaper. U.S.-born Jacques Ducharme took over in 1940 from French-Canadian Joseph Lussier, editor at the paper for thirty-three years and whose first-generation views were considerably more conservative. When forced to choose, Ducharme opted for the American in the Franco-American duality. He stated that it was more as Americans than as Franco-Americans that they must now lead their lives. Hitler had given them no choice.

While many Francos maintained cultural traditions, the American century had already begun, as had its powerful assimilating influences. For people of Lussier's generation, fidelity to French cultural identity was an imperative. Jacques Ducharme, however, repeated that Francos were more American than French. That this was said in wartime is not at all surprising, as many ethnic communities felt pressure to demonstrate their fidelity to the American nation. It is striking that in his novel *The Delusson Family* (1939), not once are Franco-Americans specifically mentioned. The year 1943, when Ducharme published his nonfiction sequel and discussed Franco-American identity at some length, represented a vastly different world. Francos expressed their joy in French at the Allied victory in May 1945, as they had in 1918. "C'EST LA VICTOIRE," read triumphant May 8 headline in Lewiston's *Le Messager*. "Jour de réjouissances," claimed a journalist at *L'Avenir National*. They hoped that France might be restored to former glory after its fall and that Frenchness in America could again be expressed without remorse and without arousing suspicion.

FRANCO-AMERICAN ACTIVISM AT *LE JOURNAL DE LOWELL*

After the Second World War, the Franco-American press entered an extended period of decline. Readership dipped as French ethnic enclaves emptied, the suburbs around industrial centers expanded, and American assimilation gained ground. Most of the extant and once daily newspapers had been forced to a weekly or monthly publishing rotation. *Le Travailleur*, as its title indicated, kept at its steady cultural work, in Manchester after the war, until the decline and death of Wilfrid Beaulieu in 1979. In the 1950s and 1960s, *L'Etoile* and *Le Travailleur* still had correspondents in different parts of the francophone world, with articles dedicated to France's last colonial war in Algeria, for instance. The FAROG Forum (Le FORUM), during this period of generalized militancy, stood with Québécois separatists. The Franco-American press expressed a keen interest in francophone and colonial issues, purposefully linking Franco-America to the rest of the francophone world. In having to answer questions about its ties to Vichy France, Franco-American newspapers convey a fluid French and francophone connection.

Le Journal de Lowell, the last traditional, printed Franco-American newspaper, represents an attempt to remain both Franco and francophone, a final effort to preserve French ethnic culture and identity in a rapidly changing world. Editors printed *Le Journal* monthly, and it was read by former or current residents of Lowell, only a small portion of whom resided outside the metropolitan area. Its influence cannot be exaggerated. It is the editors' initiative to maintain a century-old tradition of publication in French highlighting the Franco experience, however, that is pertinent. They attempted to prolong, in so doing, one of the most enduring institutions of francophone life in Lowell. As *Le Travailleur* entered its final period of activity, *Le Journal* appeared in this still actively French ethnic hub. Social club member and founder Raymond J. Barrette wanted a French-language paper for area Francos that followed in the tradition of Lowell's historic daily, *L'Etoile*. This was a necessity, he claimed in a February 1977 *Journal* cover article, particularly as the Franco-American population had begun to disperse into the surrounding region. The paper was meant to inform Francos of community news and preserve the bond between city and suburb. It aimed to encourage reading in French and keep French ethnic identity alive in the new era, which it faithfully did for more than twenty years. Two years after its founding in 1975, *Le Journal* had three hundred paying subscribers in sixteen states. Patrons in Lowell, from among the city's estimated 19,000 Franco-Americans, received their monthly edition freely at several city locations.

The first issue of *Le Journal* became available to locals in February 1975. While editors distributed it free of charge to city residents, subscribers paid a fee for shipping, with a sliding scale for U.S. subscribers, readers in Canada, and overseas supporters. Some subscribers followed cultural life from afar, in Europe or Africa. Letters from Lowell daughters and sons to the editor, published in the "Courrier" section of the paper, continued conversation on ethnic issues. At the beginning of the paper's history, the editorial team decided to print 2,500 newspapers each month for distribution to area kiosks. By the early 1980s, production had increased to 3,000 monthly copies published, a respectable circulation number, but less than some of the other French ethnic papers. For most of *Le Journal*'s run, editor Albert Côté personally delivered copies very early in the morning before beginning his day job as a teacher.[79] The paper reached a maximum circulation of 4,000 at its height in the early 1990s.

Côté claimed modestly that there was nothing particularly distinctive about Lowell and the community newspaper that served Franco-Americans (an understatement). Founder Raymond Barrette had asked him to take the editorial reins after an injury prevented him from continuing, and Côté ultimately accepted. All of the traditional industrial and ethnic centers had experienced changes, but Barrette believed that they could still support a French paper like *Le Journal*. What did set Lowell apart, Côté specified, was a collective willingness to support an ethnic newspaper. The area benefited from the community's still sizeable number of French-language speakers eager to take part in cultural activities. Many met at the French reading room, the Salle Biron, located on the ground floor at the Lowell Municipal Library, which contained thousands of French titles. For an extended period, residents had access to French television delivered by cable from Canada. Organizational synergy helped to revitalize a proactive Franco-American population intent on making its existence known in the wider francophone world.

Many local leaders took part voluntarily in community activities including the compilation of the newspaper. It was able to keep costs to a minimum in this way and remain in circulation. It was very much a family affair published for almost the entire length of its life by the Côté family and printed out of their home. The editor's spouse, a non-French speaker, was also involved in compiling the newspaper.[80] The editor's personal phone number appeared on the cover of each issue, and readers were periodically invited to contact him directly for information. In this way, the "humble gazette," as the editor called it, continued to circulate and inform year after year. Area residents still stop and ask Côté about the paper he printed. Some claim to have saved every issue.

From its modest beginnings as little more than a four-page newsletter on rigid A4 paper in 1975, *Le Journal* evolved into a more professional printed edition that typically offered twelve to sixteen pages of articles, images, and product or service advertisements, twenty during the political and holiday seasons in October, November, and December. Product endorsement for Franco-owned businesses made publication possible. The paper's middle section displayed advertisements for Côté's shoes, insurance provided by Provencher, Beaudry's roofing, limousine service offered by Marcotte, Baribeault's market, Dufresne's barbershop, the Pelletier Brothers' garage, and Archambault's funeral parlor.[81] Albert Côté continually sought more sponsors, asking readers to tell business owners that they had heard about their services through the paper. At the upper right corner, by the paper's symbolic mill bell illustration, *Le Journal* stated during its first four years of publication: "Encouragez nos annonceurs et mentionnez le journal." Like its predecessor it sought to develop a vibrant and self-sufficient community. *Le Journal* informed people outside the community that Francos continued to exist in the late twentieth century. Local politicians did not ignore this and came courting the Franco ethnic vote during political campaigns. Advertisements in French for Franco and non-Franco candidates for city council or the school board appeared. Political advertisements helped finance the publication, but translating them into French for local voters was time-consuming and costly for the editorial team.

Being a family-operated newspaper did not preclude a continued journalistic professionalism in Lowell. A prominent family that had been in the newspaper business for decades was at least partially responsible for the longevity of the paper. Louis-Alphonse Biron was the owner and longtime editor of Lowell's daily Franco and French-language newspaper, *L'Etoile*. He also ran the Franco-American paper out of nearby Nashua, New Hampshire, *L'Impartial*. Biron's daughter, Marthe Biron Péloquin, worked with him at *L'Etoile* for almost twenty years, in addition to being a journalist at *Le Travailleur* of Worcester.[82] Marthe Péloquin would go on to become a prominent member of several Franco-American organizations and was decorated for her efforts. She brought her professional expertise to *Le Journal de Lowell* and would sign many articles about her work and that of others endeavoring to support Franco-American activities.[83] Her daughter Louise Péloquin became a longtime Paris correspondent for the paper beginning in March 1983. She attempted to rekindle local Franco-American connections to France through regular interjections while living abroad. In her first piece of investigative journalism, she discussed "Pratiques culturelles des Français," a subject of some curiosity perhaps for a related but distant francophone group. The paper celebrated her academic success, and readers would hear from her for the next decade.[84] Her own daughter, Raphaële, fictitiously signed articles that Péloquin had written for *Le Journal*, representing an imaginary fourth-generation of journalism.

In addition to the individuals with professional experience, an array of people put together the gazette, former mayors, priests, and organizational leaders, who knew a great deal about what was taking place in the city. Much of the community news appeared in the columns "Faits et gestes" (Happenings and Doings), "Les Gens d'alentour" (Area People), and "Notes Brèves" (Brief Notes). Each recorded Franco weddings, vacations, and group events, as well as informal gatherings. Many of the activities took place in French and thus contributed to the extension and perpetuation of area francophonie, called "Franco-Lowellie." Like "Les Centres" and "Nouvelles du Canada" sections in other Franco-American newspapers, they most actively perpetuated a notion of French pan-Americanism.

Franco priest Armand "Spike" Morissette wrote the "Faits et gestes" column from 1975 until his death in 1991. As a priest and community leader, Morissette was certainly among the most knowledgeable about Franco affairs. When visitors sought counsel with area leaders, they met with Morissette. City officials named a thoroughfare passing along the mills and former tenements of Little Canada after him. Despite Father Morissette's engagement and influence as a spokesperson for Franco-Americans, the paper maintained a respectful but distant relationship to the Catholic Church. In religious affairs as in politics, *Le Journal* remained decidedly outside the fray. "Décès," a regularly printed obituary column, commented on the disappearance of Franco luminaries such as Morissette. Another noted death was that of Franco-American editor Wilfrid Beaulieu, who passed along with his newspaper in May 1979 as *Le Journal* was beginning to establish itself. The column, filled with images as well as text, conveys much about the shrinking of Franco-America along with efforts to sustain it. Editor Jacques Ducharme claimed that obituaries were among the most popular sections of the newspaper.[85]

As part of the proclamation of news of interest to the greater Franco-American family, pictures of Lowell's sports teams, schools, and Little Canadas frequently adorned the regular columns. Photos old and new gave an intimacy to the paper, bringing lost members and symbolic places back into the fold. *Le Journal* looked nostalgically back at parts of the Franco experience that had disappeared (the Franco ethnic enclave that had been bulldozed in the 1960s, for instance) while keeping an eye to the future. Cultural historian Robert Darnton has claimed that "the general grammar of other cultures must be imbedded in the documents that they left behind," rendering them deeply instructive objects indeed.[86]

Soon after *Le Journal* began to circulate, the Institut Français at Assumption College in Worcester, Massachusetts, opened in 1979 not only to continue to educate Franco-Americans but also to inform the nation about the little known Franco-American experience. Few institutions have done more to critically examine and support postcolonial francophone cultures in the United States. The Institut Français and its longtime director, Claire Quintal, were at the forefront of organizational activity in the 1980s and 1990s promoting greater knowledge about Franco-American culture and life. The Franco activity that they helped to generate is clearly visible in the columns of Lowell's monthly French newspaper, which reported on the annual Institute colloquia drawing scholarly as well as governmental attention to various Franco-American issues.[87] The Institute had been founded at Assumption College in order to carry forward Franco-American education in all of its facets, at a time when the College shifted its focus from educating people of mostly French-Canadian descent to a broader range of university students. All Franco-American curricular and cultural programming were left to the Institute.

At this same time, Franco-American intellectuals and activists founded ActFANE (l'Action pour les Franco-Américains du Nord-Est) to promote French ethnic interests and also more significantly to promote cohesion among the various francophone or French-descended groups in North America. ActFANE and its supporters hoped to manage, enlarge, and consolidate Franco-America: "aménager, élargir et consolider *l'espace francophone panaméricain* (my italics)."[88] Its imagining of a Panamerican francophone space is revealing. The movement claimed to be the primary intermediary between Franco-Americans, Quebec, Canada, and France.[89] Through the collaboration of the French with ActFANE and Louisiana's CODOFIL, all duly noted in *Le Journal*, there was considerable pooling of Franco-American energies from New England down to the Gulf Coast.

Le Journal de Lowell expressed a sustained focus on organizing

Franco-Americans collectively, throughout the six New England states and New York. Given their dispersal, this was a considerable task, but *Le Journal*, the Institut Français, and ActFANE collectively provided an influential platform for the brief period that they coexisted in the 1970s and 1980s. ActFANE might be considered a substitute for the New England infrastructure that never got off the ground, CODOFINE (Council for the Development of French in New England). *Le Journal* played an important role in the activity of organizations such as ActFANE, as individuals in the 1980s rediscovered the importance of their French "roots" and made efforts to recognize and honor them.[90] Franco-Americans continued to organize social clubs like the mutual aid societies that they had founded historically to promote their interests at the end of the nineteenth century. Social organizations had had a prominent place in the columns of newspapers, more recent groups such as the Cercle Jeanne-Mance, the Club Citoyens-Américains, Club Richelieu, Rochambeau, and Lafayette. Many of these Franco social clubs still have physical meeting spaces in the center of Lowell that give some sense of what remains of a distinctive, Franco-American living space. They are remnants of the place between French and American that Franco-Americans continue to occupy. The Club Passe-temps and Club Lafayette of Lowell organized Christmas parties for children and seniors in nursing homes that received annual coverage and illustrations in *Le Journal*.

Professor Paul Chassé contributed several opinion pieces to *Le Journal* in its infancy, one of which underlined the importance of *les sociétés* in the Franco-American community.[91] Social clubs allowed Francos to gather, to pool their resources, and to speak collectively with the bishop about the construction of a parish or the development of a French-language newspaper. Such organizations have served an important role in promoting Franco-American interests, and in *Le Journal*, they found an advocate as well as a promoter. Articles proclaimed news of the services and annual activities of the large mutual aid societies such as the Association Canado-Américaine and the Union Saint-Jean Baptiste. For the most part, the paper did not become involved in the debate concerning the direction of these institutions.

Le Journal de Lowell's scope ranged beyond the greater metropolitan area of central Massachusetts. The paper reported on the opening of the Centre Franco-Américain (CFA) of Manchester in 1990, one of the several Franco cultural centers operating in New England and advertised its cultural and community events (see chapter 2).[92] West of the city, the Alliance Française of Amherst/Northampton received support in the paper's columns, as did French radio programs such as *Tout en Français* on the public radio station WFCR in the same area in 1980s and 1990s.[93] For a brief period, *Le Journal* printed proceedings of the Cercle français on "Northern Ohio/ Western Pennsylvania" and "Nouvelles du Midwest," also for more distant sympathizers.

Le Journal circulated news of New England Acadian gatherings. Acadians maintained small communities in several New England towns. Fitchburg and Gardner, Massachusetts, are two such Acadian centers that were served by *Le Journal* with announcements about cultural events.[94] More broadly, *Le Journal* reported on the launching of the popular Congrès Mondial Acadien that began in 1994.[95] Acadian genealogic fervor resulted in large attendance at these very successful family gatherings. They shadowed the assertion of Cajun coolness that was just beginning to develop and of which other Franco-Americans had caught wind. Readers witnessed the birth of several Franco-American heritage festivals, including Cajun ones, in the New England area, some longer-lived than others, recognizing all members within the French diasporic family.

CODOFIL clearly represented a model of successful cultural organization for *Le Journal* and its readers. The paper printed word of one of its most successful events, le Festival international de Louisiane. Advertisements for the first festival appeared in May 1987. At this same time, in September 1987, *Le Journal* announced New England French ethnic festivals in Worcester. In summer 1991, the Kermesse Franco-Américaine de Biddeford, Maine, celebrated its ninth gathering, sponsored by ActFANE. By highlighting these events, *Le Journal* effectively promoted Franco-American as a unifying label for all groups of French descent in the United States, from *new*

New France in New England to French Louisiana. It did achieve some success in this regard. Francos were increasingly recognized by French and francophone authorities and dignitaries. The French consul paid a symbolic visit to "Franco-Lowellie" in 1979.[96] Local leaders offered the representative of France in the New England area a Franco-American flag as a token of their French cultural zeal.

Franco-Americans and francophonie became more intertwined in part due to the activities and affirmations of *Le Journal*. As an engaged mouthpiece for the greater Lowell Franco-American community, it informed readers of local participation in the international francophone summits that began to organize in the 1980s, with the support of French president François Mitterrand. Franco-Americans made certain that they were represented in the first formal international francophone meetings, headed by the Organisation internationale de la francophonie (OIF), and this was no small achievement. Paris correspondent Louise Péloquin and the Institut Français director Claire Quintal attended the first summit in Versailles in 1986, specifically as Franco-American delegates. *Le Journal* announced the existence of francophone communities in many parts of the United States: "il ne faut pas oublier qu'ici aux Etats-Unis nous trouvons de belles communautés francophones en Nouvelle-Angleterre, dans le Mid-West, en Louisiane, en Floride et en Californie."[97] Anthropologist and historian Caroline B. Brettell, in a penetrating study of the French Midwest, examines a small group of French Canadians who relocated to Illinois, a word echoing the French past in the United States. Following the charismatic Father Chiniquy, some immigrants converted to Protestantism upon settling in the northeastern corner of the state.[98]

In a follow-up article in May 1986, Péloquin noted that Francos of the United States were increasingly visible to the international francophone body. She cited three themes of the francophone summit—union, expansion, and diversity—around which all Franco-Americans could assemble.[99] The cultural paradox simultaneous diversity and unity meant that all members of the extended French family, from many different nations could find their voice in French, a message of some optimism to Francos. When compared to the current mission of the Organisation internationale de la francophonie, the goals of "la francophonie organisationnelle" and a belief in the importance of linguistic diversity in the French-speaking world have not changed substantially. Franco-Americans were some of the early pioneers of institutional francophonie.

Further summits followed immediately suggesting a continued resolve to mobilize. A second francophone summit was held in 1987 in Quebec and two years later in Dakar in 1989. A six-person Franco-American delegation attended the Dakar summit and would grow in subsequent years.[100] The summits brought more global attention to French influence in America, and to Franco-Americans. Many other smaller venues enabled Franco-Americans to publicly declare their French and francophone status, under the direction of ActFANE. The Congrès National Franco-Américain was a yearly event for a decade that received attention in Le Journal columns. Its annual meetings were held throughout Franco-America, from French New England to the French Gulf Coast.[101] This was one of the few occasions in which the Franco-American flag was unfurled.[102] It also flew at the newly inaugurated Parc de l'Amérique française in Quebec City in 1985.[103] The press gave Francos a public forum from which to publicize their existence throughout North America.

Leaders wanted to build on existing Franco-American infrastructure and resources. Franco-American advocate Louis Israël Martel affirmed a Franco right to expression in French and to multicultural rights more generally in the United States.[104] "Nous ne pouvons comprendre cette attitude d'un trop grand nombre de gens qui croient que l'on ne peut pas être bon américain qu'en parlant uniquement l'anglais. C'est faux!" Martel rejected monolinguistic patriotism and called Franco-Americans to the service of their ethnic heritage *and* American identity, in French. All Franco media sources would be required in this cultural battle for survival. Le Conseil de la vie française en Amérique, a Quebec based group, had local representation in Lowell. A Franco-American contingent that included editor Albert Côté of Le Journal attended a meeting of francophone peoples, a "Rencontre des peuples francophones," at the invitation of provincial officials in Quebec, that also included French speakers from Louisiana.[105] The umbrella organization La Fédération Féminine Franco-Américaine and its 15,000 members continued to actively promote Franco-American life, and consequently *Le Journal*. Leaders attended the sixth Congress of the Association of Franco-Americans (AFA), held at Mackinac Island, Michigan, to give Francos and Acadians, Cajuns and Creoles a sense of the dimensions of their American identity, "les vraies dimensions de leur identité américaine."[106] The number of associations created conveys the enthusiasm felt for continued French ethnic life in the United States.

This was a heady time in the development of Franco and francophone consciousness, a period when active support allowed many to believe in bright Franco-American tomorrows. The Franco media, even an obscure publication like *Le Journal*, contributed to this belief. Histories of the media and of the press generally tend to paint newspapers as "the representations that societies generate of themselves."[107] *Le Journal* made this affirmation seem realistic in the 1980s especially, by advertising a wide selection of Franco conferences, expositions, films, and performances in New England and Canada available to Franco-Americans. For a direct French phone line on cultural affairs at the consulate in Boston, *Le Journal* encouraged readers to dial or "composez 'BONJOUR'—(617) 266–5687—for more information about cultural events."[108] Many such services did not exist for very long, but they are clearly evocative of the fervor around French ethnic identity at this time.

ActFANE had gone through many changes in title and direction over the course of its existence. Since its founding in 1980, it had morphed slightly from ActFA (Action pour les Franco-Americans) to ActFANE (December 1981), to include New York State, but its primary mission remained unchanged. "Action pour les Franco-Américains est un organisme-parapluie, fondé à l'invitation du Ministère des Affaires Intergouvernementales du Québec, qui est censé de réunir tous les groupements franco-américains."[109] Quebec authorities were clearly invested in Franco-American activity and ActFANE continued to be active in supporting Franco participation in a Panamerican francophonie. Supporters of ActFANE well-known to *Le Journal* included Father Armand "Spike" Morissette, playwright Grégoire Chabot, Normand Dubé of the National Materials Development Center for French, and Claire Quintal. Each of the six New England states maintained representation in the direction of ActFANE.[110] Through the leadership of its executive council, it attempted to create support (unsuccessfully) at the state and national level, again similar to the infrastructure in Louisiana.

ActFANE was active in French cultural events small and large, from the organization of festivals to official representation at the francophone summits beginning in Quebec in 1987. After some reflection, the group concluded that Franco groups and identities were too divergent for one all-inclusive strategy. Paul Paré, longtime executive director of ActFANE, claimed aux Assises de la Francophonie américaine in Paris in 1990 that the great diversity of the French family of America prevented this type of action.[111] Delegates acknowledged the difficulties in finding common ground for action among all Franco-Americans, Cajuns, Creoles, and others. It took four years for the organization to admit this publicly in *Le Journal*, although this did not stop it from continuing its French Panamerican activities until the end of the twentieth century. *Le Journal de Lowell* continued to promote the activities of all French American groups, including les Snowbirds de la Floride. It broadened the perspectives of its readers with its consistent francophone bent. The French-Canadian and Haitian Creole populations of south Florida had created a French-language market for one of the largest and primarily commercial Franco-American papers to emerge, *Le Soleil de Floride*.[112] The seasonal migration of French Canadians to south Florida fostered a need for French linguistic and cultural services.

Paris correspondent Louise Péloquin continued to offer readers of *Le Journal* whimsical and sometimes romanticized columns about life in France and the French capital. "April in Paris" was the title of one such article making use of common French stereotypes and assumptions.[113] Péloquin let readers know that even a mythical France was not spared the realities of the modern world, with terrorist bombings that rocked the country in 1986.[114] Paris was of course a much larger, urbane place from which to consider francophone affairs than Lowell, Massachusetts. Her columns placed France, sometimes disassociated from the francophone world, squarely in the conversation of the local francophone group. She discussed Franco-American culture in Lowell and abroad from a perspective of exile.[115] She informed readers that Franco-American expressions were included in "Le Dictionnaire général de la francophonie."[116] Péloquin told them that she taught a course at the Sorbonne on the Franco-American experience, bringing it to the attention of French students.[117]

In the United States, in the early 1980s, professors Eloise Brière and Nicole Vaget had begun to examine Franco-America in the university classroom and in print, along with the Institut Français.[118] Louise Péloquin's columns echo the communication channels that were opening between Franco-America and the greater francophone world at this time. In 1982, *Le Figaro* sent correspondents to Lowell to report on Franco-American activities.[119] Five years later, *Le Journal* printed an article previously published in *Le Monde*, "Sous la Nouvelle-Angleterre la vieille France" ("Within New England, Old France").[120] The author and perhaps *Le Monde* readers were astonished at the extent to which French culture lived in Lowell because committed Franco-Americans of many stripes refused to let it expire. They subscribed to the familiar call to cultural arms in Franco-America.

Le Journal claimed that francophones worldwide were captivated by Franco *survivance*, that a francophone cultural and linguistic tradition had managed to maintain its centuries-old existence in the United States. *Le Soleil* of Dakar, Senegal, notably applauded Franco-Americans for their efforts to preserve French language and culture.[121] Articles and columns in *Le Journal* returned the favor, conveying a significant francophone interest. "Parlez-vous FRANCOPHONIE?" Péloquin asked her readers in November 1990. *Le Journal* took note of Lowell's increasingly multicultural immigrant population by celebrating its international francophone element. Poets from Haiti who had settled in the area shared their verses with the Franco community. They expressed both an interest in "Franco-Lowellie" as well their African origins.[122] African historians traveling to New England shared their scholarly thoughts with readers.[123] A long-running series on African history ran in 1990 and 1991 in *Le Journal*, written by one of the visiting scholars.[124] Through language and the press notably, a distinct example of a francophone *culture-monde* developed, a shared perspective fostered through use of technology in French, not unlike the *littérature-monde* phenomenon although more linked to the traditional and digital media.[125]

Readers studied France in noted articles on the French bicentennial, Lady Liberty, and D-day celebrations. On Quebec, *Le Journal* informed its readers of the relevance of French-language legislation ("La loi 101") as well as the Quebec leadership role in North American francophonie.[126] Franco-Americans took note of these cultural debates. Quebec's Quiet Evolution was exceedingly quiet in the columns of the paper, another example of the paper's apoliticism. Publicizing Franco-American francophonie in the United States required the focused attention of individuals as well as resources. Paul Chassé devoted one July 1979 opinion piece to "Presse, Radio, Télévision" and its importance in the Franco-American community. In the 1970s, well before the availability of TV5Monde, Franco community member Paul Blanchette was instrumental in bringing French television from Canada to Lowell. Organizers with similar objectives in other mill towns had their efforts rebuffed. As editor Albert Côté stated, cable programming in French was one of the three elements that distinguished Franco Lowell and maintained its distinctiveness for such a long period. Blanchette spent years trying to convince officials, residents, and prospective cable television providers that there was substantial local interest and a market for French-Canadian television programming in Lowell. He claimed that it would help reinforce the Franco community, and he successfully lobbied for it. According to Blanchette's daughter Suzanne and a July 25, 1973, report, "Cable subscribers now have the invaluable opportunity to hear a language which is understood and spoken in many New England homes. Furthermore, the Sherbrooke (Quebec) station broadens our outlook on the world in which we live and strengthens our ties with our northern neighbors."[127] Might the media serve to extend the life of North American francophonie? American television had worked against the *survivance* movement in the United States, but community activists hoped it might be co-opted to prolong French cultural traditions.

The Canadian consul in Boston became involved in the debate, arguing that life in French had not disappeared in the United States and that television could promote awareness of French heritage.[128] Children would be shaped by French-language television, even if they could not necessarily understand every word. Blanchette claimed, "For us, for Franco-Americans, these media have a particular influence on our language, our culture, our manner of thinking and acting. American and Franco-American cultures are not mutually exclusive but rather complement one another. It is thus necessary to work toward the fruition of our Franco-American culture through French programming."[129]

Blanchette was an ardent and effective spokesperson, having managed to persuade the television authorities of the interest in French television, as well as the willingness to pay for it, creating the rationale to offer the station to consumers. Blanchette passed away toward the end of *Le Journal*'s circulation, and the paper noted in its September 1990 homage that a square in Lowell had been named in his honor. Other Franco-Americans subsequently took up the cause of French television in Lowell.

From the late 1970s through the early 1990s, Lowell residents had access to French television programming from French Canada. The schedule appeared in the columns of *Le Journal*, informing readers and residents of the audiovisual possibilities. The daily movie in French in the evening was a particularly popular option. From the beginning of the existence of French television, residents worked to sustain this programming, and had all Franco-American residents supported it, it might have lasted even longer, advocates claimed. But by the early 1990s, *Le Journal de Lowell* reported that cable company officials from TV-9 in Sherbrooke threatened to eliminate French television access. *Le Journal* and its team went on the offensive to maintain this cultural service, describing a Franco insurrection, undertaken by culturally besieged Lowell residents refusing monolingual programming. In light of the brewing tension in 1993, *Le Journal* called its readers to battle ("aux armes"), highlighting a French republican tradition.[130] Albert Côté offered a signed petition to demonstrate local interest. Journalists reasoned that cultural survival depended on French-language media access.

At this time, a short series on "La petite histoire du câble à Lowell" by Paul Blanchette began to circulate each month, recounting the struggle to bring French television to Lowell in the first place.[131] By January 1994,

French cable television in Lowell had already become a provision from the past. Local Franco elites responded, however, with the launching of another cultural offering, their own short-lived show, *Bonjour! Le Journal* advertised it as the only French-language television show made in the United States. Singer Josée Vachon and journalist Louise Péloquin headed this Lowell and Manchester production.[132] It marked yet another symbolic but ultimately fleeting attempt to organize Franco-American media. Today, Franco-American residents in the Lowell area tune in to weekly radio shows. These broadcasts cannot replace the daily French television programming that Paul Blanchette fought to establish, but nonetheless offer a desired cultural service to the Franco-American community. Francos of southern Maine currently have access to French programming out of Sherbrooke.

The Franco-American press confirms the strong sense of collective identity expressed in an ethnic or regional literature. It also conveys the complexities of French life in the American sphere and how people maintained French cultural traditions well into the twentieth century, all the while becoming progressively American. *Le Journal de Lowell* disappeared just as the Internet age was beginning. Minor in terms of influence, this final printed newspaper expressed the collective efforts of a cultural community. *Le Journal* acknowledged in a July 1991 article, "Le Village électronique francophone." It noted the launching of TV5Monde in 1984. In January 1993, *Le Journal* published a letter from the American president-elect, "Lettre aux Franco-Américains du Président élu Bill Clinton," a sign of ethnic recognition. The following year, the paper gave voice to the activities of a new organization, the Union franco-américaine de Lowell.[133]

Had the newspaper helped to achieve the goal of the Franco press more generally, that of Franco-American recognition and respect? When one considers that the editor published *Le Journal* on a tiny budget out of his home for twenty years, the difference that one individual can make becomes clear. He helped to acknowledge a local ethnic and cultural identity, as had other Franco-American journalists before him. *Le Journal de Lowell* communicated a Franco-American consciousness and identity, one that had actively sought a recognized place in the wider francophone world. Its end announced an increasingly less francophone future, but one still half-filled with Franco-American expectations. *Le Journal*'s December 1995 edition announced to readers that it would be the last published by the Côté family. They called for others to take up the task of editing the paper, even offering assistance in the transition, but no one responded. In one of its last symbolic acts, *Le Journal* refused to take part in the recognition of English as the official language in New Hampshire.[134] It referred readers to the French-language media still available to Francos in Lowell, including *Bonjour!* on channel 61 that cable subscribers could watch on Sunday evenings, with repeats on Monday.[135]

The "humble gazette" of Lowell was the last written edition to advertise a living francophonie and carry on the Franco-American journalistic tradition. Franco activists pursued their efforts without the aid that CODOFIL has received for years (and despite ActFANE's dwindling effectiveness). The New England National Heritage Materials organization, a *Journal* supporter, received state funding to help educate about the Franco experience, but this source ultimately evaporated. Longtime advocates of the French ethnic media Marthe Biron Péloquin and Claire Quintal were recognized with the highest French and francophone honors for their work in fostering Franco-American heritage: they received the Palmes Académiques and Legion of Honor, respectively. This was a source of considerable pride for the community and for Franco-American recognition internationally. They had successfully escaped the Franco-American cultural ghetto and had gained wider recognition in the francophone world.

CHAPTER 6

Unmasking the Creole Cowboy

Popeyes restaurant chain offers French Creole cuisine, "Louisiana Fast," to patrons both in and outside of Franco-America. It makes entry into the French hinterlands of America more inviting and can extend their very borders. Louisiana's cultures are not all typically of the fast variety. Slowly simmering gumbo and meandering bayous predominate; but "fast women" of the Big Easy, a twenty-four-hour den of permissiveness, round out ambiguously mythical elements of southern-style Frenchness, all deceptively intertwined, all deliciously Creole. Vice and spice are expected and desired by those in pursuit of these Franco-American cultures. People can freely buy, sell, exchange, and otherwise transform them.

The French population of Louisiana is small in number but large in terms of its symbolic and cultural influence. This cultural capital has been essential as French Quarter economics have helped to keep the city and state afloat since the storms and floodings subsided. French Acadians or Cajuns and Creoles make up just 4 percent of the state of Louisiana's population, which perhaps served as justification for Governor Bobby Jindal cutting 40 percent of the budget for French cultural programming at the Council for the Development of French in Louisiana in 2012.[1] Jindal may have done more harm than good to the state coffers, as French is what brings tourism and tourist dollars to the Gulf city of sin and to all of the Pelican state, especially in a recovering economy. Reduction of the French cultural budget renders this Frenchness even more vulnerable, more of a minority expression, and leaves local organizers having to scramble to support programs. Will Creole traditions of the Gulf South further disintegrate, leaving Louisiana more homogenously Anglo-Protestant, more like its neighboring states that have not been as influenced by the French tradition?

It is not difficult to imagine *créolité* and catastrophe simultaneously, in light of the devastating earthquake that struck the island of Haiti on January 12, 2010. The former appears almost as a survival strategy for the latter. Historically, the impulse propelling forward the creolization process, or cultural hybridization, has been upheaval of one kind or another: revolution, exile, and slavery, as well as exploration, resettlement, and trade. Scholars associate artistic creolization in twenty-first-century New Orleans with the creative response to catastrophe.[2] The critical literature on creolization, framed by postcolonial and cultural studies, underlines the lasting impact of such phenomena. As historian Gwendolyn Midlo Hall asserts, in reference to creolization in the New World, "the colonization of the Americas was the earliest stage of the internationalization of the world," announcing a planet brought increasingly into the most intimate and very often violent forms of contact.[3]

Creolization seems a particularly useful framework for thinking about diasporic groups and cultures in the Gulf South: African slaves who arrived in Louisiana in the eighteenth century, aristocrats and wealthy planters fleeing the French and Haitian Revolutions, exiled Acadian refugees of *le Grand Dérangement*, and displaced Native American populations. Their Louisiana is very much a crossroads, at the intersection of currents in the French Atlantic, between continental France, the sugar islands, and continental America, where so many bodies, cultures, and products were exchanged. Christopher L. Miller writes that the slave trade and the cultural residue that followed in its wake connected these places, their populations, and traditions definitively.[4] Colonial Louisiana mattered little historically in the overall scheme of French colonial policy, hardly coherent as it was, yet vibrant cultural expressions emerged from the melding of traditions there. Louisiana's motley, hardscrabble frontier populations and resilient postcolonial cultures reflect this irony to some degree. Evidence of a Creole consciousness and culture, a cosmopolitanism that binds outside the usual realms of separation, is pervasive in French Louisiana and will be further explored here.

Historians of New France cite the homogeneity of French settlers in the New World, and while certainly true for settlers at the outset, the powerful force of subsequent *métissage* between indigenous and transplanted people in Franco-America both north and south is being widely explored by scholars.[5] For French cultures and populations to survive in the North American wild, they had to adopt Native American ways. Going native in the New World meant physical survival, not cultural *survivance*. The very first French settlers to endure the passage from the Old Continent and construct a New World identity, the eventually expulsed Acadians, interacted widely with Micmac and Algonquin Indians in their Canadian Maritime homes. Their descendants in the bayous of eighteenth-century Louisiana traded and intermarried with the Houma and the Chimatcha Indians.[6] Hundreds of thousands of Native Americans also died, it is important to note, from contact with European populations. Who is the trailblazing French-Canadian explorer, the fabled *coureur de bois*, other than a Métis, who essentially became Indian in order to ensure an American existence? The displaced Acadians of coastal Louisiana like *coureurs de bois* adopted Amerindian tracking, hunting, warring, dressing, cooking, and transportation customs.[7] Many individual French exiles from the Old World went native in colonial Louisiana, perhaps none as much as enterprising Jesuits. An "Amérique franco-indienne," as Havard and Vidal refer to the French colonial experiment in the Northern Hemisphere, seems accurate indeed, although this appellation may not reflect all influences at play in colonial Louisiana.[8]

This chapter examines the fusion of French, African, and indigenous experiences in North America and the ensuing journey from French to francophone on the Gulf Coast over the past four centuries. My analysis will focus on French cultural production of the past one hundred years in Louisiana, particularly creolized cultural forms in the bayou country west of New Orleans. It is indeed noteworthy that creolization did not cease at the limits of the Crescent City. Many had adopted indigenous ways to one degree or another for subsistence, thereby unsettling easy definitions. "Frenchmen could more easily become savages than savages could become French," so the saying went. The founder of the Quebec Ursuline order, Marie de l'Incarnation, who knew something about seventeenth-century cultural transformation, is sometimes credited with this belief.[9] This represents a slight exception to the traditional republican model of assimilation, in which peasants and immigrants become French, but it is perhaps more accurate in the North American context. Going native in the colonial world was risky business, nonetheless, since European standing was the defining measure of the powerful. Fears certainly existed of debilitating pure strains of Old World distinction. The French occupied the head of the social hierarchy during the fleeting colonial period, yet they sometimes enabled transgressions. In what circumstances was going native permitted and by whom?

The Jesuits certainly could not be accused of cultural treason. They set out into the American wild to convert heathens and to prevent French settlers from sleeping with Native American women. In the process, they became some of the very early Métis.[10] No one had greater knowledge of Native American languages and cultures than the devout and fearless Jesuits. While they suffered (sometimes death) in pursuit of converts, they could not help but be converted themselves in the "contact zone" of French America. The Jesuits were unsuccessful in their attempt to create a New Jerusalem among Native Americans, and most returned home. Still, they set an example of the possibilities of hybridity. In documented cases of abduction or adoption, others would be given the name White Indians, even more fully assuming Native American traditions and ways of life, preceding today's Creole Cowboys and Mardi Gras Indians.[11]

After deportation from the French shores of the future Nova Scotia and resettlement in Louisiana, Acadian tenant farmers, cooks, and musicians, among others, adopted and passed along indigenous American and African cultural traditions, darkening the lily white allegory of Evangeline in the South of Franco-America and becoming Cajun or Cadien in the process. A contemporary representation of Evangeline remains culturally relevant enough to endorse products in the French parishes of south Louisiana today. As we have seen in earlier chapters, Franco-Americans of the North sometimes self-identified as "White Niggers," conveying common struggles as well as sympathies between French communities and black groups. A French ethnic identity in the Gulf Coast allowed for such "rapprochement," the area being more accepting of racial mixing generally. Louisiana is the territory in the former French colony to have experienced *métissage* on a relatively wide scale. Certainly in no place is Franco-America as postcolonially francophone as south Louisiana, "the space of colonial encounters, the space in which peoples geographically and historically separated come into contact with each other and establish ongoing relations, usually involving conditions of coercion, radical inequality and intractable conflict."[12] It is truly a contact zone in the sense that Mary L. Pratt gave it.

White Irish, Italian, and German immigrants were assimilated into the Louisiana melting pot after their arrival in the mid-nineteenth century, adopting French creolized identities. Many had come to south Louisiana during industrialization, to build the levees, later to administer and police communities as well as to work in the oil industry. In the process they became Cajuns. Typically Irish names in south Louisiana are now unproblematically a part of the creolized Cajun family. Making traditional French music, as did fiddle player Dennis McGee in 1920 and as accordionist Steve Riley continues to do, certainly facilitated the "cajunization" process. All subsets of Cajun would become increasingly Americanized in the twentieth century. French-speaking Cajuns and Creoles left their rural occupations as well as their language for the more lucrative oil fields of Louisiana and Texas. The twentieth-century construction of Interstate 10 stretching across south Louisiana from the Mississippi Gulf to Texas facilitated this Franco-American exodus.[13] For more than a century, black urban populations have affirmed Afro-Creole traditions throughout the Zydeco Corridor, most emphatically while parading as Native Americans in New Orleans as Mardi Gras Indians.[14] Native American nations of the Gulf Coast, former slaves later assimilated into the creolized population, continue to speak Cajun French in parishes of the southern coastal wetlands.[15] One could say that passing, adopting, or making another's language and culture one's own, either temporarily or permanently, was so widespread and such a potentially volatile part of life in colonial francophone Louisiana that laws were put in place to ban it. Yet at the same time, the 1724 Code Noir articulated the existence of a hybrid, creolized third category, between white and black.[16]

Louisiana is a rather unique animal in the history of French settlement and development in the New World. The quest for a route toward the Gulf of Mexico led French explorers westward. Some had begun to hear rumors of a vast river and a few still hoped that this expanse of slowly moving water would lead to the Pacific coast. The Mississippi River represents the quest that is French America in many ways. Its far-reaching tributaries collectively conveyed the desire to stake a French claim in the New World, through contact with indigenous populations, so as not to be left behind by the other seafaring and colonial powers. The French originally named the great river St. Louis.[17] Today we know how the ramifications of the periodic flooding of the Mississippi changed the course of American history, predating the migratory shifts of the twentieth century.[18] Louis Jolliet, Robert Cavalier de la Salle, Pierre Le Moyne d'Iberville, and his brother Jean-Baptiste Le Moyne de Bienville discovered and laid claim to this part of the Gulf Coast in the late seventeenth and early eighteenth centuries, one hundred years after the founding of *La Nouvelle-France* to the north in modern Quebec. After exploration by Cavalier de la Salle, it was Iberville who was commissioned by Louis XIV to establish a French settlement where the Mississippi meets the Gulf of Mexico; Bienville is credited with founding the city of New Orleans twenty years later in 1718.[19] While French colonial policy was certainly lacking generally in cohesion, the creation of a settlement post in the Gulf Coast was part of a strategic plan to prevent the English settler colonies from expanding westward. The French and Indians formed a tightly knit if unsuccessful duo for containment.[20] While the British were ultimately victorious, it was the French and the Indians who forged a strategic and culturally compelling alliance. This bulwark proved to be a temporary solution, of course, as the French colony was first divided between English and Spanish rule, the Mississippi River separating the two, in 1763. A half century later, Napoléon Bonaparte sold the Louisiana Territory to those same Americans whom French colonialists had wanted to pin to the coast.

Louisiana had a distinct status and administrative structure, and indeed suffered from its geographic isolation. The population of New France was tiny overall and that of colonial Louisiana was tinier still, some ten thousand souls by the midpoint of the eighteenth century, most of whom lived in New Orleans.[21] Given its remote location, sweltering climate, and reputation as a tough penal colony, colonial administrators had a difficult time recruiting settlers to Louisiana. By many accounts, French colonial Louisiana attracted an assortment of people from the fringes of society: soldiers, prostitutes, bootleggers, as well as proper merchants looking for a new life and not frightened of the dangers and particularities of colonial existence. Captured slaves found themselves forcibly detained in the Louisiana Territory. The frontier element contributed again to a certain degree of interdependence and *métissage* between populations for survival's sake. Gwendolyn Hall writes that "red, white, and black met under crisis conditions."[22] The intermingling of the resident populations was simply a part of French colonial life. Louisiana is a misnomer, named in honor of the man at the head of the royal court at Versailles, Louis XIV, when the Gulf of Mexico was first breached in 1699, but it became populated by misfits, mulatos, and the popular classes.

Minuscule under French domain, a likely symptom of the rather infamous beginning to its history, New Orleans quickly grew in the hands of the American colonialists, becoming the third largest city by the mid-nineteenth century and the largest inland port.[23] The current threat to the city posed by rising tides, if one fast forwards a century, has diminished population levels, leaving it less French Creole than before. Still, it is the history of migration, slavery, and miscegenation, merging European, African, and Amerindian populations violently and pervasively, that fostered the development of French transatlantic space.[24] French roots and open fields were consequently planted by Indians, blacks, and the French in the colonial Mississippi frontier.[25] The mixing of ethnic groups was often unsupervised, even before the end of slavery. Slaves in French colonial Louisiana at times attained astonishing levels of freedom. Many came from the Senegal River basin and had been farmers, traders, and artisans.[26] Bienville encouraged a racially diverse, free market economy in which slaves were encouraged to develop small businesses and trades. They could attend market at Congo Square, now known as Louis Armstrong Park, participate in the exchange of goods, and even purchase their freedom with the money that they earned. Out of this mercantile life that brought together populations, languages, and cultures developed the Mardi Gras Indian procession that still takes place today. Ethnographer Michael P. Smith finds a tangible distinction between "the inclusive French Creole tradition vs. the exclusive Anglo-American tradition." While slavery persisted, French law established a code of conduct that regulated bondage and racial relations in ways unknown in the Anglo-American world. The Louisiana Purchase brought a Protestant ethos into the French colonial/ Creole Gulf Coast and a clear hostility toward ethnic and cultural intermingling (a tension that continued after the Civil War). Smith finds that after the Louisiana Purchase of 1803, the increasing numbers of Anglo-Protestants in French Creole Louisiana created an atmosphere less tolerant of multicultural exchange.[27]

The encounters between groups produced lively cultures, all Creole in the sense of combining Old and New World ingredients, indigenous, African, and European. Clearly, Louisiana sits in a very interesting position within the French Americas. Anthropologist Nick Spitzer has suggested that culturally the area represents an extension of Caribbean currents.[28] The late Cajun poet and teacher Richard Guidry said that all French Louisianians are Creoles. He declared that Louisiana was located somewhere between *le bon Dieu* and *le diable*, French being on the good, Godlike side, of course, and American on the bad or satanic side.[29] Questions continue to exist about whether the cultural hybridity of French Louisiana can endure in the face of American assimilation that has been at work more intensely since World War II. Are old binary antagonisms, black versus white, likely to prevail if French influence dissipates? It is perhaps more accurate to emphasize that American influence represents another ingredient thrown into the proverbial pot of gumbo and that it has been adopted as well as co-opted in the production of a distinct French Creole identity in the none too typically American South of the Gulf Coast.

Studies of race and ethnicity reveal the stain of blackness in Franco-American mixes on the Gulf Coast as well as in New England: among the downtrodden of the postcolonial French diasporic family, one finds Cajuns, Canucks, Creoles, and Coonasses, all hybrid, often displaced populations.[30] At first glance, a great deal seems to oppose groups at the crossroads of Louisiana, the southern end of the north-south axis of Franco America. Much still distinguishes the descendants of particular sets of people in this region: race, socioeconomic class, even geography. Cajun and Creole groups are often thought to occupy separate space in south Louisiana, with Cajuns in the twenty-two parishes west of the Mississippi River in Acadiana and Creoles in New Orleans.[31] Yet both of these terms, *Cajun* and *Creole*, represent murky, ever shifting categories as well as geographies.

The signifier Creole has often served to set populations apart historically, outside of creolization as a homogenizing process. White Creole distinction set more affluent Acadian populations apart from their poorer Cajun cousins in the nineteenth century.[32] To the dismay of white Creoles, *les gens de couleur libres* (free people of color) also used the Creole label to differentiate themselves from more recently freed slaves after the Civil War. Historically, socially ambitious Cajuns preferred the earlier distinctive Creole label (as did some black groups) while white Prairie Creoles opted for a Cajun identity when it became profitable to do so.[33] The Genteel Acadian / Proud Coonass disparity still points to socioeconomic and cultural differences separating poorer and wealthier Cajuns. Geographic disparities served to differentiate Acadian descendants in Louisiana. Marcia Gaudet distinguishes between "River Cajuns" along the Mississippi River north of New Orleans, "Wetland Cajuns" along southern bayous and the Atchafalaya swamp, and the "Prairie Cajuns" of the southwest interior.[34]

In the twentieth and twenty-first centuries, the meaning of Creole has become noticeably detached from its intercultural history. For some, it cannot escape an original association with African populations and cultures. The term has been linked with blackness since the slave trade at least and is often devalued as a result, despite the profusion of French Creole cultural life in New Orleans a hundred years ago. Some of its former luster has not entirely faded from memory, however, and is even resurrected in the commercialization of the Cajun/Creole brand today. Common Creole cultures developed in subtle ways that were not often acknowledged, particularly along the color line of the Jim Crow South. They circulated in the past, as remnants of them still do today. Québécois film makers opted for the title *Le Grand Mélangement* in a 2008 short film, stressing *métissage* and the French hybrid cultures of Louisiana in place of *Le Grand Dérangement*, the term used to describe Acadian uprooting, dispersal, or even ethnic cleansing.[35] The Creole Cowboy is representative of French cosmopolitanism in contemporary Louisiana. As both horseman and musician, the Creole Cowboy emphasizes mixing over cleansing.[36]

MIDDLE GROUND

One common definition of Creole can be taken from the Spanish or Portuguese experience of the Americas including slaving, beginning in the sixteenth century, designating objects, ideas, and especially people of the Old World born in the New. It identifies diasporic, multiethnic populations that fused over time. Creolization might be understood as a linguistic and cultural bridge connecting heterogeneous populations. Linguist Albert Valdman adopts Aimé Césaire's creolized view of the Creole language: "Creole is a language of which the body is French but the soul is African."[37] The authors of *Eloge de la créolité*, speaking specifically of its unifying factors for Antillian populations, claim that créolité offers an alternative model to what they consider to be "la fausse universalité, du monolinguisme et de la pureté," in other words, "l'américanité." They prefer Creole over the "false" universality of American as an identifying intranational concept. "La créolité englobe et parachève donc l'américanité," Bernabé, Chamoiseau, and Confiant observe, because of its openness to including Africans, Asians, and Europeans in a framework for cultural exchange, one that does not exclude confrontation.[38] Linguistic examples of such creolization produced through conflict and exchange are common in the Gulf South. In parts of south Louisiana and despite local tensions, some black Creoles have long spoken the predominant local variant of French, Cajun French; Cajuns have used Creole as a means of communication in communities such as Breaux Bridge and St. Martinville, for instance; and Native American groups, more than 50 percent of members of the Houma Nation, for instance, speak Cajun French as a first language.[39] Through language, a thickening agent or *roux* in culinary terms is produced, blending the local cultures.

In the creolized regions of the Gulf area, people came to share a common religion: Catholicism. New Orleans's Xavier University is the only black Roman Catholic institution in the country, founded by a prominent family (Drexel) in 1915 to educate not only African Americans but Native Americans as well. Catholic culture certainly provided middle ground in the murkiness between black and white in the French world. The Creole flag of Louisiana illustrates the hybrid nature of its cultures. The flag contains four rectangular flags in miniature, separated by a white cross symbolizing the adoption (sometimes forced) of Christianity by many African populations. In the upper left corner, a white *fleur-de-lys* is set in blue, commemorating French heritage. While formerly of royal, holy extraction, this symbol has indeed come to represent a more commonplace Frenchness in postcolonial America. In the lower right corner, one finds a castle in Castilian red in memory of tolerant Spanish rule. After 1763 under Spanish rule, African slaves could purchase their freedom. In the upper right and lower left corners, tricolor green, yellow, and red flags represent the individuals brought to Louisiana from the Mali and Senegal area. The flag has been in existence for thirty years, since 1987, a product and political emblem of C.R.E.O.L.E., Inc., which stands for "Cultural Resourceful Educational Opportunities toward Linguistic Enrichment." Its motto is "Strength in unity" (L'union fait la force).[40] The Cajun flag of Louisiana is only slightly less creolized, combining French colors and *fleur-de-lys*, the Spanish castle, and the Acadian star.

Historians suggest that the creolization process resulted in the construction of a new way of defining social and cultural groups beyond the imposing barriers of racial segregation, again a "middle ground."[41] Jim

Crow laws in the United States created a deep divide, of course, but creolization signals a curious kind of trespassing. By way of explanation, many studies point to a French tradition of tolerance and acceptance of the other. The *Code Noir*, which again set up a legal framework for relations between the races in eighteenth-century Franco America, indicates the existence of this ambiguous world between white and black.[42] The *Code Noir* arguably rendered the relations within this world more fluid than in Anglo-America. It gave slaves Sunday off (if slave masters chose to abide by it), but also branded a *fleur-de-lys* on the black bodies of fugitives, a revealing physical sign of French creolization.[43] While some studies (this one included) focus on those places where cultures collide, it is important not to overestimate or exaggerate the contours of this middle ground. The notion does not imply complicity or shared public space in colonial Louisiana. If common cultures formed, they did so silently, unofficially, and usually off the grid, for middle ground was most certainly contested.

While underlining "the chaos of French rule," Gwendolyn Hall contends that "in French Louisiana, Africans and their descendants were competent, desperately needed, and far from powerless."[44] African technologies were essential to colonial life there, she affirms. In her exhaustive study, *Africans in Colonial Louisiana*, and the development of the region's "Afro-Creole culture," Hall rightly states that easy racial and cultural binaries are far too simplistic to accurately reflect realities on the (middle) ground. Contemporary assumptions about race and race relations bear little resemblance to the social hierarchies (or lack thereof) of colonial Louisiana. African populations could physically punish whites and fear no official reprimand on the part of the colonial administration. Historian Carl Brasseaux argues that Creoles or *gens de couleur libres* were keenly aware of their rights under the *Code Noir* and used the legal system to their best advantage, to protect their families and property. Some *Creoles of the Bayou Country* not only occupied middle ground but passed completely into the white population; some possessed slaves. This is a subject of considerable unease today for Louisiana Creoles. In an interesting historical aside, Brasseaux notes that in the lower prairies of eighteenth-century south Louisiana, the cannibalism of the Attakapas Indians temporarily prevented creolization from developing.[45]

Both whites and black groups retreated from potentially deadly relations. It is important to note that French colonial policy makers in Louisiana made repeated attempts to thwart unwanted sympathies between African and Native American populations, who ultimately mingled all the same.[46] This highlights another factor within postcolonial Franco America: not all creolizations were equal or desired. People contested creolization where it might disturb the colonial (im)balance of power.

It is a French Creole, Catholic, and democratic culture that distinguishes south Louisiana from the north of the state and indeed the South more generally. This can still be seen in electoral results that distinguish French Creole Louisiana from the more traditional South, despite the inroads that the Republican Party has made throughout the region in the last fifty years. Political scientist Wayne Parent argues that this culture of tolerance is exhibited in the higher percentage of blacks registered to vote in Louisiana's French parishes prior to the 1965 Voting Rights Act than elsewhere in the South.[47] A decade before that, the University of Louisiana at Lafayette, the "Université des Acadiens" and home of the Rajun' Cajuns, became the first state school of the Deep South to desegregate in 1954.[48] The previous century, during the turmoil of the Civil War, Louisiana was the Southern state least interested in seceding from the Union.[49] This is yet another sign of Louisiana's French tradition of laissez-faire, rendering it distinctly atypical in comparison with neighboring Mississippi and Alabama. The status of New Orleans as a major commercial hub, the largest inland port in the United States in the nineteenth century, is also in part responsible for its difference.[50]

The Cajun/Creole divide, however, has long prevented many from seeing the tangible results of French hybridization. It is striking how many studies of French cultural traditions in Louisiana, of music, poetry, folktales, and foodways, indicate the very real differences that exist between Cajun and Creole expressions. What they simultaneously articulate is the cross-pollination so central to the definition of each, a fact that warrants clarification. Charles Stivale describes coming to terms with what unites and what separates Cajun and Creole in the music and dance arena.[51] The distance between peoples and cultures has become increasingly narrow as they have fused with increasing frequency and intensity. There are fewer formal boundaries between cultures, identities, or nations as a result today, particularly with the commodification of cultures in the global market-place. In their treatise on the emergence of a *culture-monde*, critics Gilles Lipovetsky and Jean Serroy argue that the parameters of culture have shifted dramatically away from typical bourgeois and popular culture oppositions, transformed by media, the market, and global currents:

> Culture-monde signifie fin de l'hétérogénéité traditionnelle de la sphère culturelle et universalisation de la culture marchande s'emparant des sphères de la vie sociale, des modes d'existence, de la quasi-totalité des activités humaines. Avec la culture-monde se répand sur tout le globe la culture de la technoscience, celle du marché, de l'individu, des médias, de la consommation. . . . Monde qui devient culture, culture qui devient monde: une culture-monde.[52]

Large-scale consumption of Cajun and Creole cultures places them within this optic, contributing to a new cosmopolitanism, a worldly arena freed from previous barriers. Individuals and individual cultures can participate in this ever-changing, perhaps increasingly democratic model of exchange.

Music offers a revealing example of such cultural transaction. In the following section, I will examine selected contemporary musical expressions of French Louisiana, where Cajun and Creole borders continue to disintegrate, despite the obstacles periodically thrown up to prevent contact. The music of French Louisiana west of the Crescent City provides a provocative example of border crossing, particularly in the age of industrialized cultural transactions. Live music captured in Lafayette, Louisiana, on YouTube videos places the intimacy of French Cajun and Creole performance on the worldwide stage of *culture-monde* continuously. French musical cultures of Louisiana and the Gulf region have been borrowing from one another constantly, from New World beginnings until this day; they are thoroughly creolized.

LE COWBOY CREOLE SINGS

Let us look more closely at Cajun music. Its very origins are creolized: French, Spanish, Acadian, American, Irish, German, African, and Native

American influences converge in the bayous. It is creolization that makes Cajun music profoundly different from Acadian music, states ethnomusicologist Barry Jean Ancelet. Each influence lent a different layer of complexity. Acadian exiles brought musical traditions and instruments such as the fiddle to the waterways of Louisiana. They borrowed extensively from the sounds, rhythms, and instruments of local populations that surrounded them, African and Native American cultures particularly. Acadian settlers learned from Native Americans "a terraced singing style and new dance rhythms; from the blacks, they learned the blues, percussion techniques, a love of syncopation and improvisational singing."[53] Black Creole or Zydeco music simply had a greater Afro-Caribbean influence, writes Ancelet, "just as Cajun music suggests the strong influence of the black Creole tradition, the lyrics as well as the forms of tunes in the Creole selections provide clues to the important influence of the Afro-Caribbean tradition of shouted music (known as *juré*) for Cajun music as well as for the most recent Creole musical form, Zydeco."[54]

Ryan Brasseaux argues that French creolized music of south Louisiana is not simply an exceptional or exotic (i.e., French) form of music. He attempts to place Cajun music within the pantheon of deeply creolized, *American* musical genres.[55] This is an unusual perspective to adopt, given that cultural expressions by francophones in Louisiana typically set themselves apart from American influence, but Brasseaux makes a convincing point. Texas hillbilly and swing among other inspirations became a part of the creolized or cosmopolitan idiom known as Cajun music coming out of French Louisiana in the mid-twentieth century. Jazz is perhaps the most recognized of America's creolized musical forms. It is typically believed to have migrated north along the Mississippi River valley and its tributaries, the Creole Corridor, between Chicago, American home of the blues, and Detroit, St. Louis, and New Orleans, all influential French ports, with Jelly Roll Morton as its most prominent innovator. Today Cajun Jazz poet Beverly Matherne carries on a deeply creolized artistic tradition.[56] John M. Barry writes that the great flood of the Mississippi River in 1927, in addition to intensifying a migration of black people already begun, placed the blues squarely in the delta.[57] The Québécois road book *Volkswagen*

Blues alludes to such traveling cultures of the Gulf South set adrift most notably along the Mississippi and that included explorers, slaves, Indians, cotton, Faulkner, and jazz.[58] "In the interplay of ethnic culture and music in New Orleans during the late nineteenth century," contends Michael P. Smith, "both secular and sacred, in the streets, in the churches, in the neighborhood enclaves, and in the great dance halls, we find the basic ingredients and chemistry of Jazz."[59]

A sign of creolization in French music of Louisiana is found at the arrival of the accordion onto the scene in the 1920s. A product of Germany, sold by Jewish merchants in Louisiana, its sounds and rhythms produced by African populations greatly influenced the makers of French Cajun/Creole music.[60] Following its introduction, the accordion consequently transformed the music coming out of French Louisiana because voices that accompanied it had to be pitched just so to be heard over the soaring riffs. Annie Proulx's novel *Accordion Crimes* traces the trajectory of an instrument shared by many immigrant communities from the Louisiana bayou to musical soirées of New England. Black Creole accordionist and vocalist Amédé Ardoin helped to promote the instrument's big sound, playing to white and black audiences in the informal house dances (*bals de maison*) and country balls (*fais do-do*) of south Louisiana. He and exuberant Cajun fiddler Dennis McGee are responsible for putting together many standards from the "Cajun" repertoire, despite the racial barriers and segregation of the period.[61] The appeal of cosmopolitan French music trumped social convention, and the economics of the transaction trumped all. The two musicians could make more money playing to black and white audiences. Ardoin was, however, almost beaten to death for transgressing the rigid boundary of white womanhood, after accepting a handkerchief from a reveler to wipe his brow.[62] This again underscores the peril of creolization, even French; it took place sometimes at considerable personal risk. Ardoin was reportedly never the same man or musician following the beating.[63]

Standards from the 1920s and 1930s like the "Eunice Two-Step" and "Les Blues/Barres de la prison" have become thoroughly creolized in their interpretations.[64] These tunes can be performed in either tradition of postcolonial Franco America of the South. "Les Blues de la prison" echo the "bad times" that so often accompany the good in the French music tradition of Louisiana, for black and white alike:

O parti à la prison pour un condamné
La balance de mes jours, O la balance de mes jours.
Ma pauvre maman s'ennuie autant et elle peut pas me rejoindre.

O jusqu'à, yaïe, O la porte de la prison fermée sur moi,
Ils ont oublié la clef. Je crois ils l'ont jetée,
Ils vont jamais la retrouver encore.[65]

The subject of the song is jail-bound, the key to the prison lost, and a mother left to lament. All hope seems gone, the voice and instruments suggest. The fiddle and the rub board can still distinguish Cajun from Creole music, respectively, but there is a wailing, plaintive character in both musical expressions. Indeed one finds echoes of tragedy, heartache, and mourning in each, in response to unrequited love, betrayal, poverty, and death. Compilations of contemporary Cajun standards feature "Creole" artists such as Canray Fontenot playing traditional tunes.[66] More evidence of this phenomenon lies in the recorded, noncommercial music preserved in the Cajun and Creole archives at the University of Louisiana at Lafayette. The classic "Jolie Blonde," in which a young woman leaves her lover for another, is performed by both white and black musicians, each equally plaintive due to the sentimental burden that jilted men are forced to carry:

Jolie blonde, regardez donc quoi t'as fait
Tu m'as quitté pour t'en aller,
Pour t'en aller avec un autre, oui, que moi
Quel espoir et quel avenir, mais moi, je
vas avoir.[67]

A century ago, Cajun and Creole sharecroppers picked cotton under the same Louisiana sun and could authentically sing the French Creole blues. One hears this in the voice of Nathan Abshire, an illiterate accordionist and music maker whose renditions of the Cajun blues were shaped by teacher Amédé Ardoin.[68] To the largely illiterate, working-class French

Creole and Cajun populations of the prairies and bayous, music was a language understood and consumed by all.

The accordion dominated the French music scene until the 1930s; then it passed out of favor before being brought back by Cajun GIs nostalgic for more traditional music after the Second World War. The Hackberry Ramblers' rendition of "Jolie Blonde" aided this evolution. Creole musician Canray Fontenot opted for the more traditional fiddle in the postwar period, instead of the accordion that his father, Adam Fontenot, played, often alongside friend Amédé Ardoin. Canray claimed that Ardoin and his father could pass off the instrument between them without missing a beat at dances.[69] Accordionist Alphonse "Bois Sec" Ardoin, Amédé's cousin, and Canray Fontenot played traditional French Creole songs together, not Zydeco, for some forty years.[70] Labels sometimes marketed their music as French Cajun or "traditional," which is often synonymous for white. This provides further examples of cultural mixing, of Creole eliding into Cajun and Cajun merging with Creole. "Bois Sec" Ardoin claimed that to make true French music in Louisiana, the seed had to be planted within the family.[71] Music is very much a part of the French family tree in south Louisiana as the Ardoin, Balfa, Chavis, Michot, and Savoy clans attest, with well-established roots and very often hybrid fruit. Marc Savoy has long been an innovator in the fabrication of traditional accordions that accompany and often lead newly interpreted Cajun and Creole music.

More contemporary musicians like accordion player Geno Delafose, who followed his father into the music arena, have a style that places them between Cajun and Creole. Indeed, some in the younger generation of musicians move easily between traditions, between rub board and fiddle, although there are no "Cajun" artists on some Creole greatest hits compilations.[72] Cedric Watson, fiddler and vocalist for the Pine Leaf Boys for several years, developed his Cajun repertoire there, before returning to the black Creole sounds of his youth in his band Bijou Creole. Soulful Cajun crooner Courtney Granger, of the Balfa music family, collaborates with the Pine Leaf Boys, but also performs with Creole musicians like Delafose and traditional Cajun artists such as Balfa Toujours. Since the 1980s, Wayne Toups and his ZydeCajun band, and Horace Trahan and the Ossun Express more recently, sing both Creole and Cajun style, transgressing boundaries, ruffling feathers, but advancing the culture and genres with their music.

On his daily French language program devoted to local music and the arts, *Bonjour Louisiane* host Pete Bergeron plays not only the Cajun and Creole standards that define the music but the more recent tunes that demonstrate current trends where traditions merge.[73] The *Encore* program sponsored through the same KRVS public radio station, Radio Acadie, airs music and folklore that take inspiration from the archives at the University of Louisiana at Lafayette. In both recorded and live performances of Louisiana French music, the popular reinterpretations of current musicians fuse artistic and scholarly pursuits. Joshua McCafferty's *Traditional Music of Coastal Louisiana* provides a critical anthology of the original 1934 field recordings of rural Louisiana musicians by Alan and John Lomax. The Lomaxes traveled through south Louisiana recording "tropical French music" that echoed an eerie authenticity that they feared would soon disappear entirely. The access of young Cajun and Creole musicians to the John and Alan Lomax collection of recorded songs makes the sounds, rhythms, and lyrics timeless; contemporary artists continually reinterpret standards.[74] Barry Jean Ancelet helped to repatriate to Louisiana recordings that the Lomaxes first filed at the National Archives in Washington so that they could continue to inspire new creations.

Texan transplant Cedric Watson, who learned to play fiddle and speak French, is representative of the Creole Cowboy phenomenon, of the hybrid, cosmopolitan cultures of south Louisiana. Use of the Creole Cowboy as a metaphor for French hybridization, one should note, has some historical legitimacy. The horse and the horseman are central to Creole francophone cultures of the Gulf Coast, both black and white. Cattle ranching required cowboys of remarkable fortitude to lead herds over land and water on the wide prairies of south Louisiana and Texas. Black horsemen such as Floyd "Mano" Clifton were legendary for their skills.[75] A core belief in freedom defined them, like *coureurs de bois* in the North.[76] Some traditional Mardi Gras runnings or "courirs" in rural communities in Louisiana today, which exemplify contemporary performances of *cajunitude* and *créolité*, take place on horseback. The Federation of Black Cowboys sponsors trail rides that perpetuate tradition. Female Mardi Gras runs demonstrate that men are not the only creators of French Louisiana cultures.

In a 2007 CD, Geno Delafose plays "La Porte d'en arrière," a Cajun standard made famous by D. L. Menard in 1962. He calls it "La Porte en arriere," a slightly modified transcription into unaccented French.[77] Delafose sings in Louisiana French, in the language of Boudreaux, the Cajun everyman of local mythology. Delafose and his French Rockin' Boogie band advertise their CD as "100% Louisiana Creole Zydeco." Delafose's production of hybrid musical forms most certainly contains Cajun country elements as well. Such authenticity derives from the French experience, it is important to note. Traditional Cajun and Creole music in south Louisiana today is sung primarily in French. In addition to playing more contemporary Zydeco, the great Clifton Chenier claimed to enjoy playing the "authentic" French Creole music of his youth in French.

The French experience in America typically meant entering through the "back door" as a minority group. Geno Delafose uses French syntax to signal his Frenchness and to set himself apart from his main rival to the crown, Jeffery Broussard and the Creole Cowboys. Note the English syntax in the band's name, in contrast to Geno Delafose's Le Cowboy Creole. This is significant, as Delafose not only sings in French but speaks French unlike many Creole musicians today. Delafose is one of the featured Louisiana Francophones in the 2002 documentary *Gumb-oh! là! là!* This was the first film reportedly recorded in Louisiana French.[78] Undeterred by the challenge, Jeffery Broussard took up French Creole fiddling.

Zachary Richard and Beausoleil are two of the most widely known French musical groups of America who also embody some of its most radicalized elements. They represent a modern creolization process that has been taking place in Cajun music since its inception. Both Richard and Beausoleil have experimented with styles and genres that express a profound respect for traditional French music, but that also take it in new directions, including fusion that harkens back to the Afro-Caribbean tradition noted earlier. Richard has experimented with Cajun reggae and rap. Beausoleil's experimental *Cajunization* (1999) also attempts to expand the parameters of traditional French Acadian music. Recently, Grammy winners Steve Riley and the Mamou Playboys as well as the Lost Bayou Ramblers have taken traditional French music from Louisiana honky-tonks to mainstream airways. Chris Ardoin brings an R&B and hip-hop swagger to what is generally a more traditional Franco-American folk music genre. Soul Creole, composed notably of Lost Bayou Ramblers Louis Michot on fiddle and Corey Ledet on accordion, also relishes in the play of nontraditional music. Music has certainly helped to make it acceptable, even fashionable, to be Cajun perhaps and has helped to ease the modern transgressing of the color line. Louisiana Creole musicians cross the color line today by taking part in the local Acadian cultural scene, after the Un-Cajun Committee of the 1980s established clear boundaries between white and black.[79]

French music in Louisiana has traditionally been male dominated, but a few women can be identified. Christine Balfa of the Balfa clan and Ann Savoy are two of the best known today. They were preceded by pioneering women in the traditional "Cajun music and dance arena," who were little known outside of Louisiana. Cleoma Breaux is one of the old-time and pervasive influences. Small in stature but large in volume and stage presence, she was very much a fixture on the local dance hall scene like Amédé Ardoin. She and her husband, Joe Falcon, collaborated on the first Cajun music recording in 1928.[80] Women have long been at the heart of Franco-American musical traditions, the objects of unloving, cheating, and otherwise absent Franco men in verse or singing about them. There is a tradition of women singing love songs in kitchens and on porches, unrecorded music mostly captured in the archives and brought back to life.[81] Women also nurture the culture through the recording of song for children, another way of maintaining French linguistic and cultural traditions in Acadiana.

Adopted Cajun matriarch Ann Savoy became involved in recording music in order to help transmit French cultures of Louisiana. Her Magnolia Sisters present classic Cajun and Creole songs to children of Franco descent.[82] Many of these songs have faded from living memory and are no longer actively sung by children or adults. Michael Doucet of Beausoleil has also recorded French song, folklore, and culture for children.[83] Listeners relate to the swamp mosquitoes and crocodiles (*cocodris*, in Louisiana French). The selections, including "Jolie Blonde," Creole classic "Zydeco Gris-Gris," and the Louisiana French version of the "Hokey Pokey," are presented bilingually as sing-alongs meant to foster cultural appreciation. Contemporary Creole singer and accordion player Rosie Ledet and the Zydeco Playboys offer substantially more adult fare than Ann Savoy or Cleoma Breaux. Ledet gained a regional and even wider audience for her high-energy performances and sexualized lyrics.[84] They are full of double entendres and play on French stereotypes of promiscuity that sell. These performers and performances have drawn increased attention to French Creole music.

Like Mardi Gras, the large festivals featuring live Cajun and Creole music, the fall Festivals Acadiens (now called the Festivals Acadiens et Créoles) and the Festival International de Louisiane in spring, draw attention to not one but all of the lively French art forms of south Louisiana. Their success lies in an appealing presentation of food, music, French language, and culture over several days each year. It is impossible to revive French cultures during the course of a festival weekend, but annual celebrations can perhaps (re)kindle interest. Once cultural forms like music had attained an appreciable currency among people, such manifestations were in a position to prosper. The 1964 Newport Folk Festival helped to facilitate the transcendence of French music of Louisiana. The Cajun fiddler Dewey Balfa attended the event half expecting the audience to dislike the local music that he and others had previously played only to intimate crowds in Louisiana, often to friends and family at the popular country and home dances. It had been discounted as "chang-chang" music not worthy of attention.[85] Instead of scorn, Balfa received a standing ovation in Newport, Rhode Island, and returned with a missionary zeal to revive French traditions through music. He reportedly wanted to bring the glow of that ovation back to south Louisiana.

Dewey Balfa's experience paved the way for other Cajun and Creole musicians to play for regional, national, and international audiences, taking their music out of the bayous and into the Smithsonian and beyond. Balfa ultimately found an ally in the leadership of the Council for the

Development of French in Louisiana (CODOFIL), which had begun to spearhead efforts to teach and preserve Louisiana French cultures.[86] Balfa and other Cajun/Creole musicians brought their instruments and sounds to classrooms in southwestern Louisiana in order to use this powerful artistic form to stir interest in linguistic and cultural identity. Music has indeed been a part of CODOFIL's strategic planning for cultural rebirth since the very beginning, and its effectiveness is perhaps confirmed in the desire of young Cajun musicians to sing in French.

CODOFIL was the initial sponsor and supporter of Festivals Acadiens organized in order to help transmit and promote Cajun/Cadien cultures over the course of its three-day celebration. Such a state-supported festival aimed to make known to younger generations the traditional musical cultures that had developed in the area. Organizers conceived of this first manifestation as a strictly seated affair, a marked change in style, as fans were used to dancing at the *bals de maison* when French music was played. Sponsors decided that if people actually listened rather than danced to the music, they might better appreciate the talent of the musicians. They could not hope to keep them from dancing for very long.

The very first music concert of the Festivals Acadiens held at Blackham Coliseum on the University of Louisiana at Lafayette campus on March 26, 1974, was a defining moment in the emergence of French Louisiana cultures. CODOFIL needed such a signature event, dubbed "A Tribute to Cajun Music," to promote its cultural programming in south Louisiana and had invited francophone journalists to witness the expression of French cultures. On March 26, musicians played, people cheered, and an indigenous French culture in the United States was affirmed. The lineup included many Cajun and Creole legends including Dennis McGee, Bois Sec Ardoin, Canray Fontenot, Clifton Chenier, Nathan Abshire, Marc Savoy, and the Balfa brothers, clearly not just a tribute to strictly Cajun music. CODOFIL director Jimmie Domengeaux allegedly did not want to confuse matters by including Creole in the concert title.[87] For more than thirty years it remained an Acadian festival in title, although the Cajun/Creole influences were present from the start. Festival documentation reveals the consistent inclusion of Creole cultures.

10. Poster for the Festivals Acadiens et Créoles, 2013, Lafayette, Louisiana.

The second festival starred Zachary Richard and the Bayou des mystères, who performed "Réveille" with raised white fists and politicized ethnic consciousness, crying, "Awaken!" to all who would hear. Dancing was permitted following the successful first experiment, and the modern outdoor festival emerged the following year. CODOFIL discontinued its sponsorship of the event by 1980, but it grew bigger, adding food and artisanry to its cultural offerings and programming names. The French plural name Festivals Acadiens comes from the fusion of independent music, food, and craft venues. For the last twenty years, not only could cultures be sampled there, but through the *Atelier* and Workshop tents, festival-goers were encouraged to learn to produce art themselves. Cooking and Jam sessions with musicians are part of the cultural programming. In this way, all can become involved in the preservation of Louisiana's French and francophone cultures, through hands-on instruction and practice.

It was in 2008 that the Creole contribution to the event was formally acknowledged by name. The 2014 celebration marked the fortieth year of the Festivals Acadiens et Créoles. The Festival International de Louisiane, less Cajun perhaps but proudly francophone and Creole in scope, was first organized by CODOFIL in 1986 and has since become the largest French music event in the United States. Conceived to bring together the visual and performing arts, today it draws some of the biggest names in traditional French Creole music of South Louisiana and beyond and hundreds of thousands of people. In 2009, TV5Monde's *Acoustic* program presented broadcasts from Lafayette, drawing greater attention to its lively music, dancing, and cultural scene. Both before and after festival season, local radio stations play traditional Cajun/Creole music in French and English each day of the year, maintaining the culture and keeping it fresh.[88]

LES BONS TEMPS AFTER THE FLOOD

Music may be able to keep French Creole cultures alive in Louisiana (afloat might be the more appropriate metaphor), if young people like Courtney Granger, Wilson Savoy, Horace Trahan, Cedric Watson, Cory Ledet, and Louis Michot continue to sing in French when playing Cajun and Creole standards. Some have pessimistically claimed, however, that the only French spoken in south Louisiana at some point will come from the lips of predominantly monolingual (i.e., English) singers.[89] Others like historian Shane Bernard are highly critical of CODOFIL for failing to produce French speakers in their immersion programs in south Louisiana. At the very least, CODOFIL has held the powerful forces of English at bay for several decades by keeping French pertinent. Residents of south Louisiana want access to French and lobby for immersion schools. The reality of the cultural climate in south Louisiana is that most people no longer know, for instance, the traditional Mardi Gras songs that crews sing as they "cut up." Bystanders participate by singing along to live music, radio broadcasts, and CDs.

French Louisianans such as Richard Guidry tell us that language is essential to the vitality of culture and to its specificity. There are fewer francophone residents in the state than thirty or forty years ago, but the latest census data from 2010 indicate that French Creoles are helping to sustain the overall number of French speakers in the United States. Even French third way categories have departed in many respects. As early as the Reconstruction period, Union officials refused to recognize elevated Creole social and cultural status. One hundred years later, the black power movement of the 1960s and 1970s did away with some of the black/Creole distinctions as Creoles of color came out as black.[90] It was indeed more difficult to be Creole when "Black Is Beautiful." French Louisiana's demise has been proclaimed many times in the past. But "On est toujours icitte!" / "We're still here!" remains a rallying cry for Franco-Americans in Louisiana and elsewhere.[91]

Entrepreneurs will not easily let French cultural distinction fade, because they know that French branding can stimulate business.[92] French cultural symbols are packaged and distributed, sometimes widely, because of the value that is tied directly to their Frenchness. While French cultural meanings surely change as a result of commercialization, there is a constant in such advertising: French defined as spicy, exotic, sexually permissive, and symbolized by the good times of the *Vieux Carré* in carnivalesque New Orleans, at least a century past its francophone heyday. This French joie de vivre further greases the merchandizing wheels, increasing circulation of T-shirts, postcards, CDs, and foods. Throughout French Louisiana and indeed well beyond its limited borders, one finds "Cajun" campgrounds, pizzerias, and grocery stores, most doing little if any business in French.

The Creole/Cajun label clearly adds to the luster of a given product, providing an appealing sales pitch to American consumers in search of a local or regional exotic, a contradiction in terms, but one very evocative of French Louisiana. Chef and cable television mogul Emeril Lagasse's "Bayou Blast" condiment makes reference to its Cajun heritage, but also its zest as a Creole seasoning. Today, a confusing array of commercial Creole and Cajun food products exist not only in the Gulf Coast but nationally. Regional supermarket chains from Louisiana to New England have a zesty Cajun section. As mentioned, both Cajun and Creole can help to move merchandise, and the two are often used simultaneously to describe the same item. In cuisine, both possess a cultural capital that is acknowledged in the branding of a particular product. Advertising as Cajun and Creole, often an attempt to profit commercially from both labels, represents a contradiction in meaning to many, although it echoes the hybridity suggested here. Food represents a cultural tradition upon which many South Louisianans can concur.

The borders between Cajun and Creole are clearly ambiguous but ultimately unproblematic at table with dishes like gumbo, which can be served in one, the other, or increasingly both styles.[93] The transnational itineraries of "French" foods of the Gulf South region, stews, sausages, and sauces, are the subject of lively scholarly debate. Recipes in the French postcolonial world are certainly cultural roadmaps. While one could most certainly construct an argument around culinary creolization in contemporary French Louisiana, I will touch only briefly on the area's culinary traditions and refer readers to a growing literature on the subject.[94]

Marcelle Bienvenu's book *Can You Make a Roux, Are You Catholic, and Who's Your Momma?* conveys the importance of cooking alongside religion and family in French Louisiana. One of the most common examples of French Creole gastronomy can be found in festival stands as well as in private and public kitchens, in a simmering pot of gumbo. The roux, a mixture of equal parts fat and flour, glazed to a copper complexion, from whence the gumbo originates, is at the base of almost all south Louisiana cooking. The rice that is a common denominator to many French Creole meals is a product of the French Atlantic slave trade. Crawfish étouffée, gumbos, and jambalayas are consumed by all ethnic groups in Louisiana; they are clearly multicultural, cosmopolitan dishes that refer back to Spanish, French, African, and Native American heritage, acknowledged in both the Cajan and Creole flags. The kitchen is the center of the traditional French universe in south Louisiana, the very hearth of the Cajun and Creole home.[95] It was as much a performance space as other more recognized venues, a place where cooks and consumers met joyously. European, African, and Native American traditions all share a Creole culinary expression.[96] If you are what you eat, then francophones in South Louisiana are all pretty much the same. Theirs is the food of the working classes, featuring the morsels first hunted or harvested, dishes lovingly prepared with the toughest of cuts and simmered to tenderness. Now some of these traditional favorites have gained national prominence. Black and white French Louisianans remember only having "couche-couche" to eat, fried cornmeal that could be sweetened with sugar and milk. Couche-couche is now served at swank eateries reviewed in the Sunday *New York Times*.[97]

The adjective Cajun and Creole can be found attached to dishes in restaurants across the country, both high and low end, many with very little authentic link to south Louisiana cuisine. "Louisiana fast food" emerged as a mostly regional chain of restaurants that opened in the 1970s and later expanded nationally. Popeyes Louisiana Kitchen now brings its original chicken but also seafood and more traditional Cajun/Creole dishes to Americans and other nations with 1,800 franchises in the United States and in twenty countries. Shane K. Bernard credits Popeyes with popularizing the Cajun gastronomic brand.[98] Beginning in 2008, Popeye's television spokeswoman Annie offered "Louisiana Fast" to hungry patrons, many in African American communities. Branches presented Franco-American light fare in 2011, "Cajun Leaux" (pronounced "low" as is low calorie), in order to cash in on healthier diet concerns, and people needing encouragement to "Get up and geaux"[99] (pronounced "go"). Countless other restaurants and menu items attempt to take advantage of the popularity of French

Cajun branding, including McDonald's, whose franchises offer loosely defined regional fare periodically, from McLobster sandwiches in Maine to Crispy Chicken Cajun Deluxe sandwiches in Louisiana.[100] Seasonal specialties like the Mardi Gras King Cake appear in local bakeries during the Carnival season, decorated in purple, gold, and green. Consuming the cake is tasty and ritualistic, as eaters find a bean or *fève*, making the lucky person who finds it king for a day. According to tradition, that person is responsible for buying the next King Cake.

Charismatic and evangelical television chefs like Lagasse have certainly contributed to and profited from the Cajun/Creole boon. The transformation of Cajuns and Cajun culture, from regional peasant fare to national chic, can be witnessed through foodways.[101] French Louisianans, nonetheless, are still known today as being willing eaters of anything that they can capture. The lowly New World crawfish has come to symbolize the piquant Frenchness of Louisiana perhaps as much as the *fleur-de-lys* and recall the original earthiness of these now recognized delicacies. Legend has it that during the journey from old Acadie in the North to *L'Acadie tropicale* in Louisiana, lobsters exhausted by their travails shriveled down to the size of crawfish.[102] Thirty years ago, crawfish, or mud bugs, as they are sometimes called, were a subject of shame that no one readily or publicly admitted eating. Now they are celebrated in festivals as a national delicacy and reinterpreted tradition. Popeye's brought crawfish to a national audience beginning in 1989, and since 2008 it sponsors an annual crawfish festival. Crawfish boils in people's homes provide a way of participating in a local French cultural tradition on a smaller scale. Food preparation and consumption are identity-affirming activities, like *la boucherie*, when families gathered to slaughter pigs for collective meat sharing. They are for the most part an event of the past, but crawfish boils continue to draw together Cajun families as well as culinary tourists.[103] Writer Rheta G. Johnson suggests that even outsiders become sensitized to the sensory elements of Poor Man's Provence, as she calls Cajun country.[104] At what point does tourism and mass production pervert the authenticity of cultural production? Rather than say that tourism defiles, critic Kevin Fox claims that new definitions of authentic culture emerge from increased tourism taking place in New Orleans's French Quarter as well as the Ninth Ward.[105]

FRENCH CREOLE CREATION

Mardi Gras draws together French music, dance, performance, and identity formation, outside of New Orleans, in the backwaters of Acadiana. The histories of Mardi Gras, the Mardi Gras Indians, and Carnival have been explored by scholars and will certainly continue to elicit much general interest. The HBO series *Treme* is based on the multicultural allure of the Indians and their cultural relevance to post-Katrina Creole New Orleans. The television drama also neatly folds in Cajun specificities (as well as some fictions) on western shores of the Mississippi. Country Mardi Gras in southwest Louisiana represent less well known but culturally significant enactments of French Cajun and Creole ethnic identity today. The world over, Mardi Gras and Carnival generally are immersed in notions of socioeconomic difference, of the inversion of social norms, about excess before deprivation, making permissible (albeit temporarily) what is usually taboo. For almost two hundred years, Francos have reenacted the Mardi Gras ritual as a last act of communal revelry before the austerity of Lent.

People began celebrating as early as the 1820s and 1830s with the first recorded Mardi Gras celebration registered in the *New Orleans Picayune* in 1837.[106] In 1857 the Krewe of Comus organized the first exclusive parade and balls for the city's elite, making the affair a highly ritualized and racialized formal event. Urban Mardi Gras had been segregated, not just racially but sexually and socioeconomically, for well over a century. In New Orleans, the Krewes of Rex and Comus were linked to white supremacists. Blacks were not allowed to wear masks due to fear of passing. For more than a hundred years, the Zulu Krewe (1909–2009) defied many codes by dressing in blackface, shocking some black and white revelers. Zulu "throws" have been some of the most prized gifts dispersed to participants of the parade historically, although the coconuts were more recently handed over to avoid injury. Over the twentieth century, an essentially private Mardi Gras affair became more public and partially desegregated as Louisianans realized the cultural and commercial potential of Carnival.

The "throws" from privileged Mardi Gras krewes still symbolically represent a redistribution of resources from the elite to working classes. Yet Mardi Gras retains little of its religious meaning and is much more an expression of acceptable social mixing, of hybridity in many ways today. Within the confines of established norms, slightly promiscuous interaction is permissible. In Acadiana, "the runs represent ethnic heritage, but also a specifically regional way of life: prairie Cajunness, in distinction from life in Louisiana's swamps, marshes, and cities," says historian Carolyn Ware.[107] As she notes, this kind of regional affirmation simultaneously constitutes an expression of whiteness alongside more hybrid Creole articulations. Food, Swamp Pop and dance, and urban and country cultures also express the many ways of being Cajun.

The traditional *courir* (or run) *du Mardi Gras* is a medieval affair demonstrating French links to an ancient history from the Old World. Masked men typically ran wild begging for ingredients for a communal gumbo, although the performance could also serve to settle scores. The country Mardi Gras run was pretty strictly segregated between Cajun and Creole populations in terms of participation. Anthropologists confirm this separation, although the two krewes did patronize some of the same homes in black and white rural communities and periodically crossed paths as they paraded.[108] Creole revelers believed their Cajun counterparts to be much more rowdy, drunken, and potentially violent. In places like Tee Mamou (Iota), Eunice, and Basile, Louisiana, the runs have been going on for decades. Lafayette's larger urban area and more recent reenactment draws large crowds today to a family-friendly celebration. Black Creoles long held tight to their distinctive French identity, expressed during Creole Mardi Gras. Many of their cultural traditions eroded as the elder generations passed and as younger blacks became more assimilated into the American twentieth century. The Creole celebration in L'Anse de 'Prien Noir, a traditionally black enclave in south Louisiana, speaks of past traditions.[109]

The Creole Mardi Gras Krewe consisted of some thirty masked men, or clowns, one strong-willed captain to keep the excited clowns in check, and assorted musicians including Alphonse "Bois Sec" Ardoin of L'Anse de 'Prien Noir. The captain led the group from house to house along a meandering route while the musicians played. The clowns begged for *charité* along the way or for chickens for a communal gumbo after the procession. They begged with ritualized and repeated phrases, "Une poule par an c'est pas souvent" (One chicken per year is not a lot) and "On n'a pas souvent beaucoup fait ça" (We have not often done that). It was a rite of passage for young clowns to catch Mardi Gras chickens. The captains entered into dialogue with households asking if krewes could perform for *charité*. If met with a positive response, the clowns would sing and dance to the music. These Creole Mardi Gras did not wear anything resembling the elaborate costumes of the Mardi Gras Indians; in fact the clowns' costumes were mostly store bought. The L'Anse de 'Prien Noir crew would typically leave early in the morning on Fat Tuesday and return in the afternoon to the Ardoin family dance hall in L'Anse de 'Prien Noir, where the communal gumbo would be shared and a dance would be held until midnight.[110] As many observed Lent the following day, Mardi Gras dances ended punctually.

Creole krewes were segregated not only by race but also by sex. While the men were out chasing chickens, the women were typically at home.[111] Cajun women were responsible for cooking the communal chickens that had been collected during the Mardi Gras run. Today those chickens are more often than not purchased in stores, and Cajun women continue a surprisingly long tradition of Mardi Gras runs in the rural spaces of south Louisiana. There are twenty Creole and Cajun, male and female, and even a few coed *courirs de Mardi Gras*, taking place annually today in communities in southwest Louisiana. Women Mardi Gras arrive more often than not in trucks now, and the performance ("cutting up") is more symbolic than utilitarian (the chickens do not have to be caught). Interest in cultural traditions and identity led Cajun women to get involved in this male-dominated sphere and to form their own associations. There existed a women's run in the 1920s, but it was during the postwar period that they became more active.[112] Local families enjoyed having women entertain at their home because they tended to be respectful of private property and were not overly drunk or disorderly. Coed runs were initially an affront to local mores, promoting unsavory mixing of the married and unmarried, and so enterprising women organized family and single-sex runs. Male

Mardi Gras posed a symbolic threat to protected womanhood in French Catholic Acadiana, with masked paraders attempting to scare women or pretending to carry them off. Even at traditional home dances, there were separate spaces for men (*la cage aux chiens*) and women in order to protect the virtue of unmarried girls.

Educational concerns have served as motivation for French Louisianans and Mardi Gras. In the communities of Basile and Tee Mamou, women Mardi Gras teach young girls about Cajun and Creole culture. The Basile Mardi Gras Association helped develop the children's run in 1986 to preserve the tradition, which seemed to be dying. People were not speaking French anymore, and no one knew the Mardi Gras song. Organizers began visiting the local schools to encourage interest. Cajun children learn to strut in the bayou countryside, and social and cultural organizations help them to better understand Louisiana French tradition. The National Prairie Cajun Center in Eunice profits from the colorful historic and pedagogic lure of Mardi Gras to teach about French cultural traditions. The Tee Mamou Mardi Gras Association maintains printed song sheets, and while helping to teach, there is almost no variation of the performance. The Carnival song originates from old French and French-Canadian drinking songs, and provides an example of reinterpreted Franco-American tradition.[113] The Creole Mardi Gras song is similar to that sung in Eunice, Iota, Basile, or Mamou during Cajun renditions.

CREOLIZED PRANKS, PROSE, AND POETRY

Live music and performances maintain the vibrant oral component of Cajun/Creole culture, and some efforts to record them have been met with resistance. Traditional musicians believed that in order for the performance to be authentic (i.e., French), it had to be live. Some vociferously preferred that their music die with them rather than be recorded, although thankfully their wishes were not always respected. The prevalence of oral cultures in south Louisiana explains perhaps why written French expression often takes on a lyric or poetic form. Cajun and Creole raconteurs, musicians, and lay poets continue to express *les bons* (and bad) *temps* today. There is a connection between the music, folktales, and poetic tradition of south

Louisiana, all oral practices conveying something of the French popular working-class experience from one generation to another; each medium, in fact, tends to inform the others. People from the French South were not widely educated, but curiously became makers of culture appreciated nationally today. Not all can be accurately transcribed, and so there is something lost in the translation (and transformation) of French Creole cultures. Modern publication is now putting oral culture to paper, an activity required perhaps to save remnants of endangered traditions. Regional presses publish French Louisiana dictionaries and record regional patois that vary from parish to parish, however incomplete they may be.[114]

The poetics of Cajun and Creole "authors" are unassuming. Poets are heralds and ambassadors for French Louisiana cultures like musicians, although quieter ones; they are scribes of a proud and effusive French people. They tell the story of Louisiana Creole identity, through imagery, melody, and language, using a variety of linguistic and artistic strategies. Poets and poetry must be defined loosely in the context of south Louisiana, for few if any Cajuns or Creoles made their living by writing verse and fewer still aspired to literary recognition. Theirs is an art created by bus drivers, carpenters, and factory workers by day, taking on the role of lyric expression at their leisure. Renaissance men and a few women articulated a Blue Collar Bayou.[115]

In the 1970s makeshift poets began to assemble in conjunction with the first Rencontre des Francophones de L'Amérique du Nord in 1978.[116] Some were certainly familiar with verse as musicians, and all knew the rhythms of south Louisiana. There is little difference between the artistic genres as they are presented in the anthology *Cris sur le bayou: Naissance d'une poésie acadienne en Louisiane*. The book represented an ambitious attempt to give birth to a Cajun cultural movement, one that combined poetics and politics, verse and song. Musicians try their hand at poetry, and the lines convey much of the melodies of French oral cultures. Word and image indeed pay tribute to the rich musical tradition in south Louisiana. All contents of the anthology recount hardscrabble lives lived in French and the constant search for love and validation. *Cris sur le bayou* amply illustrates that there is no clear distinction in fact between storytelling, music, and poetry. They each tell the same narrative of French efforts not only to survive but to fully live in the Gulf South, to different audiences perhaps. It is a distinctly Acadian struggle of poets fighting for cultural survival with some attention paid to Creole specificities.

Music and language, as well as food and performance, were uniting powerfully to produce a climate propitious for the recognition of under-valued French cultures in Louisiana. Jean Arceneaux, pen name of Barry Jean Ancelet, captured this important moment in a January 1979 poem entitled "Exil II":

Richard, Broussard, Guidry,
Jeunes Cadiens s'attachent à des nourrices
Pour se préparer pour une rerenaissance,
Cette fois vraie, née d'un marriage légitime
La musique ayant enfin épousé la langue.[117]

To their credit, the organizers of CODOFIL recognized this influential combination of language, culture, and music and attempted to profit from it during ethnic festival time. Arceneaux can be credited with insisting on these points of artistic convergence, and for recognizing their power to persuade. At the same early festivals organized by CODOFIL that brought together so many of the cultural arts, poets inspired founder Jimmie Domengeaux to the point that after first attempting to cleanse Cajun language and culture of its ethnic grit, he wanted to celebrate it for what it was, an authentically American and French Creole construction. It is in this light that the CODOFIL-led French Cajun and Creole renaissance emerged.

The poems contained within *Cris sur le bayou* speak of a linguistic and cultural resistance to American assimilation. Titles like "Assimilation" and "Resistance" articulate a call to arms. As Louisiana had been colo-nized, resistance was necessary, although the local French population had most certainly become creolized and the creolization process involved English or American elements. The poems included in the volume affirm the Franco-American language and identity of the Cajuns, although they distinguish between a generally bad kind of colonization (American) and a good one (French) in the telling of the French narrative of America.

Arceneaux speaks of "*schizophrénie linguistique*" in one of his verses. "I will not speak French on the school grounds. I will not speak French on the school grounds," conveys the stigmatization of French internalized by a generation. While Arceneaux's poems offer a strong critique of Americanization in French, he saves some of his strongest criticism for Cajuns themselves, "proud Coonasses qui make better lovers because they eat anything." In "Colonihilisme," the author suggests that Cajuns need only to look in the mirror to find their cultural executioners.[118] "Les school boards étaient composes, De Babineaux, d'Arceneaux et de LeBlanc. C'est-tu des noms américains, ça?" Arceneaux is quick to point an accusatory finger at Cajuns who have not advanced the culture, who have been too ashamed to embrace it, perhaps after decades of officially imposed cultural shame. Louisiana's English-only laws date back to 1916 and 1921.

"Dix ans après la renaissance de la Louisiane-française, On se retrouve avec une orpheline retardée, Qui sait pas encore s'expliquer elle-même. . . . Et asteur, elle est incapable de se défendre." Ten years following the birth of CODOFIL, Louisiana is still burdened with a "retarded orphan" incapable of self-expression, suggests Arceneaux. These words echo an impatient, piercing evaluation from within of the organization's outcomes. The author claimed that culturally dependent Cajuns only advanced through the assistance of foreigners (teachers) who spoke with a different accent, a less than oblique shot at CODOFIL immersion programs. Historian Shawn Bernard disassociated Cajun identity from language in fact, expressing an inevitable cultural decline and an Anglo future of non-francophone Cajuns.[119] CODOFIL remained sensitive to the "colonial" efforts of French officials in the area and the need to protect and preserve local variants of French.

"Fragment of a longer work" speaks specifically to the process of creolization in South Louisiana.[120] The French family of America is made up of Africans and Europeans as well as Native Americans, not specifically mentioned in the poem. "Mais Noirs et Blancs, riches et pauvres, maîtres et esclaves, nobles et paysans, nous sommes venus et nous sommes restés." "We came and remained," claims Arceneaux for black and white, rich and poor, master and slave, lord and peasant. Passage by ocean and river (the

Mississippi) brought these populations to Louisiana where they would fuse, all parts of a larger French work. All are French of America and would continue to be so. "Il y aura des Français d'Amérique jusqu'à la fin du temps. Et nous, Français de Louisiane, nous sommes une branche de cet arbre. Nous sommes de cette race qui ne sait pas mourir." The perseverance of the French race of America recalls the affirmation of author Félix-Antoine Savard's *Menaud, maître-draveur* of the Canadian North, heralding the fortitude of pioneers of French ancestry.

Some of the defining poems included in the anthology read lyrically as music, as they were written by renowned artists such as Iry Lejeune and Zachary Richard. The text includes photos of musicians. "A la musique" is dedicated to legendary Nathan Abshire. Arcenenaux himself was an amateur musician playing cymbals in bands at the time French Creole cultures were brewing in the 1970s. The poems pay tribute to the French musical heritage of Louisiana, such as in "Northbound and down," which dissects the protagonist of the musical standard "Jolie Blonde," who was not really Cajun but from Mississippi, thus explaining her vanity and departure. A real "Fille cadienne" could not be a heartbreaker. Several poems/songs, "Blues de Bosco," "La valse du pont d'amour," "Grand Duralde," "Grande nuit," "Jolie catin," and "La Grosse erreur," refer back to the familiar French Cajun/Creole themes of broken heartedness and abandonment, and many find their origin in the primal source of sadness, Le Grand Dérangement. Zachary Richard's signature song is listed as poetry, once again confusing the frontiers of verse and music: "Réveille Réveille c'est les goddams qui viennent, / brûler la récolte. Réveille, Réveille, hommes acadiens, pour sauver le village. . . . Réveille, Réveille hommes Acadiens pour sauver l'héritage." A French cultural awakening is indeed necessary to combat the forces of assimilation. Like legendary resistant Beausoleil, people took up arms (and instruments) against the invaders. "La Balade de Beausoleil" tells their story.[121]

It is not insignificant that the collection *Cris sur le bayou* was published in Montreal, from whence the Québécois struggle for Franco-American dignity and sovereignty was often waged. The diversity of the North American French experience as well as common themes of celebration and revolution, discrimination and mourning come out clearly in this call for recognition of the French marking of the New World. Several poems voice the fleeting exuberance of Mardi Gras. They are defined as Acadien, but the collection includes a few verses from the Creole experience. Some of Arceneaux's Cajun and Creole storytellers wax poetic in Creole French. Those crafted by Debbie Clifton are distinct in terms of their form as well as content. Cajun/Creole poems give some indication of the variety of Louisiana French spellings, as Areceneaux states in *Cris sur le bayou*. The text includes a glossary of local terms.

We know that a French linguistic renaissance ended up being one of the objectives of CODOFIL. The Council supported a stage for Cajun culture and put *L'Acadie tropicale* on the francophone map. The role of Barry Jean Ancelet and alter ego Jean Arceneaux in the development of French cultural life in Louisiana should not be understated, as he has had a hand in Cajun and Creole music, storytelling, and poetry, not only producing it but collecting it, studying it, and making it available to others. As spokespersons for the francophone United States, both he and Debbie Clifton have pursued cultural reflection through the poetic voice in more recent publications.[122] Ancelet remains the MC at a music and dance event, the Rendez-Vous des Cajuns, at the Liberty Theatre in Eunice, Louisiana, and a host at the Festivals Acadiens et Créoles.

The older generation of poets inspired a handful of younger artists, musicians, and cultural ambassadors who are active in south Louisiana. Kirby Jambon, a teacher in CODOFIL's French immersion program in Acadiana, published his first book of poems, *L'École Gombo*, which was awarded the 2006 Prix Mondes Francophones. As the title suggests, many of the poems echo the cultural creolization process in south Louisiana, as well as the affirmation of ethnic identity. "French Kiss" and "A l'écoute" delve into the biculturalism and bilingualism that are at the heart of Cajun identity. In "Qui'c'qu'on est," Jambon writes, "On est Français, mais pas Français d'la France, on est, mais on est pas tout à fait, Acadien, tout en étant *American*, mais pas Américain." We are American in English only, Jambon suggests, not in French. The "on" that he uses to describe "us" French Louisianans is thoroughly creolized, distinctly so.

On parle le vieux français, on parle cadien ou créole, ou au moins on parle anglais *flat*, on dit *sha*, *dis* and *dat*, un accent dans les deux langues, on parle les deux en même temps, ou peut-être juste une langue avec un ou deux accents, ou peut-être que pas...

On a des récolteurs et des pêcheurs, on est catholiques et pêcheurs, on a des conteurs et des menteurs, on est raconteurs et radoteurs, on a des fêtes et des festivals tout l'temps, toute l'année où on laisse les bons temps rouler toute la nuit et toute la journée où on cris "lâchez-les," ou Hé là-bas, comment ça va?" ou peut-être que pas."[123]

Whether speaking French or English, Cajuns/Cadiens may have an accent, cites Jambon. They may or may not be ... scavengers, fishermen, partiers, Catholics and sinners. French Louisianans defy stereotypes. They are everything and everyone. Jambon concludes the opening piece on French Louisiana simply by stating "on est là," the familiar Franco-American anthem. Jambon's poems evoke a much more contemporary and a slightly less militant portrayal of the French experience in the American South compared with *Cris sur le bayou*. His poetry expresses many of the joys and tribulations of being French. It examines the food, music, Mardi Gras, of course, as well as specific cultural institutions of Acadiana.

Several poems combine verse with local history. "Héritage culturel" written in 2001 at the founding of the African American Museum in St. Martinville, Louisiana, comments on cultural loss and common exile and pain among French Creoles, all in the same metaphoric slave or deportation ship. They have only to walk side by side to realize this: "On est tous dans le meme bateau soit les navires de déportation, d'exploration ou d'esclavage on a tous passé à travers on le fait asteur on le ferait encore ça se fait on a juste pour marcher côte à côte pour commencer." The poem "Acadie en fête" was written for the opening of the Museum of the Acadian Monument, in symbolic proximity next door to the African American Museum.[124] Kirby Jambon is not the only CODOFIL cultural ambassador who is also a poet. David Cheramie, former CODOFIL director, is a published French Louisiana poet.[125] The poets and poetry of south Louisiana affirm that "Ici on parle français" (Here we speak French) in song, verse, and prose as well as through other artistic expressions. This assertion is a part of the process of eliminating the shame and embracing what it means to be a Franco-American. In 2013, Jambon published *Petites Communions*, which was formally recognized by the French Academy with the 2014 Prix Henri de Régnier. While read at regional, national, and international French and francophone conferences and increasingly recognized, Jambon's poems remain an expression of the everyday Cajun experience, written by a Franco-Louisianais for others. A digital recording of his *École gombo* verses makes them accessible to those who cannot read.

CODOFIL teacher and storyteller Richard Guidry wanted to translate oral cultures into printed text so that they could be performed in the late twentieth century for illiterate French Louisianans. He wrote short monologues designed to be read on the radio or on stage. He transcribed the voices he grew up with, voices unfamiliar with professional recordings, so that they could easily and unselfconsciously be heard. Guidry dedicated the publication "Pour ma tante Dot" (For my Aunt Dot). These are familiar stories of Cajuns adapting and surviving, their "dying" culture right along with them. In the very first story, "Hallo cher, Gramma's fin, an y'all" (Hello Dear, Grandma's fine and you), readers discover the assimilation process at work in south Louisiana. Grandma thinks things have changed quite a lot, for the only line of communication is "Hallo, Gramma's fine, an y'all" between the younger, more Americanized generation and older Louisiana francophones. She understands why people did not want to teach French to their kids when they were physically reprimanded for speaking French. She grew up hearing, "You-muss-speak—Anglish li'l-girl." There were clear divisions between the French that was spoken among French Louisianans anyway. Gramma expresses scorn for uppity urban Cajuns, or Creoles, who think they are superior because they have left the bayou. The young folks want no part of the old French ways. Just talking about it makes them grimace: "Les jeunes d'asteur, tu yeux parles de ça, i' faisont des grimaces."[126] "C'est p'us pareil" (Things ain't the same).

In these stories, readers learn about the old ways: *la boucherie* (slaughter of meat), eating *couche-couche* (fried cornmeal), *barbues* (catfish), *ouaoua-rons* (bull frogs), *écrevisses* (crawfish), and *chevrettes* (shrimp). Together they constitute a Cajun linguistic and culinary lexicon.[127] Many of the old ways are recorded in cultural and ecological studies of the traditional Cajun life and its evolution.[128] There are examples of Cajun speak in the recorded stories, one being usage of the word *Neg'* as a term of endearment among Cajuns. This word tends to arouse objections, like Coonass; it is embraced by some and rejected by others. The old French ways included the traditional gathering of family around a hearth for warmth, good cheer, and food. "On a passé des veillées et d'aut's veillées autour du réchaud à écouter des contes," says Grandma. The tales that she tells are unmistakably nostalgic. In the good ol' days, people were poor, but they were free, autonomous, as far as Grandma remembered, free of debt notably as they never purchased on credit. Now the catfish doesn't taste the same.[129] "Non, c'est p'us pareil," Grandma repeats to her listeners, real and figurative children and grandchildren.

Today people are not respectful of the past and of tradition as they once were if Grandma Guidry is believed. They want to put old people in homes, but she's determined to remain where she and her late husband, Sosthène, have always been. In the *Cajuns of the Atchafalya Basin*, woodland expert/photographer Greg Guirard documents a fiercely independent way of life maintained until the very end by elderly individuals in Guidry's stories. The Cajun voices recorded in Richard Guidry's tales are still hopeful in some ways. We see how the oil industry affected Cajun culture positively and adversely in the 1980s, in "14 et 14," for instance, referring to fourteen days on the oil rig and fourteen days off. Well-paying jobs in the oil industry brought newfound comforts to the bayou, television and automobiles, but also destroyed traditional life, *veillées*, and French language. Many had moved to "Grand Texas," as lamented in Cajun song, indicating the power of assimilation.

The family man on the rig has more available income but barely knows his children, whom he calls his wife's kids. He is hopeful that life will be better for his son, who will know his own children. His daughter can make her *roux* in the microwave at the touch of a button: "Et ma fille elle, a' pourra faire son roux dans ein 'microwave' et toucher ein bouton pour allumer le réchaud. Les Bons Vieux Temps sont asteur."[130] The good times may indeed be right now in many ways because the old days were tough. Good riddance for more than one modern Cajun. The last story recorded in Guidry's short text is called "L'espoir" (Hope), a tale told in Louisiana creole. Here Guidry acts as a ventriloquist for Louisiana Creoles, as does Kirby Jambon. French Creoles have fewer scribes today than Cajuns. Creoles were faced with similar challenges and opportunities by the changing world around them in the second half of the twentieth century, one transformed by oil.

Guidry's recorded stories read practically as folktales reminiscent of dying ways. Much less explored than music or poetry are the rich folktales as well as the ethnic jokes of French Cajun and Creole Louisiana that offer a bounty of cultural signifiers.[131] Stories and jokes have been passed down vertically from generation to generation but also horizontally from friend to acquaintance. Robert Darnton contends that folktales "communicated traits, values, attitudes, and a way of construing the world that was particularly French."[132] We gain intimate access to French Louisiana cultures through this oral tradition. Just about everyone from different social and racial groups in south Louisiana knows a Boudreaux story or joke about the Cajun you love to hate, make fun of, *and* cheer. Boudreaux stories are folktales about the old ways in many regards. Boudreaux is an antihero, an everyman in whom people can recognize their own foibles. He is someone who triumphs despite himself, like a previously discussed character named Ti-Jean in the Franco-American tradition in New England. Boudreaux is a similarly comic-tragic figure, one who is genuinely likeable in the francophone lore of Louisiana. Boudreaux is a Cajun working Joe, with a bumbling nature but also a resiliency. Boudreaux is someone who is going to find a way whether in the bayou or the French Quarter. "A Cajun is a guy that's gonna make it no what matter what," claims a descendant.[133]

In written form, Boudreau(x) is a fairly nondescript Cajun man of thirty to forty years, casually dressed, sometimes wearing a baseball hat. The fictional and legendary figure, sometimes written as Boudreau in another spelling, has a whole cast of characters who assist in his many adventures. His long-suffering wife is Marie, often depicted as an ugly woman. Boudreaux's pal and partner in crime is Thibodeau(x) or Thibodo, and he also has an ugly wife by the name of Clotile. His dog is playfully named Phideaux (pronounced "phi-do," e.g., a Franco American version of Fido).[134] The pair of friends find themselves involved in much mischief. Boudreaux is a country boy at heart, huntin', trappin', and outsmartin' the devil. Boudreaux is a problem solver, curiously, and while he is certainly not the sharpest, he still manages to get by, even succeed (briefly). These stories help to translate the Cajun way of viewing the world. Some of the tales involve going to heaven or to hell, voicing the contours of a sometimes problematic French Catholic upbringing. Others talk about catching Boudreaux or one of his cronies in the act of doing something not entirely Catholic (although not too bad). Animals fear for their lives in the presence of Cajun hunters like Boudreaux. The Cajun zoo states not only the names of species but also their preferred method of cooking.

Boudreaux jokes are a kind of self-deprecating humor acceptable today when told by Louisiana Cajuns to other Cajuns, offering people the chance to self-reflect and laugh. They are usually read by members of the extended Boudreaux family. Versions of the stories as well as the spellings vary from edition to edition. Illustrations often accompany contemporary stories of Boudreaux at the Atlanta Olympics, ice fishing at the Cajundome (a University of Lafayette sporting arena), poaching game in the bayou, and again consuming anything that walks, swims, flies, or crawls, scheming not to lose his disability check, and dealing with an ugly, jealous wife.[135] One Boudreaux storyteller and illustrator includes local Cajun recipes along with the sketches of the capers of his protagonist. This is mostly a regional cultural production, but some national circulation can be identified outside of south Louisiana.[136] Folktales, even those as "low brow" as Boudreaux jokes, speak to local concerns and fears, as well as creolized cultural influences. Boudreaux stories make light of the difficult circumstances of the exiled Acadian experience in Louisiana.

Boudreaux is as much a part of popular culture now as lore or folktale. Boudreaux songs, jokes, and stories are widely available on CD, DVD, and the Internet. Modern Cajun musicians sing about Boudreaux. He has been marketed and anthologized by local *raconteurs*. While these stories were certainly once only told by word of mouth, today the array of publications and recordings make consumption all the easier. Most Boudreaux jokes and stories are now narrated and packaged in English, although they tend to include (sometimes misspelled) French words and often glossaries. As translations, they give new life to old cultural forms, disseminating them to more people and places. Folktales themselves are a product of linguistic and cultural creolization, combining European, African, and Native American influences. They often include a Creole hero who similarly outsmarts his adversaries, like Boudreaux and Ti-Jean.[137] Creole tales of Br'er Rabbit are ancient and less widely circulated electronically today, but continue to be examined by specialists. Through written and oral tradition, we see common French creolized expressions from the Gulf Coast to New England.

Food, Mardi Gras, and music all tell an epic and persistent French story. They are powerful cultural conveyors, appealing to many and consumed by those with a hankering for something authentically American and colorfully French. They are a part of the "holy trinity" of Louisiana French cultures.[138] The 2010 Super Bowl champion New Orleans Saints and their signature *fleur-de-lys* emblem likely did more for publicizing French creolized influence than anything else in the last decade.[139] A Boudreaux story claims that Hell must in fact have frozen over if the Saints (Aints) had won. Designer Mignon Faget's jewelry and accessories with replicas of the *fleur-de-lys* represent the higher end of New Orleans French culture, a symbol of the renaissance of a smaller and demographically altered Crescent City after the 2005 hurricane. They serve as still more props with which to express Frenchness. While the city is less heterogeneous racially and socioeconomically than before, less Creole, signs of its cosmopolitan cultures remain. Tattoos of the *fleur-de-lys* emblem and expressions of "Who Dat," the unofficial Saints rallying cry, speak to the more common, marginalized, and creolized French cultures of the area. CODOFIL translated "Who Dat" as "Qui Ça" in French and "Ki Ça" in Louisiana Creole.[140]

The coolness of the Cajun renaissance that has been experienced for the last three decades has not fully "outed" closeted Franco-Americans, hidden from view because of the shame associated with working-class

Frenchness. Deep racial and class divisions exist in Louisiana today, despite the legacy of more tolerant French legal traditions (i.e., *Code Noir*), many of which are still in place. Today creolization, hybridization, and cultural exchange are fostered, temporarily or superficially, one might interject, during the Mardi Gras revelry, during the annual rite that is participation in Carnival festivities. Far from Bourbon Street and the Vieux Carré, the Mardi Gras Indians proceed through the streets of poorer communities, oblivious to storms, singing and dancing with no set route, performing Afro-Caribbean traditions expressed also in Cuba, Panama, and Martinique. With the Mardi Gras Indians back in twenty-first-century New Orleans, creolization and rejuvenation continue. They parade perhaps in honor of the Buffalo Soldiers who borrowed more from Indians than fought them in the nineteenth century, or to pay tribute to the Native American tribes who harbored African slaves when they took flight. Indian krewes such as the "Creole Wild West" indicate that the cowboy or ranching tradition of black Creoles has not been forgotten.[141] Ever endangered and constantly changing, these hybrid Franco cultures ramble on.

Conclusion

We were American as tarte aux pommes. *—Memere*

How can an ethnic group acknowledge an adopted American identity but also maintain its French cultural traditions? Recognition of a common core of Americanness can be as validating as the distinction of French heritage. The intolerance faced by members of the Franco family and the determined desire to be, somehow, both French and American in the United States have created compelling Franco-American sensibilities despite varying experiences, trajectories, and labels. Although older generations experienced the trauma of rejection, others, including those who had not dealt firsthand with disapproval, have helped to revive a culture. It is in the effort to preserve vital expressions and to exist biculturally (if not multiculturally) that similarities emerge between the various zones of Frenchness. The French Atlantic sojourn does certainly render Louisiana's francophone groups distinct, yet they possess the common chords of a minority French experience. The willingness to transform Old World cultures into contemporary modes of life for Francos of North America reflects an ongoing creolization process.

Some thirty years ago in 1986, in commemoration of the French gift of the Statue of Liberty to the United States, Franco-American novelist Normand Beaupré offered thoughts in verse:

Les Canadiens-Français qui passent la frontière,
    Deviennent Américains sans faire de manière;
Car c'est avec le Coeur qu'ils servent leur patrie,
    Pour elle ils sont prêts à sacrifier leur vie
Obéissant aux lois, ils ont juré, c'est vrai,
    De ne pas oublier leur langage Français.

Franco-Américains, marchez la tête haute,
    Vous avez un passé et sans tâche et sans faute;
Priez que vos enfants; comme vous désormais,
    Soient fiers de leurs aïeux, car ils étaient Français.

Les Canadiens-Français, malgré tant de souffrance;
    Ont tous bien conservé les traditions de France;
En Dieu ils ont la foi et pour toujours s'engagent,
    Même aux Etats-Unis à garder leur langage;
Franco-Américains, il faut parler l'Anglais,
    Mais nos aïeux nous disent: "conservez le Français."[1]

The poem, like the opening song from the first chapter, conveys an evolution of Franco identity articulated by the use of four qualifiers: French-Canadian, American, Franco-American, and French. While one can identify a chronological transformation, from French to French-Canadian, on to Franco-American and American, all four can and are used simultaneously and confusingly to describe the Franco experience today. Tension clearly lingers between preserved Frenchness and assimilated Americanness for immigrants of French descent in the United States, between the various states of national identification, linguistic fluency, and religious beliefs that they exhibit. An abiding faith in Frenchness, despite historic suffering, has kept fellow travelers culturally anchored. As people encountered obligations to uphold both strictly French and American cultural identities, from familial, organizational, or governmental authorities, they responded with resistance to each absolute. In the end, many opted to become Franco-American, proportionally, as they saw fit.

In the cited documentary on contemporary Franco-American life, *Waking Up French . . . ! Réveil*, a young man asks if he could still be Franco-American without being able to articulate ideas in his native French language. Can someone similarly be Franco if she has lost her Catholic faith and no longer attends mass, even in English? What if contemporaries cannot or do not want to uphold the ideals of *la survivance française*? Is memory of a distant French past enough to sustain a Franco-American present and future? The producers of French ethnic culture have indeed, in the last half century, sought to demonstrate that Franco-Americans exist, that some still speak, think, write, pray, laugh, and cry in French as well as English, and that they remain living participants in the francophone world. As writers in English, some Francos have demonstrated how cultural worlds can be extended. Journalists, novelists, poets, pranksters, storytellers, and musicians have long insisted that they are Franco and uniquely intercultural through their various artistic media. While fewer of these ambassadors remain active today, they continue to pursue cultural work, sometimes with assistance in the wider Franco community.[2]

The Statue of Liberty has remained a curiously relevant kind of symbol for Franco-Americans, even for those who had not emigrated transatlantically. It is for this reason that it has appeared strategically in the Franco-American press, at moments when Francos felt it important to express their dual identity. Most monuments to French activity in North America are, however, far less prominent. Robert Aldrich examined "the ways in which the imperial vocation was consciously mapped onto the built landscape" in France.[3] He found evidence throughout the French Hexagon, but the construction of memory in a place like the United States where French influences were widely dispersed is more subtly presented. The Statue of Liberty did acknowledge French American opportunities as well as struggles to make a life in urban industrial America, and *Le Journal de Lowell* noted its centennial along with other French affiliates.

Franco-Americans in Lowell had their own symbolic Liberty Bell, like the more famous cracked version in Philadelphia. It was inaugurated in

Le Journal de Lowell

Notre 21e année

Albert V. Côte
Éditeur

Téléphone (508) 453-1780

BULK RATE
U.S. Postage
PAID
PERMIT NO. 257

COMPLIMENTAIRE

VOLUME 21 NUMERO 5   LOWELL, MASSACHUSETTS   JUIN 1995

25e ANNIVERSAIRE

La Semaine Franco-Américaine DE LOWELL

Curtis J. LeMay, président général du Comité de la Semaine Franco-Américaine de Lowell annonce que les activités pour 1995 iront du 17 au 24 juin. Le Comité célèbre cette année son 25e anniversaire car c'est en 1970 qu'un comité se forma pour ranimer la pratique de célébrer La Saint-Jean-Baptiste le 24 juin.

Comme préliminaire à l'ouverture officielle cette année, le comité patronnera une Tournée Kérouacienne, le samedi matin 17 juin, en concert avec le Parc national de Lowell. L'entrée est libre, mais il est nécessaire se faire réserver une place à l'avance en composant le (508) 970-5000.

La Messe, ouverture officielle de la semaine, aura lieu en l'Église Ste-Thérèse de Dracut à 9h, dimanche matin, le 18 juin, après quoi suivra une réception et l'annonce de la nomination de la Personne Franco-Américaine de l'Année.

Une Messe à la mémoire des vétérans franco-américains sera célébrée en fin de l'après-midi le lundi 19 juin. Suivant cette célébration eucharistique à 5h40 au Sanctuaire St-Joseph, rue Lee, les Vétérans, en procession, se rendront au Parc Boarding House pour une soirée de divertissement. Le public est invité à la messe ainsi qu'à la soirée musicale présentée par la troupe Les Franco-Américains qui commencera à 7h. L'entrée est libre, mais on doit vous prévenir que le palais des spectateurs sera tempté par la disponibilité de mets québécois. S'il fait mauvais ces festivités auront lieu au centre Smith Baker, rue Merrimack.

Le soir suivant, c'est-à-dire, mardi le 20 juin, le comité participera à une partie de balle-molle sur le champ Harry Allen, rue West Sixth à Lowell. Comme opposition ils feront face aux membres du Club des Citoyens-Américains. On

Curtis J. LeMay

lancera la première balle à 7 heures et l'entrée est libre.

Un *Spectacle de Variété à la Orion* sera présenté en la salle Durgin de l'Université de Massachusetts à Lowell

(Cont. à la page 6)

11. *Le Journal de Lowell*, June 1995, Lowell, Massachusetts.

1974 as Lowell's Franco-American monument by the city's mayor, Armand Lemay. Signaling not independence but rather physical and cultural presence, the Franco bell tolled sonorically the parameters of the working day. Its sounds had structured the waking and laboring hours of the population, chiming when people came to work, when they stopped for lunch, and when they returned home at the end of the day. From 1975 until 1995, the Franco Mill Bell appeared on each and every cover of *Le Journal de Lowell*, most often in black ink but also in red (May 1992–June 1995) and holiday green (December 1994) during periods of journalistic experimentation. The physical monument still sits just outside the main entrance to the Lowell city hall.

Franco-Americans came to Lowell as the industrial revolution gained traction in New England and as word of the opportunities it afforded spread north across the Canadian border. For many Canadiens français in search of a life beyond their native Canada, Lowell was the final destination. Like in many industrial towns of New England, the train carrying emigrants stopped directly in front of the clamoring textile mills. For Franco-American families, coming to industrial America, however long the stay, often equated a positive change in economic stability. They could save as well as spend, send money home, and travel back to Canada. The number of Franco-Americans who distinguished themselves in some way during their time in Lowell is striking: Calixa Lavallée, composer of "O Canada," the Canadian national anthem; Louis Cyr, the reputed strongest man in the world; prominent Franco journalist Wilfrid Beaulieu; and of course beatnik *and* Franco novelist Jack Kerouac—all share a common passage in Lowell. Even if Frederick Douglass lectured in Lowell about the parallels between slavery and mill work, employment meant financial freedom and an expanded social and cultural universe, particularly for Franco-American women. With a newly acquired disposable income, Mill Girls could participate in the developing consumer society that accompanied the industrial revolution.

Contemporary scholarship is in need of more exploration of French ethnic mill girls or *demoiselles de Lowell* such as the fictive Vic from the novel *Canuck*. More industrious than frivolous, as the narrative suggests, young women like her shopped at Lowell's very own downtown Bon Marché department store, a cultural appropriation from the Parisian flagship store opened in 1869.[4] Newspaper advertisements in French, in the local daily newspaper *l'Etoile*, encouraged them to peruse the store for all of their needs: "Gilets pour Demoiselles" (Cardigans for young ladies), "Sous-vêtements pour hommes" (Undergarments for men), and "Robes de première communion" (First communion dresses).[5] By taking part in the spoils of the industrial revolution, shoppers were participating in a transformative commercial and cultural exchange and thereby becoming more fully Franco-American. French author Emile Zola spoke of the "democratisation du luxe," the democratization of luxury, in his novel based on the Bon Marché, and so could thrifty shoppers in Lowell find style at *moitié prix!* (half price), as store sales announced.[6] They could access fashion, inherently French, at American prices; there was no need to travel to Paris to dress the part of the stylish mademoiselle. Lowell's Bon Marché store was a commercial fixture on Merrimack Street for practically a century before its closing in 1976.

Each summer in Lowell today, Franco-Americans publicly acknowledge their heritage with a weeklong celebration. Ethnic parades and demonstrations announce membership to those within the clan. Francos and the Franco-American Day Committee have officially affirmed postcolonial francophone traditions in central Massachusetts every year since 1970, marking forty years of cultural life in 2010 with an especially festive demonstration. The annual affirmation of French life in Lowell includes a ceremonial French mass in a local parish. A Haitian priest led the community in prayer in 2014, a noteworthy event as many of the French ethnic churches have closed, and French-speaking priests are increasingly rare. Francos also congregated at the city's Little Canada monument, built with the stone from the last standing tenement in the ethnic enclave. The site names all of the razed streets that once made up the French neighborhood in Lowell.

The ethnic celebration reaches its zenith on Franco-American Day (June 24), with public speeches and displays. City residents spend hours during the week talking, praying, listening to music, dancing, and eating together in the Franco-American tradition. The ham and bean supper is often the most popular event. Program organizers often feature a Québécois film festival, and in 2014 it included a showing of *Louis Cyr*, the highest grossing Quebec film of 2013. The week's activities also incorporate academic discussion of Franco-American history led by specialists. What does it mean that hundreds of people attend the Franco Day and Week events each year? It translates a desire to take part in a still breathing culture. Expressing Franco-American identity requires planning, resources, commitment, and cooperation; it is not simply an ethnic veneer easily put on and later discarded.

Francos are just one of many groups in Lowell to engage in ethnic pride demonstrations and to receive recognition from city officials. Each immigrant group has an assigned day at the Lowell city hall, reserved for the expression of cultural distinction. The Polish, Portuguese, and Armenian communities have also erected commemorative shrines. Like Franco-Americans, these groups have actively developed their own expressions of difference and sameness (Americanness). The Franco-American monument continues to remind residents of Lowell's French past and present, a factor easily lost in the current multiethnic city. Each year, the honored Franco-Américain(e) of the Year poses beside the Mill Bell along with the festival's director. The 2010 Franco-Americaine winner was the twelfth woman in four decades to be recognized for her work in maintaining French language, cultural traditions, and heritage in Lowell. Perhaps the most meaningful event occurs at city hall with multiple Franco flag raisings. Each year the demonstration expresses the diversity that exists within French ethnic identity in North America. Past and present municipal officials attend the celebration, many of whom are Franco-Americans themselves, including previous Franco city counselor Curtis Lemay and his father, former mayor Armand Lemay, the first Franco-American of the Year forty years ago. In 2010, on the municipal office steps, the younger, more assimilated Lemay led the crowd in singing the American national anthem, and his father then directed the Canadian anthem in French. Organizers listed the French anthem, "La Marseillaise," in the program, but it was not sung, a subtle reminder of a more dormant French identity.

The Franco-Americaine of the Year in 2010 had the honor of raising the Quebec national flag, joining the American one already unfolded and on high. This was presumably in recognition of the descendants of the thousands of French Canadians who began arriving two centuries ago and who remain in the United States, if not necessarily in Lowell. The unfamiliar Franco-American flag fluttered at eye level alongside the better-known flags. At its center, a white *fleur-de-lys* sits within an American star in a blue reminiscent of Franco-American hybridity, much lighter than the blue of the Quebec national symbol. The flag, designed by Robert Coutourier, was first flown in 1983, and it joined the many other emblems of the French cultural tradition in North America.[7] While most Franco-Americans today would probably not recognize it, the flag is suggestive of their hidden French past.

Franco-American Day concludes with the ceremonial march of Franco war veterans, each of whom carries aloft a flag announcing intertwined French and American histories and traditions. In 2010, eight veterans marched out from the city hall and reassembled by the Franco-American monument, with their flags in the following order: American, French, Canadian, Quebec, old Quebec, Franco-American of New England, Massachusetts, and Lowell. The city, state, regional, national, international, and cultural affinities expressed relate the many affiliations and national or cultural symbols operating in the Franco-American world today. The number of flags unfurled in a given year depends on the dwindling number of Franco-American war veterans who are able to carry them. These symbols proclaim the Franco connection to places real and imagined, known and ignored. The pull of old Acadie is still powerful, voicing the lasting drama of *le Grand Dérangement*, the Evangeline legend, and enduring and sober French lives in America. In 2012, nine war veterans marched, one of whom carried the Acadian flag, signaling the recognition of the still distinct group within the Franco-American community. Acadians, Cajuns, Creoles, and Canucks can all lay claim to their status as Franco-Americans.

Scholars, officials, and even activists have had a tendency to stress the isolation of French life in America. While such enclave mentality persists, stressing nomadic or exiled existence in a cultural desert, activities in Lowell indicate that Francos have not forgotten a common cultural heritage. Bill Marshall suggests that we better understand the relationship between these places/spaces: "It is networks rather than boundaries, routes rather than roots, that characterize their extensive and profound relationship."[8] Collectively they represent a consciously preserved French way of American life. Those who inhabit these spaces have illustrated a common desire to live their Franco-American identity in ways that were sometimes impossible in the past.

Franco-Americans of New England, as well as the U.S. government, offer tribute to neighboring Quebec in a twenty-first-century monument erected along the banks of the St. Lawrence River, just south of Quebec City, where the French began their colonial experiment in the New World. It stands as a tribute to the French-Canadian populations and cultures that traveled south and established themselves permanently in the United States. It also marks their symbolic return to their ancestral Canada, a return that would not be realized by many French-Canadian immigrants while living. Francos of North America still remember from whence they came (*Je me souviens*). Insisting that the descendants of immigrants have not forgotten their roots or the routes that they have taken, the Franco-American monument transcribes the topographic and imaginary space where France and America converge. Its existence is an acknowledgment of transnational French and francophone cultures. The fleeting nature of life, francophone and otherwise, renders memory in all of its manifestations profoundly meaningful.

Inaugurated on the symbolic date of July 2, 2008, precisely four hundred years following the establishment of the French on North American shores, the Monument de l'Amitié recalls past alliances that outweigh more recent squabbles. The attendance of distinguished guests including then Quebec prime minister Jean Charest marked the occasion. The American, French, and Canadian flags fly alongside the site, as does the provincial symbol of Quebec, and the Franco-American emblem. The riverside site actually includes three distinct commemorative statues honoring the United States, Vermont, and New England. The singling out of Vermont is due to the naming of the state's largest lake, Lake Champlain, for its explorer, as well as the economics of state financing. The sites pay homage to France and Quebec, ancestral homes to the invisible American immigrants from the north. The predominant New England monument lists all of the towns where Franco-Americans settled and established homes according to a 1940 survey. Little Canadas, parishes, churches, schools, even the rivers along whose banks many immigrants settled, receive written recognition. It is a fitting tribute indeed, as they evoke the meanderings of Franco-America.

As some monuments rise, others eventually fall, suggesting that little is truly permanent. Sponsors still memorialize Samuel de Champlain's efforts with new sites recently constructed (in English) on Cape Cod and on the campus of Champlain College in Vermont. Ethnic churches, however, continue to fall. Historic *Notre Dame-des-Canadiens* in the center of Worcester awaits demolition. The former Sacred Heart Church school of Northampton, Massachusetts, razed but remembered in stone in the very place where it once stood, saw its commemorative monument unceremoniously removed and laid at the back of the new church and parish. Some of the signs of "Bienvenue/Welcome," which city residents fought to erect at the entrance to their communities, have also come down.[9] One finds an interesting episode of selective remembering at Jack Kerouac's restored gravesite in Lowell. The "Ti Jean" commemorative stone mentioned in chapter 4 lay flush to the ground for decades. The new burial site constructed in 2014 includes a prominent piece of Vermont granite significantly more visible to visitors. While the unassuming former site contained a fragment of Kerouac's French past ("Ti Jean"), the new one bears the Beat author's signature and the phrase "The Road is Life."[10] Kerouac's Franco-American heritage remains thus obscured.

How can one read remaining Franco-American sites of ethnic and cultural memory, those discovered, altered, or still otherwise unknown? A few appear to be regularly seen and remembered, although we know little about how such sites are used. Certain aspects of Franco life have been immortalized on film and in literature, but many elements will reside underground until unearthed. I have argued for their recognition as an understated assertion of francophone life in the United States. Glimpses of French life do appear intermittently and surprisingly in contemporary

American culture, such as in the Clint Eastwood film or *West Wing* episode mentioned, where Francos make short cameo appearances.

Is there danger in remembering too fondly or nostalgically le Petit Canada, in not only identifying but essentializing French ethnic enclaves and cultures? Critics take Pierre Nora to task for exoticizing the past in his monumental series of volumes, *Les Lieux de mémoire*. Nora is interested primarily in national symbols, not those whose import is regional, ethnic, or minority based. French places are always in relationship to a mythical center, and most cultures are regional by nature. Even French national literature can be read as regional in the context of Europe and globalization.[11] The decentering of France may very well enable critical thought to acknowledge the intrinsic nature of minor literatures, monuments, newspapers, and organizations. Such outlying cultures may seem bucolic in nature, but can certainly contain hidden threats.[12] They echo the scattered and far-flung Frenchness that is the residue of the colonial experiment. Franco-American sites articulate to observers evolving yet resistant ethnic cultures of North America. French cultures remain vulnerable, but they circulate still (and sell) along open waterways such as the Mississippi River and on the shores of the St. Lawrence River, as well as along land conduits such as the Northway (Route 87) leading through New York into Canada.[13] The Northwind, or Le Vent du Nord, as a traditional Québécois musical group calls itself, keeps creolized traffic moving and mixing.

These French signs or signposts say a number of things to the people who are genuinely interested. They express a French *joie de vivre* but also *mélancholie*. They often honor the dead, and so there is clearly an element of mourning and of sadness, but there is also joy felt in being present despite everything, despite assimilation, poverty, invisibility. French life in America has been far from dreamlike, but individuals continue to find opportunities for reinvention and rebirth. They have not yet let go of the potato (*Lâche pas la patate!*). A French life constructed by resolute dreamers has rebuffed dominant cultural forces. Franco-Americans are still in the process of making themselves. They are American à *la française*, as American as *tarte aux pommes* (apple pie), subjects in the Franco version of the American story, choosing to air their laundry, dirty or otherwise.

INTRODUCTION

1. See Gitlin, *The Bourgeois Frontier*. See also Abrahams et al., *Blues for New Orleans*.
2. See Salhi, *Francophone Post-Colonial Cultures* and Forsdick and Murphy, *Francophone Postcolonial Studies*. See also Forsdick and Murphy, *Postcolonial Thought in the French-Speaking World* and Murdoch and Fagyal, *Francophone Cultures and Geographies of Identity* for more recent work.
3. Watts, *In This Remote Country*.
4. Carroll, *Evidences invisibles*.
5. Said, *Culture and Imperialism*.
6. Bancel et al., *Ruptures postcoloniales*.
7. Gilroy, *The Black Atlantic*; Marshall, *The French Atlantic*.
8. Le Bris and Rouard, *Pour une littérature-monde*.
9. Forsdick and Murphy, *Postcolonial Thought in the French-Speaking World*.
10. Hargreaves, Forsdick, and Murphy, *Transnational French Studies*, 3.
11. Forsdick and Murphy, *Postcolonial Thought in the French-Speaking World*, 18.
12. Bancel, Blanchard, and Vergès, *La République coloniale*.
13. Bouchard, *Genèse des nations et cultures du Nouveau Monde*.

14. Bensmaïa, *Experimental Nations*.

15. See Bourdieu, "The Forms of Capital."

16. Louder and Waddell, *Franco-Amérique*.

17. See McDermott and Samson, "White Racial and Ethnic Identity in the United States."

18. Louder and Waddell, *Franco-Amérique*, 14.

19. See Doyle and Pamplona, *Nationalism in the New World* and Shukla and Tinsman, *Imagining Our Americas*.

20. Murdoch and Fagyal, *Francophone Cultures and Geographies of Identity*. 2.

21. Aldrich, *Vestiges of the Colonial Empire in France*, 218.

22. Paul Gilroy's metaphoric ship traversing the ocean is a watery casket. See Gilroy, *The Black Atlantic*.

23. Beaulieu and Bergeron, *Amérique française*, 64.

24. See Dash, *The Other America*.

25. Brettell, *Following Father Chiniquy*.

26. Havard and Vidal, *Histoire de l'Amérique française*.

27. Hartford, *Working People of Holyoke*.

28. Richard, *Loyal but French*, 150. See also Richard's new book, *Not a Catholic Nation*.

29. Beaulieu and Bergeron, *Amérique française*.

30. Thériault, *Critique de l'américanité*.

31. Nora, *Les Lieux de Mémoires*.

32. Aldrich, *Vestiges of the Colonial Empire in France*.

33. Bancel et al., *Ruptures postcoloniales*, 17.

34. Tellingly, Jack Kerouac's modest headstone received a refurbishing in 2014.

35. See Anctil's *Sur les traces de Kerouac*.

36. See Hurley, *National Performance*.

37. Hémon, *Maria Chapdelaine*, 193.

1. BETWEEN DREAM AND REALITY

1. Beaulieu and Bergeron, *Amérique française*, 5.

2. Louder and Waddell, *French America*, 8

3. See Louder, Morisset, and Waddell, *Visions and Visages de la Franco-Amérique* and *Franco-Amérique*. In their earlier writings from the 1980s, they described Amérique française or French America.

4. Marshall, *The French Atlantic*, 302.

5. See Nora, *Les Lieux de Mémoire*.

6. Beaulieu and Bergeron, *Amérique française,* 7.

7. Nadeau and Barlow, *The Story of French,* 359–60.

8. Eccles, *France in America,* 27, 41.

9. Havard and Vidal, *Histoire de l'Amérique française,* 361.

10. Eccles, *France in America,* 52–53.

11. Bouchard, *Genèse des nations et cultures du Nouveau Monde,* 22.

12. See Brecher, *Losing a Continent.* See also Eccles, *France in America.*

13. *Hamilton* the musical is based on Ron Chernow's definitive biography, *Hamilton.*

14. For a sardonic account of French American history, see Vowell, *Lafayette in the Somewhat United States.*

15. See Bourdieu, "Deux imperialismes de l'universel."

16. See Hayward, *Fragmented France.*

17. Chapman "Flourishing in a Tough Climate," 7.

18. Schiff, *A Great Improvisation.*

19. Quoted from Thériault, *Critique de l'américanité,* 51.

20. Thériault, *Critique de l'américanité,* 71.

21. Parkman, *Pioneers of France in the New World,* viii–ix.

22. Parkman, *Pioneers of France in the New World,* x.

23. Watts, *In This Remote Country,* 73.

24. Parkman, *Pioneers of France in the New World,* x.

25. DeJean, *The Essence of Style.*

26. Bancel et al., *Ruptures postcoloniales,* 11.

27. See article by Pam Bellock, "Long Scorned in Maine, French Has Renaissance," *New York Times,* 4 June 2006, A1, 20.

28. Tidwell, *Bayou Farewell.*

29. See Perrin, *Acadian Redemption.*

30. See Doyle and Pamplona, *Nationalism in the New World.*

31. See the official website of the Congrès mondial acadien, http://www.cma2014.com/fr/.

32. Wilkerson, *The Warmth of Other Suns,* xi.

33. Robbins, *Wednesday's Child,* 56.

34. Vallières, *Nègres blancs d'Amérique.*

35. Michelle Lalonde's poem "Speak White" was first published in 1974 by Editions de l'Hexagone in Montreal.

36. See Roediger, *The Wages of Whiteness.*

37. Richards, "Corralling the Wild Ponies," 149.

38. Hobbs, "La Représentation ambivalente de l'Autochtone," 361.

39. Desroches, "Quebec and Postcolonial Theory."

40. Ashcroft, Griffiths, and Tifin, *The Empire Writes Back*, 15.

41. Havard and Vidal, *Histoire de l'Amérique française*, 12, 168.

42. Greer, *The People of New France*, 120.

43. Brasseaux, *French, Cajun, Creole, Houma*, 129.

44. Havard and Vidal, *Histoire de l'Amérique française*, 92.

45. Havard and Vidal, *Histoire de l'Amérique française*, 98.

46. Eccles, *France in America*, 125.

47. Eccles, *France in America*, 361.

48. Eccles, *France in America*, 80.

49. Havard and Vidal, *Histoire de l'Amérique française*, 160–61.

50. Eccles, *France in America*, 76.

51. Havard and Vidal, *Histoire de l'Amérique française*, 401.

52. Moogk, *La Nouvelle France*, 14.

53. Banks, *Chasing Empire across the Sea*; Marchand, *Ghost Empire*; Pritchard, *In Search of Empire*.

54. Pritchard, *In Search of Empire*, xxxi. The concluding chapter of Pritchard's study is entitled "Elusive Empire."

55. Eccles, *France in America*, 1.

56. Moogk, *La Nouvelle France*, 119.

57. Brecher, *Losing a Continent*, 9.

58. Eccles, *France in America*, 187.

59. Mathieu, *La Nouvelle-France*, 37.

60. Eccles, *France in America*, 14.

61. Havard and Vidal, *Histoire de l'Amérique française*, 42.

62. Joan DeJean calls Louis XIV the original male peacock. See DeJean, *The Essence of Style*, 162.

63. Havard and Vidal, *Histoire de l'Amérique française*, 58.

64. Eccles, *France in America*, 81.

65. Mathieu, *La Nouvelle-France*, 67.

66. A museum and commemorative plaque in Quebec City pay tribute to these young women pioneers of New France.

67. See description in Landry's *Histoires des Amériques*, 132.

68. Mathieu, *La Nouvelle-France*, 71, 54.

69. Choquette, *Frenchmen into Peasants*.

70. Mathieu, *La Nouvelle-France*, 247.

71. Moogk, *La Nouvelle France*, 25.

72. Greer, *The People of New France.*
73. Mathieu, *La Nouvelle-France.*
74. Eccles, *France in America,* 230–31.
75. Katz, *French America.*
76. Weil, *Les Franco-Américains,* 124.
77. New Hampshire Welcome/Bienvenue signs have been updated and are still currently displayed at state borders.
78. See Marshall, *France and the Americas.* The three-volume set provides students, teachers, and researchers with an encyclopedia of information about French America.
79. Tocqueville, *De la Démocratie en Amérique,* 76.
80. The University of Louisiana at Lafayette is home to the Ragin' Cajuns athletic brand.
81. Quintal, *Steeples and Smokestacks.*
82. See the historical Franco-American novel *Mirbah* by Emma Dumas.
83. The French name Dubois became Woods, for instance, and Leblanc became White.
84. Marshall, *The French Atlantic,* 302. Marshall speaks of far-flung "hinges" of French influence in the Atlantic world.
85. Abrahams et al., *Blues for New Orleans,* 1.
86. Baron and Cara, *Creolization as Cultural Creativity.*
87. Weil, *Les Franco-Américains,* 28.
88. Hartford, *Working People of Holyoke,* 86–87, 152.
89. Weil, *Les Franco-Américains,* 31.
90. Péloquin-Faré identifies these cultural institutions in her presentation of Franco-American life, *L'identité culturelle.*
91. *Springfield's Ethnic Heritage,* 25.
92. Brault, *The French-Canadian Heritage in New England,* 68.
93. Weil, *Les Franco-Américains,* 177.
94. Roby, *Les Franco-Américains de la Nouvelle-Angleterre.*
95. Péloquin-Faré, *L'identité culturelle,* 34–35.
96. Perreault, "Les Franco-Américains de Manchester, New Hampshire," 29.
97. See Pam Bellock, "Long Scorned in Maine, French Has Renaissance," *New York Times,* 4 June 2006, A1, 20, and Richard Fausset, "In Louisiana, Desire for a French Renaissance," *New York Times,* 14 February 2015.
98. Alexis Berthier, "La Fierté d'un héritage francophone," *France-Amérique,* 8–14 April 2006, 16.

99. Jean-Louis, Turlin, "L'Hymne américain en français dans le Maine," *France-Amérique*, 25–31 March 2006, 17.

100. Todd, *Le Destin des immigrés*.

101. French and other foreign language practices in the United States, as recorded in the 2000 census, can be easily accessed through the MLA Language Maps found at www.mla.org. The software provides tables, pie charts, and other information.

102. Ryan, "Language Use in the United States: 2011," 7, 8.

103. U.S. Census Bureau, "Language Use in the United States," 1, 3.

104. See Camille Ryan, U.S. Census Bureau, "Language Use in the United States: 2011," *American Community Survey Reports*, August 2013.

105. Michael Parent and Greg Boardman, *Chantons—Let's Sing" (in French and English)*. L/A Arts, 2000, compact disc.

106. Ben Levine, *Réveil . . . Waking Up French*, Watch Place Productions, 2001, DVD.

107. Robbins, *Wednesday's Child*.

108. Abby Paige, *Piecework: When We Were French*, self-published, 2013, DVD.

109. See Salhi, *Francophone Post-Colonial Cultures*.

2. CULTURAL INSTITUTIONS

1. Beaulieu and Bergeron, *Amérique française*, 41.

2. Roby, *Les Franco-Américains de la Nouvelle-Angleterre*, 192. See also Quintal, *Steeples and Smokestacks*.

3. French newspaper, radio, and television access has been a politicized object of contention in Lowell, Massachusetts, for instance. Details can be found in chapter 5.

4. See Moynihan's *Assumption College*.

5. Brault, *The French-Canadian Heritage in New England*.

6. See the American International College website (www.aic.edu/about /history).

7. See website addresses for museums: Millyard Museum (www .manchesterhistoric.org/millyard-museum), Museum of Work and Culture (www.ci.woonsocket.ri.us/museum.htm); and Museum L-A (www .museumla.org).

8. See website from the National Park Service (www.nps.gov/lowe /historyculture/mogan-cultural-center.htm).

9. Since 2004 the exhibit in Waterville, Maine, takes pedestrians on a tour through the former French ethnic neighborhood, with thirty

panels displaying archival images and bilingual text. See www
.themuseuminthestreets.com/maine_towns.html.

10. Bourdieu, *Distinction*.

11. Much related data can be found on the official *Alliance Française de Paris* website: www.alliancefr.org.

12. Bruézière, *L'Alliance française*, 176.

13. See Gabrielle Parker's article "'Francophonie' and 'Universalité': Evolution of Two Notions Conjoined."

14. Dubosclard, *Histoire de la Fédération des Alliances Françaises aux Etats-Unis*, 21.

15. See Bruézière, *L'Alliance française*.

16. "L'Alliance Française, au fond, est née d'une idée simple: laisser les étrangers eux-mêmes propager la culture française, céder partiellement la responsabilité de l'action culturelle de la France." Dubosclard, *Histoire de la Fédération des Alliances Françaises aux Etats-Unis*, 143. All French to English translations are my own unless otherwise noted.

17. See Peter McGuire, "African Immigrants Drive French-Speaking Renaissance in Maine," *Portland Press Herald*, 31 July 2016.

18. In 2014, there were 114 Alliance Française chapters.

19. No current Alliance chapters exist in Alaska, Wyoming, Arkansas, North Dakota, or South Dakota.

20. *France-Amérique*, 23–29 October 2004, 17.

21. *France-Amérique*, 23–29 October 2004, 17.

22. This is made clear on the "French-American Friendship" page of the official Federation of Alliances Françaises, USA website (www.afusa.org) under "French Culture."

23. *Hartford Courant*, 23 March 2005, B9.

24. Bruézière, *L'Alliance française*, 126–32.

25. "Si le combat contre le nazisme était un combat pour la défense de la culture française, la fédération américaine n'a-t-elle pas failli à sa mission?" Dubosclard, *Histoire de la Fédération des Alliances Françaises aux Etats-Unis*, 94.

26. See Ozouf, *L'Ecole, l'Eglise et la République*.

27. Bruézière, *L'Alliance française*, 12.

28. This phenomenon is explored in detail in Nadeau and Barlow, *The Story of French*.

29. Bancel, Blanchard, and Vergès, *La République coloniale*.

30. Agulhon, *Les Métamorphoses de Marianne*. See also Agulhon, Bonte, and Chagny, *Entre Liberté, République et France* and Manceron, *Marianne et les colonies*.

31. Bruézière, *L'Alliance française*, 62.

32. The Marianne representations come from early AF materials and group membership brochures.

33. Manceron, *Marianne et les colonies*.

34. Bruézière, *L'Alliance française*, 42–43, 95–96.

35. AF chapters in Worcester and Boston used this particular Marianne figure from the 1940s through the 1980s.

36. See Brault, *The French-Canadian Heritage in New England*; Roby, *Les Franco-Américains de la Nouvelle-Angleterre*; Quintal, *Steeples and Smokestacks*; and Weil, *Les Franco-Américains*.

37. Dubosclard, *Histoire de la Fédération des Alliances Françaises aux Etats-Unis*, 74.

38. Weil, *Les Franco-Américains*, 26.

39. Dubosclard, *Histoire de la Fédération des Alliances Françaises aux Etats-Unis*, 31–2.

40. Clément, *L'Alliance française de Lowell*.

41. "Un instrument de culture pour toute notre élite et un moyen de remplir pleinement des exigences des esprits les plus cultivés parmi l'élément d'origine canadienne-française. Conserver chez nous l'amour de la langue française et rehausser le prestige des Franco-Américains aux yeux des autres éléments américains qui les entourent, tel est le but que réalise de mieux en mieux le cercle régénéré de Lowell depuis cinq ans." Clément, *L'Alliance française de Lowell*, 22–23.

42. Alliance Française–Groupe de Worcester archives, Institut Français, Assumption College, Worcester, MA.

43. AF–Groupe de Worcester archives.

44. *France-Amérique*, 30 December 1962, 12.

45. Interview with former AF–Groupe de Worcester president, 18 March 2005.

46. A list of chapters is provided in *Alliance* 2 (Fall 1977): 24. This is the short-lived bilingual magazine published by the French Institute/Alliance Française (FIAF) of New York.

47. My research included interviews with several past and present chapter presidents of the Alliance Française in 2005. AF de St. Louis, 15 March, Alliance Française de Boston, 16 March, AF de Portland, 17 March, AF de Worcester, 18 March, AF d'Amherst, 23 March, AF du Lac Champlain, 30 March, AF de Manchester, 8 April, and AF de Lowell, 15 April.

48. Beaulieu and Bergeron, *Amérique française*, 7.

49. The Let's Talk Language School in Waterville, Maine, for instance, offers French language classes to heritage learners. See the school's website at www.letstalklanguageschool.org.

50. *France-Amérique*, 26 March–1 April 2005, 3.

51. Serrano, *Against the Postcolonial*.

52. Manning, *Francophone Sub-Saharan Africa*, 182.

53. *Federation Forum*, Winter 2004, 1.

54. *Federation Forum*, Winter 2005, 7.

55. Refer to the "Community" section of the Federation of Alliances Françaises website (www.afusa.org).

56. "Faire tout ce qui est nécessaire pour encourager le développement, l'utilisation et la préservation du français tel qu'il existe en Louisiane pour le plus grand bien culturel, économique et touristique pour l'état."

57. This is according to Louisiana State Senate Bill no. 800 of the regular session 2010, which included some slight changes to the organization's structure.

58. CODOFIL Strategic Plan 2005–2010, 2.

59. Louisiana State Senate Bill no. 800, 4.

60. Cajun French is sometimes referred to disparagingly as Nigger French.

61. Jeff Adelson, "CODOFIL Stunned by Gov. Bobby Jindal's Line-Item Veto of Much of Its Budget," *Times-Picayune*, 27 June 2012.

62. CODOFIL poster, "La vie commence à 40 ans," 2008.

63. "Enrichir, développer et soutenir la communauté francophone de Lafayette et de ses environs par l'enseignement du français et de ses variantes locales, par la valorisation de l'héritage français en ses multiples expressions, grâce à une programmation culturelle variée et adaptée." Mission statement, Dossier de candidature, AF de Lafayette, Louisiana, 18 July 2005, 18

64. Dossier de candidature, AF de Lafayette LA, 4.

65. "Le CODOFIL offre des bourses d'études à l'étranger pour étudiants et travaille à consolider les relations communautaires entre francophones." Dossier de candidature, AF de Lafayette, 10.

66. Dossier de candidature, AF de Lafayette, 5.

67. *Patates Nouvelles*, le bulletin-courriel du CODOFIL, 13 November 2009.

68. Interview with former CODOFIL executive director David Cheramie, 19 July 2005.

69. CODOFIL Strategic Plan 2005–10, 1.

70. CODOFIL, French Language Foreign Associate Teacher Placement Chart, 2004–5.

71. CODOFIL Strategic Plan 2005–10, Appendix Vision 2020, 10.

72. CODOFIL document 2004–5.

73. CODOFIL Strategic Plan 2005–10, 3.

74. See Lindner, "Attitudes toward Cajun French."

75. Email interview with CODOFIL instructor, 11 November 2011.

76. I communicated with a total of three CODOFIL instructors, one French, one Cajun, and one Ivorienne. They explained the challenges of teaching French in Louisiana.

77. Bernard, *The Cajuns*.

78. Interview with CODOFIL executive director David Cheramie, 29 July 2005.

79. I attended several meals at Dwyer's Restaurant in Lafayette on Wednesdays at 7 a.m.

80. Interview with Cheramie.

81. *Le Bulletin du Calendrier*, CODOFIL, 12 May 2006.

82. CODOFIL Strategic Plan 2005–10, Philosophy, 2.

83. See *Patates Nouvelles*, Le bulletin-courriel du CODOFIL, 11 December 2009. Community Outreach thanked Clifford Johnson for his translation into Louisiana Creole.

84. *Le Bulletin du Calendrier*, CODOFIL, 20 January 2006.

85. Interview with Cheramie.

86. Interview with Cheramie.

87. See "About FAC" section of the organization website (www.facnh.com /about.html).

88. In July 2005, for instance, the French flag flew to indicate that the ACA/ Franco-American Center was also home to Manchester's chapter of the Alliance Française.

89. See Samuel Blumenfeld, "Clint Eastwood, le vieil homme et la guerre," *Le Temps*, 28 October 2006, 40–41.

90. *France-Amérique*, 10–16 December 2005, 19.

91. Alliance française de Manchester archives.

92. Interview with Christine Davis, former executive director of the Centre Franco-Américain, 15 February 2008.

93. See Perreault, "Les Franco-Américains de Manchester, New Hampshire."

94. "Célébrons notre Histoire–Assurons notre avenir," Franco-American Heritage Center at St. Mary's Case Statement, 2.

95. "Célébrons notre Histoire–Assurons notre avenir," 2.

96. See www.francocenter.org.

97. Former organization website (www.francoamericanheritage.org/public /index.cfm).

98. Interview with FAHC executive director Rita Dubé, 25 June 2009.

99. See Hathaway, *Food Lovers' Guide to Maine*.

100. Third annual Franco Fun Festival program, 1–3 August 2008, 21.

101. Fourth annual Franco Fun Festival program, 19–21 June 2009, 3–4.

102. See Annie Murphy, "In Maine, a Little French Goes a Long Way" (www/pri .org/stories/2014-03-13/us-english-king-surprising-number-people-maine -also-speak-french/).

103. Juliana L'Heureux, "Franco-Americans in Print," *Press Herald* online, 26 October 2010. (www.pressherald.com/2010/10/26/franco-americans-in-print/).

104. Le Messager d'Aujourd'hui, *Today's Messenger*, no. 5 (April 2008): 2–3.

105. Joshua Shea, "Q&A: Rita Dube," *Lewiston-Auburn Magazine*, January/February 2013 (www.la-mag.com/rita-dube/).

106. Murphy, "In Maine, a Little French Goes a Long Way."

107. See www.facebook.com/FrenchHeritageCenter.

108. See Mass Live blog reports "French Heritage Center Lecture Series at Elms College in Chicopee Continues Look at Canadian Immigration," 22 October 2013, and "French Heritage Center to Commemorate D-Day with Chicopee Event," 23 April 2014 (http://blog.masslive.com).

109. Franco-American Women's Institute (www.fawi.net/).

110. Franco-American Women's Institute (www.fawi.net/).

111. Rhea Côté Robbins seeks to draw attention to the cultural work of francophone women. See Robbins, *Heliotrope*.

112. Franco-American Women's Institute (www.fawi.net/).

3. WOMEN'S SOCIAL CLUBS

1. I discovered this myself on several occasions, by chance stumbling across commemorative Franco sites of memory in postindustrial America.

2. Baker, *Fraternity among the French Peasantry*, 52.

3. Wylie, *Village in the Vaucluse*, 274–77.

4. Franco-American Women's Association meeting, 12 November 2009.

5. L'Association des Dames Franco-Amércaines de Chicopee, member directory, 2008–9; L'Association des Dames Franco-Américaines de Saint Rose de Lima Church de Chicopee, member directory, 2011–12.

6. Gans, "Symbolic Ethnicity," 1–20.

7. I attended my first meeting of les Dames franco-américaines on 26 May 2005 and became a regular attendee between January 2008 and May 2012. Members welcomed me back on several occasions. I was often the only man present and dealt with some friendly chiding about my obvious penchant for older ladies. Over the years, my presence came to feel normal and even expected.

8. Darnton, *The Great Cat Massacre*, 260.

9. L'Association des Dames Franco-Amércaines de Chicopee, member directory, 2008–9; L'Association des Dames Franco-Américaines de Saint Rose de Lima Church de Chicopee, member directory, 2011–12.

10. I attended a ceremony held on 9 November 2009 in honor of deceased members in Nativity Church before the regular meeting that followed and another gathering to pay respects in November 2015 in the Saint Rose de Lima Church sanctuary.

11. Richard, *Loyal but French*, 77.

12. See Alvarez, *How the García Girls Lost Their Accents*.

13. I witnessed this myself during group meetings. Because I was an outsider, some native French speakers felt more at ease speaking with me in English.

14. Franco-American Women's Association meeting, 27 May 2010.

15. See Weil, *Les Franco-Américains* and Faré-Peloquin, *L'identité culturelle*.

16. Jeannette Deforge, "French classes propagate heritage," *Republican*, 11 September 2003.

17. Brault, *The French-Canadian Heritage in New England*, 172–73.

18. See Michael Parent's website (www.michael-parent.com) for a description of his education and cultural activities.

19. The 30 percent figure for Franco-Americans in New Hampshire was a slight exaggeration, according to census data. See chapter 1.

20. See special issue of *Food & Foodways* 23, nos. 1–2 (2015), particularly Durmelat, "Tasting Displacement: Couscous and Culinary Citizenship in Maghrebi-French Diasporic Cinema," 108.

21. Interview with former Chicopee City treasurer and French Nite organizer, Ernest Laflamme, 11 February 2008.

22. See Gaudet and McDonald, *Mardi Gras, Gumbo, and Zydeco*.

23. Several similar Cajun and Creole maman's recipe books exist. See *Mais Oui, Marie: Creole Cookin. Life and Flavor in the Creole Tradition*.

24. Parent and Boardman, *Chantons! Let's Sing*.

25. See Langellier, "Performing Family Stories, Forming Cultural Identity," 53, 56–73. For an expanded version of analysis, see Langellier and Peterson, *Storytelling in Daily Life*.

26. Parent and Boardman, "Bonsoir, mes amis," track 13, *Chantons! Let's Sing.*

27. See Hartford, *Working People of Holyoke*, 152.

28. Etta Walsh, "French Group Keeps Cultural Roots Alive," *Chicopee Plus*, 28 September 2005. This is a weekly publication printed each Wednesday for communities in the Chicopee area.

29. Rev. Gérard Lafleur, "Tribut final," *Le Bulletin de la Fédération Féminine Franco-Américaine* 32, nos. 1/2 (Winter-Spring 1984).

30. "Le but du Cercle est d'encourager les lettres françaises et le bon parler français, de promouvoir l'intérêt de ses membres et du groupement franco-américain au moyen de réunions et d'oeuvres philanthropiques." Cercle des Dames Françaises, 2004–2006 booklet, 17.

31. Walsh, "French Group Keeps Cultural Roots Alive."

32. "Esprit Saint, Roi de Lumière et d'Amour, veuillez nous accorder votre secours. Aidez-nous à bien comprendre nos devoirs et donnez-nous la force d'agir avec sagesse afin que nous sachions toujours travailler dans un esprit chrétien et patriotique. Bénissez nos soeurs, bénissez notre travail afin que nous soyons dignes de recevoir la récompense du succès. Amen." Cercle des Dames françaises, Adieu proceedings, 24 June 2007.

33. Walsh, "French Group Keeps Cultural Roots Alive."

34. See Graham, *Our Kind of People*.

35. Cercle des Dames Françaises, 2004–2006 booklet, article III, 17.

36. Interview with former *Cercle* member and official, 11 February 2008.

37. Stoler and Cooper, *Tensions of Empire*, 155.

38. Claire Quintal, address to the Cercle des Dames Françaises, 75th year anniversary celebration, 2 October 2005.

39. Cercle des Dames Françaises, *Le Bulletin*, April 2004.

40. Murielle Banas to Cercle des Dames Françaises, 19 January 2006.

41. See announcement for the adieu in Hometown Notes, *Chicopee Plus*, 13 June 2007, as well as John P. O'Connor, "Your Ancestors Often Joined Clubs, Societies," *Chicopee Plus*, 20 June 2007.

42. Interview with Cécile Provencher, Cercle Jeanne Mance de Lowell member and Franco-American of the Year 2010, 7 July 2010.

43. Interview with Claudette Gagnon, Cercle Jeanne Mance president, 14 July 2010.

44. According to the September 1952 version of the Cercle Jeanne Mance's constitution, these ten women met at the home of the first president, Mme. Joseph T. Roberge, who later became Mme. Frank Loveland. The identity of the female founder is twice hidden behind the traditional matrimonial title.

45. "Le but de cette association sera de promouvoir l'avancement de ses membres dans l'étude de la langue française, la religion, les sciences et la littérature." Constitution du Cercle Jeanne Mance, Worcester, MA, 1921–22, article II, 2

46. Constitution du Cercle Jeanne Mance, Worcester, MA, 1921–22, article VI, 3.

47. Cercle Jeanne Mance, Programme de l'exercice 1933–34. September, October, and January meetings included card games.

48. Mme. Edouard-A. Brodeur, Historique du Cercle Jeanne-Mance, 1913–1963, 50th year organization program, 5.

49. "Fêtes inoubliables qui ont eu lieu à Worcester," *La Liberté*, Fitchburg, MA, 17 November 1938.

50. Cercle Jeanne Mance, Programme de l'exercice, 1933–34. Classes listed under November activities.

51. Constitution du Cercle Jeanne Mance, Worcester, MA, September 1952, article III, 1.

52. Cercle Jeanne Mance, Programme de la saison 1914–15 includes many musical performances. See also "Musicale," sous la direction de Mlle M.-Rose Rochelle. Cercle Jeanne Mance, la Salle David Hale Fanning, Worcester, MA, 24 January 1928. A 22 May 1928 Cercle performance was entitled "Revue musicale et comédie."

53. "Carlita Opérette en deux actes," Donnée par le Cercle Jeanne Mance, la Salle paroissale Saint Nom de Jésus, Worcester, MA, 28 May 1934.

54. Brodeur, Historique du Cercle Jeanne Mance, 10.

55. "Le but du Cercle Jeanne Mance est d'encourager l'étude de la langue française, *de mettre en relief le rôle de la culture française et de la religion dans la vie américaine*, de soutenir les oeuvres de charité et d'éducation et de favoriser la vie sociale de ses membres." Constitution du Cercle Jeanne Mance. Worcester, MA, September 1952, article II, 1.

56. "Jubilé d'argent–Acrostiche en prose–Jeanne Mance, la patronne du Cercle Jeanne Mance de Worcester," 17–24 November 1938.

57. "France to Decorate Retired City Teacher," *Worcester Daily Telegram*, 25 September 1957.

58. Cercle Jeanne Mance, application submitted for consideration to become an honor club, Mrs. Edwin P. Meyer, publicity chairman, 22 October 1955.

59. Cercle Jeanne Mance. Bulletin–September 1953. Signed by "Secrétaire" Mme. Armand C. Jetté.

60. Historique de la Fédération Féminine Franco-Américaine, 1951–2001, 1.

61. Article 4, Statuts et règlements de la Fédération Féminine Franco-Américaine, revised November 1988 (hereafter Statuts et règlements).

62. Article 8, Statuts et règlements.

63. Historique de la Fédération Féminine Franco-Américaine 1951–2001, chronology.

64. "Américaine de naissance, parfaitement bilingue, épouse, mère, animatrice sociale, conférencière, artiste, pianiste, initiée même à la fonction publique, elle apporte au mouvement de base une connaissance complète du milieu et sait proposer des moyens pratiques pour la consolidation du réseau féminin." *Le Bulletin de la Fédération Féminine Franco-Américaine* 32, nos. 1/2 (Winter/Spring 1984): 2.

65. "La Fédération Féminine Franco-Américaine a pour objet de grouper les femmes franco-américaines catholiques et les femmes francophones de la Nouvelle-Angleterre en vue de fortifier par l'union leur action française ainsi que leur promotion de la langue française dans la famille et dans la société," Article 1, Statuts et règlements.

66. Article 10, Statuts et règlements.

67. Interview with Claire Quintal, 18 March 2005.

68. "Tout groupement mixte peut aussi être affilié mais il doit être représenté par une femme." Article 12, Statuts et règlements.

69. Article 20, Statuts et règlements.

70. *Le Bulletin* will be "un lien entre les groupements affiliés et les tiendra au courant de ce qui se passe chez les Franco-Américaines. Il vous parlera de leurs activités. Plus nous grandirons, plus le BULLETIN sera intéressant." *Le Bulletin de la Fédération Féminine Franco-Américaine* 1, no. 1 (January 1953): 1.

71. Péloquin-Faré, *L'identité culturelle*, 102.

72. "La recette est bien simple: nous voulons du français? Eh bien! Parlons français, surtout dans nos foyers. C'est le premier moyen, c'est le grand moyen, c'est l'unique moyen de commencer notre travail aussi noble que nécessaire." *Le Bulletin* 1, no. 1 (January 1953): 1.

73. Article 11, Statuts et règlements.

74. The Waterbury CT chapter of the Alliance Française publicized its activities in the bulletin like other Franco-American organizations. *Le Bulletin* 30, nos. 3/4 (Summer/Autumn 1982): 6.

75. *Le Bulletin* 1, no. 2 (April 1953): 1.

76. "Nous demandons solennellement, à chacun des membres de la Fédération Féminine Franco-Américaine, de s'abonner à un journal franco-américain et de trouver au moins une autre abonnée pour le journal de votre choix. . . . Tous nos journaux sont catholiques, patriotiques et dévoués à nos intérêts." *Le Bulletin* 1, no. 2 (April 1953): 2.

77. "Le Congrès constitue l'autorité suprême dans la Fédération." Article 15, Statuts et règlements.

78. "The Woman in the French life movement" (1954); "Franco-American education" (1956); "French in the family, at school, and among youth" (1965); "The Teaching of French in parochial and public schools" (1967); "Woman, her transformation, and social action" (1975); "The Franco-American woman, her role, rights and responsibilities vis-à-vis bilingualism and biculturalism in our society" (1979); "The Francophone woman in the United States" (1984).

79. Tenth anniversary, "Persuade and act for our *refrancisation*" (1961); twentieth anniversary, "Renaissance of French in the 20th century" (1971).

80. *Le Petit Bulletin* was edited by Marthe W. Whalon, a native of France.

81. Fédération Féminine Franco-Américaine, *Le Petit Bulletin*, no. 2 (Autumn 1993): 3.

82. Cercle des Dames Françaises, *Bulletin*, October 2001. The Fédération president voiced hope of increasing the amount left for educational purpose, but donations did not follow.

83. Historique de la Fédération Féminine Franco-Américaine, 1951–2001, 2.

4. FRANCO-AMERICAN CULTURES

1. While Franco-American literature may not be entirely "cosmopolitan" or "global," it is located between physical and metaphoric worlds. Donald Morrison and Antoine Compagnon refer to a "world" literature in French, in *The Death of French Culture*, 32.

2. Le Bris and Rouaud, *Pour une littérature-monde*.

3. The Winthrop-King Institute for Contemporary French and Francophone Studies at Florida State University held an international conference entitled "Littérature-Monde: New Wave or New Hype?" 12–14 February 2009.

The twentieth meeting of the Association des professeurs des littératures acadienne et québécoise de l'Atlantique (APLAQA) examined "Trajectoires et dérives de la littérature-monde," 21–23 October 2010. Issues of the journals *Contemporary French and Francophone Studies* and the *International Journal of Francophone Studies* are devoted to this subject. See the book edited by Hargreaves, *Transnational French Studies*.

4. Richards, "Putting Québec Studies on the Map," 81–89.

5. See special issues of the *French Review*: "La Francophonie aux États-Unis," 80, no. 6 (May 2007) and "Le Français a-t-il un avenir aux États-Unis," 86, no. 6 (May 2013).

6. Megharbi et al., *Pause-Café*; Schultz and Tranvouez, *Réseau*. Both locate Francophone minorities not just in Louisiana but in New England as well.

7. Redonnet et al., *Héritages francophones*.

8. Louder and Waddell, *Franco-Amérique*.

9. Greer, *The People of New France*, 22, 26.

10. Weil, *Les Franco-Américains*.

11. Ben Jelloun Barbery et al., "Pour Une 'Littérature-Monde' en français," *Le Monde*, 16 March 2007, 1.

12. Abdou Diouf, "La Francophonie, une réalité oubliée," *Le Monde*, 19 March 2007.

13. Thomas, "Decolonizing France," 47–55.

14. Gitlin, *The Bourgeois Frontier*.

15. Louder and Waddell, *Franco-Amérique*.

16. Francophone literature is, of course, alive and well in *la Belle Province*. The publishing houses of Montreal and Quebec City have played a central role in the writing of the French experience in America.

17. See, for instance, Beaupré's *Deux femmes, deux rêves*.

18. Some fifty years earlier, Camille Lessard-Bissonnette wrote *Canuck*.

19. Other noteworthy histories of Franco-Americans include Roby, *Les Franco-Américains de la Nouvelle-Angleterre* and Brault, *The French-Canadian Heritage in New England*.

20. Senécal, *The Franco-American Bibliographic File Project*.

21. See, for instance, Jambon's *L'Ecole Gombo*.

22. Le Bris and Rouaud, *Pour une littérature-monde*, 61.

23. Le Bris and Rouaud, *Pour une littérature-monde*, 24.

24. See, for instance, Dash, *The Other America*.

25. Senécal, *The Franco-American Bibliographic File Project*.

26. Beaugrand, *Jeanne la fileuse*.

27. Belisle, *Histoire de la presse franco-américaine*, 14.

28. Belisle, *Histoire de la presse franco-américaine*, 341–42.

29. Weil, *Les Franco-Américains*, 26, 32.

30. Rhea Côté Robbins provides useful biographical information in her English-language edition of *Canuck*. See Robbins, *Canuck and Other Stories*.

31. See Lees, "Exploring Rural and Urban Space."

32. Robbins, *Canuck and Other Stories*, 23.

33. Robbins, *Canuck and Other Stories*, 14, 39.

34. See Robinson, *Loom & Spindle; or, Life among the Early Mill Girls*. Noyes, *Yvonne of the Amoskeag Textile Mills* provides a closer look at a young Franco-American mill girl.

35. Robbins, *Canuck and Other Stories*, 40.

36. Maillet, *Pélagie-la-charette*, 108, 312.

37. Maillet, *Pélagie-la-charette*, 312.

38. Hémon, *Maria Chapdelaine*, 193.

39. Hémon, *Maria Chapdelaine* 189.

40. "Que faire d'un roman écrit par un Français pour un public français?" editors Michel Biron, François Dumont, and Élisabeth Nardout-Lafarge ask specifically. See *Histoire de la littérature québécoise*, 200.

41. The French verb *gagner* means to win.

42. Hémon, *Maria Chapdelaine*, 156

43. Hémon, *Maria Chapdelaine*, 87–88.

44. Hémon, *Maria Chapdelaine*, 23.

45. Savard, *Menaud, maître-draveur*, 40, 77.

46. See, e.g., Bouchard, *Genèse des nations et cultures du Nouveau Monde*.

47. Savard, *Menaud, maître-draveur*, 40, 77, 101, 133.

48. Biron, Dumont, and Nardout-Lafarge, *Histoire de la Littérature Québécoise*, 12. "Dès le XIXe siècle, cette littérature s'est définie comme un projet 'national.'"

49. Ringuet, *Trente Arpents*, 51, 146.

50. Ringuet, *Trente Arpents*, 202.

51. This is a reference to Louis Chevalier's classic, *Classes laborieuses et classes dangereuses à Paris pendant la première moitié du XIXe siècle*.

52. Weil, *Les Franco-Américains*, 146.

53. Ringuet, *Trente Arpents*, 103, 286.

54. Ringuet, *Trente Arpents*, 123.

55. Ringuet, *Trente Arpents*, 248, 254.

56. Marshall, *The French Atlantic*.

57. See Ernest Renan's 1882 lecture, "Qu'est-ce qu'une nation?"

58. Moogk, *La Nouvelle France*, 14.

59. Biron, Dumont, and Nardout-Lafarge, *Histoire de la Littérature Québécoise*, 20.

60. Like other Franco-American novels, Hémon's *Maria Chapdelaine* first appeared in several serial segments in Montreal and in book form five years later in Paris.

61. Quote taken from Thériault, *Critique de l'américanité*, 51.

62. Thériault, *Critique de l'américanité*, 317.

63. Bouchard, *Genèse des nations et cultures du Nouveau Monde*, 22.

64. Bouchard and Lamonde, *Québécois et Américains*, 17.

65. See article by Gabriel Anctil, "Sur le chemin," *Le Devoir*, 4 September 2008.

66. For details on Jack Kerouac's trans-American itinerary, see Anctil and Nuovo, *Sur les traces de Kerouac*.

67. Weil, *Les Franco-Américains*, 26.

68. Gabriel Anctil makes this point clear in his article.

69. Plante, *American Ghosts*, 247.

70. "Le *Canuck* iroquois d'origine bretonne." See Anctil and Nuovo, *Sur les traces de Kerouac*, 6.

71. A review of Kerouac's *The Town and the City* written by Yvonne Le Maitre appeared in Worcester's French-language weekly, *Le Travailleur*, 23 March 1950, 7.

72. Biron, Dumont, and Nardout-Lafarge, *Histoire de la littérature québécoise*, 573.

73. Ducharme, *The Shadows of the Trees*, 18.

74. Jacques Ducharme, "Profession de foi," *La Justice*, 6 June 1940, 1.

75. For some, the only visible, noteworthy, and highly ambiguous reference to "Franco-American" was found on the label of "SpaghettiOs" cans.

76. Rhea Côté Robbins is founder of the Franco-Americans Women's Institute (www.fawi.net), which uses social networking sites to communicate.

77. Robbins, *Wednesday's Child*, 62.

78. Robbins, *Wednesday's Child*, 81.

79. See *New York Times* cover article by Pam Belluck, "Long-Scorned in Maine, French Has Renaissance," 4 June 2006, as well as Richard Fausset, "In Louisiana, Desire for a French Renaissance," 4 February 2015.

80. Plante, *American Ghosts*, 5.

81. Plante, *American Ghosts*, 7.

82. Plante, *American Ghosts*, 86.

83. Plante, *American Ghosts*, 59–60.

84. Plante, *American Ghosts*, 194. He also mentions the Native American ancestral connection so common to the hybrid French experience in North America.

85. Hebert, *Never Back Down,* 5, 255.

86. See Guglielmo and Salerno, *Are Italians White? How Race Is Made in America.*

87. Pelletier, *Little Pine to King Spruce*, 175.

88. See, for instance, Chute's *The Beans of Egypt.*

89. Beaugrand, *Jeanne la fileuse*, 120.

90. Ducharme, *Shadows of the Trees*, 11.

91. Parent and Olivier, *Of Kings and Fools.*

92. See Thériault, *Critique de l'américanité.*

93. Laferrière, *Je suis fatigué*, 93.

94. Le Clézio, *Le Chercheur d'or.*

95. Cloonan, "Littérature-Monde and the Novel in 2007."

5. ETHNIC IDENTITY

1. Guillet, "French Ethnic Literature and Culture in an American City," 82, 89.

2. Guillet, *Essai de journalisme.*

3. Weil, *Les Franco-Américains*, 99.

4. See, for instance, Roby, *Les Franco-Américains de la Nouvelle-Angleterre*; Quintal, *Steeples and Smokestacks.* The Dreyfus affair in France similarly only became a national discussion because of an influential French press.

5. Louder and Waddell, *Franco-Amérique*, 120.

6. See Senécal, *The Franco-American Bibliographic File Project.*

7. Weil, *Les Franco-Américains*, 90.

8. Senécal, *The Franco-American Bibliographic File Project.*

9. Tétrault, *Le Rôle de la presse dans l'évolution du peuple franco-américain.*

10. Anderson, *Imagined Communities*, 62.

11. Mezzasalma, *A la Une: La Presse de la gazette à Internet*, 174.

12. Senécal, *The Franco-American Bibliographic File Project.*

13. This is Mark Paul Richard's assertion in *Loyal but French*, 226. By the 1940s, daily production had dropped to five thousand copies.

14. Brousseau, "*Le FAROG Forum*: Autopsie d'un journal d'éveil et de combat."

15. Guillet, "French Ethnic Literature and Culture in an American City," 3.

16. "Le Tricentenaire de Québec," *L'Avenir national*, 17 July 1908, 1, 2; "Les Fêtes de Québec" and "La Fondation de Québec," *L'Avenir national*, 20 July 1908, 1, 2.

17. "Le IIIe centenaire du Québec," *L'Etoile*, 20 July 1908, cover. "Allez à Québec," *L'Etoile*, 21 July 1908, encouraged readers to make the ancestral trip to Quebec as did many Franco newspapers, often around the Saint John the Baptist celebration on 24 June.

18. *L'Avenir national*, 19 January 1948, 4.

19. Anderson, *Imagined Communities*.

20. Ducharme, *The Shadows of the Trees*, 123–24. Four years earlier, Ducharme published an autobiographical novel, *The Delusson Family*, that brought the author a certain amount of attention in the Franco community.

21. Mark Paul Richard finds this in *Loyal but French,* his study of Franco-Americans in Lewiston, Maine.

22. Ducharme, *The Shadows of the Trees*, 124.

23. See the fictional series entitled "Amour," *Le National*, 9 January 1894, 3.

24. Péloquin-Faré confirms the influential role of women in the traditional Franco home. *L'Identité culturelle*, 40.

25. "Conte du soir," *L'Avenir national*, 6 July 1931.

26. The series began in *Le Travailleur* on 28 January 1932.

27. *Le Travailleur*, 10 September 1931, 12. A poem, "A Ferdinand Gagnon," also appeared in the inaugural edition.

28. Wilfrid Beaulieu, "Notre premier numéro," *Le Travailleur*, 10 September 1931, 1.

29. *Le Travailleur*, 10 September 1931, 4.

30. Ernest d'Amour, "Franco-Américanisme et Catholicisme," *Le Travailleur*, 10 September 1931, 3.

31. Weil, *Les Franco-Américains*, 147. See table 4.2

32. Dollard, "A qui nos Ecoles? A nous!" *Le Travailleur*, 17 September 1931, 1, 2.

33. *L'Avenir national*, 1 July 1939, 7.

34. *L'Avenir national*, 14 July 1939, 4.

35. Biron, Dumont, and Nordout-Lafare, *Histoire de la littérature québécoise*, 456–62.

36. See editorial by *La Justice* director Joseph Lussier entitled "American French," 9 January, 1913, 4.

37. Chanoine Emile Chartier, "Le patois canadien-français," *Le Travailleur*, 7, 14, 28 April 1932.

38. See "Nos enfants Américains et nous," *La Justice*, 25 April 1940, 6.

39. Weil, *Les Franco-Américains*, 212.

40. "We specifically address Franco-Americans, that is all compatriots of French-Canadian descent, all those who still have the blood of their ancestors in their veins, in their brains a spirit particular to their ancestral race, in their heart the sense of pride of belonging to that subset of good Americans called Francos." "Parlons français," *La Justice*, 28 March 1940, 4.

41. "La langue et la race," *Le Travailleur*, 10 September 1931, 3.

42. Sainte Thérèse, "Le Collège de l'Assomption," *Le Travailleur*, 17 September 1931, 2.

43. *Le Travailleur*, 28 January 1932, 1, 8.

44. See *Le Travailleur*, 9 and 16 May 1935. "Plus de 50,000 personnes lisent 'Le Travailleur,'" reads a right cover statement.

45. William-B. Munro, "Les Etats-Unis Désunis," *Le Travailleur*, 25 February 1932.

46. See "Noël!" *Le Travailleur*, 24 December 1931.

47. Rodolphe Laplante, "Traditions ancestrales," *Le Travailleur*, 31 December 1931, 7.

48. Ducharme, *The Shadows of the Trees*, 181–82.

49. See Ryan, "The American Parade."

50. "La St. Jean-Baptiste," *Le Messager*, 21 June 1926.

51. Richard, *Loyal but French*.

52. *La Justice*, 4 July 1940.

53. See *L'Avenir national*, 3 July 1914, 1.

54. Richard, *Loyal but French*, 77, 80.

55. Antoine Dumouchel, M.D., "Nos sociétés nationales," *Le Travailleur*, 17 December 1931, 13.

56. "Vive la France," *L'Avenir national*, 5 September 1914. France had just declared war on Germany.

57. The entire second page was devoted to patriotic hymns. *L'Avenir national*, 3 July 1918.

58. "Victoire!" *L'Avenir national*, 11 November 1918.

59. "La Déclaration d'indépendance," *L'Avenir national*, 3 July 1939, 4.

60. Elphège–J. Daignault, "Franco-Américains! 'On est ce qu'on est, c'est bien clair,'" *Le Travailleur*, 1 October 1931, 2.

61. Alexandra, "La Patrie," *Le Travailleur*, 19 November 1931, 1.

62. "La Lutte," *Le Travailleur*, 8 October 1931, 1.

63. L'Ermite, "Patriotisme à l'école," *Le Travailleur*, 5 November 1931, 1.

64. Antoine Dumouchel, M.D., "L'Union des peuples de langue française," *Le Travailleur*, 5 May 1932.

65. Weil, *Les Franco-Américains*, 177.

66. Lussier, "La France éternelle," *La Justice*, 6 August 1914, 4.

67. See Lebovics, *True France*.

68. Hobsbawm and Ranger, *The Invention of Tradition*.

69. "Yes, long live eternal France, the France always ready to promote good causes, a generous France never intending to do wrong to anyone, the beloved France patron of the fine arts, the France to whom we owe the best of ourselves; long live our faith, our language, our national spirit, the independence even of the United States, that we love." "Fête nationale de la France," *L'Avenir national*, 13 July 1939, 4.

70. See Hunt, *Politics, Culture, and Class in the French Revolution*.

71. "Le Maréchal Pétain," *Le Travailleur*, 5 November 1931, 1.

72. "Pétain et les Canadiens français," *L'Avenir national*, 21 June 1939, 4.

73. "La France entière," *Le Travailleur*, 10 April 1941, 3-A.

74. Ducharme, *The Shadow of the Trees*, 18.

75. Doty, "'Monsieur Maurras est ici,'" 527–38.

76. Winock, *La Fièvre hexagonale*, chapter 7.

77. See Lebovics, *True France*.

78. Ducharme, "Aux Armes!" *La Justice*, 11 July 1940, 4. This is a call to arms against fascist France, or Vichy France.

79. Interview with Albert Côté, 5 August 2008.

80. This may explain some of the errors that crept into *Le Journal's* French print.

81. This selection of Franco services could be found in the June 1978 issue.

82. See photograph and descriptive caption about the Biron-Péloquin journalistic family in *Le Journal de Lowell*, April 1980, 4.

83. Interview with Marthe Biron Péloquin, 15 April 2005.

84. The September 1981 edition of *Le Journal* mentioned the successful completion of Louise Péloquin's doctorate at the University of Paris. Franco recognition in the French capital was certainly a subject of some local ethnic pride. The paper would additionally advertise the book version of her dissertation.

85. Ducharme, *The Shadow of the Trees*, 124.

86. Darnton, *The Great Cat Massacre*, 262.

87. The fourth annual conference of the French Institute held 11–12 March 1983 was entitled "Le Journalisme de langue française aux Etats-Unis," February 1983, cover.

88. "Guy Rivard parle à ActFANE," *Le Journal de Lowell*, May 1991, 7.

89. "Qu'est-ce que l'ActFANE?" *Le Journal de Lowell*, March 1991, 4.

90. An article by Marthe Biron Péloquin gives some indication of the relevance to Franco-Americans of Alex Haley's book and television series, *Roots*, on African American life. See "'Roots' franco-américaines à la Lowell City Library," *Le Journal de Lowell*, June 1980, 4.

91. Paul Chassé, "Les Sociétés," *Le Journal de Lowell*, March 1980, 2.

92. "Nouveau centre Franco-Américain," *Le Journal de Lowell*, May 1990, 5.

93. See advertisement for the AF Amherst/Northampton, October 1984. *Tout en français* aired thirteen one-hour interviews of fifty-two Franco-Americans on Northampton's FM dial in the early 1980s. Lionel Delevingne conceived the idea of a photographic essay to accompany the interviews and was aided by professors Eloise Brière and Nicole Vaget. The Massachusetts Council on the Arts funded the research as well as a regional and international tour of the photo exhibit.

94. See "Fête nationale des Acadiens," *Le Journal de Lowell*, September 1983, 3.

95. *Le Journal* began advertising the event in a January 1990 cover article, "Congrès Mondial Acadien."

96. "Le Consul de France, l'invité du Cercle Jeanne-Mance de Lowell," *Le Journal de Lowell*, April 1979, cover.

97. "Premier Sommet francophone voit la participation de 39 pays," *Le Journal de Lowell*, April 1986, 2. Canada, Europe, Africa, Asia, the Caribbean, and the United States had representation at the meeting.

98. Brettell, *Following Father Chiniquy*.

99. "Le Premier sommet francophone–la citoyenneté de la langue," *Le Journal de Lowell*, May 1986, 2.

100. "La francophonie mondiale," *Le Journal de Lowell*, July 1989, cover.

101. The Third Franco-American Congress was held in Lafayette, Louisiana, 28–30 March 1980.

102. See the Ninth Franco-American National Congress in Nashua, New Hampshire, in 1987.

103. "Un parc de l'Amérique française à Québec," *Le Journal de Lowell*, December 1985, 12.

104. The official discourse of the Second Franco-American Congress was printed in *Le Journal*, July 1979, 8–9.

105. See cover article, *Le Journal de Lowell*, August 1979.

106. "Congrès AFA," *Le Journal de Lowell*, June 1983, 6.

107. Jeanneney, *Une histoire des médias*, 7. My translation of "la représentation que les sociétés se font d'elles-mêmes et des autres."

108. *Le Journal de Lowell*, March 1987, cover.

109. Photograph of ActFA reunion and description, *Le Journal*, October 1980, 8.

110. See "Qu'est-ce que l'ActFANE?" *Le Journal de Lowell*, March 1991, 4.

111. Paul Paré, "Une francophonie surprenante et variée," *Le Journal de Lowell*, January 1994, 3.

112. "Lancement du premier journal francophone de Floride," *Le Journal de Lowell*, February 1981, 2. Printing had been set at 35,000 copies for the 250,000 francophone residents of south Florida.

113. Louise P. Faré, "April in Paris," *Le Journal de Lowell*, June 1984, 2. English title, French prose.

114. Louise P. Faré, "Terrorisme? N'en parlons pas!" *Le Journal de Lowell*, June 1986, 2.

115. Louise P. Faré, "Les gens de chez nous," *Le Journal de Lowell*, July 1991, 2.

116. Louise P. Faré, "Le Dictionnaire général de la francophonie," *Le Journal de Lowell*, December 1987, 2.

117. Louise P. Faré, "Les 'Francos'–sujet de cours à la Sorbonne," *Le Journal de Lowell*, March 1987, 2. Franco-American study in France was a subject of some pride in Lowell.

118. Eloise Brière and Nicole Grangeat-Vaget coauthored *Franco-American Viewpoints*, along with photographer Lionel Delavigne. See Nicole Grangeat-Vaget, "Nos Cousins d'Amérique," *Le Journal*, July 1981.

119. "Le Figaro à Lowell," *Le Journal de Lowell*, September 1982, 2.

120. Originally published by Jean-Pierre Péroncel-Hugoz in *Le Monde*, 12 December 1987.

121. Claire Quintal, "Les sommets francophones," *Le Journal*, July 1989.

122. Hervé Bellevue, "Ô Lowell," *Le Journal*, January 1982, 3; Hervé Bellevue, "Pays de mes ancêtres," *Le Journal*, March 1982, 4. Another Lowell poet of Haitian descent, Michel-Yves Danger, was published in *Le Journal*.

123. Roger J. Brunelle, "Délégation africaine visite Lowell," *Le Journal de Lowell*, October 1989, 8.

124. Dr. Georges Okouya, "Les grandes phases de l'histoire sénégalo-mauritanienne de la colonisation à nos jours," *Le Journal de Lowell*, June 1990, 7.

125. Lipovetsky and Serroy, *La Culture-monde*.

126. See the February 1989 and February 1991 *Journal* editions.

127. "La petite histoire du câble à Lowell," *Le Journal de Lowell*, March 1994, 6.

128. "La petite histoire du câble à Lowell," part 7, *Le Journal de Lowell*, May 1994, 7

129. "Pour nous, Franco-Américains, ces médias ont une influence particulière sur notre langue, notre culture, notre manière de penser et d'agir. Les cultures américaines et franco-américaines ne s'excluent pas mais au contraire se complètent. Il faut donc travailler vers l'épanouissement de notre culture franco-américaine à travers une programmation française." Conclusion to "La petite histoire du câble à Lowell," *Le Journal de Lowell*, July 1994, 8.

130. "Aux armes citoyens," *Le Journal de Lowell*, June 1993, cover.

131. In a 1988 historical drama called *The Mills of Power*, a struggle resembling that in Lowell to maintain French television access, aired in Quebec.

132. "Bonjour! . . . Bienvenue à Lowell," *Le Journal de Lowell*, September 1994.

133. "Franco ES-TU LA?" *Le Journal de Lowell*, May 1994, cover.

134. "Médias francophones à Lowell," *Le Journal de Lowell*, October 1995.

135. Two New England businessmen who succeeded without mention of a French cultural connection are William Aubuchon of Aubuchon Hardware and Paul d'Amour of the Big Y Supermarket chain.

6. UNMASKING THE CREOLE COWBOY

1. Jeff Adelson, "CODOFIL Stunned by Gov. Bobby Jindal's Line-Item Veto of Much of Its Budget," *Times-Picayune*, 27 June 2012.

2. Abrahams et al., *Blues for New Orleans*.

3. Hall, *Africans in Colonial Louisiana*, 2.

4. See Miller, *The French Atlantic Triangle*.

5. See Havard and Vidal, *Histoire de l'Amérique française*; Greer, *The People of New France*; Axtall, *The Invasion Within*.

6. Brasseaux, *French, Cajun, Creole, Houma*, 127.

7. Eccles, *France in America*.

8. Havard and Vidal, *Histoire de l'Amérique française*, 168.

9. Havard and Vidal, *Histoire de l'Amérique française*, 347, attribute this thought to colonial *intendant* Champigny in 1699.

10. Axtell, *The Invasion Within*.

11. The last chapter of Axtell's *The Invasion Within* is entitled "White Indians."

12. Pratt, *Imperial Eyes*, 6.

13. Bernard, *The Cajuns*, 78–79.

14. See Smith, *Mardi Gras Indians*.

15. Brasseaux, *French, Cajun, Creole, Houma*.

16. See Brasseaux, Fontenot, and Oubre, *Creoles of Color in the Bayou Country*.

17. Tocqueville, *De la Démocratie en Amérique*, 76.

18. See Barry, *Rising Tide*.

19. Beaulieu and Bergeron, *Amérique française*, 35.

20. See Axtall, *The Invasion Within*.

21. Mathieu, *La Nouvelle-France*, 247.

22. Hall, *Africans in Colonial Louisiana*, 238.

23. Gotham, *Authentic New Orleans*, 26.

24. Miller, *The French Atlantic Triangle*.

25. Eckberg, *French Roots in the Illinois Country*.

26. Hall, *Africans in Colonial Louisiana*, 34.

27. Smith, *Mardi Gras Indians*, 24, 95, 78.

28. The Greater Caribbean is Spitzer's chosen term. Abrahams et al., *Blues for New Orleans*, 13.

29. See episode 1 with Richard Guidry, *Gumb-oh là! là!* Lafayette: Louisiane à la carte, 2002, DVD.

30. *Coonass* is a pejorative and controversial term that has been both appropriated and rejected by Cajun populations. See Bernard, *The Cajuns*, 96–97.

31. The word *Acadiana* dates back to the 1970s and is a conflation of Louisiana and Acadia.

32. Brasseaux, *Acadian to Cajun*, 150–51.

33. Kate Chopin's late nineteenth-century short stories relate Cajun and Creole interaction and circulate widely today (www.katechopin.org). See also Seyersted, *The Complete Works of Kate Chopin*.

34. Gaudet and McDonald, *Mardi Gras, Gumbo, and Zydeco*, ix.

35. Saël Lacroix and Frédéric Julien, *Le Grand Mélangement*, Montréal: L'Envers, 2008, film.

36. The Mardi Gras Indians are another thoroughly evocative representation of Louisiana's melting pot of cultures. I will return to their performance of creolized identity further in the essay.

37. Dormon, *Creoles of Color of the Gulf South*, 163.

38. Barnabé, Chamoiseau, and Confiant, *Eloge de la créolité*, 28, 31.

39. Brasseaux, *French, Cajun, Creole, Houma*, 129.

40. Dormon, *Creoles of Color of the Gulf South*, 7, 173.

41. Dormon, *Creoles of Color of the Gulf South*, xi.

42. Brasseaux, Fontenot, and Oubre, *Creoles of Color in the Bayou Country*, 40.

43. Hall, *Africans in Colonial Louisiana*, 141, 143.

44. Hall, *Africans in Colonial Louisiana*, 155.

45. Brasseaux, Fontenot, and Oubre, *Creoles of Color in the Bayou Country*, 6, 44.

46. Hall, *Africans in Colonial Louisiana,* 99.

47. Parent, *Inside the Carnival,* 19.

48. Bernard, *The Cajuns,* 57. In the 1980s, the Un-Cajun Committee of Lafayette took issue with calling the university's athletes, the Rajun' Cajuns. They argued that black Creoles were simply "un-Cajun."

49. Parent, *Inside the Carnival,* 16.

50. Gotham, *Authentic New Orleans,* 26.

51. See Stivale, *Disenchanting les Bons Temps.*

52. Lipovetsky and Serroy, *La Culture-monde,* 9–10.

53. Ancelet, *Cajun Music,* 1, 15, 17.

54. Stivale, *Disenchanting Les Bons Temps,* 135.

55. Brasseaux, *Cajun Breakdown,* 4.

56. See Beverly Matherne, *Le Blues braillant, The Blues Cryin',* Saulnierville, Nova Scotia, 1999, compact disc.

57. Barry, *Rising Tide,* 334.

58. Poulin, *Volkswagen Blues,* 117–18.

59. Smith, *Mardi Gras Indians,* 143.

60. Brasseaux, *Cajun Breakdown,* 22. German origins of accordion affirmed in Cajun and Creole Archives, University of Louisiana at Lafayette, Ancelet Collection access number: AN1.094.

61. Cajun and Creole Archives, University of Louisiana at Lafayette, Ancelet Collection access number: AN1.048. See documentary by Les Blank, Chris Strachwitz, and Maureen Gosling, eds., *J'ai été au bal (I Went to the Dance): The Cajun and Zydeco Music of Louisiana,* El Cervito, Brazos, 1989, video.

62. Stivale, *Disenchanting les Bons Temps,* 146.

63. Cajun and Creole Archives, University of Louisiana at Lafayette, Ancelet Collection access number: AN1.072.

64. Tisserand, *The Kingdom of Zydeco,* 5.

65. Ancelet, *Cajun and Creole Music Makers,* 23.

66. *15 Louisiana Cajun Classics,* American Masters, Arhoolie Productions, 1996, vol. 3, compact disc.

67. Ancelet, *Cajun and Creole Music Makers,* 24.

68. Ancelet, *Cajun and Creole Music Makers,* 101–3.

69. Cajun and Creole Archives, University of Louisiana at Lafayette, Ancelet Collection access number AN1.102.

70. Cajun and Creole Archives, University of Louisiana at Lafayette, Ancelet Collection access number: AN1.022.

71. Ancelet, *Cajun and Creole Music Makers*, 87.

72. *15 Louisiana Zydeco Classics*, American Masters, Arhoolie Productions, 1997, vol. 5, compact disc 105.

73. "Bonjour Louisiane" is recorded at Lafayette's public radio station KRVS, on the university campus, and airs every weekday morning from 5 a.m. until 7 a.m. Live streaming via the Internet is available at www.krvs.org.

74. See the new recording *Brand New Old Songs: Recycling the Lomax Recordings*, Festivals Acadiens et Créoles, Center for Louisiana Studies, 2014, compact disc.

75. Jones, *Louisiana Cowboys*, 58.

76. Brasseaux, *Cajun Breakdown*, 149.

77. See track 11, Geno Delafose, *Le Cowboy Creole*, Silva Screen Music, 2007, compact disc.

78. The 2002 DVD *"Gumb-Oh! Là! Là!"* contains thirteen video recordings of French Louisiana's cultural ambassadors speaking in French about their work: musicians, teachers, and activists among others. Of the thirteen, five are music makers, which speaks to the centrality of music to the culture.

79. Bernard, *The Cajuns,* 142.

80. Brasseaux, *Cajun Breakdown*, 59, 62.

81. See track 6, *Brand New Old Songs*.

82. Magnolia Sisters, "Lapin, Lapin," *Chansons Cajuns et Creoles pour les enfants*, LA Division of the Arts, 2005, compact disc.

83. Michael "Beausoleil" Doucet with Family and Friends, "Le Hoogie Boogie," *Louisiana French Music for Children*, Rounder, 1992, compact disc 8022.

84. Ledet's lyrics are full of double entendres, "Eat my poussière" being one example

85. Ancelet, "The History of Festivals Acadiens et Créoles," keynote address, University of Louisiana at Lafayette, 9 October 2014. This academic conference accompanied the fortieth annual celebration of the Festivals Acadiens in 2014.

86. Ancelet, "The History of Festivals Acadiens et Créoles."

87. Ancelet, "The History of Festivals Acadiens et Créoles."

88. See Kbon (www.kbon.com) and KRVS (www.krvs.org).

89. Henry and Banston, *Blue Collar Bayou*, 218.

90. Brasseaux, Fontenot, and Oubre, *Creoles of Color in the Bayou Country,* 104, 124–25.

91. See the cover of Louder and Waddell, *Franco-Amérique*.

92. CODOFIL organizes French immersion classes in local primary schools as well as annual cultural festivities drawing thousands to Lafayette. The monthly newsletter of the organization, *Patates Nouvelles*, is trilingual, written in regionally colored French, English, and Creole.

93. Gaudet and McDonald, *Mardi Gras, Gumbo, and Zydeco*, 152.

94. Bienvenu, Brasseaux and Brasseaux, *Stir the Pot*.

95. Bienvenu, Brasseaux, and Brasseaux, *Stir the Pot*, 175.

96. Gaudet and McDonald, *Mardi Gras, Gumbo, and Zydeco*, 55.

97. The "Zydeco Brunch" at Café des Amis in Breaux Bridges, Louisiana, combining pulsating music, two-stepping, and food every Saturday morning, has attracted national attention.

98. Bernard, *The Cajuns*, 117–18.

99. See the official website of the Popeye's Louisiana Kitchen, founded in 1972 in New Orleans by Al Copeland (www.popeyes.com).

100. Bernard, *The Cajuns*, 117.

101. See Gutierrez, *Cajun Foodways*.

102. Bienvenu, *Who's Your Mama*, 17.

103. Bienvenu, Brasseaux, and Brasseaux, *Stir the Pot*, 84.

104. See Johnson, *Poor Man's Provence*.

105. See Gotham, *Authentic New Orleans*.

106. Gotham, *Authentic New Orleans*, 25.

107. Ware, *Cajun Women and Mardi Gras*, 3.

108. Ware, *Cajun Women and Mardi Gras*, 100.

109. Dormon, *Creoles of Color of the Gulf South*, 63, 90–91.

110. Dormon, *Creoles of Color of the Gulf South*, 91, 98, 93, 116, 99.

111. Dormon, *Creoles of Color of the Gulf South*, 113–14.

112. Ware, *Cajun Women and Mardi Gras*, 1, 50.

113. Ware, *Cajun Women and Mardi Gras*, 50, 76, 44, 110–11.

114. See Valdman, *Dictionary of Louisiana French*.

115. See Henry and Bankson, *Blue Collar Bayou*.

116. Arceneaux et al., *Cris sur le bayou*, 9.

117. Arceneaux et al., *Cris sur le bayou*, 37.

118. Arceneaux et al., *Cris sur le bayou*, 16–17, 26.

119. Bernard, *The Cajuns*, 114.

120. Arceneaux et al., *Cris sur le bayou*, 82.

121. Arceneaux et al., *Cris sur le bayou*, 51–53, 113, 116–17.

122. See Clifton, *À Cette heure, la louve*, and more recently Arceneaux, *Le Trou dans le mur*.

123. Jambon, *L'École Gombo*, 23.

124. Jambon, *L'École Gombo*, 147–49, 151.

125. Cheramie, *Lait à mère*.

126. Guidry, *C'est p'us pareil*, 2–4, 15.

127. For an exhaustive list of terms, see Valdman, *Dictionary of Louisiana French*.

128. See Guirard, *Cajun Families of the Atchafalaya*. He records stories of people drinking the water in which they swam, not knowing they were poor, and eating everything they could catch in the Atchafalaya Basin.

129. Guidry, *C'est p'us pareil*, 8, 16.

130. Guidry, *C'est p'us pareil*, 17, 21.

131. Ancelet, *Cajun and Creole Folktales*, xxxii.

132. Darnton, *The Great Cat Massacre*, 63.

133. Guirard, *Cajun Families of the Atchafalaya*, 22.

134. Boudreaux, *Dat Boudreaux ain't me, it's ma cousin*, 22.

135. Bergeron, *Original Boudreau an' Tibodeau Jokes*.

136. Reneaux, *Cajun Folktales*. The book was produced "Pour les Cadiens partout." This is the same publishing house that printed Franco-American folktales from New England.

137. See collections of French folktales mentioned in chapter 4, as well as Thomas, *It's Good to Tell You: French Folk Tales*.

138. Gotham, *Authentic New Orleans*, 20.

139. Joe Lapointe, "Saints Aren't the First to Call on Fleur Power," *New York Times*, 2 February 2010, 2.

140. CODOFIL, "Patates nouvelles," February 2010, 1 (codofil.blogspot.com).

141. Smith, *Mardi Gras Indians*, 102, 107–8.

CONCLUSION

Epigraph: Hebert, *Never Back Down*, frontispiece.

1. Normand Beaupré, "Franco-Américain," *Le Journal de Lowell*, June 1986, 5.

2. Peter McGuire, "African Immigrants Drive French-Speaking Renaissance in Maine," *Portland Press Herald*, 31 July 2016.

3. Aldrich, *Vestiges of the Colonial Empire in France*, 6.

4. See Miller, *The Bon Marché*.

5. See *l'Etoile*, 12 June 1890, 3, and *l'Etoile*, 5 November 1891, 3, for examples.

6. Zola, *Au Bonheur des Dames*.

7. Brault, *The French-Canadian Heritage in New England*, 160–61.

8. Marshall, *The French Atlantic*, 21.

9. This is the case in Waterville, Maine, where visitors are no longer welcomed in French.

10. James Sullivan, "Lowell Monument Captures Jack Kerouac's Spirit," *Boston Globe*, 30 September 2014.

11. Bancel et al., "Écrire le postcolonial depuis la langue française," in *Ruptures postcoloniales: Les nouveaux visages de la société française*, 179.

12. See Dainotto, *Place in Literature*.

13. Brière, *J'aime New York*.

BIBLIOGRAPHY

ARCHIVES

Alliance Française de Worcester, Massachusetts, Assumption College
L'Association des Dames Franco-Américaines, Chicopee, Massachusetts
Cajun and Creole Archives, University of Louisiana, Lafayette
Centre Franco-Américain, Manchester, New Hampshire
Le Cercle des Dames Françaises, Springfield, Massachusetts
Le Cercle Jeanne Mance, Lowell and Worcester, Massachusetts
Conseil pour le développement du français en Louisiane (CODOFIL), Lafayette
Fédération Féminine Franco-Américaine
Franco-American Heritage Center, Lewiston, Maine
French Press of New England:

    L'Avenir National (1895–1949), daily publication, Manchester, New Hampshire
    L'Etoile (1886–1957), daily publication, Lowell, Massachusetts
    Le Journal de Lowell (1975–95), monthly publication, Lowell, Massachusetts
    La Justice (1904–64), weekly publication, Holyoke, Massachusetts
    Le Messager (1880–1968), daily publication, Lewiston, Maine
    Le Travailleur (1931–78), weekly publication, Worcester, Massachusetts

PUBLISHED WORKS

Abrahams, Roger D., Nick Spitzer, John F. Szwed, and Robert F. Thompson, eds. *Blues for New Orleans: Mardi Gras and America's Creole Soul*. Philadelphia: University of Pennsylvania Press, 2006.

Agulhon, Maurice. *Les Métamorphoses de Marianne: L'imagerie et la symbolique républicaines de 1914 à nos jours*. Paris: Flammarion, 2001.

Agulhon, Maurice, Pierre Bonte, and Robert Chagny, eds. *Entre Liberté, République et France: Les Représentations de Marianne de 1792 à nos jours*. Vizille: Musée de la Révolution française, 2003.

Aldrich, Robert. *Vestiges of the Colonial Empire in France: Monuments, Museums, and Colonial Memories*. New York: Palgrave-Macmillan, 2005.

Alvarez, Julia. *How the García Girls Lost their Accents*. New York: Plume, 1992.

Ancelet, Barry Jean, ed. *Cajun and Creole Folktales: The French Oral Tradition of South Louisiana*. New York: Garland, 1994.

———. *Cajun and Creole Music Makers*. Jackson: University Press of Mississippi, 1999.

———. *Cajun Music: Its Origins and Development*. Lafayette: University Press of Southwestern Louisiana, 1989.

———. "The History of Festivals Acadiens et Créoles." Keynote address, University of Louisiana at Lafayette, October 9, 2014.

Anctil, Gabriel, and Franco Nuovo. *Sur les traces de Kerouac* (ebook). Montréal: Radio-Canada, 2014.

Anderson, Benedict. *Imagined Communities: Reflections on the Origin and Spread of Nationalism*. New York: Verso, 1983, 1991.

Appell, Louise S. *Forever and Ever*. Bloomington IN: Author House, 2009.

———. *Forgive Me Father for I Have Sinned*. Bloomington IN: Author House, 2005.

———. *Thy Will Be Done*. Bloomington IN: Author House, 2006.

Arceneaux, Jean. *Le Trou dans le mur: Fabliaux cadiens*. Moncton CA: Editions Perce-Neige, 2012.

Arceneaux, Jean, et al. *Cris sur le bayou: Naissance d'une poésie acadienne en Louisiane*. Montréal: Les Editions Intermède, 1980.

Ashcroft, Bill, Gareth Griffiths, and Helen Tiffin, eds. *The Empire Writes Back: Theory and Practice in Post-Colonial Literatures*. 2nd ed. London: Routledge, 2002.

Axtell, James. *The Invasion Within: The Contest of Cultures in Colonial North America*. New York: Oxford University Press, 1985.

Baker, Alan R. H. *Fraternity among the French Peasantry: Sociability and Voluntary Associations in the Loire Valley, 1815–1914*. Cambridge: Cambridge University Press, 1999.

Bancel, Nicolas, Florence Bernault, Pascal Blanchard, Ahmed Boubeker, Achille Mbembe, and Françoise Vergès, eds. *Ruptures postcoloniales: Les nouveaux visages de la société française*. Paris: La Découverte, 2010.

Bancel, Nicolas, Pascal Blanchard, and Françoise Vergès, eds. *La République coloniale: Essai sur une utopie*. Paris: Albin Michel, 2003.

Banks, Kenneth J. *Chasing Empire across the Sea: Communications and the State in the French Atlantic, 1713–1763*. Montreal: McGill-Queen's University Press, 2006.

Barnabé, Jean, Patrick Chamoiseau, and Raphaël Confiant. *Eloge de la créolité*. Paris: Gallimard, 1989.

Baron, Robert, and Ana C. Cara, eds. *Creolization as Cultural Creativity*. Jackson: University Press of Mississippi, 2011.

Barry, John M. *Rising Tide: The Great Mississippi Flood of 1927 and How It Changed America*. New York: Touchstone, 1998.

Beaugrand, Honoré. *Jeanne la fileuse*. Bedford NH: National Materials Development Center for French, 1980. Originally published in 1878.

Beaulieu, Alain, and Yves Bergeron. *Amérique francaise: L'aventure*. Québec, QC: Editions Fides, 2002.

Beaupré, Normand. *Deux femmes, deux rêves*. Coral Springs FL: Llumina, 2005.

———. *Le Petit Mangeur de fleurs*. Chicoutimi, QC: Les Editions JCL, 1999.

Belisle, Alexandre. *Histoire de la presse franco-américaine*. Worcester MA: L'Opinion publique, 1911.

Bensmaïa, Réda. *Experimental Nations; or, The Invention of the Maghreb*. Translated by Alyson Waters. Princeton: Princeton University Press, 2003.

Bergeron, John. *Original Boudreau an' Tibodeau Jokes*. Vol. 1. Abbeville LA: Gulf South Printing and Specialties, 1996.

Bernard, Shane. *The Cajuns: Americanization of a People*. Jackson: University Press of Mississippi, 2003.

Bhabha, Homi. *Nation and Narration*. London: Routledge, 1990.

Bienvenu, Marcelle. *Who's Your Mama, Are You Catholic, and Can You Make a Roux?* Lafayette LA: Acadian House, 2006.

Bienvenu, Marcelle, Carl Brasseaux, and Ryan Brasseaux. *Stir the Pot: The History of Cajun Cuisine*. New York: Hippocrene, 2005.

Biron, Michel, François Dumont, and Élisabeth Nardout-Lafarge, eds. *Histoire de la littérature québécoise*. Montréal: Boréal, 2008.

Bouchard, Gérard. *Genèse des nations et cultures du Nouveau Monde*. Montréal: Boreal, 2000.

Bouchard, Gérard, and Yvan Lamonde, eds. *Québécois et Américains: La culture québécoise au XIXe et XXe siècles*. Montréal: Editions Fides, 1995.

Boudreaux, Larry. *Dat Boudreaux ain't me, it's ma cousin*. 5th ed. Baton Rouge: Boudreaux Cajun General Store, 1999.

Bourdieu, Pierre. "Deux imperialismes de l'universel." In *L'Amérique des Français*. Fauré, Christine and Bishop, Tom, eds. Paris: Editions François Bourin, 1992.

———. *Distinction: A Social Critique of the Judgement of Taste*. Translated by Richard Nice. Cambridge MA: Harvard University Press, 1984.

———. "The Forms of Capital." In *Handbook of Theory and Research for the Sociology of Education*, edited by J. Richardson, 241–58. New York: Greenwood, 1986.

Brasseaux, Carl. *Acadian to Cajun: Transformation of a People, 1803–1877*. Jackson: University Press of Mississippi, 1992.

———. *French, Cajun, Creole, Houma: A Primer*. Baton Rouge: Louisiana State University Press, 2005.

Brasseaux, Carl, Keith P. Fontenot, and Claude F. Oubre. *Creoles of Color in the Bayou Country*. Jackson: University Press of Mississippi, 1994.

Brasseaux, Ryan. *Cajun Breakdown*. Oxford: Oxford University Press, 2009.

Brault, Gerard J. *The French-Canadian Heritage in New England*. Hanover NH: University Press of New England, 1986.

Brecher, Frank W. *Losing a Continent: France's North American Policy, 1753–1763*. Westport CT: Greenwood, 1998.

Brettell, Caroline B. *Following Father Chiniquy: Immigration, Religious Schism, and Social Change in Nineteenth-Century Illinois*. Carbondale: Southern Illinois University Press, 2015.

Brière, Eloise A., ed. *J'aime New York: A Bilingual Guide to the French Heritage of New York State*. 2nd ed. Albany: State University of New York Press, 2012.

Brière, Eloise, and Nicole Grangeat-Vaget. *Franco-American Viewpoints*. Photographs by Lionel Delavigne. Northampton MA: Nouveau Monde Press, 1988.

Brousseau, Yves. "Le FAROG Forum: Autopsie d'un journal d'éveil et de combat." Thesis, Université Laval, 1983.

Bruézière, Maurice. *L'Alliance francaise: Histoire d'une institution*. Paris: Hachette, 1983.

Carroll, Raymonde. *Evidences invisibles: Américains et Français au quotidien.* Paris: Seuil, 1987.

Chapman, Herrick. "Flourishing in a Tough Climate." *French Politics, Culture, and Society* 32, no. 2 (Summer 2014): 1–7.

Cheramie, David. *Lait à mère.* Montréal: Prise de parole, 1997.

Chernow, Ron. *Hamilton.* New York: Penguin, 2005.

Chevalier, Louis. *Classes laborieuses et classes dangereuses à Paris pendant la première moitié du XIXe siècle.* Paris: Plon, 1958.

Choquette, Leslie. *Frenchmen into Peasants: Modernity and Tradition in the Peopling of French Canada.* Cambridge MA: Harvard University Press, 1997.

Chute, Carolyn. *The Beans of Egypt, Maine.* New York: Ticknor & Fields, 1985.

Clément, Antoine. *L'Alliance française de Lowell.* Manchester NH: L'Imprimerie de l'Avenir National, 1937.

Clifton, Deborah J. *À Cette heure, la louve.* Moncton CA: Editions Perce-Neige, 1999.

Cloonan, William. "Littérature-Monde and the Novel in 2007." *French Review* 82, no. 1 (October 2008): 33–50.

Dainotto, Roberto. *Place in Literature: Regions, Cultures, Communities.* Ithaca NY: Cornell University Press, 2000.

Darnton, Robert. *The Great Cat Massacre.* New York: Basic, 1984.

Dash, J. Michael. *The Other America: Caribbean Literature in a New World Context.* Charlottesville: University Press of Virginia, 1998.

DeJean, Joan. *The Essence of Style: How the French Invented High Fashion, Fine Food, Chic Cafés, Style, Sophistication, and Glamour.* New York: Free Press, 2005.

Desroches, Vincent. "Quebec and Postcolonial Theory." *Quebec Studies* 35 (Spring/Summer 2003).

Dormon, James. *Creoles of Color of the Gulf South.* Knoxville: University Press of Tennessee, 1996.

Doty, C. Stewart. "'Monsieur Maurras est ici': French Fascism in Franco-American New England." *Journal of Contemporary History* 32, no. 4 (October 1997): 527–38.

Doyle, Don H., and Marco A. Pamplona, eds. *Nationalism in the New World.* Athens: University of Georgia Press, 2006.

Dubosclard, Alain. *Histoire de la Fédération des Alliances Françaises aux Etats-Unis (1902–1997): L'Alliance au coeur.* Paris: L'Harmattan, 1998.

Ducharme, Jacques. *The Delusson Family: A Novel.* New York: Funk and Wagnalls, 1939.

————. *The Shadows of the Trees: The Story of French Canadians in New England*. New York: Harper and Brothers, 1943.

Dumas, Emma. *Mirbah*. Bedford NH: National Materials Development Center for French, 1979. First published in Holyoke MA between 1910 and 1912.

Durmelat, Sylvie. "Tasting Displacement: Couscous and Culinary Citizenship in Maghrebi-French Diasporic Cinema." *Food & Foodways* 23, nos. 1–2 (2015): 104–26.

Eccles, W. J. *France in America*. East Lansing: Michigan State University Press, 1990.

Ekberg, Carl J. *French Roots in the Illinois Country: The Mississippi Frontier in Colonial Times*. Urbana: University of Illinois Press, 1998.

Ellison, Ralph. *Invisible Man*. New York: Random House, 1952.

Fischer, David Hackett. *Champlain's Dream*. New York: Simon and Schuster, 2008.

Forsdick, Charles, and David Murphy, eds. *Francophone Postcolonial Studies: A Critical Introduction*. London: Arnold, 2003.

————. *Postcolonial Thought in the French-Speaking World*. Liverpool: Liverpool University Press, 2009.

Gans, Herbert J. "Symbolic Ethnicity: The Future of Ethnic Groups and Cultures in America." *Ethnic and Racial Studies* 2, no. 1 (1979): 1–20.

Gaudet, Marci, and James C. McDonald, eds. *Mardi Gras, Gumbo, and Zydeco: Readings in Louisiana Culture*. Jackson: University Press of Mississippi, 2003.

Gilroy, Paul. *The Black Atlantic: Modernity and Double-Consciousness*. Cambridge MA: Harvard University Press, 1993.

Gitlin, Jay. *The Bourgeois Frontier: French Towns, French Traders, and American Expansion*. New Haven CT: Yale University Press, 2010.

Gotham, Kevin Fox. *Authentic New Orleans: Tourism, Culture, and Race in the Big Easy*. New York: New York University Press, 2007.

Graham, Lawrence O. *Our Kind of People: Inside America's Black Upper Class*. New York: Harper Perennial, 1999.

Greer, Allan. *The People of New France*. Toronto: University of Toronto Press, 1997.

Guglielmo, Jennifer, and Salvatore Salerno, eds. *Are Italians White? How Race Is Made in America*. New York: Routledge, 2003.

Guidry, Richard. *C'est p'us pareil*. Lafayette LA: Center for Louisiana Studies, University of Southwestern Louisiana, 1982.

Guillet, Ernest B. *Essai de journalisme*. Bedford NH: National Materials Development Center, 1981.

————. "French Ethnic Literature and Culture in an American City: Holyoke MA." PhD diss., University of Massachusetts, 1978.

Guirard, Greg. *Cajun Families of the Atchafalaya*. 3rd ed. Louisville KY: Friesens Canada, 1999.

Gutierrez, C. Paige. *Cajun Foodways*. Jackson: University Press of Mississippi, 1992.

Hall, Gwendolyn Midlo. *Africans in Colonial Louisiana: The Development of Afro-Creole Culture in the Eighteenth Century*. Baton Rouge: Louisiana State University Press, 1992.

Hargreaves, Alec. G., Charles Forsdick, and David Murphy, eds. *Transnational French Studies: Postcolonialism and Littérature-monde*. Liverpool: Liverpool University Press, 2010.

Hartford, William F. *Working People of Holyoke: Class and Ethnicity in a Massachusetts Mill Town, 1850–1960*. New Brunswick NJ: Rutgers University Press, 1990.

Hathaway, Margaret. *Food Lovers' Guide to Maine*. Guilford CT: Globe Pequot, 2011.

Havard, Gilles, and Cécile Vidal. *Histoire de l'Amérique française*. Paris: Flammarion, 2003.

Hayward, Jack. *Fragmented France: Two Centuries of Disputed Identity*. Oxford: Oxford University Press, 2007

Hebert, Ernest. *Never Back Down*. Jaffrey NH: David R. Godine, 2012.

Hémon, Louis. *Maria Chapdelaine*. Montréal: J.-A. Lefebvre, 1916.

Henry, Jacques, and Carl Bankston III. *Blue Collar Bayou: Louisiana Cajuns in the New Economy of Ethnicity*. Westport CT: Praeger, 2002.

Hobbs, Sandra. "La Représentation ambivalente de l'Autochtone dans le roman québécois: vers une perspective postcoloniale." *International Journal of Francophone Studies* 9, no. 3 (November 2006): 347–64.

Hobsbawm, Eric, and Terrence Ranger, eds. *The Invention of Tradition*. Cambridge: Cambridge University Press, 2012.

Hunt, Lynn. *Politics, Culture, and Class in the French Revolution*. Berkeley: University of California Press, 1984.

Hurley, Erin. *National Performance: Representing Quebec from Expo 67 to Céline Dion*. Toronto: University of Toronto Press, 2011.

Jambon, Kirby. *L'École Gombo*. Shreveport LA: Les Cahiers du Tintamarre, 2006.
———. *Petites Communions: Poèmes, chansons et jonglements*. Shreveport LA: Tintamarre, 2013.

Jeanneney, Jean-Noël. *Une histoire des médias: Des origines à nos jours*. Paris: Seuil, 1996.

Johnson, Rheat Grimsley. *Poor Man's Provence: Finding Myself in Cajun Louisiana*. Montgomery AL: NewSouth, 2008.

Jones, Bill. *Louisiana Cowboys*. Gretna LA: Pelican, 2007.

Katz, Ron. *French America: French Architecture from Colonization to the Birth of a Nation*. New York: French Heritage Society, 2004.

Kerouac, Jack. *Doctor Sax*. New York: Grove Press, 1959.

———. *On the Road*. New York: Viking Press, 1957.

———. *The Town and the City*. New York: Harcourt, Brace, 1950.

Laferrière, Dany. *Je suis fatigué*. Outremont, QC: Lanctôt Editeur, 2001.

Landry, Pierre. *Histoires des Amériques*. Montreal: Musée d'art contemporain de Montreal, 2004.

Langellier, Kristen M. "Performing Family Stories, Forming Cultural Identity: Franco American Mémère Stories." *Communication Studies* 53, no. 1 (2002): 56–73.

Langellier, K. M., and E. E. Peterson. *Storytelling in Daily Life: Performing Narrative*. Philadelphia: Temple University Press, 2004.

Lebovics, Herman. *True France: The Wars over Cultural Identity*. Ithaca NY: Cornell University Press, 1994.

Le Bris, Michel, and Jean Rouard, eds. *Pour une littérature-monde*. Paris: Gallimard, 2007.

Le Clézio, J. M. G. *Le Chercheur d'or*. Paris: Gallimard, 1985.

Lees, Cynthia. "Exploring Rural and Urban Space in *Jeanne la fileuse* and *Canuck*." *French Review* 90, no. 2 (December 2016): 47–60.

Lessard-Bissonnette, Camille. *Canuck*. Bedford NH: National Materials Development Center for French, 1980. Originally published in 1936.

Lindner, Tamara. "Attitudes toward Cajun French and International French in South Louisiana: A Study of High School Students." PhD diss., Indiana University, 2008.

Lipovetsky, Gilles, and Jean Serroy. *La Culture-monde: Réponse à une société désorientée*. Paris: Odile Jacob, 2008.

Longfellow, Henry Wadsworth. *Evangeline: A Tale of Acadie*. Halifax NS: Nimbus, 2003. Originally published in 1847.

Louder, Dean, Jean Morisset, and Éric Waddell, eds. *Visions and Visages de la Franco-Amérique*. Sillery QC: Septentrion: 2001.

Louder, Dean, and Éric Waddell, eds. *Franco-Amérique*. Sillery, QC: Septentrion, 2008.

———. *French America: Mobility, Identity, and Minority Experience across the Continent*. Baton Rouge: Louisiana State University Press, 1993.

Maillet, Antonine. *Pélagie-la-charette*. Montréal: Leméac, 1979.

Mais Oui, Marie: Creole Cookin. Life and Flavor in the Creole Tradition. Opelousas, LA: Marie's Catering, 1999.

Manceron, Gilles. *Marianne et les colonies: Une Introduction à l'histoire coloniale de la France.* Paris: La Découverte, 2003.

Manning, Patrick. *Francophone Sub-Saharan Africa, 1880–1995.* Cambridge: Cambridge University Press, 1998.

Marchand, Philip. *Ghost Empire: How the French Almost Conquered North America.* Toronto: McClelland & Stewart, 2006.

Marshall, Bill, ed. *France and the Americas: Culture, Politics, and History.* Santa Barbara CA: ABC-CLIO, 2005.

———. *The French Atlantic: Travels in Culture and History.* Liverpool: Liverpool University Press, 2009.

Mathieu, Jacques. *La Nouvelle-France: Les Français en Amérique du Nord XVIe–XVIIIe siècle.* Québec, QC: Les Presses de l'Université Laval, 2001.

Mathy, Jean-Philippe. *French Resistance: The French-American Culture Wars.* Minneapolis: University of Minnesota Press, 2000.

McCafferty, Josh. *Traditional Music in Coastal Louisiana.* Baton Rouge: Louisiana State University Press, 2013.

McDermott, Monic, and Frank L. Samson. "White Racial and Ethnic Identity in the United States." *Annual Review of Sociology* 3 (2005): 245–61.

Megharbi, Nora, et al. *Pause-Café.* New York: McGraw-Hill, 2009.

Mezzasalma, Philippe, ed. *A la Une: La Presse de la gazette à Internet.* Paris: BNF, 2012.

Miller, Christopher L. *The French Atlantic Triangle: Literature and Culture of the Slave Trade.* Durham NC: Duke University Press, 2008.

Miller, Michael B. *The Bon Marché: Bourgeois Culture and the Department Store, 1869–1920.* Princeton NJ: Princeton University Press, 1981.

Moogk, Peter. *La Nouvelle France: The Making of French Canada. A Cultural History.* East Lansing: Michigan State University Press, 2000.

Morisset, Jean, and Éric Waddell, eds. *Amériques.* Montréal: Éditions de l'Hexagone, 2000.

Morrison, Donald, and Antonie Compagnon. *The Death of French Culture.* Cambridge UK: Polity, 2010.

Moynihan, Kenneth. *Assumption College: A Centennial History, 1904–2004.* Worcester MA: Assumption College, 2004.

Murdoch, H. Adlai, and Zsuzsanna Fagyal, eds. *Francophone Cultures and Geographies of Identity.* Newcastle upon Tyne: Cambridge Scholars, 2013.

Nadeau, Jean-Benoît, and Julie Barlow. *The Story of French*. New York: St. Martin's Press, 2006.

Nora, Pierre. *Les Lieux de Mémoires*. Paris: Seuil, 1984.

Noyes, Alice Daley. *Yvonne of the Amoskeag Textile Mills*. Manchester NH: ATC, 2000.

Ozouf, Mona. *L'Ecole, l'Eglise, et la République, 1871–1914*. Paris: Seuil, 2007.

Parent, Michael, and Julien Olivier, eds. *Of Kings and Fools: Stories of the French Tradition in North America*. Little Rock AR: August House, 1996.

Parent, Wayne. *Inside the Carnival: Unmasking Louisiana Politics*. Baton Rouge: Louisiana State University Press, 2004.

Parker, Gabrielle. "'Francophonie' and 'Universalité': Evolution of Two Notions Conjoined." In *Francophone Postcolonial Studies: A Critical Introduction*, eds. David Murphy and Charles Forsdick. London: Arnold, 2003.

Parkman, Francis. *Pioneers of France in the New World*. Boston: Little, Brown, 1867.

Pelletier, Fran. *Little Pine to King Spruce: A Franco-American Childhood*. Gardiner ME: Tilbury House, 2003.

Péloquin-Faré, Louise. *L'identité culturelle: Les Franco-Américains de la Nouvelle-Angleterre*. Paris: Crédif, 1983.

Perreault, Robert. "Les Franco-Américains de Manchester, New Hampshire: Réalités en 2011." *International Journal of Canadian Studies* 44 (2011): 23–32.

———. *L'Héritage*. Durham NH: National Materials Development Center for French, 1983.

Perrin, Warren A. *Acadian Redemption: From Beausoleil Broussard to the Queen's Royal Proclamation*. Opelousas LA: Andrepont, 2004.

Plante, David. *American Ghosts*. Boston: Beacon, 2005.

Poulin, Jacques. *Volkswagen Blues*. Montréal: Québec Amérique, 1984.

Pratt, Mary L. *Imperial Eyes: Travel Writing and Transculturation*. London: Routledge, 1992.

Pritchard, James. *In Search of Empire: The French in the Americas, 1670–1730*. Cambridge: Cambridge University Press, 2007.

Proulx, Annie. *Accordion Crimes*. New York: Scribner, 1997.

Quintal, Claire, ed. *Steeples and Smokestacks: A Collection of Essays on the Franco-American Experience in New England*. Worcester MA: Institut Français, 1996.

Redonnet, J. C., R. St. Onge, S. St. Onge, and J. Nielsen. *Héritages francophones: Enquêtes interculturelles*. New Haven CT: Yale University Press, 2010.

Reed, Revon. *Lâche pas la patate: Portrait des Acadiens de la Louisiane*. Montréal: Editions Parti Pris, 1976.

Renan, Ernest. *Qu'est-ce qu'une nation?* Paris: 11 March 1882 lecture at the Sorbonne.

Reneaux, J. J. *Cajun Folktales*. Little Rock AR: August House, 1992.

Richard, Mark Paul. *Loyal but French: The Negotiation of Identity by French Canadian Descendants in the United States*. East Lansing: Michigan State University Press, 2008.

———. *Not a Catholic Nation: The Ku Klux Klan Confronts New England in the 1920s*. Amherst: University of Massachusetts Press, 2015.

Richards, Marvin. "Corralling the Wild Ponies: Correspondences between Quebec and the Postcolonial." *Quebec Studies* 35 (Spring/Summer 2003): 133–52.

———. "Putting Québec Studies on the Map." *Contemporary French and Francophone Studies* 13, no. 1 (January 2009): 81–89.

Ringuet. *Trente Arpents*. Paris: Flammarion, 1938.

Robbins, Rhea Côté, ed. *Canuck and Other Stories*. Translated by Sylvie Charron, Sue Huseman, Jeannine Bacon Roy, Madeleine C. Paré Roy. Brewer ME: Rheta, 2006.

———. *Heliotrope: French Heritage Women Create*. Brewer ME: Rheta, 2016.

———. *Wednesday's Child*. Brewer ME: Rheta, 1997.

Robichaud, Gérard. *Papa Martel*. Orono: University of Maine Press, 2003. Originally published in 1961.

Robinson, Harriet H. *Loom & Spindle; or, Life among the Early Mill Girls*. Kailua HI: Press Pacifica, 1976.

Roby, Yves. *Les Franco-Américains de la Nouvelle-Angleterre: Rêve et réalités*. Sillery QC: Septentrion, 2000.

Roediger, David R. *The Wages of Whiteness: Race and the Making of the American Working Class*. London: Verso, 1991.

Ryan, Camille. "Language Use in the United States: 2011." *American Community Survey Reports*, August 2013.

Ryan, Mary. "The American Parade: Representations of the Nineteenth-Century Social Order Representations." In *The New Cultural History*, ed. Lynn Hunt, 131–53. Berkeley: University of California Press, 1989.

Said, Edward W. *Culture and Imperialism*. New York: Alfred A. Knopf, 1993.

Saldívar, José David. *Border Matters: Remapping American Cultural Studies*. Berkeley: University of California Press, 1997.

Salhi, Kamal, ed. *Francophone Post-Colonial Cultures: Critical Essays*. Lanham MD: Lexington, 2003.

Savard, Félix-Antoine. *Menaud, maître-draveur*. Québec, QC: Garneau, 1937.

Schiff, Stacy. *A Great Improvisation: Franklin, France, and the Birth of America*. New York: Henry Holt, 2005.

Schubart, Bill. *The Lamoille Stories: Uncle Benoit's Wake and Other Tales from Vermont*. White River Junction VT: White River, 2008.

Schultz, Jean Marie, and Marie-Paule Tranvouez. *Réseau*. Upper Saddle River NJ: Prentice Hall, 2010.

Senécal, Joseph-André. *The Franco-American Bibliographic File Project: Newspapers and Periodicals. A Preliminary Checklist*. Burlington VT: CREFANE, 1995.

Serrano, Richard. *Against the Postcolonial: "Francophone" Writers at the Ends of French Empire*. Lanham MD: Lexington, 2005.

Seyersted, Per, ed. *The Complete Works of Kate Chopin*. Baton Rouge: Louisiana State University Press, 2006.

Shukla, Sandhya, and Heidi Tinsman, eds. *Imagining Our Americas: Toward a Transnational Frame*. Durham NC: Duke University Press, 2007.

Smith, Michael. *Mardi Gras Indians*. Gretna LA: Pelican, 1994.

Springfield's Ethnic Heritage: The French and French-Canadian Community. Springfield MA: USA Bicentennial Committee of Springfield, 1976.

Stivale, Charles. *Disenchanting Les Bons Temps: Identity and Authenticity in Cajun Music and Dance*. Durham: Duke University Press, 2003.

Stoler, Ann L., and Frederick Cooper, eds. *Tensions of Empire: Colonial Cultures in a Bourgeois World*. Berkeley: University of California Press, 1997.

Tétrault, Maximilienne. *Le Rôle de la presse dans l'évolution du peuple franco-américain de la Nouvelle Angleterre*. Marseille: Imprimerie Ferran, 1935.

Thériault, Joseph Yvon. *Critique de l'américanité: Mémoire et démocratie au Québec*. Montréal: Editions Québec Amérique, 2002.

Thomas, Dominic. *Black France: Colonialism, Immigration and Transnationalism*. Bloomington: Indiana University Press, 2007.

———. "Decolonizing France: From National Literatures to World Literatures." *Contemporary French and Francophone Studies* 14, no. 1 (January 2010): 47–55.

Thomas, Rosemary. *It's Good to Tell You: French Folk Tales*. Columbia: University of Missouri Press, 1982.

Tidwell, Mike. *Bayou Farewell: The Rich Life and Tragic Death of Louisiana's Cajun Coast*. New York: Vintage, 2003.

Tisserand, Michael. *The Kingdom of Zydeco*. New York: Avon, 1998.

Tocqueville, Alexis de. *De la Démocratie en Amérique*. Paris: Flammarion, 1981. Originally published in 1835.

Todd, Emmanuel. *Le Destin des immigrés*. Paris: Editions du Seuil, 1994.

Valdman, Albert, ed. *Dictionary of Louisiana French as Spoken in Cajun, Creole, and American Indian Communities*. Jackson: University Press of Mississippi, 2010.

Vallières, Pierre. *Nègres blancs d'Amérique*. Montréal: Editions Parti Pris, 1968.

Vowell, Sarah. *Lafayette in the Somewhat United States*. New York: Riverhead, 2015.

Ware, Carolyn E. *Cajun Women and Mardi Gras: Reading the Rules Backward*. Urbana: University of Illinois Press, 2007.

Watts, Edward. *In This Remote Country: French Colonial Culture in the Anglo-American Imagination, 1780–1860*. Chapel Hill: University of North Carolina, 2006.

Weil, François. *Les Franco-Américains*. Paris: Belin, 1989.

Wilkerson, Isabel. *The Warmth of Other Suns: The Epic Story of America's Great Migration*. New York: Random House, 2010.

Winock, Michel. *La Fièvre hexagonale: Les grandes crises politiques, 1871–1968*. Paris: Calmann-Lévy, 1986.

Wylie, Lawrence. *Village in the Vaucluse*. Cambridge MA: Harvard University Press, 1957.

INDEX

Page numbers in italic indicate illustrations.

Abshire, Nathan, 249, 255, 269
Acadian people: and Cajun music, 247, 255, *256*; and the Catholic Church, 52–53; CODOFIL events for, 92; and Evangeline site memorial, 34–35; exile of, 33, 34, 153; and French education, 48–49; news circulation about, 223
Acadian World Congress, 34, 35
Accordion Crimes (Proulx), 248
ActFANE organization, 221–22, 225, 226, 227
African American Museum, 94, 271
African Americans, 35, 95, 123, 131, 243
Alliance Française (AF): community outreach efforts by, 82–83; cultural centers, 78–79; description of,

66–67; early history of, 77–78; establishment of, 68–69; first bulletin, 73, *74*; and Franco-America, 76–83; and francophonie, 81–83, 89; and French republicanism, 71–76; individual chapters, 66, 68, 79–81, 87, 88, 97–98; introduction to, 16; language promotion by, 72–73; leaders of, 73; objectives of, 77; personal enrichment through, 70; public relations work by, 67; reference sources, 68; role of, 78; and Second World War, 66, 72; transnational past, 67, 68
Amaron, Reverend Calvin E., 63
American Association of Teachers of French (AATF), 69, 85
American Federation of Alliance Françaises (FAF), 76, 97, 99

American Ghosts (Plante), 180, 181

American identity, 29–30, 202, 204, 210, 279

américanité, 29, 30, 242

Amerindian populations, 75, 239

Ancelet, Barry Jean, 247, 251, 267, 270

Anderson, Benedict, 5, 26, 192

Ardoin, Alphonse "Boise Sec," 250, 263

Ardoin, Amédé, 248, 249, 250

Association Canado-Américaine (ACA), 16, 53, 93, 96

Assumption College, 62, 63, *64*, 203, 221

Atlantic World, 31, 41, 42, 61, 183

L'Avenir National newspaper, 194, *207*, 208

Balfa, Dewey, 254–55

Barry, John M, 247

Bastille Day, 98, 133, 209, 210, 214

Beaugrand, Honoré, 159, 160, 183, 190

Beaulieu, Wilfrid, 190, 198–99, 203, 212–14, 216

Beaupré, Normand, 155, 156

Beausoleil musical group, 252–53

Bernard, Shane K., 258, 260

Bhabha, Homi, 34, 132

bienvenue, 45, 46, 47, 288. *See also* welcome signs

bilingualism, 118, 200, 270

bilingual parochial schools, 16, 51, 62

Biron, Louis-A, 190, 219

Blanchette, Paul, 229, 230

Bonaparte, Napoléon, 38, 45, 239

Bonjour Louisiane program, 93, 251

Bouchard, Gérard, 5, 173–74

Boudreaux, 274–76

Bourdieu, Pierre, 28, 66, 158

Brasseaux, Carl, 244

Brasseaux, Ryan, 247

Breaux, Cleoma, 253

Le Bulletin publication, 145, 146

Cajun country/people: Boudreaux as a working Joe for, 274–77; *fleur-de-lys* symbol in, 46; and French education, 48–49, 92; and French heritage, 55; and literary works, 265–77; and musical expressions, 246–57; and poets and poetry, 266–70; social mobility for, 62; stories about, 273–74. *See also* Creole culture/population; Louisiana

Canadian national anthem, 114, 115, 133, 142

Canuck epithet, 23, 31, 65, 118, 241, 286

Canuck (Lessard-Bissonnette), 160–63

Can You Make a Roux, Are You Catholic, and Who's Your Momma? (Bienvenu), 259

card party, 117, 120, 126, 127, 128

Carnival celebrations, 262

Cartier, Jacques, 41

Catholic Church, 51–53, 120, 180, 191, 220

Cercle des Dames Françaises, 110, 111, 129–36, 148

Cercle Jeanne Mance, 109, 110, 111, 136–41

Champlain, Samuel de, 8, 9, 13, 38, 172, 287, 288

Chassé, Paul, 222, 229

Chinese of the East, 46

Christmas celebration, 120, 134, 204–5

civil rights movement, 36, 144

Clémentine Poirier Scholarships, 134–35

Code Noir, 38, 238, 244, 277

colonial activity, 2, 31, 37, 40, 72

colonial populations, 40, 109

commemorative sites, 27, 34, 39

communautarisme, 32

community news, 48, 52, 197, 217, 220

Coonass, 23, 31, 241

Côté, Albert, 217, 218, 229, 230

Côté Robbins, Rhea, 35, 58, 59, 104–5, 179–81

couche-couche, 260, 272

Council for the Development of French in Louisiana (CODOFIL), 16–17; budget issues, 83, 86; and Cajun and Creole renaissance, 267, 271; community relations office of, 93–95; culture promotion by, 84–85; and francophone world, 87, 93; and French immersion classes, 85–86, 89–90, 92–93, 270, 320n92; and French speakers, 258; and *Le Journal de Lowell*, 223–24; legal status of, 84; mission of, 83–84; and music festivals, 255, *256*, 257; and Native Americans, 94–95; objectives of, 33, 84–85, 90; signature sign, 87; teaching corps, 90–92; weekly bulletin, 94. *See also* Alliance Française (AF)

Council for the Development of French in New England (CODO-FINE), 95, 96, 222

country Mardi Gras run, 262, 263

coureurs de bois, 15, 27, 39, 44, 164, 167, 235, 251

Le Courrier newspaper, 191, 195

crawfish, 260, 261, 272

Creole/Cajun label, 259, 260

Creole Corridor, 15, 247

Creole Cowboy, 19, 39, 236, 242, 246, 251, 252

Creole culture/population: blackness term linked with, 242; common definition of, 242–43; French speakers, 56, 243; Haitian, 227; introduction to, 49; and live music, 265–77; Mardi Gras Krewe, 263–64; and poets and poetry, 266–70. *See also* Louisiana

Creole nation, 2, 35

creolization process, 49, 234, 241–45, 248, 276–77

Cris sur le bayou (Arceneaux), 266–70, 271

cue cards, 114, 116, 124

culinary traditions, 259–62

cultural and teaching institutions: access to, 62, 70, 86, 98; Alliance Française, 66–71, 76–83; Assumption College, 62, 63, *64*, 203, 221; factories-turned-museums, 65; and Franco-America, 76–83; and French outreach in Gulf South, 83–95; and French Third Republic, 71–76; historical site at Lowell, 65–66; introduction to, 61–62; University of Louisiana, 62, 88, 92, 95, 245. *See also* social clubs

cultural elites, 135, 158, 163, 194, 201

cultural journey, 15–16; conclusion about, 59; and Franco-American future, 45–53; and Franco-Amérique entity, 23; and French ethnic revival, 53–59; and French presence in America, 24–26; and New World, 27–38; and settlements, 38–45; and threat to traditions, 22

cultural production, 151, 152, 236, 261, 275

culture-monde movement, 228, 246

Cyr, Louis, 283, 285

Les Dames Franco-Américaines. *See* Franco-Americans

Darnton, Robert, 114, 221, 274

debutante balls, 132–33, 136

Delafose, Geno, 250, 252

de l'Incarnation, Marie, 109, 110, 236

The Delusson Family (Ducharme), 177, 178, 216, 311n20

Dion, Céline, 13

Doctor Sax (Kerouac), 175

Domengeaux, James, 83, 85, 86, 89, 95

Douglass, Frederick, 283

Dubosclard, Alain, 68, 70, 72

Ducharme, Jacques, 177, 178, 197–98, 205, 214–15, 216

Eloge de la créolité (Bernabé, Chamoiseau, Confiant), 242–43

Encore program, 251

English speakers: in French America, 45; introduction to, 9; priests, 51–52, 118; at social clubs, 120, 126, 128

ethnic hubs, 190, 196–97

ethnic identity. *See* identity issues

ethnic media, 25, 51, 56, 232

ethnic neighborhoods, 16, 102, 113, 153, 296–97n9

L'Etoile newspaper, 78, 79, 192–96, 219, 284

European populations, 37, 44, 235

Evangeline poem (Longfellow), 34, 165, 171

FAROG Forum, 52, 193, 216

Fat Tuesday. *See* Mardi Gras celebrations

Fédération Féminine Franco-Américaine, 141–49

Federation of Alliances in the United States, 68, 73

Festivals Acadiens, 255, *256*, 257

fiction works: *Canuck*, 160–63; *Jeanne la Fileuse*, 159–60; *Maria*

Chapdelaine, 14, 18, 163–66, 171, 172; *Menaud, maître draveur*, 166–68; *Pélagie-la-charette*, 162–63, 185; *Trente Arpents*, 168–70, 184

filles du roi, 8, 43, 104, 109

First World War, 61, 140, 177, 205–8

Flags of Our Fathers (Eastwood), 97

fleur-de-lys French symbol, 9, 46, 47, 62, 107, 122, 133, 138, 142, 243, 244, 261, 276, 286

Fontenot, Canray, 250

Foreign Language Newspaper Association, 196

Forever and Ever (Appell), 176

Forgive Me Father for I Have Sinned (Appell), 176, 184

France: Americanization of, 29; immigrants to, 55; imperial foothold in North America, 38; and United States, 28–29. *See also* Alliance Française (AF)

France-Amérique newspaper, 26, 62, 79, 83

Franco-America, 4–5, 11–12, 76–83

Franco-American Centers, 96, 99–102, 223

Franco-American Day, 19–20, 54, 137, 284, 286

Franco-American flag, 286, 287

Franco-American literary cultures: and cultural fissures, 174–86; introduction to, 17–18; and *littérature-monde* movement, 4, 151–52, 154–55, 157, 186–87; and *survivance* movement, 186–87; transcribing la Franco-Américaine, 155–74; and transnational literature, 151, 152, 153, 170, 186

Franco-American press: access to, 218, 230, 231, 296n3; and American identity, 29–30, 202, 204, 210, 279; *L'Avenir National* newspaper, 194, 207, 208; *Le Bulletin* publication,

145, 146; and Christmas celebration, 204–5; community-based, 191; *Le Courrier* newspaper, 191, 195; decline in, 192–93, 216; *L'Etoile* newspaper, 78, 79, 192–96, 219, 284; and female readership, 197–98; and francophonie, 223–32; introduction to, 146, 189–90; *Le Journal de Lowell* newspaper, 195, 216–32, *282*; journalists and editors of, 190, 196, 201–2; *La Justice* newspaper, 178, 194–95, 202, 215; *Le Messager* newspaper, 101, 193–94, 206; and nationalism, 206–16; and newspaper circulation, 191–94, 217; and Philippe Pétain, 211–12; race issues, 203; *Le Travailleur* newspaper, 79, 158–59, 189–91, 198–206, 208–17

Franco-Americans: accents of, 119; assimilation issues, 182, 184; celebrations for, 33; choosing to live as French, 24–25; conclusion about, 279–89; cookbook proposed by, 125–26; "culinary citizenship" practice, 125; description of, 3–4; devotion of, 209; disintegration of, 31–32; and *Evangeline* poem, 34; and FAWI, 104–5, 149; fiction works related to, 159–171; first governor, 51; future of, 45–53; heritage center for, 99–101; immigrant experience of, 153; and Irish Americans, 51; leadership positions of, 103; in Massachusetts, 112; meetings of, 112–16; members' induction at, 121; memorabilia collection of, 102; migration of, 35–36; and multiculturalism, 94, 100; and music, 246–57; in New England, 95–105; as objects of ridicule, 31; and religious faith,

130–31, 200; scholarships awarded to, 117–18, 120–21, 128, 132, 134–35; and Second World War, 53, 216; and sense of inferiority, 52–53; and St. Georges School, 121–23; tracing history of, 104; and *Le Travailleur* newspaper, 198–206; tributes to, 96–97; and usual prayers, 117; war veterans, 97, 286; and welcome signs, 46–47, 295n77; Women's Association, 112–23. *See also* Cajun country/people; cultural and teaching institutions; identity issues

Franco-American Women's Institute (FAWI), 104–5, 149

Franco elites, 2, 6, 132, 139, 231

François I, 41, 42

francophone culture/world: and Alliance Française, 82; and CODOFIL, 87, 93; introduction to, 1, 7, 9; outside of Quebec, 13; postcolonial studies, 2, 4, 8, 11, 20, 187; promoting, 25–26; teachers from, 90–91

francophone groups, 219, 227, 279

francophone summit, 224, 225, 227

francophonie: and Alliance Française, 81–83, 89; census information about, 59; and Franco-American press, 223–32

Franklin, Ben, 29

French Canadians: Americanness issues, 30; ethnic hubs created by, 190, 196–97; French descent generations as, 23; introduction to, 8–11, 15, 16; language of communication for families of, 45; migration of, 49–50, 203; tributes to, 287. *See also* Franco-American literary cultures; Franco-American press; social clubs

French churches, 50–52

French colonial activity, 2, 31, 37, 42

French culture. *See* cultural and teaching institutions

French diaspora, 156, 173, 195

French education, 48–49, 201

French ethnic press, 156, 158

French flag, 76, 97, 300n88

French immersion classes, 85–86, 89–90, 92–93, 270, 320n92

French language: access to, 84, 86, 92; census information about, 59; controversial, 201; and identity issues, 200–202; instruction related to, 84–85, 139; and *littérature-monde* movement, 157; Mass, 116; newspapers, 26, 48, 189–92; practices related to, 296n101; preservation of, 53, 66; promoting, 9, 72–73; sponsoring teaching of, 87; television station, 25. *See also* social clubs

French language press. *See* Franco-American press

French mass, 116, 136, 137

French neighborhoods welcome sign, 45, *46*

French Nite, 123–26

French populations, 22–24, 37, 44, 46, 233–34

French presence: official celebration of, 13, 28; physical traces of, 47; significance of, 24

French Republic, 32, 107, 215

French Republicanism, 71–76

French Revolution, 68, 211

French settlers, 235, 236

French-speaking populations/world: and Alliance Française, 76; census data about, 56–57, 59; and

CODOFIL, 258; and Creole culture, 56, 243; and francophonie, 81; introduction to, 25, 26; in North America, 2; in Quebec, 9; snowbirds, 58; at social clubs, 127–30, 138–40, 144, 146–47

French teachers, 90–91

fund raising, 117, 120, 125, 135, 141

Gagnon, Ferdinand, 158, 159, 160, 190, 191

Gaulle, Charles de, 72, 212, 214

Gitlin, Jay, 27, 155

"God Bless America," 117, 126, 133

good night, my friends, 126–28

Le Grand Dérangement, 33, 234, 242, 286

Greer, Allan, 37, 153

Guidry, Richard, 240, 258, 272–74

Gulf South. *See* Louisiana

habitant, 8, 27, 44, 164, 165, 169

Haitian Revolution, 7, 234

Hall, Gwendolyn Midlo, 234, 239, 244

Hamilton musical, 27

Havard, Gilles, 37, 39

higher learning institutions. *See* cultural and teaching institutions

historical site, 65–66

Houma Nation, 37–38, 85, 243

Hurricane Katrina, 10, 25, 49, 83

identity issues: and accents issue, 119; ethnic identity, 32–33, 48, 79, 128; and evolution and formation of identity, 23–24, 280; and French language, 200–202; introduction to, 19; and literary works, 158–59, 168–73; and people of color, 35; and religion, 51, 52, 130–31, 200; and TV shows, 124

immigration law, 55

industrial cities, 35, 103, 111, 158
In Search of Empire (Pritchard), 41
Institut Français, 63, 221, 222, 224, 228
institutions. *See* cultural and teaching
  institutions
International Francophone Day, 54
In This Remote Country (Watts), 31
Iraq War, 28, 71, 158

Jambon, Kirby, 270, 271, 272, 274
Jeanne la fileuse (Beaugrand), 159, 183
Je me souviens slogan, 9, 87, 287
Jesuits (Black Robes), 43, 44, 236
Jim Crow laws, 35, 242, 243, 244
Jindal, Bobby, 83, 233
"Jolie Blonde" song, 249, 250, 254, 269
Le Journal de Lowell newspaper, 195,
  216–32, 282
La Justice newspaper, 178, 202, 215

Kerouac, Jack, 12, 172, 174, *185*, 288
Ku Klux Klan, 11

Lafayette, Marquis de, 27, 28
Lagasse, Emeril, 259, 261
Lamoille Stories (Schubart), 183
Lavallée, Calixa, 283
Le Clézio, J.M.G., 186, 187
Lescarbot, Marc, 8, 172
Lessard-Bissonnette, Camille, 160, 161
Les Lieux de mémoire (Nora), 289
linguistic diversity, 154, 225
literary works. *See* fiction works
littérature-monde movement, 4, 151–52,
  154–55, 157, 186–87
Little Canada, 16, 66, 78, 199, 208, 288.
  See also *petit Canada*
Little Pine to King Spruce (Pelletier), 183
live music and performances, 265–77

Louder, Dean, 7, 23
Louis XIV, 41, 42, 43, 47, 109, 294n62
Louisiana: blackness issues, 241, 242;
  Cajun/Creole divide in, 245; and
  Creole/Cajun label, 259; and Creole creation, 262–65; and Creolized
  pranks, 265–77; and culinary
  traditions, 259–62; cultural decline
  in, 156; cultural hybridity of, 240,
  242; cultural renewal in, 53–59; and
  cultural symbols, 258–59; ethnic
  groups in, 240; Evangeline site,
  34; flag of, 243; French education
  in, 48–49; French heritage in, 55;
  French outreach in, 83–95; French
  population of, 22, 23, 233–34; and
  French settlement, 238–39; French
  speakers in, 57; geographic isolation
  of, 239; introduction to, 12, 13,
  16–19; legal system in, 38; and
  music expressions, 246–57; as an
  official bilingual state, 84. *See also*
  Franco-Americans
"Louisiana fast food," 233, 260
Lowell. *See* New England
Lussier, Joseph, 190, 209, 215

Maillet, Antonine, 162, 163, 185
Maine, French speakers in, 57
la Maison Française, 62, 63, *64*
Mance, Jeanne, 109, 110, 129, 138, 304n44
Mardi Gras celebrations, 19, 134, 254,
  262–65, 276–77
Mardi Gras Indians, 19, 49, 236, 277
Maria Chapdelaine (Hémon), 14, 18,
  163–66, 171, 172
Marianne the emblem, 73, *74*, 75, 76, 211
Marshall, Bill, 23, 287
Massachusetts, French speakers in, 57

McGee, Dennis, 237, 248
media forms, 25–26
mémére, 104, 125, 184, 279
Menaud, maître draveur (Savard), 166–68
Le Messager d'aujourd'hui newsletter, 101, 193–95, 206
métissage, 234, 235, 237, 239
migration: of French Americans, 35–36; of French Canadians, 49–50, 203; law related to, 55; from Quebec, 49–50, 203
Mill Bell, 219, 283, 285
Miller, Christopher L., 234–35
Mississippi River, 1, 15, 21, 39, 47, 238, 239, 241, 247
Le Monde newspaper, 153, 154
Monument National, *3*
monuments: *dame de la renaissance française*, 17, 107, *108*; image of, *3*; James Domengeaux, 95; de l'amitié, 287; Mill Bell, 281, 283; postcolonial, 19; Samuel de Champlain, 9
Moogk, Peter, 40, 41, 171
Morrissette, Armand "Spike," 220, 226
multiculturalism, 94, 100
music festivals, 255, *256*, 257

nationalism, 72, 166, 167, 206–16
National Revolution, 168, 212, 214
Nation and Narration (Bhabha), 34
Native Americans: and CODOFIL, 94–95; and French settlers, 235, 237; and Houma Nation, 37–38; introduction to, 10, 13; and New France, 43–44
Nativity Church, 112, 120, 124, 125, 302n10
naturalization law, 55
Nazi ideal/Nazism, 72, 213
Never Back Down (Hebert), 182

New England: cultural renewal in, 53–59; ethnic celebrations in, 284–85; Franco-Americans' organizations in, 110–11; Franco grassroots in, 95–105; and French newspapers, 48; French population in, 58; French prosperity in, 50–51; growth of, 30; introduction to, 12, 13, 15–18; statues honoring, 287–88; welcome signs in, 45–47, 295n77. *See also* Franco-American literary cultures; Franco-Americans
New England Foreign Language Newspaper Association, 196
New France: and colonization efforts, 40; expansion of, 30; and French settlers, 235, 236; introduction to, 27; loss of, 45; and Native Americans, 43–44; new history of, 37–38; population of, 239; powerful men's interest in, 41; remaking of, 50
New Orleans, 49, 87–89, 233, 236–39, 241–43, 262
newspapers. *See* Franco-American press
New World: colonial presence in, 40–43; cultural study, 7–8; French, 27–39; introduction to, 6–7; women's role in, 109
North America: colonial activity in, 2, 31, 37, 42; France's imperial foothold in, 38; Frenchness in, 14; French speakers in, 2. *See also* Franco-Americans
Notre Dame-des-Canadiens Church, 288
la Nouvelle-France, 38, 39, 40, 45, 68, 134, 157, 195, 238

"O Canada" national anthem, 114, 115, 133, 142
Old Bull in the Bowery (Kerouac), 174
Old World cultures, 10, 27, 279
On the Road (Kerouac), 174, 175
oral cultures, 2, 6, 265, 266, 272
Organisation internationale de la Francophonie (OIF), 82, 85, 98, 154, 224, 225

Paige, Abby, 59
Papa Martel (Robichaud), 183
Parent, Michael, 58, 127
Parisian institution, 67, 78, 81
Parisian publishing houses, 75, 156
Parkman, Francis, 30, 31, 39, 173
Pélagie-la-charette (Maillet), 162–63, 185
Péloquin, Louise, 224, 227, 228, 231, 313n84
Péloquin, Marthe Biron, 144, 232, 314n90
people of color, 7, 35, 59, 241
Perreault, Robert, 155, 156
Pétain, Philippe, 53, 211, 212, 215
petit Canada, 16, 50, 113, 119, 131, 195
Pine Leaf Boys musical group, 250
Plante, David, 175, 180, 181
Pledge of Allegiance, 114
poets and poetry, 266–70
Popeyes restaurant, 233, 260
postcolonial cultures, 2, 11, 235
Precious Blood Church, 48
print cultures, 5, 6, 14
Protestants, 8, 37

Quebec: Americanness in, 29–30; colonial settlement in, 38; demographic history of, 44; francophone culture outside of, 13; French speakers in, 9; language of communication in, 45; migration from, 49–50, 203. *See also* Franco-American literary cultures; social clubs
Quiet Evolution, 56, 229
Quiet Revolution, 44, 52, 120, 202
Quintal, Claire, 135, 144, 221, 224, 232

Radio France Internationale (RFI), 26, 62, 83
religious elites, 51, 160
religious faith, 130–31, 200
Richard, Zachary, 13, 25, 252, 257, 269
Richards, Marvin, 36, 152
Rivier College, 63, 147
Robert, Jane, 69, 70
Rochambeau, Comte de, 27
romans de la terre, 162, 168, 169, 183
roux, 259–60

Sacred Heart Church, 288
Saint John the Baptist Day, 8, 33, 98, 205–6, 212
Saldívar, José David, 9
Savoy, Ann, 253, 254
Savoy, Marc, 250
scholarships for Franco-Americans, 117–18, 120–21, 128, 132, 134–35
"screw your neighbor" game, 127
Second World War: and Alliance Française, 66, 72; and Franco-Americans, 53, 216; and literary works, 175–76
the *Sentinelle* affair, 191
settlements and French transatlantic voyages, 38–45
Shadows of the Trees, The (Ducharme), 177, 184, 197, 311n20

slave trade, 234, 242, 260

Smith, Michael P., 240, 248

"Snowbirds" French people, 58, 227

social clubs: cultural activities for, 115–17, 123, 134–35, 144–45; English speakers at, 120, 126, 128; Fédération Féminine Franco-Américaine, 141–49; French Nite, 123–26; fund raising for, 117, 120, 125, 135, 141; and "good night, my dear friends," 126–28; introduction to, 17, 107, 109; Le Cercle des Dames Françaises, 111, 129–36; Le Cercle Jeanne Mance, 136–41; Les Dames Franco-Américaines, 112–23; membership dues for, 137; social events for, 117, 120, 133, 135, 138. See also French-speaking populations/world

social elites, 27, 129, 131

soupe aux pois, 124, 125, 126, 184

"Speak White" poem, 22, 36

Spitzer, Nick, 49, 240

St. Anselm College, 63, 99

Statue of Liberty, 55, 207, 208, 280, 281

St. Georges School, 121, 122, 123, 136

Stival, Charles, 245

St. Lawrence River, 9, 287, 289

St. Mary's Church, 99

St. Rose de Lima Church, 112, 113, 116, 120

Sur le Chemin (Kerouac), 174

survivance movement, 77, 79, 135, 141, 177, 186–87, 192, 204, 229, 235, 281

teaching institutions. See cultural and teaching institutions

television programming, 25, 124, 218, 229–31

Thériault, Joseph Yvon, 11, 173

Third Republic, 71–76

Thy Will Be Done (Appell), 176

Ti-Jean, 184, 185, 186, 274, 276, 288

Tocqueville, Alexis de, 15, 29

tourtiére, 124, 125, 126, 184

The Town and City (Kerouac), 175

Traditional Music of Coastal Louisiana (McCafferty), 251

transnational literature, 151, 152, 153, 170, 186

Le Travailleur newspaper, 79, 158–59, 189–91, 198–206, 208–17

Treme (television series), 262

Trente Arpents (Panneton), 168–70, 184

True France, 210, 211, 215

TV5Monde, 25, 83, 101, 229, 257

Union Saint-Jean Baptiste (USJB), 16, 53

United States: continental divide issues, 28–29; ethnic identity in, 32–33; immigrants to, 55; imperial status of, 37; statues honoring, 287–88

universalism, 28, 32, 157

University of Louisiana, Lafayette (ULL), 16, 62, 63, 88, 92, 95, 245, 255

Vachon, Josée, 15, 22, 33, 123, 124

veillées, 111, 184, 273

Vichy France, 18, 53, 72, 206–16

Vidal, Cécile, 37, 39

Visions of Gerard (Kerouac), 175

Volkswagen Blues (Poulin), 247–48

Waddell, Eric, 7, 23

Waking Up French!... Réveil, 58, 59, 281

"war brides," 78, 132

The Warmth of Other Suns: The Epic Story of America's Great Migration (Wilkerson), 35

war veterans, 19, 97, 145, 286

Watson, Cedric, 250, 251

Wednesday's Child (Côté Robbins), 35, 179

Weil, François, 53, 209

welcome signs, 45, *46*, 47, 295n77. See also *bienvenue*

West Wing (TV series), 124, 289

white ethnic identity, 7, 36, 182

White Niggers, 36, 181, 186, 237

Wilkerson, Isabel, 35, 36

women organizations. *See* social clubs

women's rights, 142, 144, 147

Xavier University, 243

Zydeco Corridor, 15, 237

Regeneration through Empire:
French Pronatalists and Colonial
Settlement in the Third Republic
Margaret Cook Andersen

To Hell and Back:
The Life of Samira Bellil
Samira Bellil
Translated by Lucy R. McNair
Introduction by Alec G. Hargreaves

Colonial Metropolis: The Urban
Grounds of Anti-Imperialism and
Feminism in Interwar Paris
Jennifer Anne Boittin

Paradise Destroyed: Catastrophe and
Citizenship in the French Caribbean
Christopher M. Church

The French Navy and the
Seven Years' War
Jonathan R. Dull

I, Nadia, Wife of a Terrorist
Baya Gacemi

Transnational Spaces and Identities
in the Francophone World
Edited by Hafid Gafaïti, Patricia M.
E. Lorcin, and David G. Troyansky

Contesting French West Africa:
Battles over Schools and the
Colonial Order, 1900–1950
Harry Gamble

Black French Women and the
Struggle for Equality, 1848–2016
Edited and with an introduction by
Félix Germain and Silyane Larcher

The French Army and Its African
Soldiers: The Years of Decolonization
Ruth Ginio

French Colonialism Unmasked:
The Vichy Years in French West Africa
Ruth Ginio

Bourdieu in Algeria: Colonial
Politics, Ethnographic Practices,
Theoretical Developments
Edited and with an introduction
by Jane E. Goodman
and Paul A. Silverstein

Franco America in the Making:
The Creole Nation Within
Jonathan K. Gosnell

Endgame 1758: The Promise,
the Glory, and the Despair of
Louisbourg's Last Decade
A. J. B. Johnston

Colonial Suspects: Suspicion,
Imperial Rule, and Colonial Society
in Interwar French West Africa
Kathleen Keller

French Mediterraneans:
Transnational and Imperial Histories
Edited and with an introduction
by Patricia M. E. Lorcin
and Todd Shepard

The Cult of the Modern:
Trans-Mediterranean France and the
Construction of French Modernity
Gavin Murray-Miller

Cinema in an Age of Terror:
North Africa, Victimization,
and Colonial History
Michael F. O'Riley

Medical Imperialism in French North
Africa: Regenerating the Jewish
Community of Colonial Tunis
Richard C. Parks

Making the Voyageur World:
Travelers and Traders in the
North American Fur Trade
Carolyn Podruchny

A Workman Is Worthy of His Meat:
Food and Colonialism in Gabon
Jeremy Rich

The Moroccan Soul: French
Education, Colonial Ethnology, and
Muslim Resistance, 1912–1956
Spencer D. Segalla

Silence Is Death: The Life and
Work of Tahar Djaout
Julija Šukys

The French Colonial Mind,
Volume 1: Mental Maps of Empire
and Colonial Encounters
Edited and with an introduction
by Martin Thomas

The French Colonial Mind,
Volume 2: Violence, Military
Encounters, and Colonialism
Edited and with an introduction
by Martin Thomas

Beyond Papillon: The French Overseas
Penal Colonies, 1854–1952
Stephen A. Toth

Madah-Sartre: The Kidnapping, Trial,
and Conver(sat/s)ion of Jean-Paul
Sartre and Simone de Beauvoir
Written and translated by
Alek Baylee Toumi
With an introduction by
James D. Le Sueur

To order or obtain more information on these or other University
of Nebraska Press titles, visit nebraskapress.unl.edu.

9 780803 285279